LEO

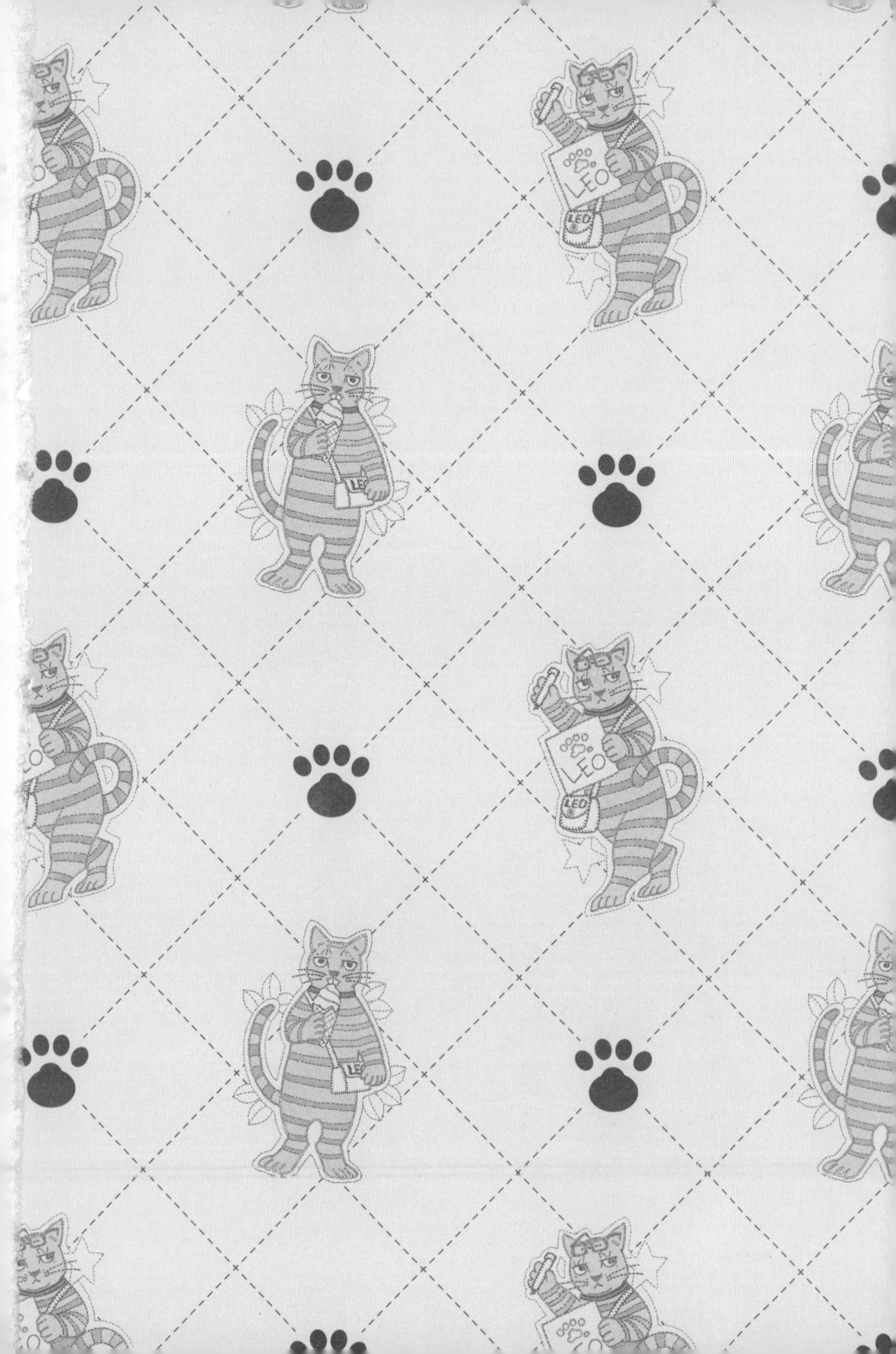
LEO

Lil' Leo

Moto Hagio

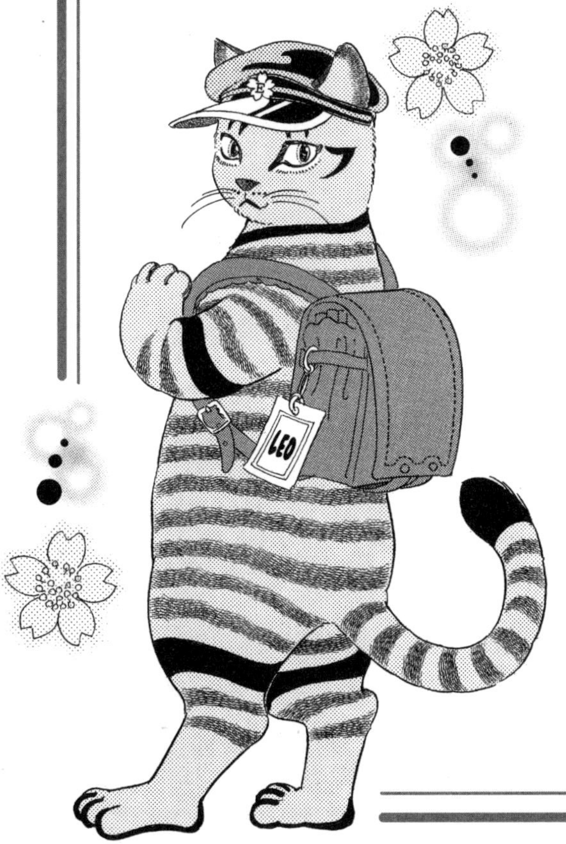
LEO

CONTENTS

1 Lil' Leo the First-Grader

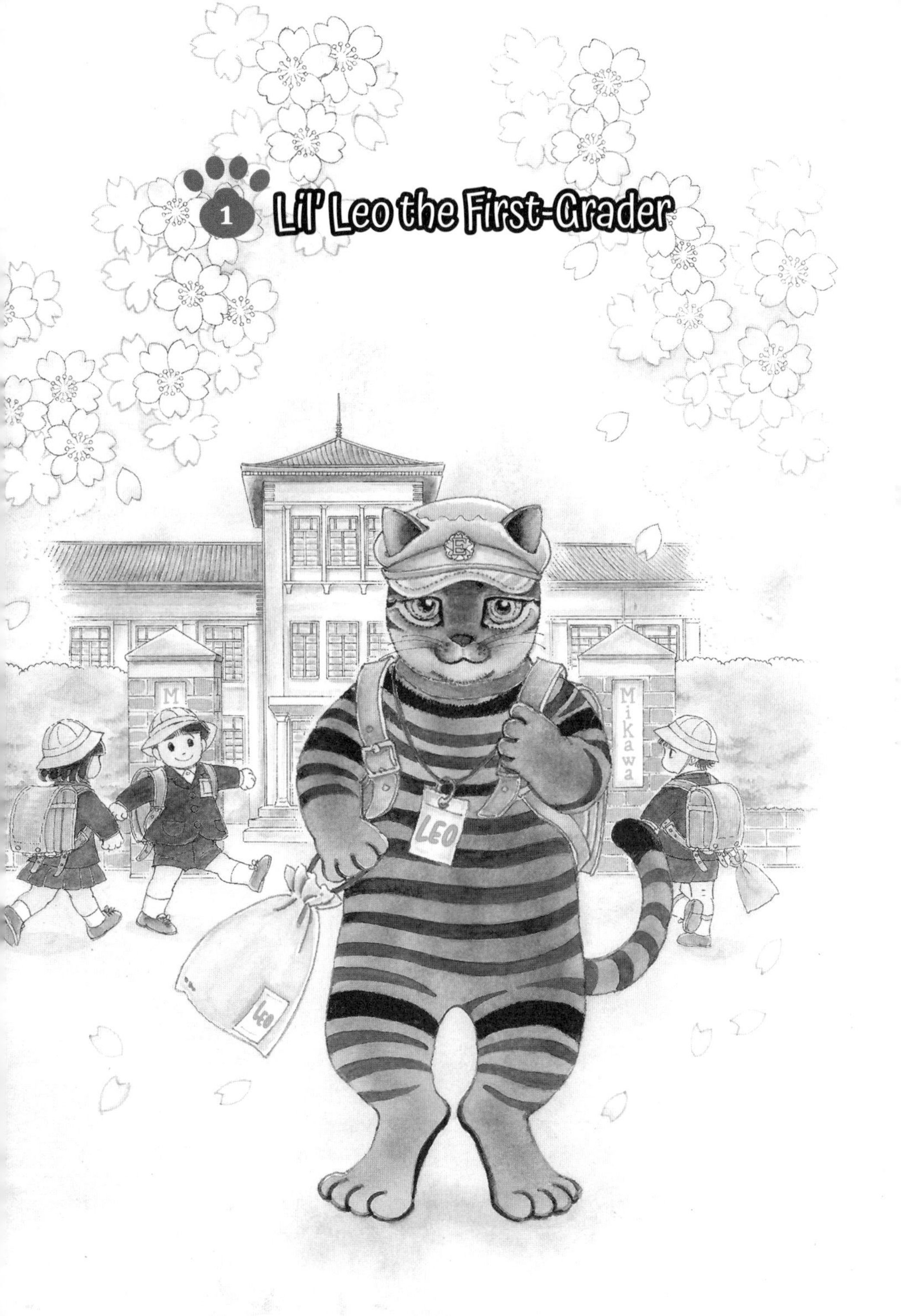
M
Mikawa
LEO
LEO

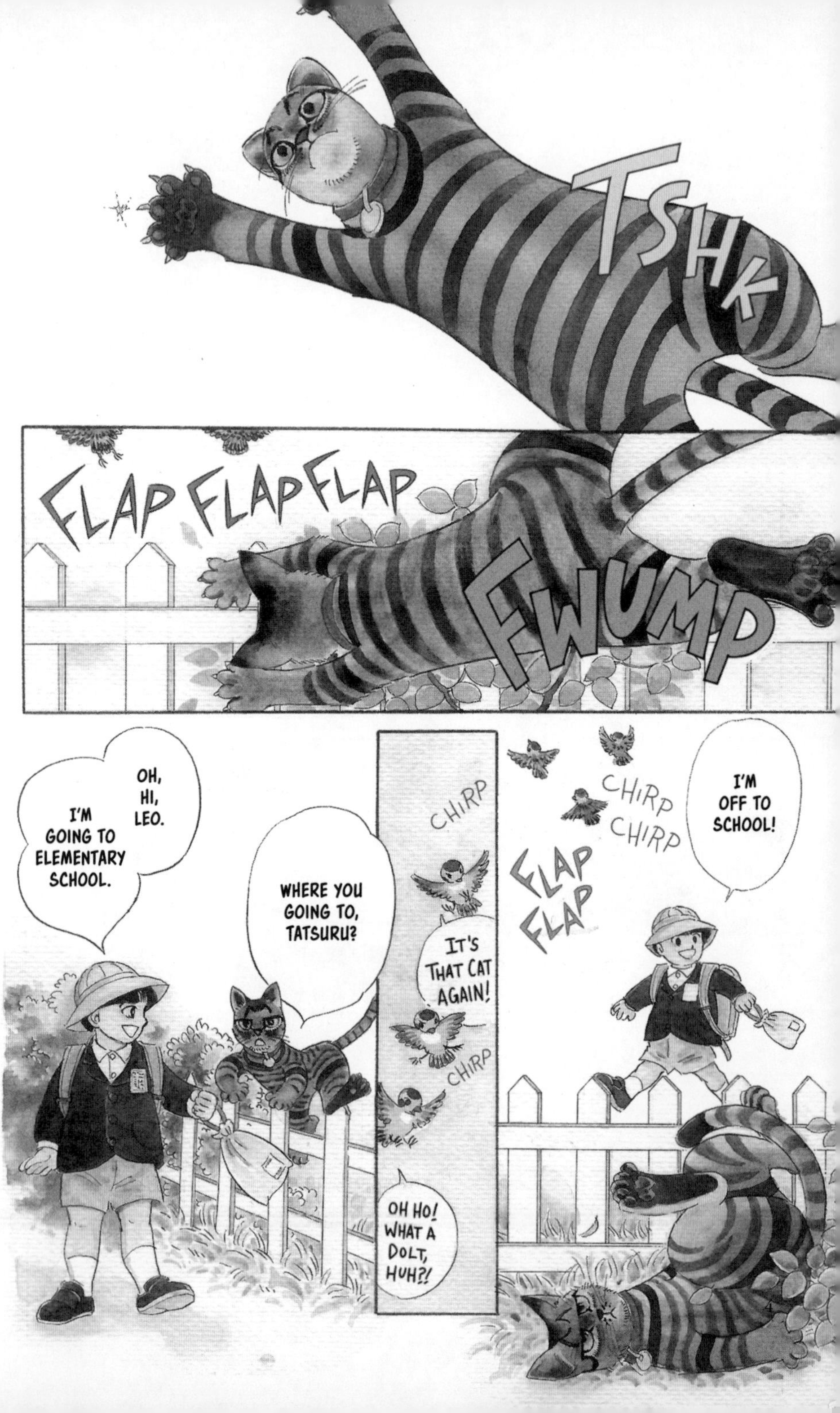
TSHK
FWUMP
FLAP FLAP FLAP
I'M OFF TO SCHOOL!
CHIRP
CHIRP
FLAP
FLAP
CHIRP
IT'S THAT CAT AGAIN!
CHIRP
OH HO! WHAT A DOLT, HUH?!
WHERE YOU GOING TO, TATSURU?
OH, HI, LEO. I'M GOING TO ELEMENTARY SCHOOL.

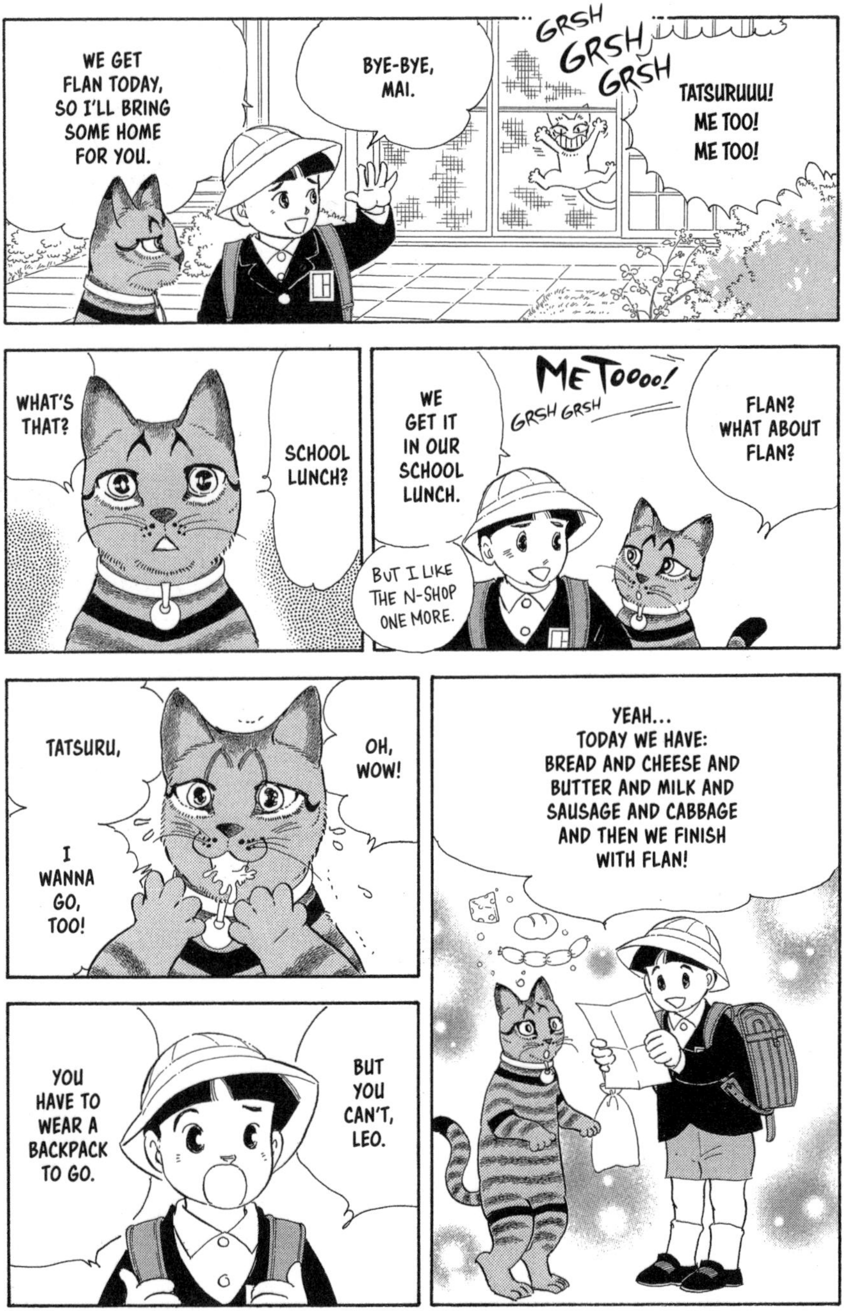
GRSH GRSH GRSH
TATSURUUU! ME TOO! ME TOO!
BYE-BYE, MAI.
WE GET FLAN TODAY, SO I'LL BRING SOME HOME FOR YOU.
FLAN? WHAT ABOUT FLAN?
ME Toooo!
GRSH GRSH
WE GET IT IN OUR SCHOOL LUNCH.
BUT I LIKE THE N-SHOP ONE MORE.
SCHOOL LUNCH?
WHAT'S THAT?
YEAH... TODAY WE HAVE: BREAD AND CHEESE AND BUTTER AND MILK AND SAUSAGE AND CABBAGE AND THEN WE FINISH WITH FLAN!
OH, WOW!
TATSURU,
I WANNA GO, TOO!
BUT YOU CAN'T, LEO.
YOU HAVE TO WEAR A BACKPACK TO GO.

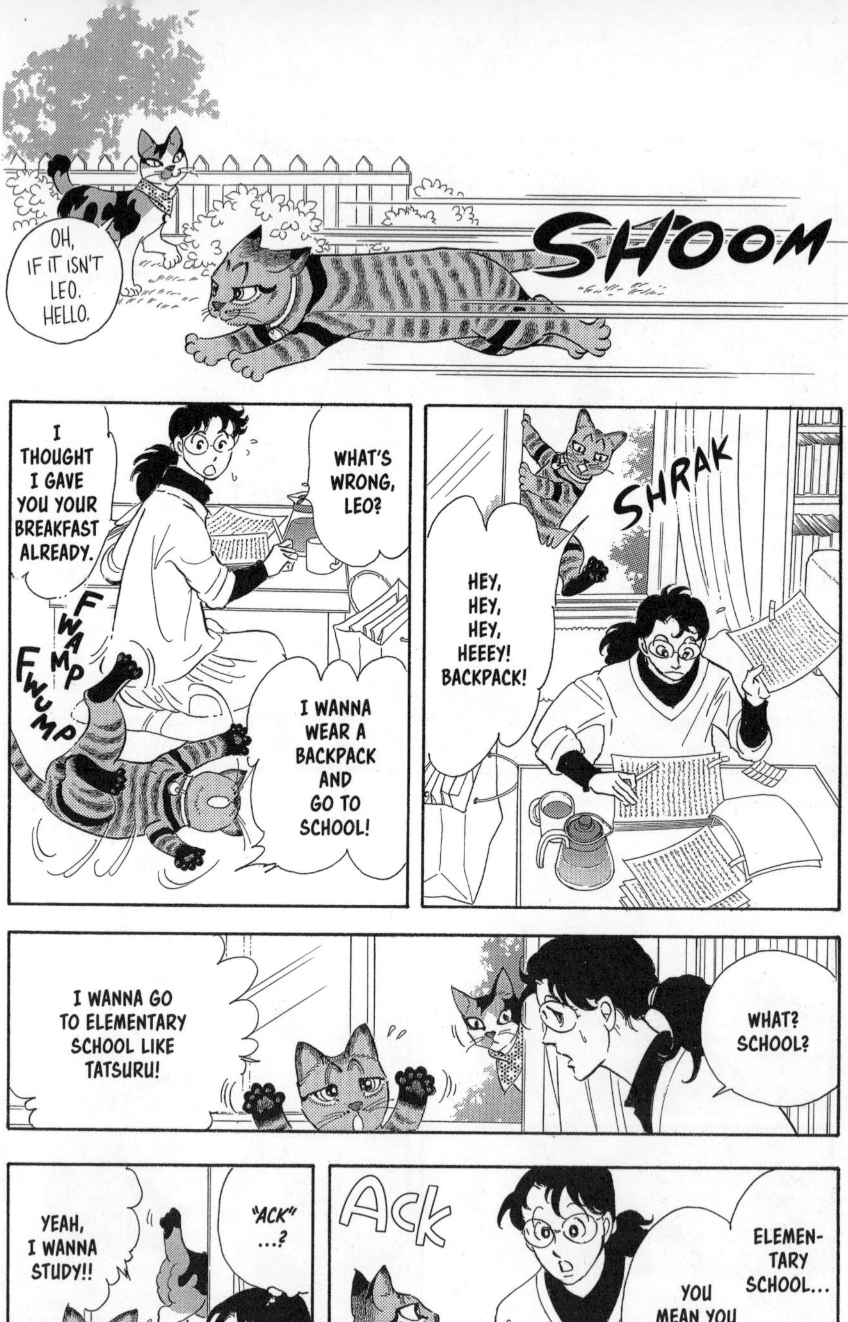
SHOOM
OH, IF IT ISN'T LEO. HELLO.
SHRAK
HEY, HEY, HEY, HEEEY! BACKPACK!
WHAT'S WRONG, LEO?
I THOUGHT I GAVE YOU YOUR BREAKFAST ALREADY.
FWAMP
FWUMP
I WANNA WEAR A BACKPACK AND GO TO SCHOOL!
WHAT? SCHOOL?
I WANNA GO TO ELEMENTARY SCHOOL LIKE TATSURU!
ELEMENTARY SCHOOL...
YOU MEAN YOU WANT TO STUDY?
Ack
"ACK" ...?
YEAH, I WANNA STUDY!!

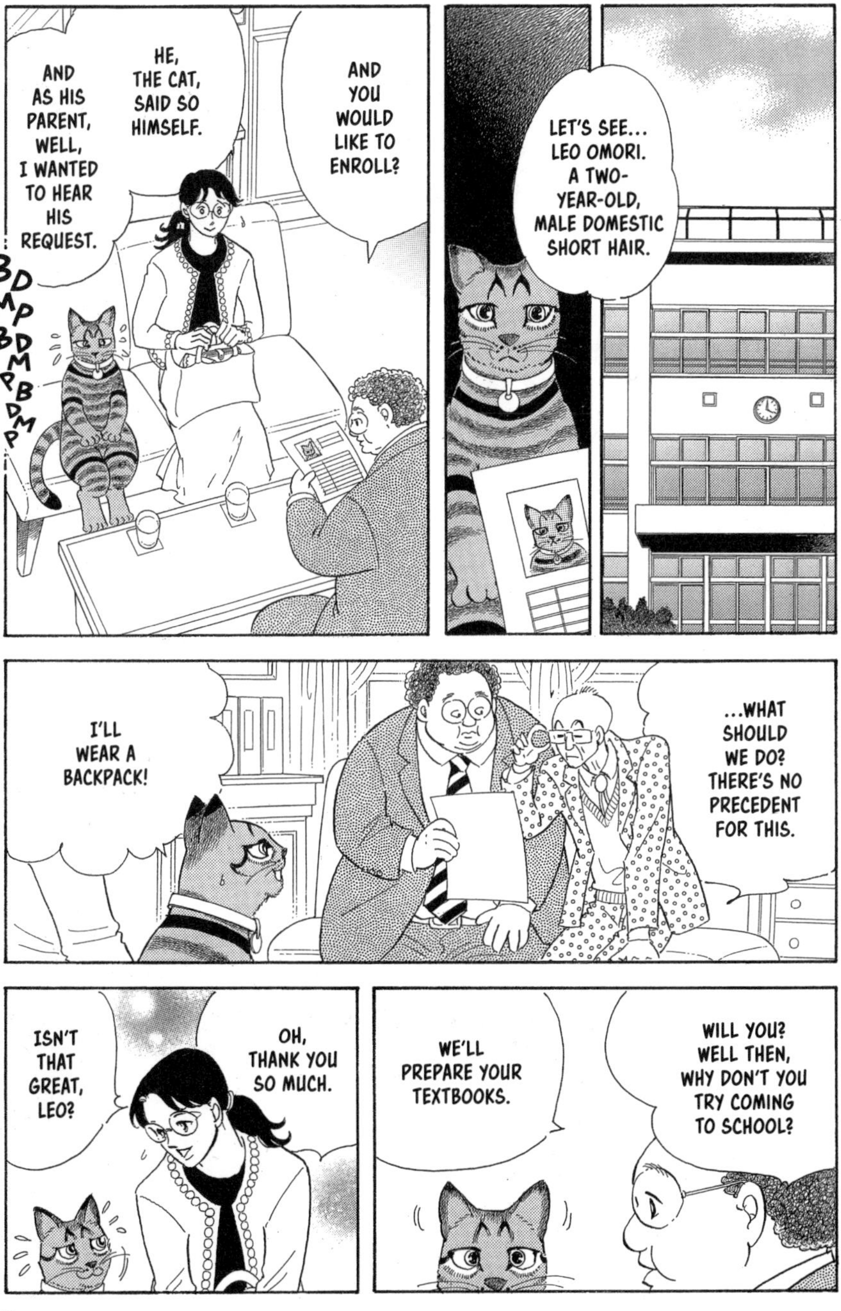
LET'S SEE... LEO OMORI. A TWO-YEAR-OLD, MALE DOMESTIC SHORT HAIR.
AND YOU WOULD LIKE TO ENROLL?
HE, THE CAT, SAID SO HIMSELF.
AND AS HIS PARENT, WELL, I WANTED TO HEAR HIS REQUEST.
BDMP BDMP BDMP
...WHAT SHOULD WE DO? THERE'S NO PRECEDENT FOR THIS.
I'LL WEAR A BACKPACK!
WILL YOU? WELL THEN, WHY DON'T YOU TRY COMING TO SCHOOL?
WE'LL PREPARE YOUR TEXTBOOKS.
OH, THANK YOU SO MUCH.
ISN'T THAT GREAT, LEO?

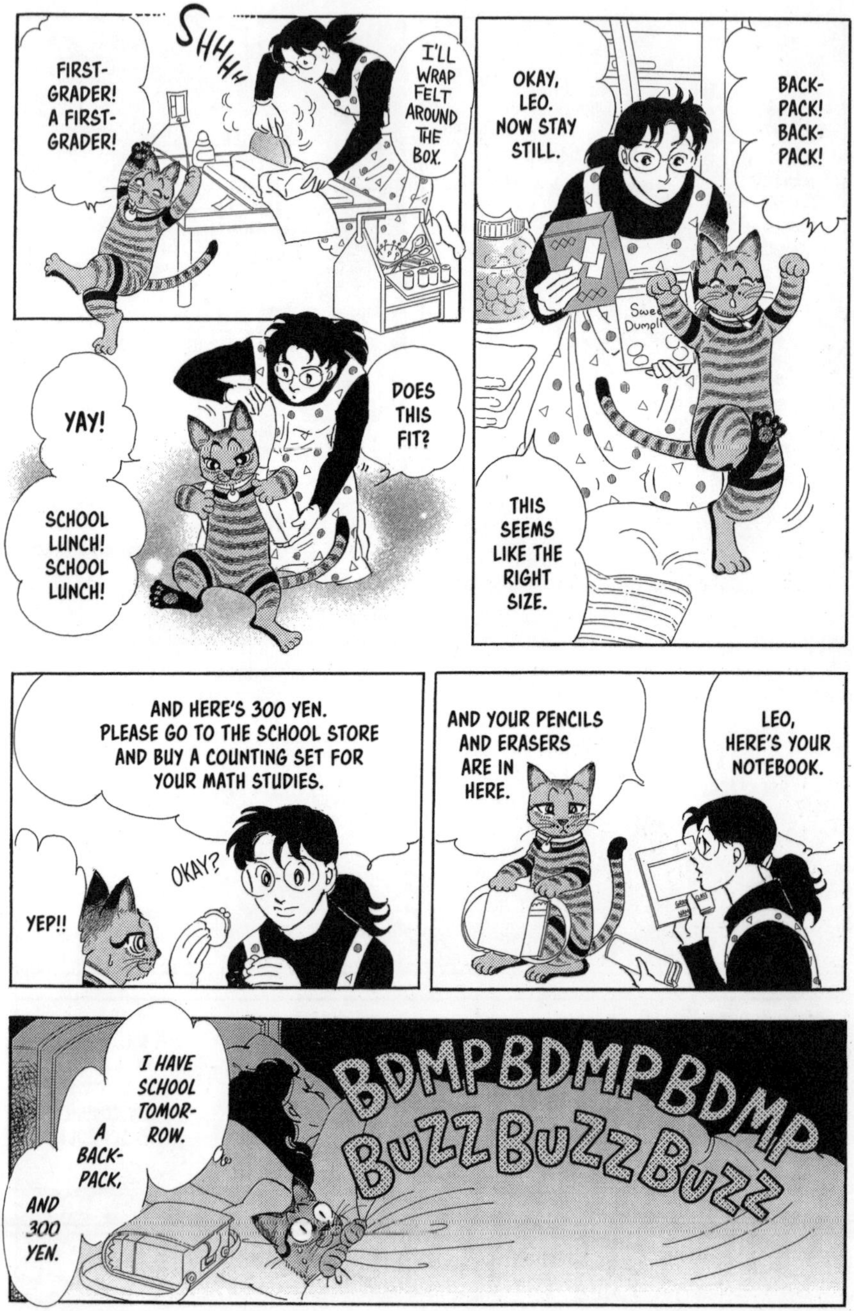
BACK-PACK! BACK-PACK!
OKAY, LEO. NOW STAY STILL.
THIS SEEMS LIKE THE RIGHT SIZE.
I'LL WRAP FELT AROUND THE BOX.
SHHHH
FIRST-GRADER! A FIRST-GRADER!
DOES THIS FIT?
YAY!
SCHOOL LUNCH! SCHOOL LUNCH!
LEO, HERE'S YOUR NOTEBOOK.
AND YOUR PENCILS AND ERASERS ARE IN HERE.
AND HERE'S 300 YEN. PLEASE GO TO THE SCHOOL STORE AND BUY A COUNTING SET FOR YOUR MATH STUDIES.
OKAY?
YEP!!
BDMP BDMP BDMP BDMP
BUZZ BUZZ BUZZ
I HAVE SCHOOL TOMORROW.
A BACKPACK,
AND 300 YEN.

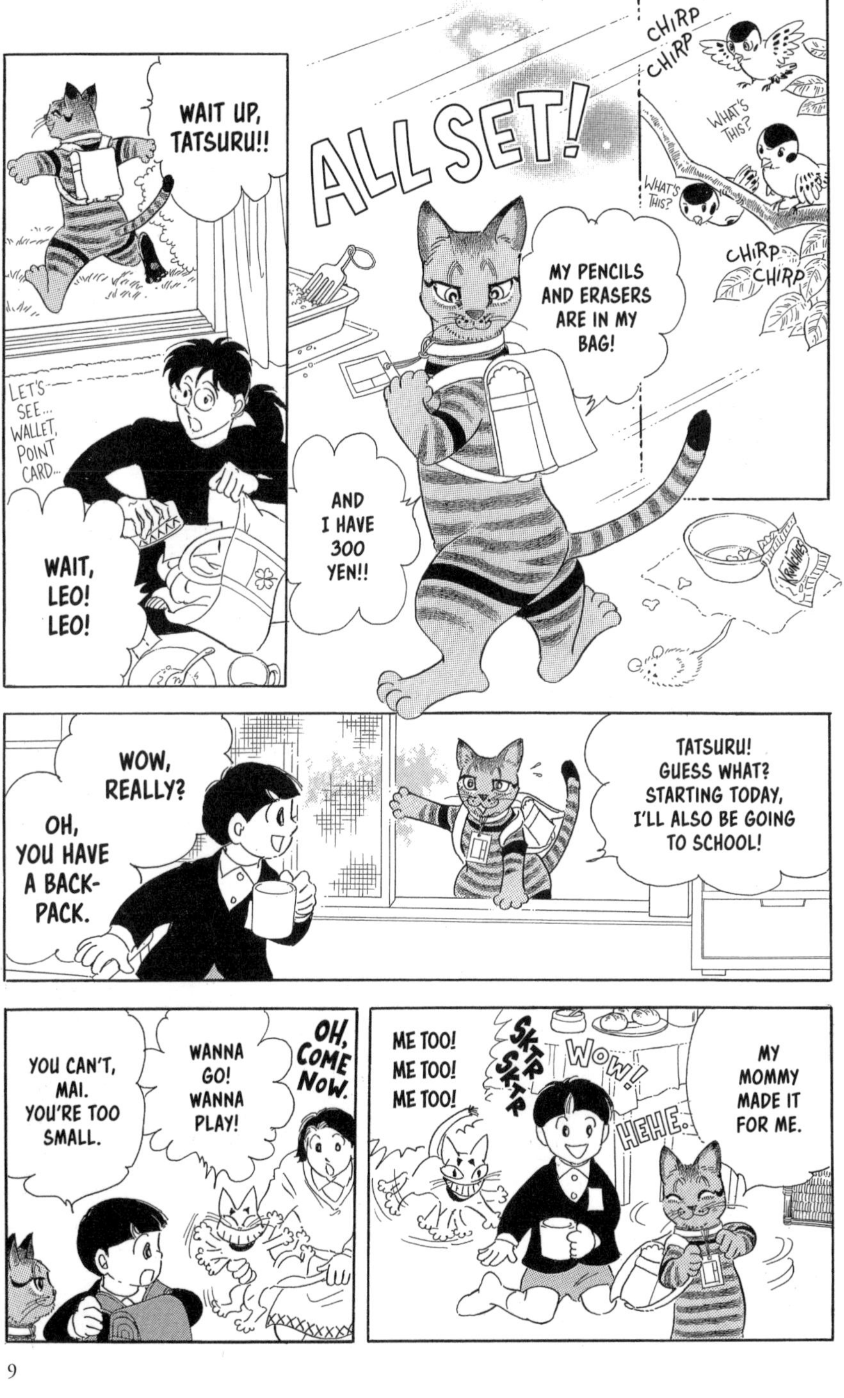
CHIRP CHIRP
WHAT'S THIS?
WHAT'S THIS?
CHIRP CHIRP
ALL SET!
MY PENCILS AND ERASERS ARE IN MY BAG!
AND I HAVE 300 YEN!!
WAIT UP, TATSURU!!
LET'S SEE... WALLET, POINT CARD...
WAIT, LEO! LEO!
TATSURU! GUESS WHAT? STARTING TODAY, I'LL ALSO BE GOING TO SCHOOL!
WOW, REALLY?
OH, YOU HAVE A BACK-PACK.
MY MOMMY MADE IT FOR ME.
HEHE.
WOW!
SKTR SKTR
ME TOO! ME TOO! ME TOO!
OH, COME NOW.
WANNA GO! WANNA PLAY!
YOU CAN'T, MAI. YOU'RE TOO SMALL.

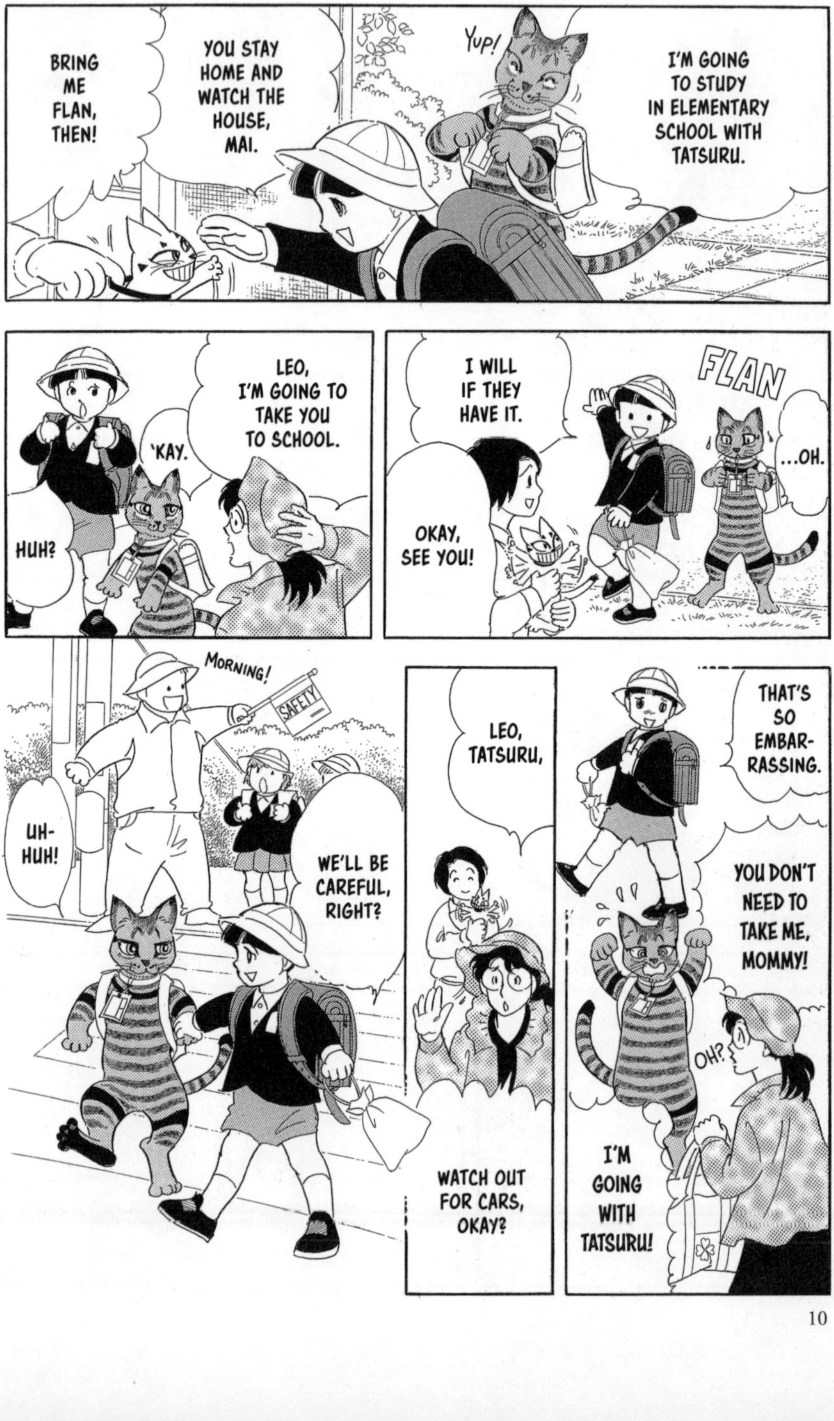
I'M GOING TO STUDY IN ELEMENTARY SCHOOL WITH TATSURU.
YUP!
YOU STAY HOME AND WATCH THE HOUSE, MAI.
BRING ME FLAN, THEN!
FLAN
...OH.
I WILL IF THEY HAVE IT.
OKAY, SEE YOU!
LEO, I'M GOING TO TAKE YOU TO SCHOOL.
'KAY.
HUH?
THAT'S SO EMBARRASSING.
YOU DON'T NEED TO TAKE ME, MOMMY!
OH?
I'M GOING WITH TATSURU!
LEO, TATSURU,
WATCH OUT FOR CARS, OKAY?
MORNING!
SAFETY
WE'LL BE CAREFUL, RIGHT?
UH-HUH!

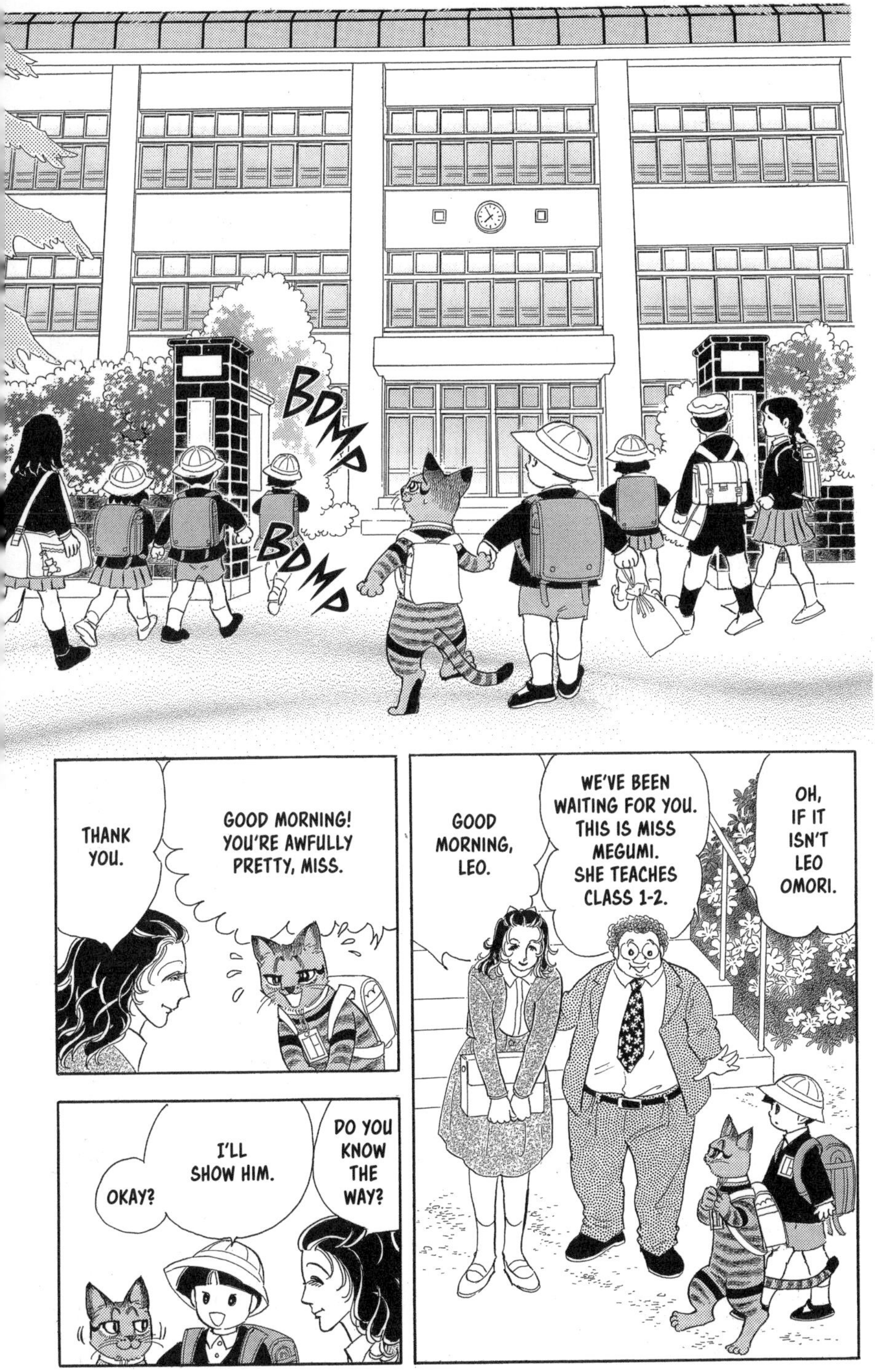
BDMP
BDMP
OH, IF IT ISN'T LEO OMORI.
WE'VE BEEN WAITING FOR YOU. THIS IS MISS MEGUMI. SHE TEACHES CLASS 1-2.
GOOD MORNING, LEO.
GOOD MORNING! YOU'RE AWFULLY PRETTY, MISS.
THANK YOU.
DO YOU KNOW THE WAY?
I'LL SHOW HIM.
OKAY?

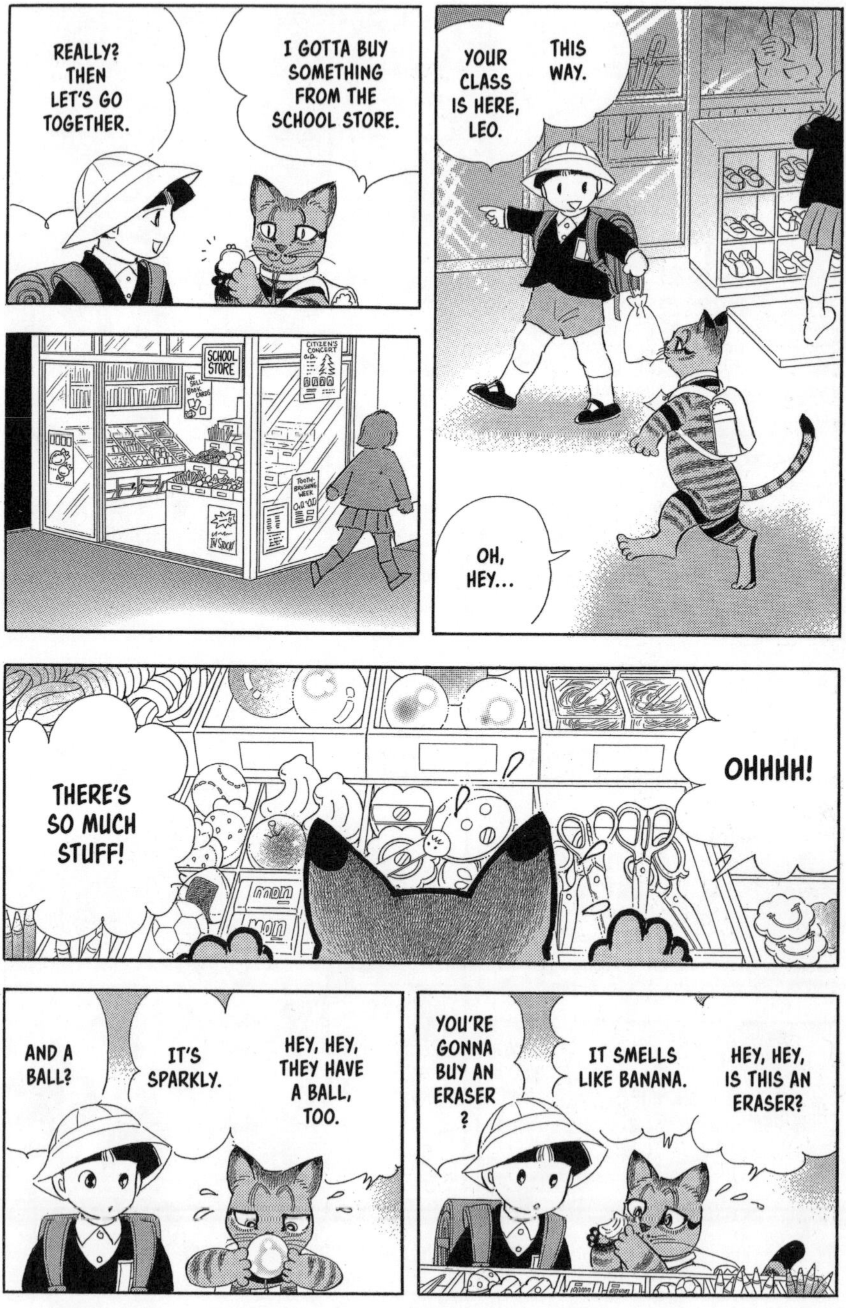
THIS WAY.
YOUR CLASS IS HERE, LEO.
OH, HEY...
I GOTTA BUY SOMETHING FROM THE SCHOOL STORE.
REALLY? THEN LET'S GO TOGETHER.
CITIZEN'S CONCERT
SCHOOL STORE
WE SELL BOOK CARDS
TOOTH-BRUSHING WEEK
IN STOCK!
OHHHH!
THERE'S SO MUCH STUFF!
HEY, HEY, IS THIS AN ERASER?
IT SMELLS LIKE BANANA.
YOU'RE GONNA BUY AN ERASER?
HEY, HEY, THEY HAVE A BALL, TOO.
IT'S SPARKLY.
AND A BALL?

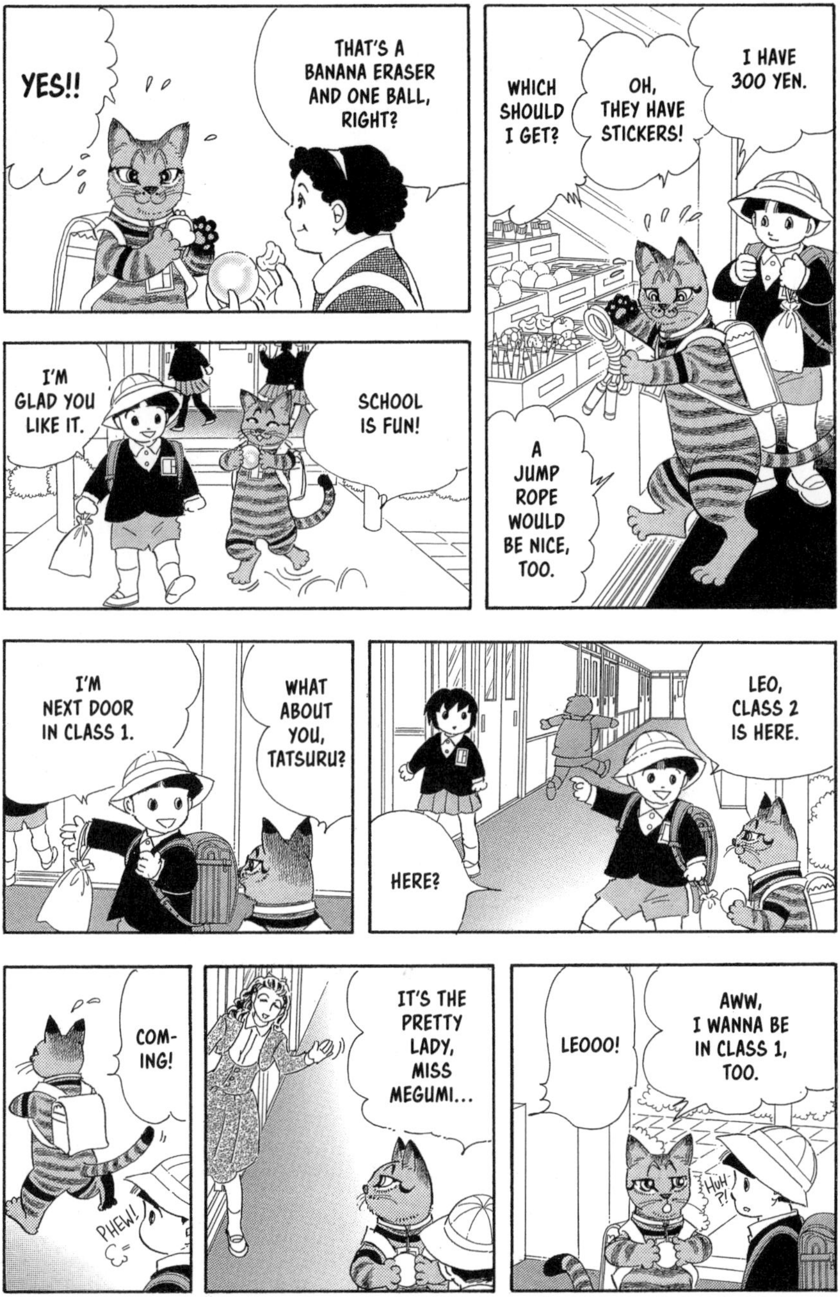
I HAVE 300 YEN.
OH, THEY HAVE STICKERS!
WHICH SHOULD I GET?
A JUMP ROPE WOULD BE NICE, TOO.
THAT'S A BANANA ERASER AND ONE BALL, RIGHT?
YES!!
SCHOOL IS FUN!
I'M GLAD YOU LIKE IT.
LEO, CLASS 2 IS HERE.
HERE?
WHAT ABOUT YOU, TATSURU?
I'M NEXT DOOR IN CLASS 1.
AWW, I WANNA BE IN CLASS 1, TOO.
LEOOO!
HUH?!
IT'S THE PRETTY LADY, MISS MEGUMI...
COM-ING!
PHEW!

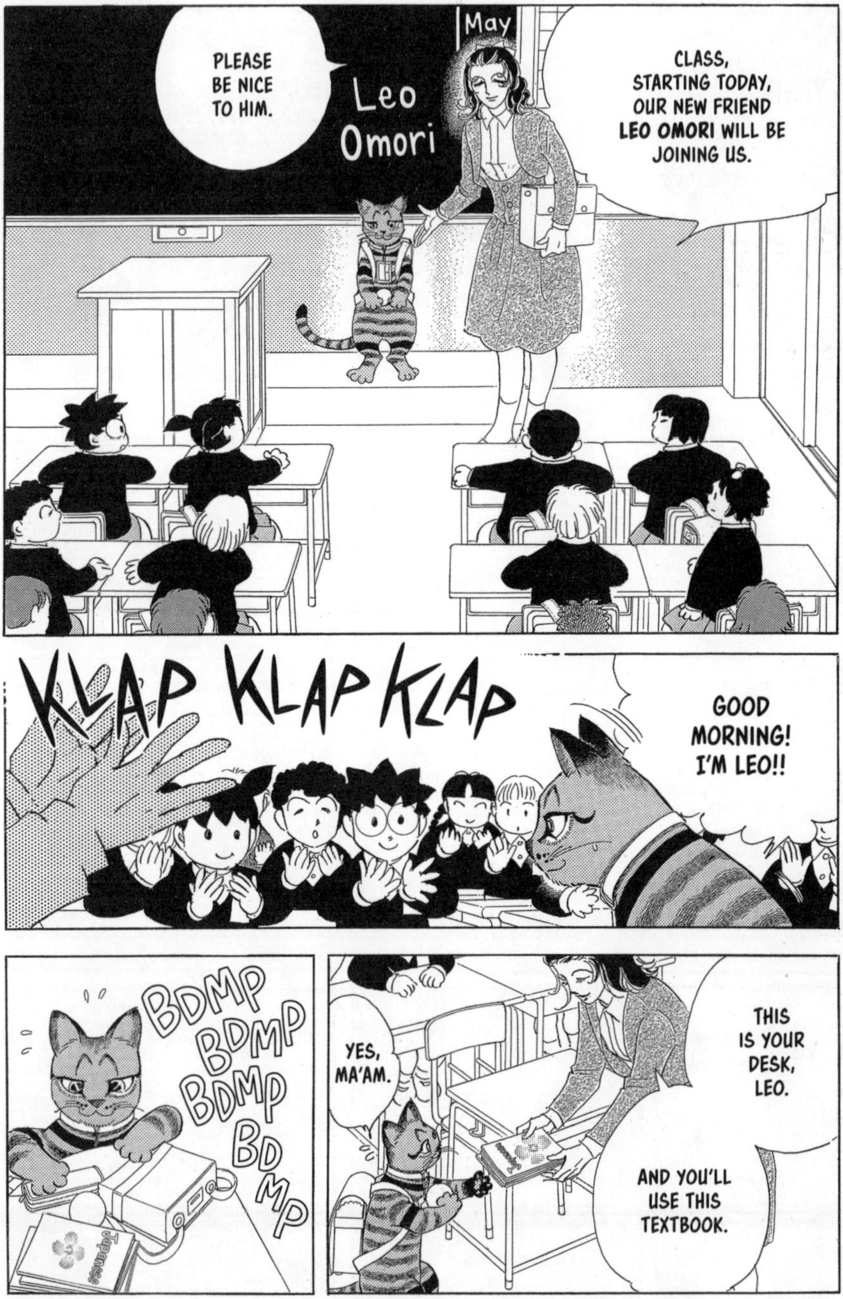

CLASS, STARTING TODAY, OUR NEW FRIEND LEO OMORI WILL BE JOINING US.
May
Leo Omori
PLEASE BE NICE TO HIM.
GOOD MORNING! I'M LEO!!
KLAP KLAP KLAP
THIS IS YOUR DESK, LEO.
AND YOU'LL USE THIS TEXTBOOK.
YES, MA'AM.
BDMP BDMP BDMP BDMP
Japanese

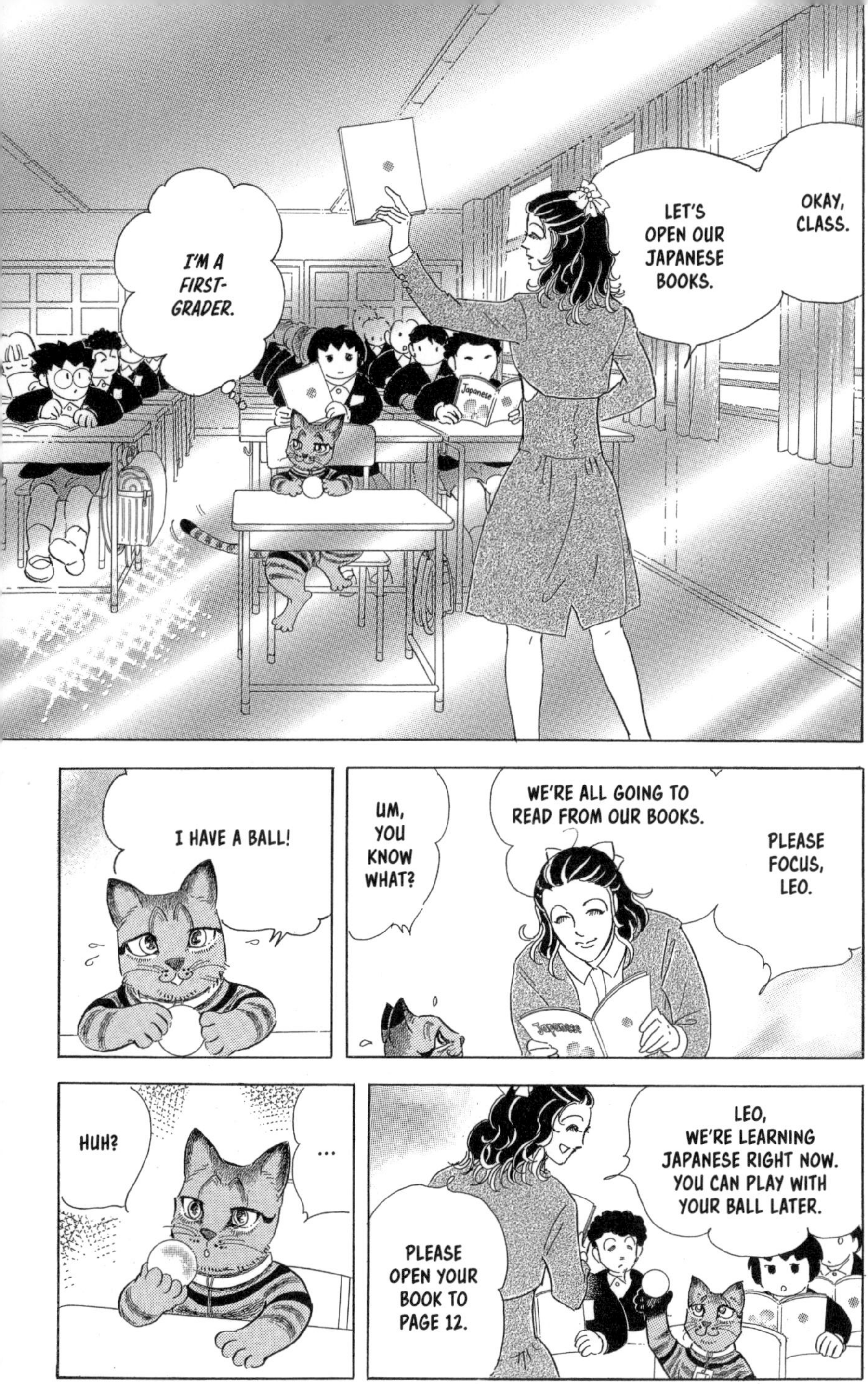
OKAY, CLASS.
LET'S OPEN OUR JAPANESE BOOKS.
I'M A FIRST-GRADER.
PLEASE FOCUS, LEO.
WE'RE ALL GOING TO READ FROM OUR BOOKS.
UM, YOU KNOW WHAT?
I HAVE A BALL!
LEO, WE'RE LEARNING JAPANESE RIGHT NOW. YOU CAN PLAY WITH YOUR BALL LATER.
PLEASE OPEN YOUR BOOK TO PAGE 12.
...
HUH?

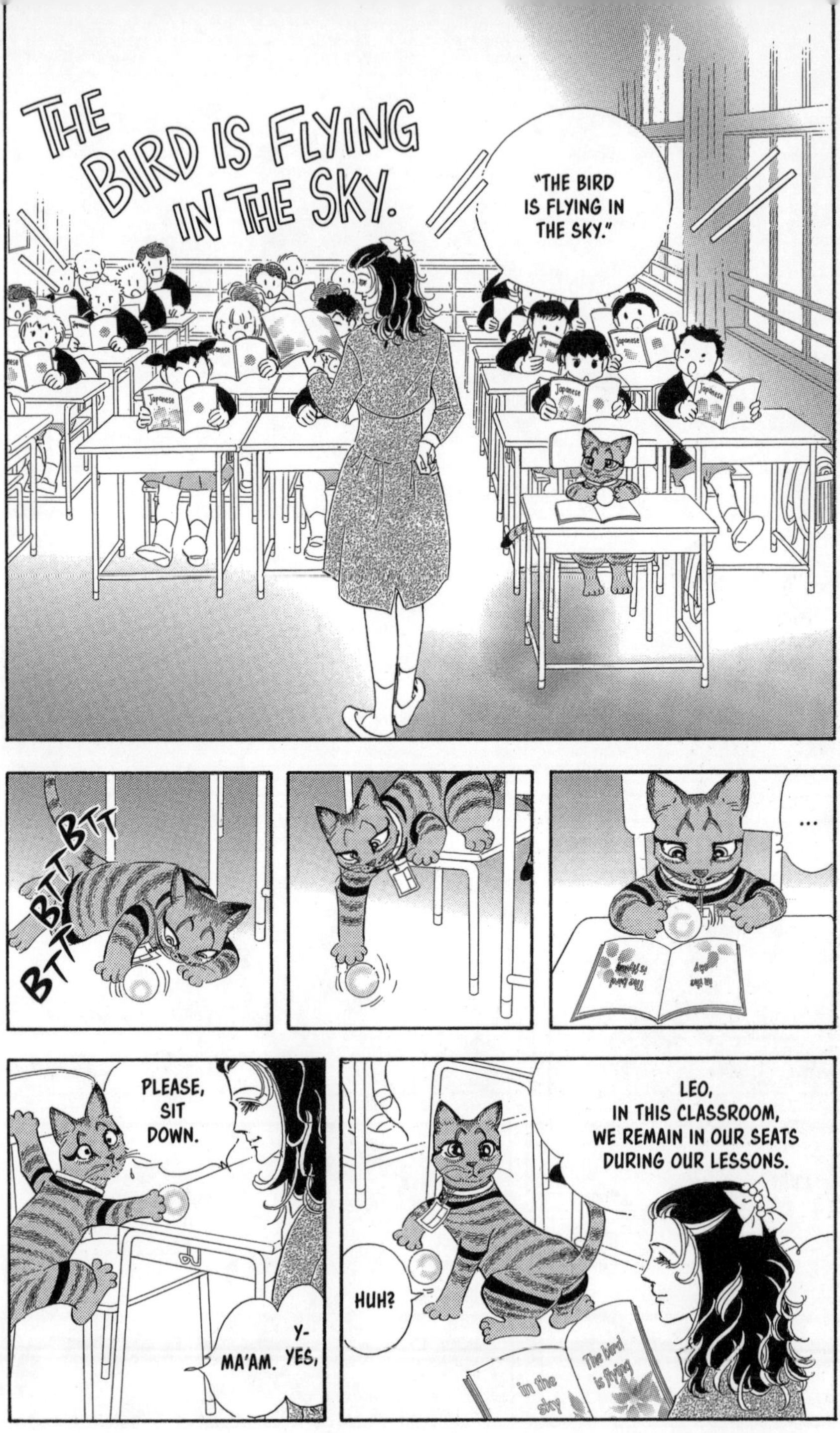
"THE BIRD IS FLYING IN THE SKY."
THE BIRD IS FLYING IN THE SKY.
...
BTT BTT BTT
LEO, IN THIS CLASSROOM, WE REMAIN IN OUR SEATS DURING OUR LESSONS.
HUH?
The bird is flying
in the sky
PLEASE, SIT DOWN.
Y- YES, MA'AM.

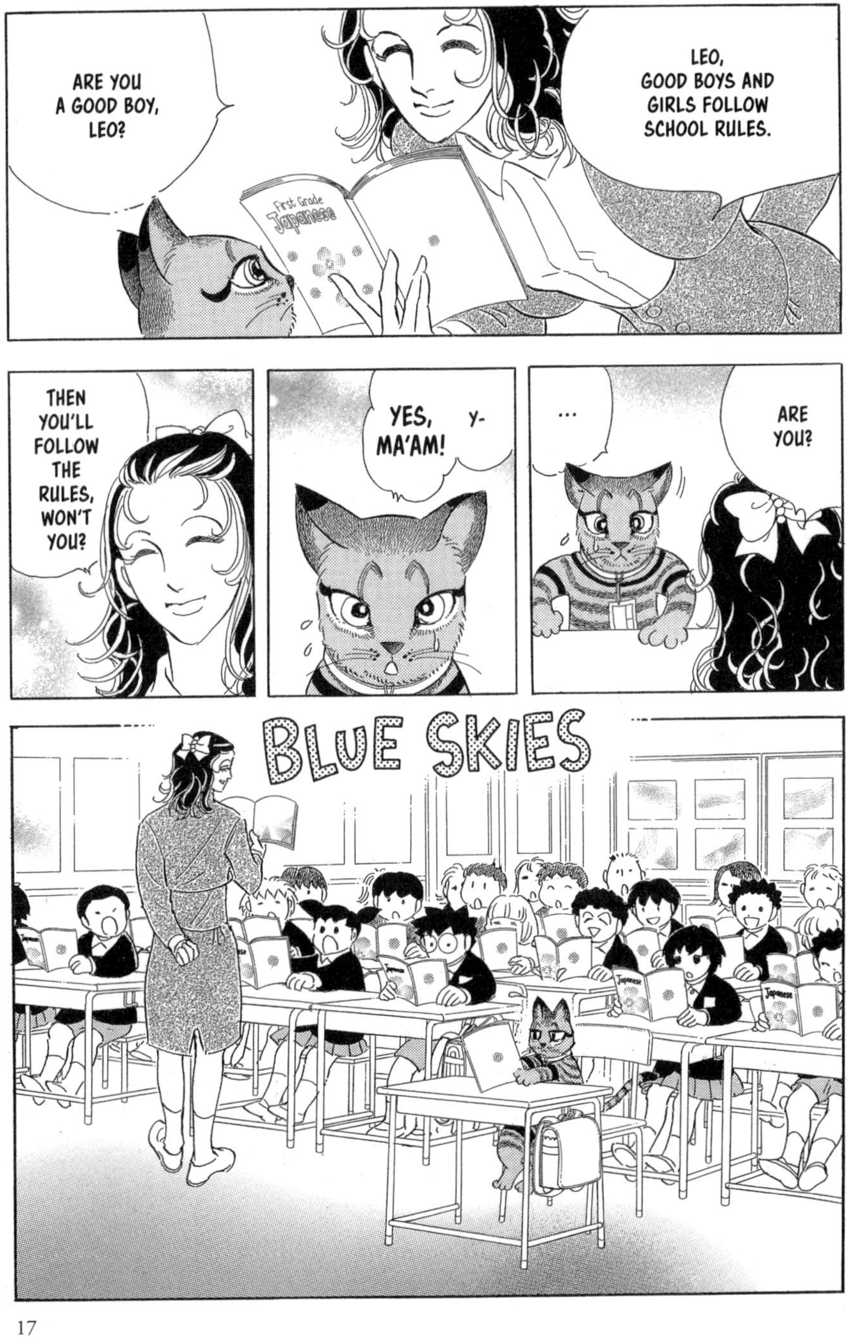
LEO, GOOD BOYS AND GIRLS FOLLOW SCHOOL RULES.
ARE YOU A GOOD BOY, LEO?
First Grade Japanese
ARE YOU?
...
Y- YES, MA'AM!
THEN YOU'LL FOLLOW THE RULES, WON'T YOU?
BLUE SKIES

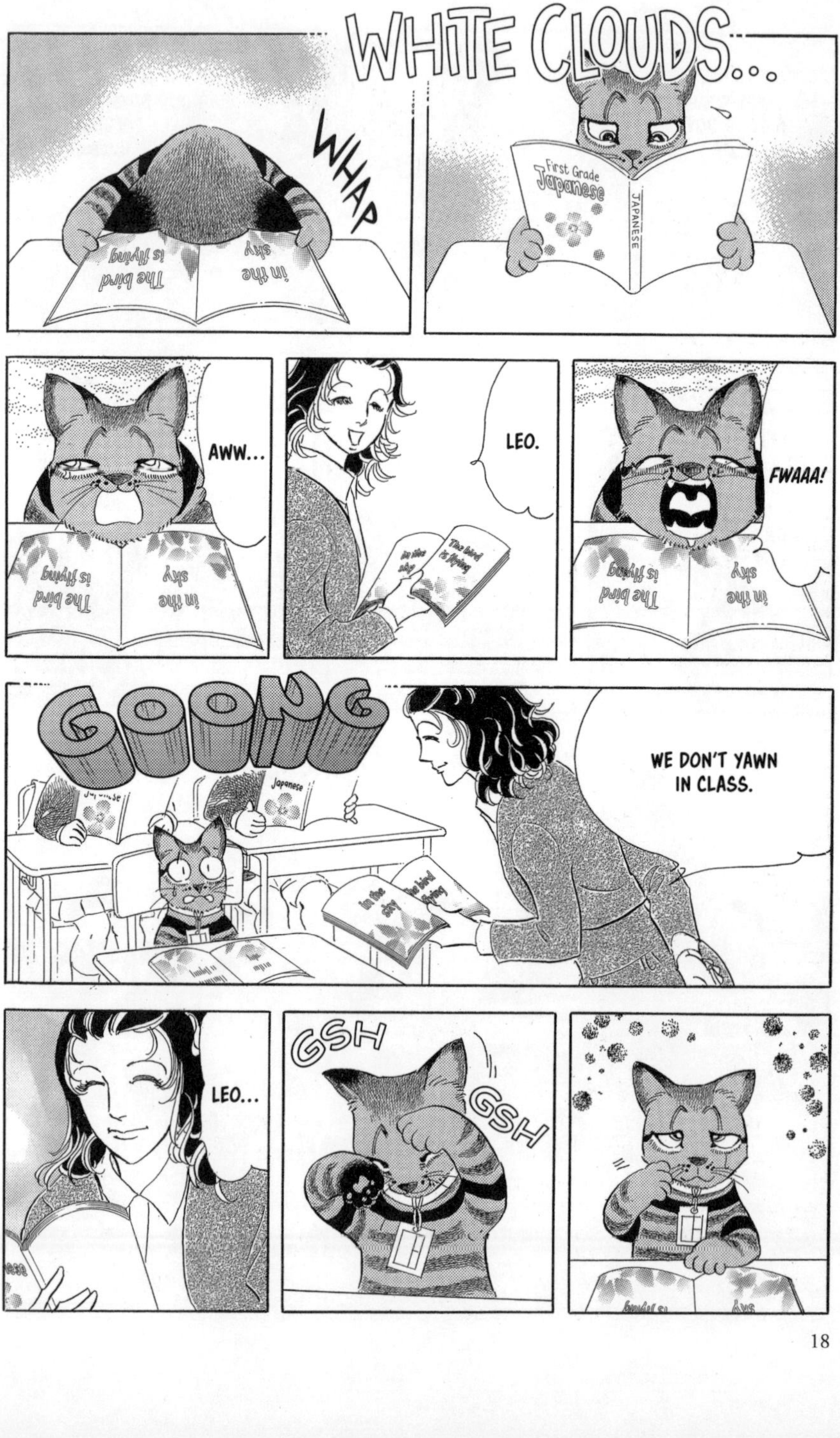
WHITE CLOUDS...
First Grade Japanese
JAPANESE
WHAP
FWAAA!
LEO.
The bird is flying
in the sky
AWW...
WE DON'T YAWN IN CLASS.
GOONG
Japanese
in the sky
The bird is flying
GSH
GSH
LEO...

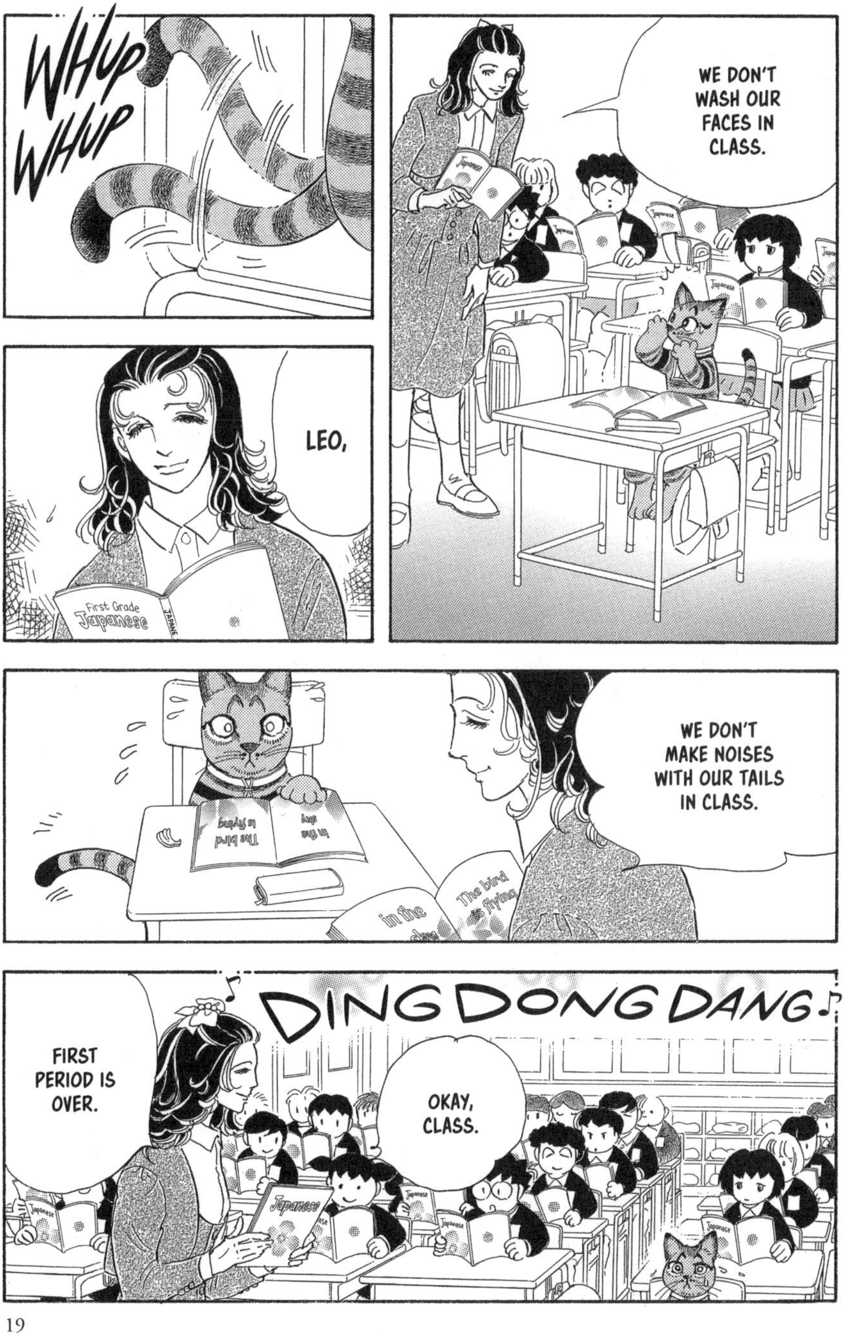
WE DON'T WASH OUR FACES IN CLASS.
WHUP WHUP
LEO,
First Grade Japanese
WE DON'T MAKE NOISES WITH OUR TAILS IN CLASS.
The bird is flying in the sky
DING DONG DANG
OKAY, CLASS.
FIRST PERIOD IS OVER.

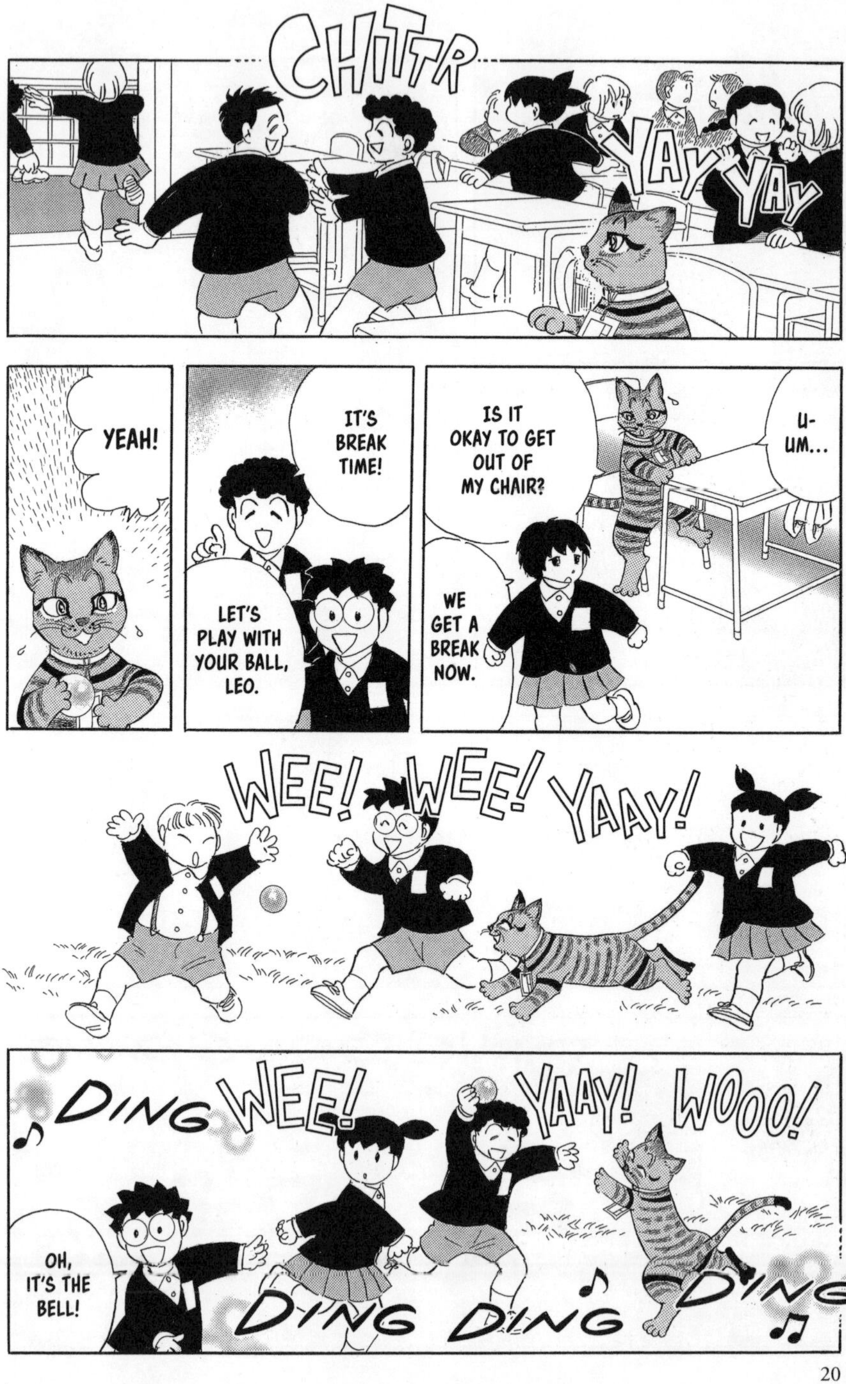
CHITTR
YAY YAY
U-UM...
IS IT OKAY TO GET OUT OF MY CHAIR?
WE GET A BREAK NOW.
IT'S BREAK TIME!
LET'S PLAY WITH YOUR BALL, LEO.
YEAH!
YAAY!
WEE! WEE!
WOOO!
YAAY!
WEE!
DING
DING
DING DING
OH, IT'S THE BELL!

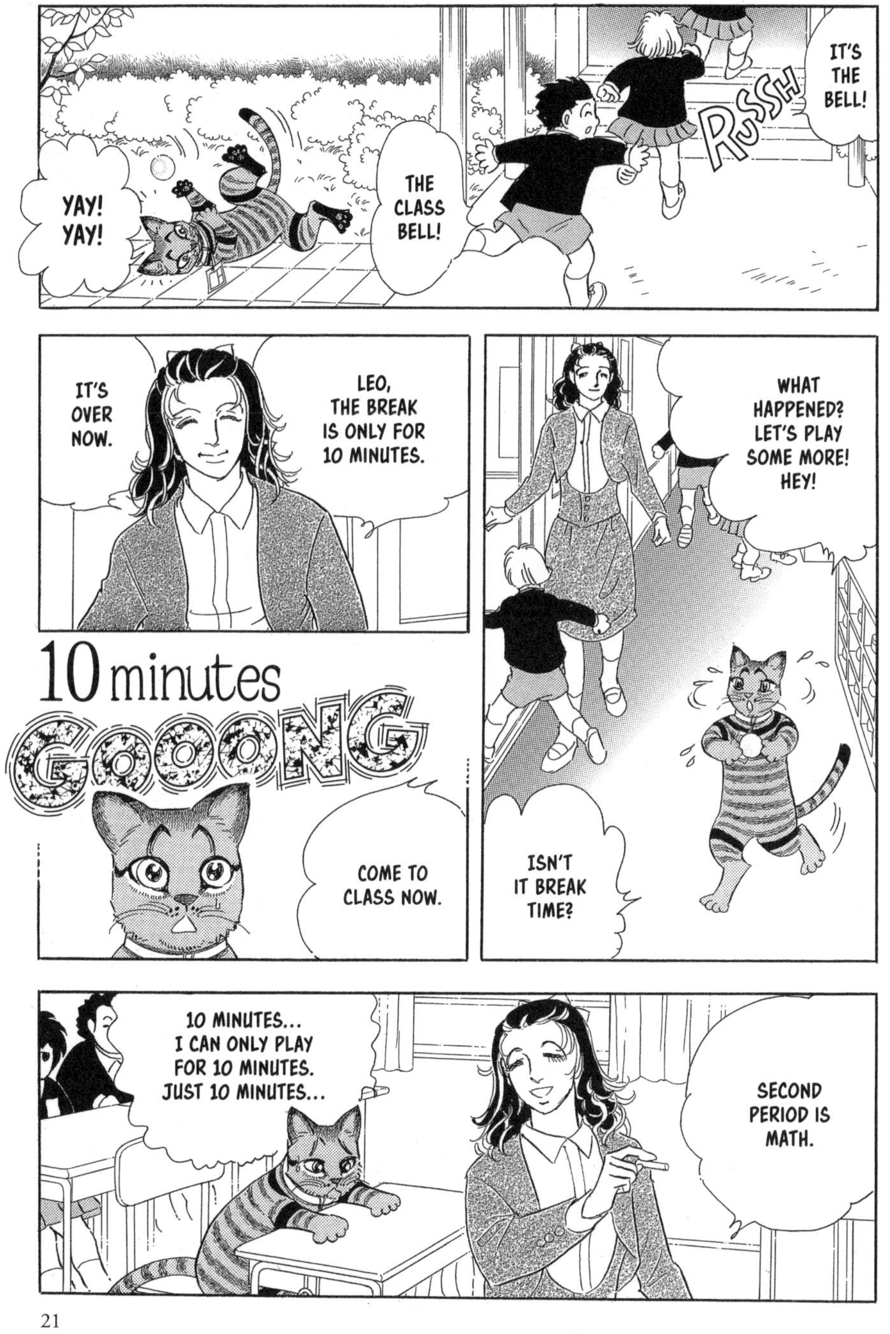
IT'S THE BELL!
RSSSH
THE CLASS BELL!
YAY! YAY!
WHAT HAPPENED? LET'S PLAY SOME MORE! HEY!
ISN'T IT BREAK TIME?
LEO, THE BREAK IS ONLY FOR 10 MINUTES.
IT'S OVER NOW.
10 minutes
GOOONG
COME TO CLASS NOW.
SECOND PERIOD IS MATH.
10 MINUTES... I CAN ONLY PLAY FOR 10 MINUTES. JUST 10 MINUTES...

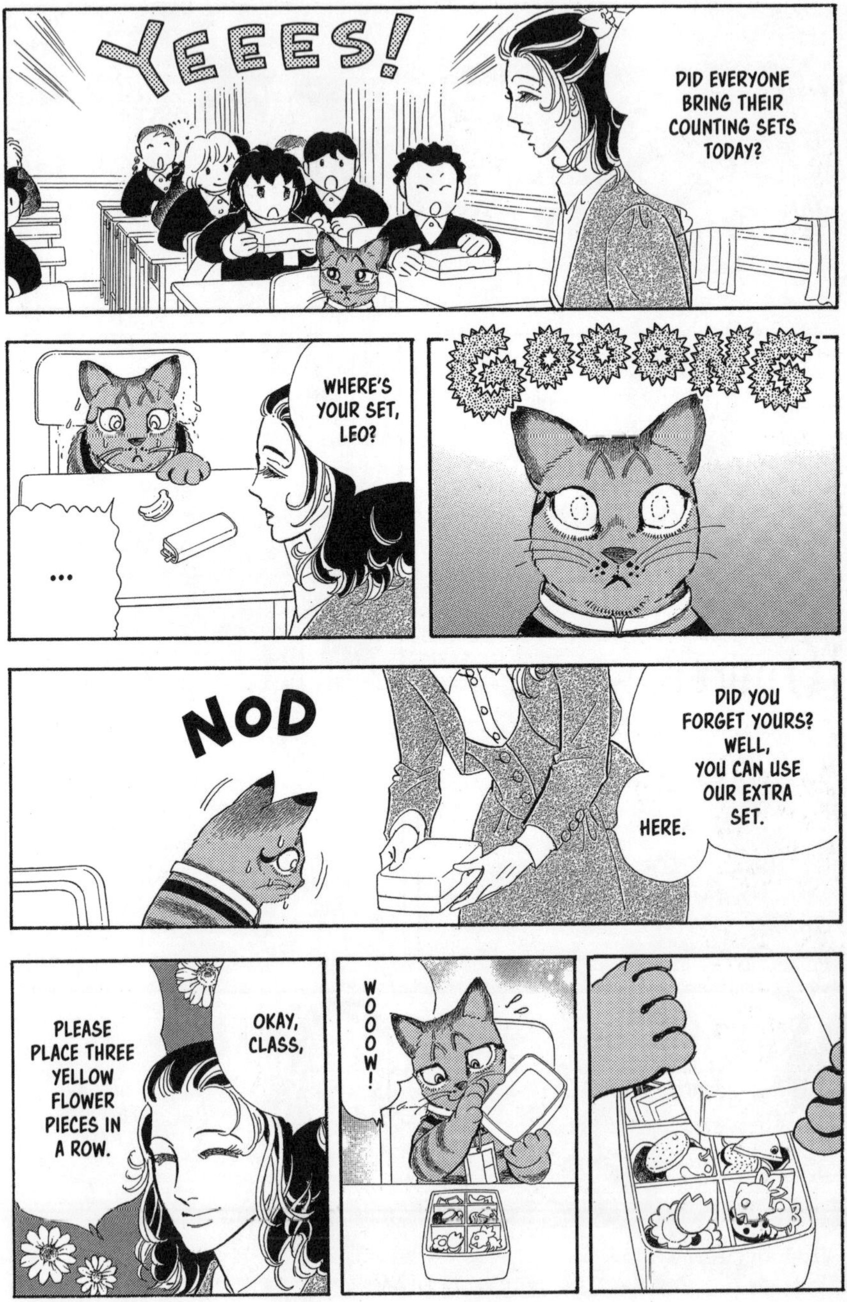
DID EVERYONE BRING THEIR COUNTING SETS TODAY?
YEEES!
GOONG
WHERE'S YOUR SET, LEO?
...
DID YOU FORGET YOURS? WELL, YOU CAN USE OUR EXTRA SET.
HERE.
NOD
WOOOOW!
OKAY, CLASS,
PLEASE PLACE THREE YELLOW FLOWER PIECES IN A ROW.

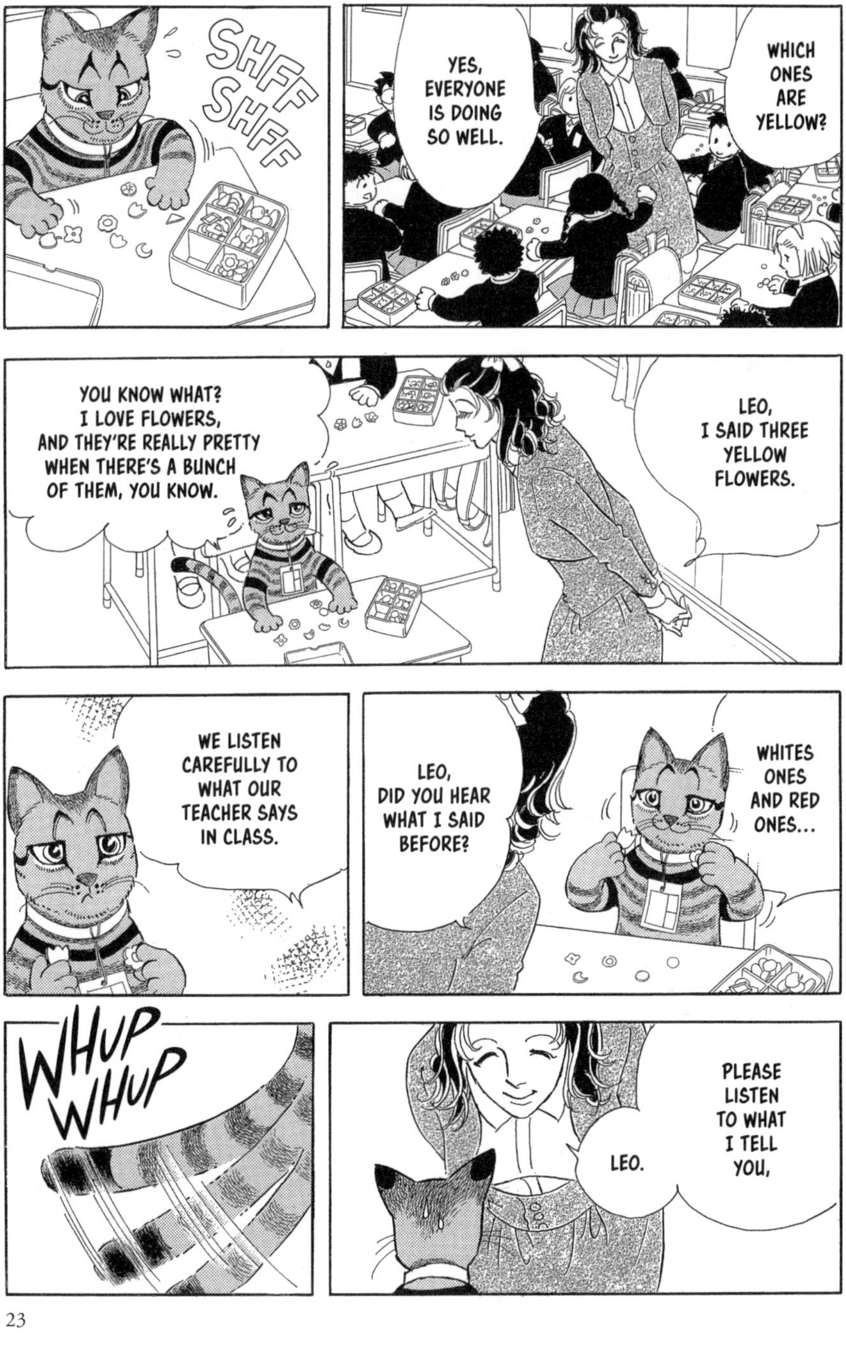
WHICH ONES ARE YELLOW?
YES, EVERYONE IS DOING SO WELL.
SHFF SHFF
LEO, I SAID THREE YELLOW FLOWERS.
YOU KNOW WHAT? I LOVE FLOWERS, AND THEY'RE REALLY PRETTY WHEN THERE'S A BUNCH OF THEM, YOU KNOW.
WHITES ONES AND RED ONES...
LEO, DID YOU HEAR WHAT I SAID BEFORE?
WE LISTEN CAREFULLY TO WHAT OUR TEACHER SAYS IN CLASS.
PLEASE LISTEN TO WHAT I TELL YOU,
LEO.
WHUP WHUP

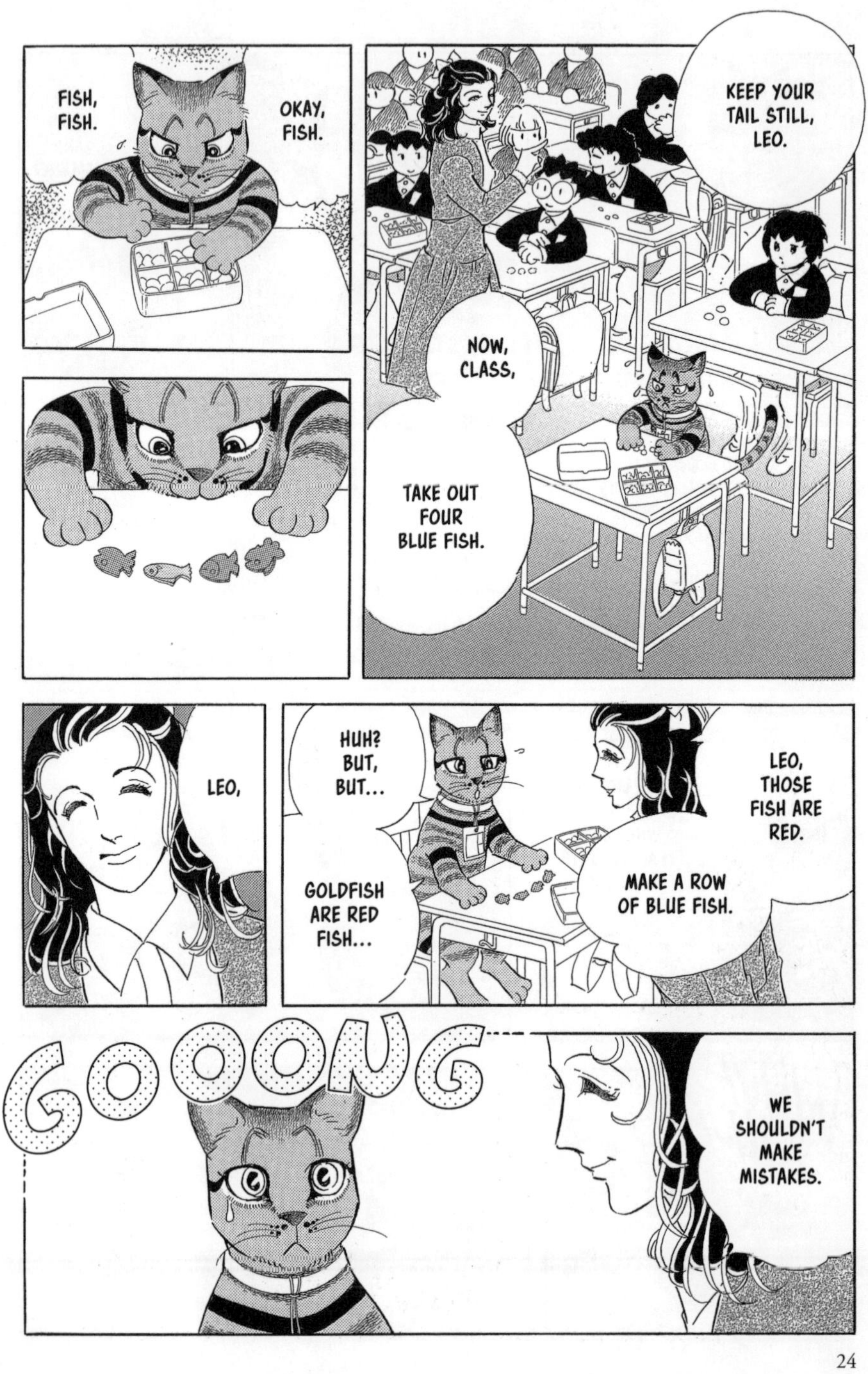
KEEP YOUR TAIL STILL, LEO.
NOW, CLASS,
TAKE OUT FOUR BLUE FISH.
OKAY, FISH.
FISH, FISH.
LEO, THOSE FISH ARE RED.
MAKE A ROW OF BLUE FISH.
HUH? BUT, BUT...
GOLDFISH ARE RED FISH...
LEO,
WE SHOULDN'T MAKE MISTAKES.
GOOONG

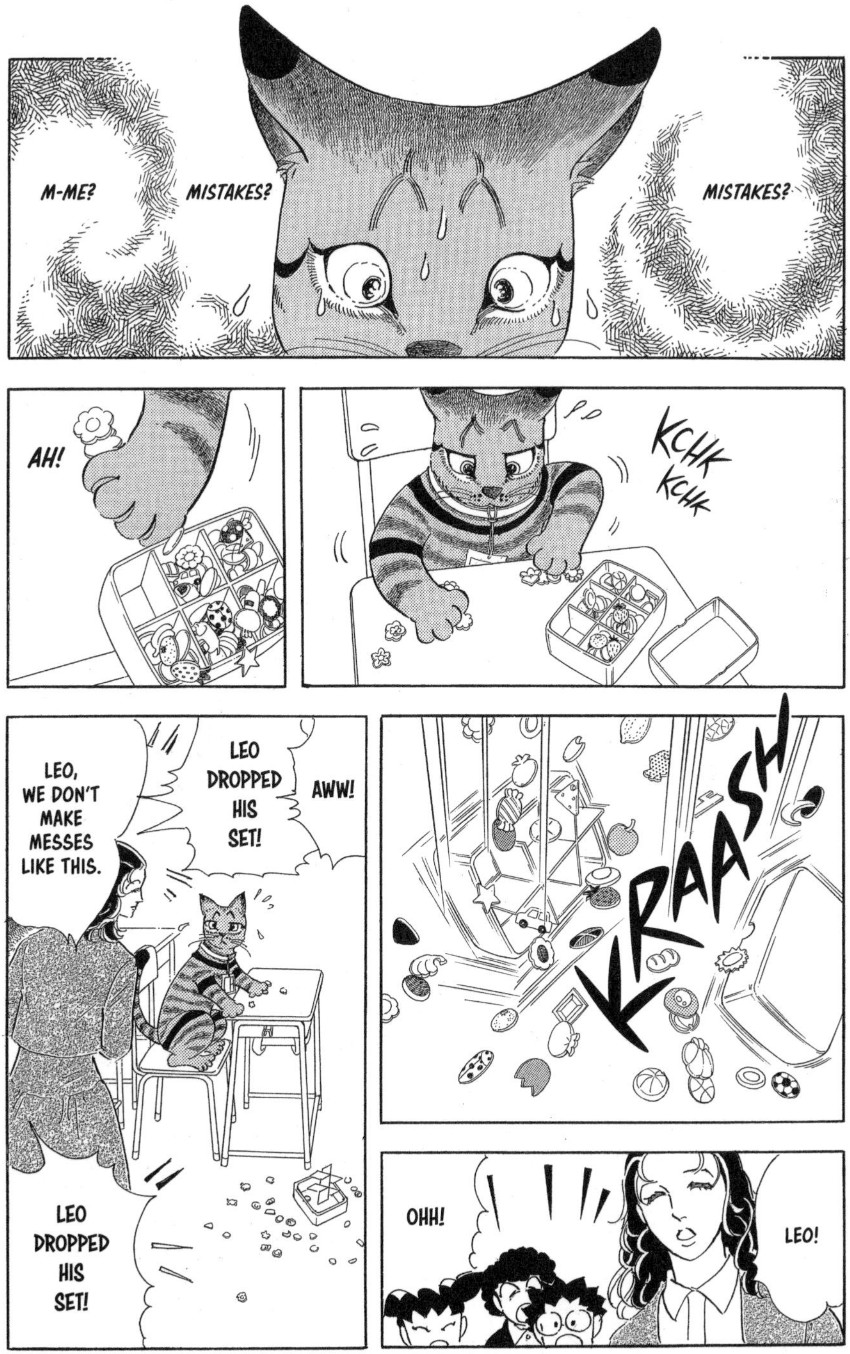
MISTAKES?
MISTAKES?
M-ME?
KCHK KCHK
AH!
KRAASH
LEO!
OHH!
AWW!
LEO DROPPED HIS SET!
LEO, WE DON'T MAKE MESSES LIKE THIS.
LEO DROPPED HIS SET!

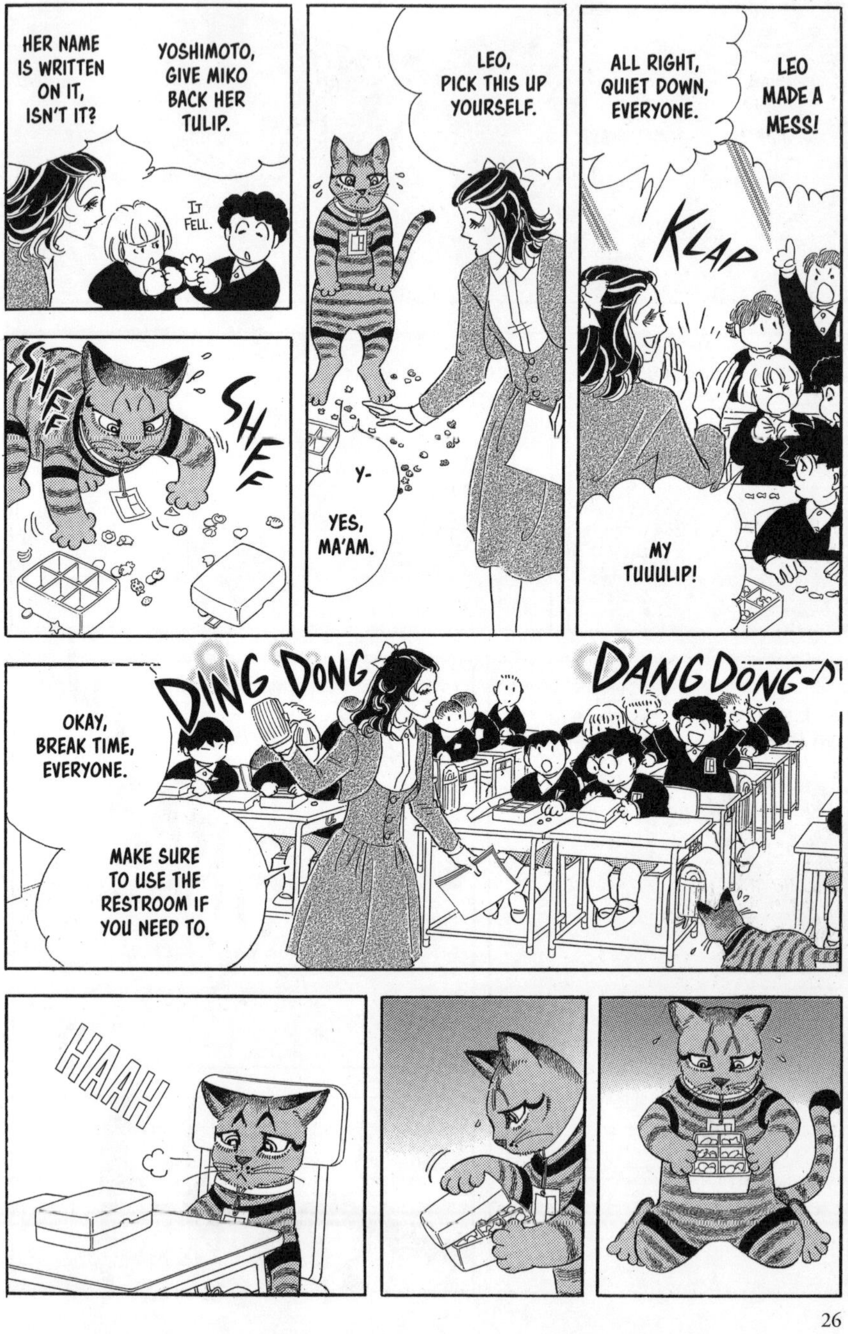

LEO MADE A MESS!
ALL RIGHT, QUIET DOWN, EVERYONE.
KLAP
MY TUUULIP!
LEO, PICK THIS UP YOURSELF.
Y-
YES, MA'AM.
YOSHIMOTO, GIVE MIKO BACK HER TULIP.
HER NAME IS WRITTEN ON IT, ISN'T IT?
IT FELL.
SHEFF
SHEFF
DANG DONG
DING DONG
OKAY, BREAK TIME, EVERYONE.
MAKE SURE TO USE THE RESTROOM IF YOU NEED TO.
HAAH

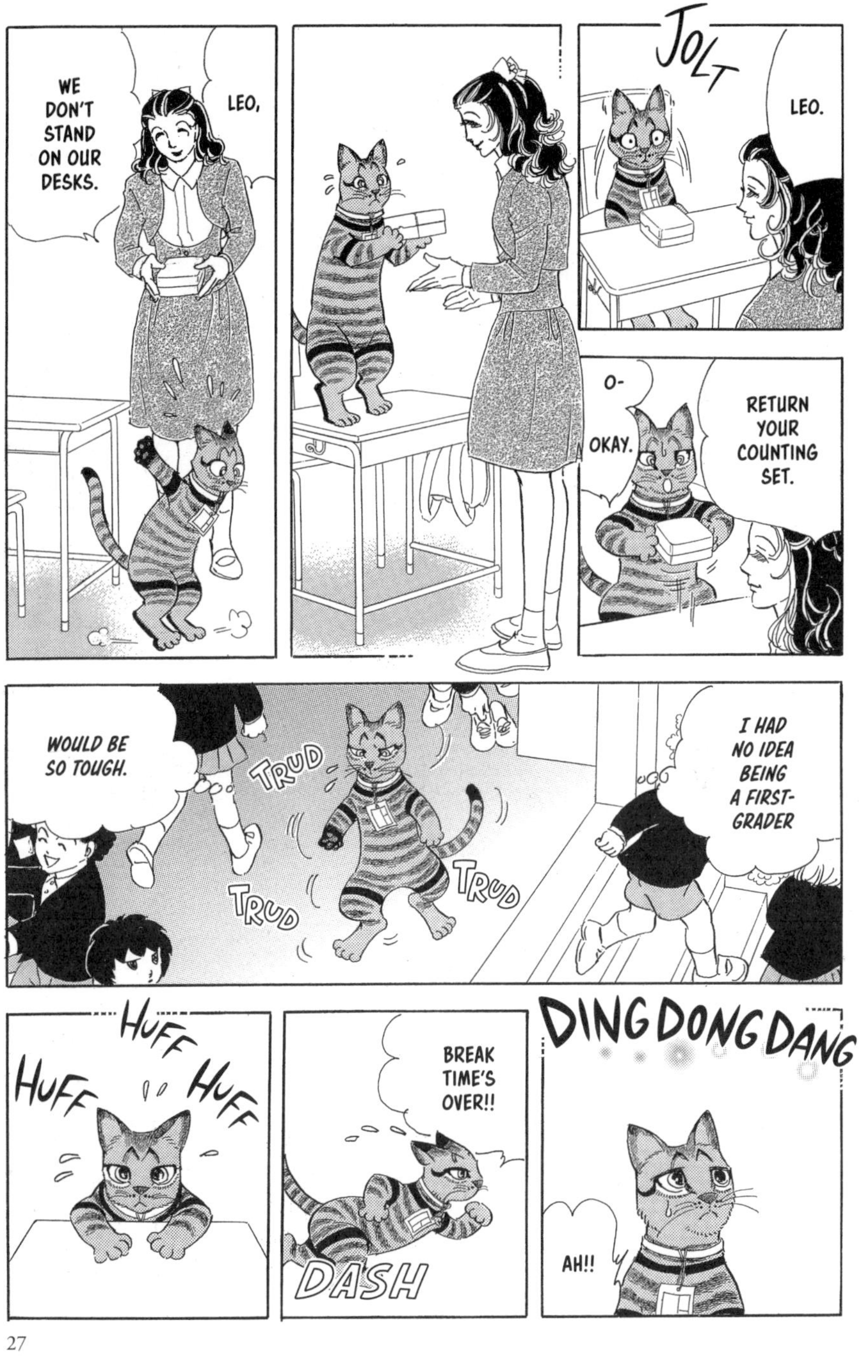
JOLT
LEO.
RETURN YOUR COUNTING SET.
O-
OKAY.
LEO,
WE DON'T STAND ON OUR DESKS.
I HAD NO IDEA BEING A FIRST-GRADER
WOULD BE SO TOUGH.
TRUD
TRUD
TRUD
DING DONG DANG
AH!!
BREAK TIME'S OVER!!
DASH
HUFF
HUFF
HUFF

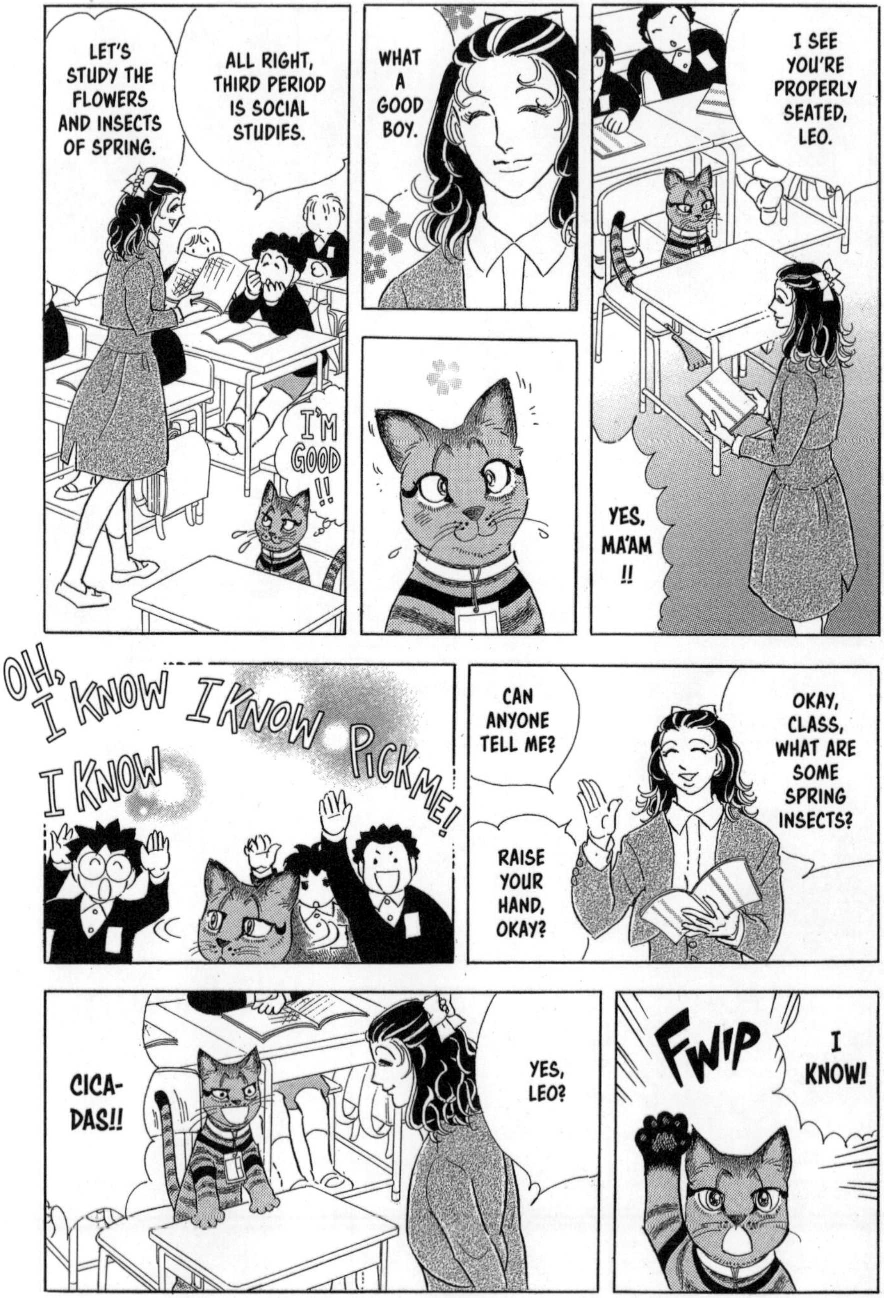
I SEE YOU'RE PROPERLY SEATED, LEO.
YES, MA'AM!!
WHAT A GOOD BOY.
ALL RIGHT, THIRD PERIOD IS SOCIAL STUDIES.
LET'S STUDY THE FLOWERS AND INSECTS OF SPRING.
I'M GOOD!!
OKAY, CLASS, WHAT ARE SOME SPRING INSECTS?
CAN ANYONE TELL ME?
RAISE YOUR HAND, OKAY?
PICK ME!
I KNOW
OH, I KNOW
I KNOW
FWIP
I KNOW!
YES, LEO?
CICA-DAS!!

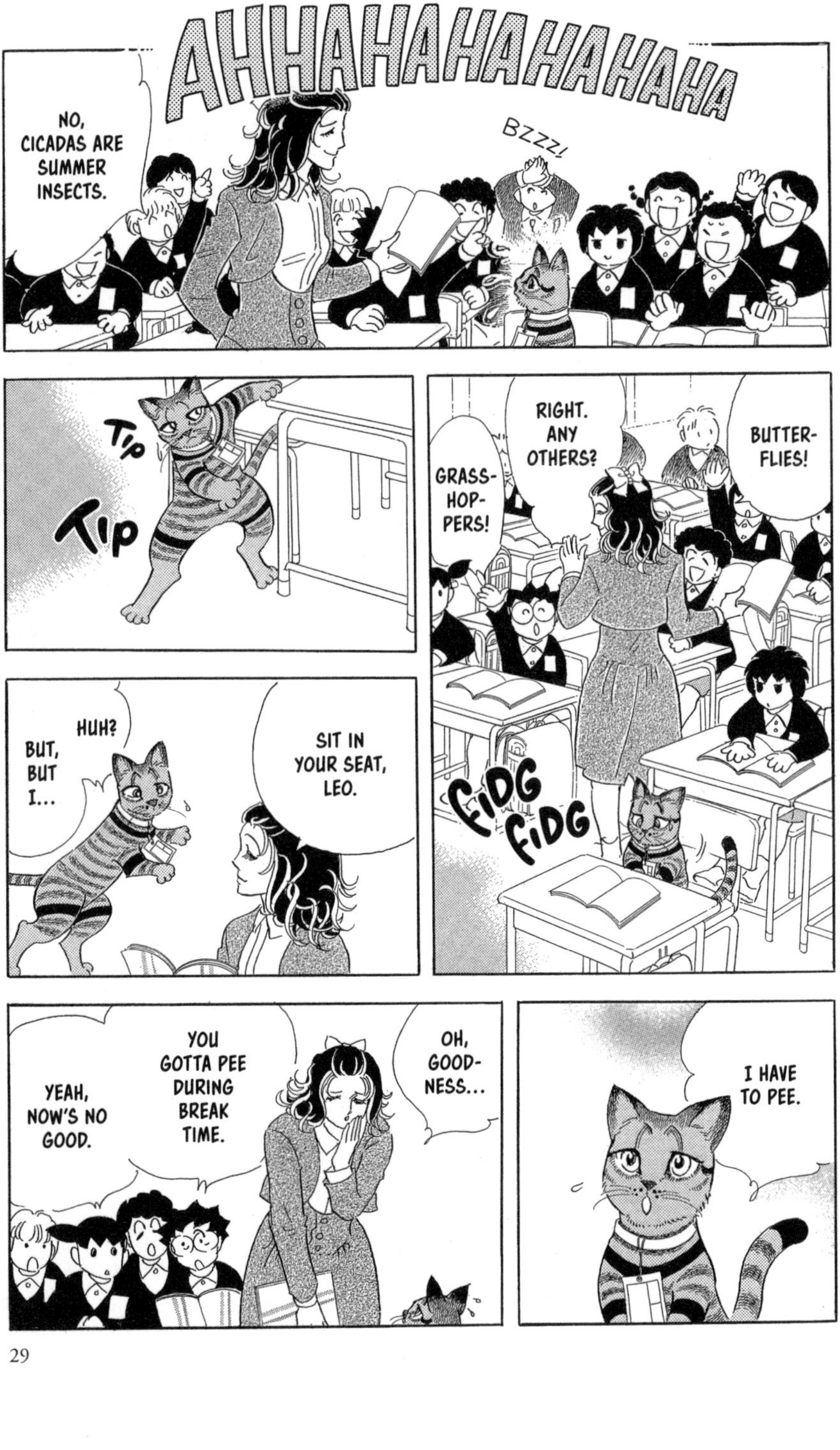
AHHAHAHAHAHAHAHA
BZZZ!
NO, CICADAS ARE SUMMER INSECTS.
BUTTER-FLIES!
RIGHT. ANY OTHERS?
GRASS-HOP-PERS!
FIDG FIDG
TIP
TIP
SIT IN YOUR SEAT, LEO.
HUH?
BUT, BUT I...
I HAVE TO PEE.
OH, GOOD-NESS...
YOU GOTTA PEE DURING BREAK TIME.
YEAH, NOW'S NO GOOD.

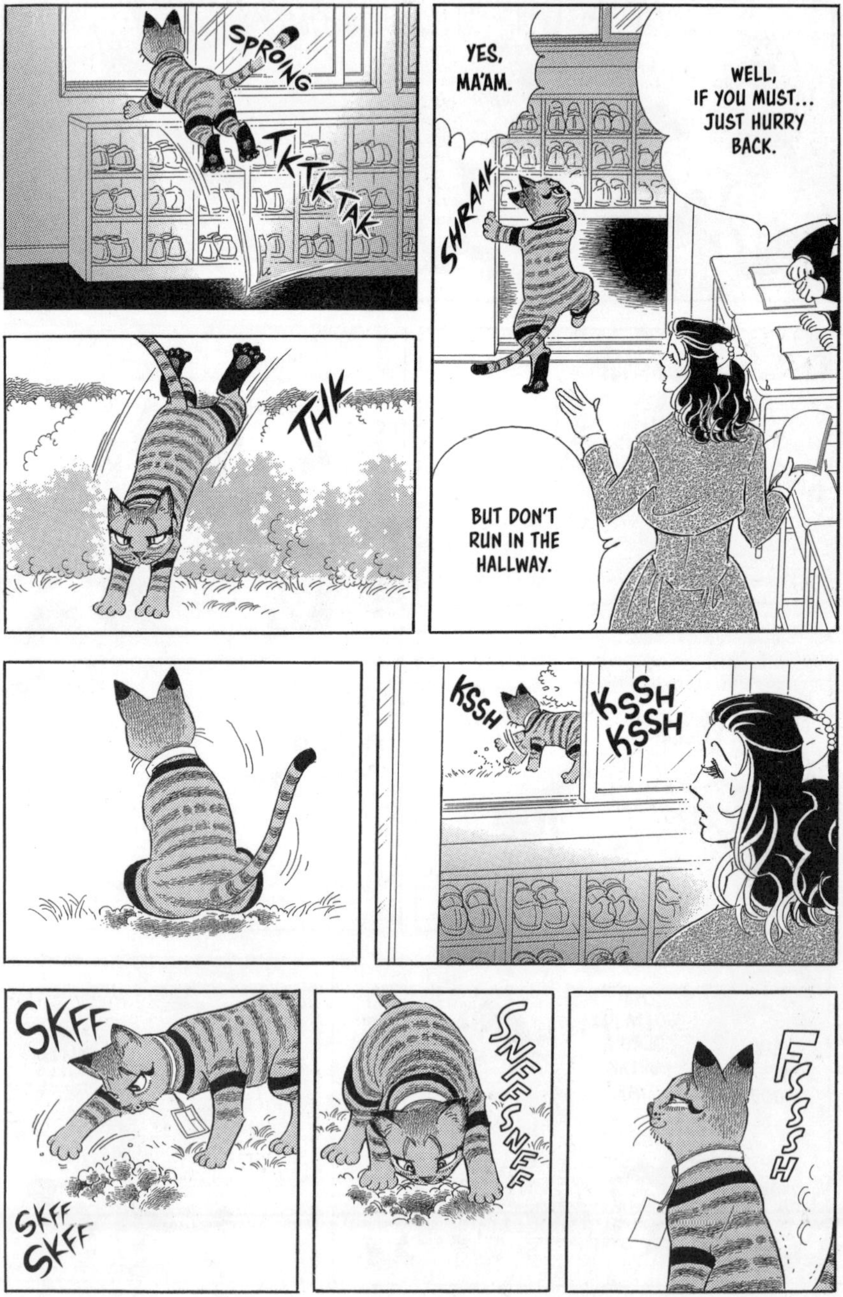
WELL, IF YOU MUST... JUST HURRY BACK.
YES, MA'AM.
SHRAAK
BUT DON'T RUN IN THE HALLWAY.
SPROING
TKTKTAK
THK
KSSH KSSH
KSSH
FSSSSH
SNFFSNFF
SKFF
SKFF SKFF

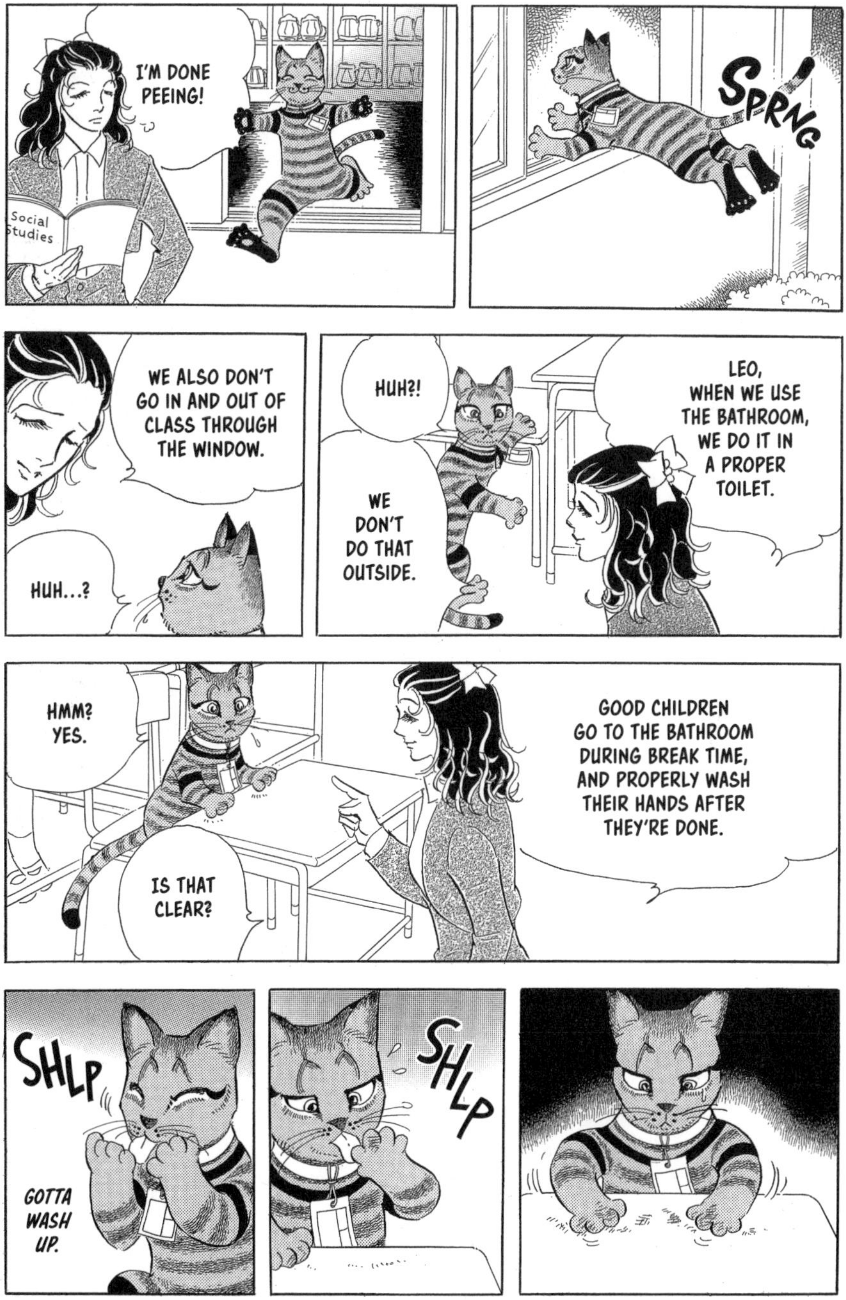
SPRNG
I'M DONE PEEING!
Social Studies
LEO, WHEN WE USE THE BATHROOM, WE DO IT IN A PROPER TOILET.
HUH?!
WE DON'T DO THAT OUTSIDE.
WE ALSO DON'T GO IN AND OUT OF CLASS THROUGH THE WINDOW.
HUH...?
GOOD CHILDREN GO TO THE BATHROOM DURING BREAK TIME, AND PROPERLY WASH THEIR HANDS AFTER THEY'RE DONE.
IS THAT CLEAR?
HMM? YES.
SHLP
SHLP
GOTTA WASH UP.

KWIP
SHLP
SHLP
SHLP
LEO,
WE DON'T LICK OUR BEHINDS IN CLASS.
GOONG
DING DONG DAAANG♪
ALRIGHT! THIRD PERIOD IS OVER.
YOU CAN'T LICK YOUR BEHIND!
YEAH!
YOU CAN'T DO THAT!
YOU CAN'T PEE OUTSIDE, EITHER!
TIP TIP
YOU CAN'T DO THAT, LEO!
AUGHH!

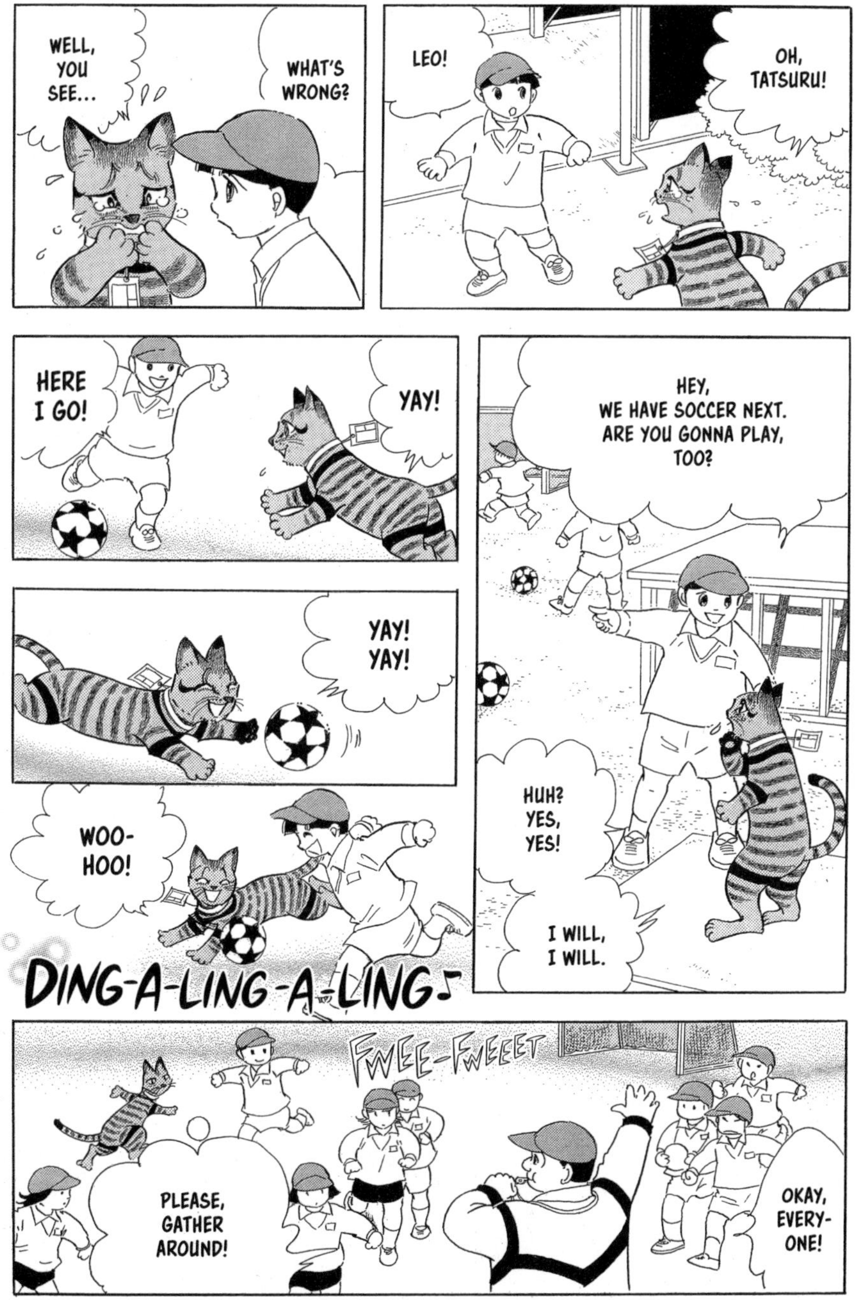
OH, TATSURU!
LEO!
WHAT'S WRONG?
WELL, YOU SEE...
HEY, WE HAVE SOCCER NEXT. ARE YOU GONNA PLAY, TOO?
HUH? YES, YES!
I WILL, I WILL.
YAY!
HERE I GO!
YAY! YAY!
WOO-HOO!
DING-A-LING-A-LING
FWEE-FWEEET
OKAY, EVERY-ONE!
PLEASE, GATHER AROUND!

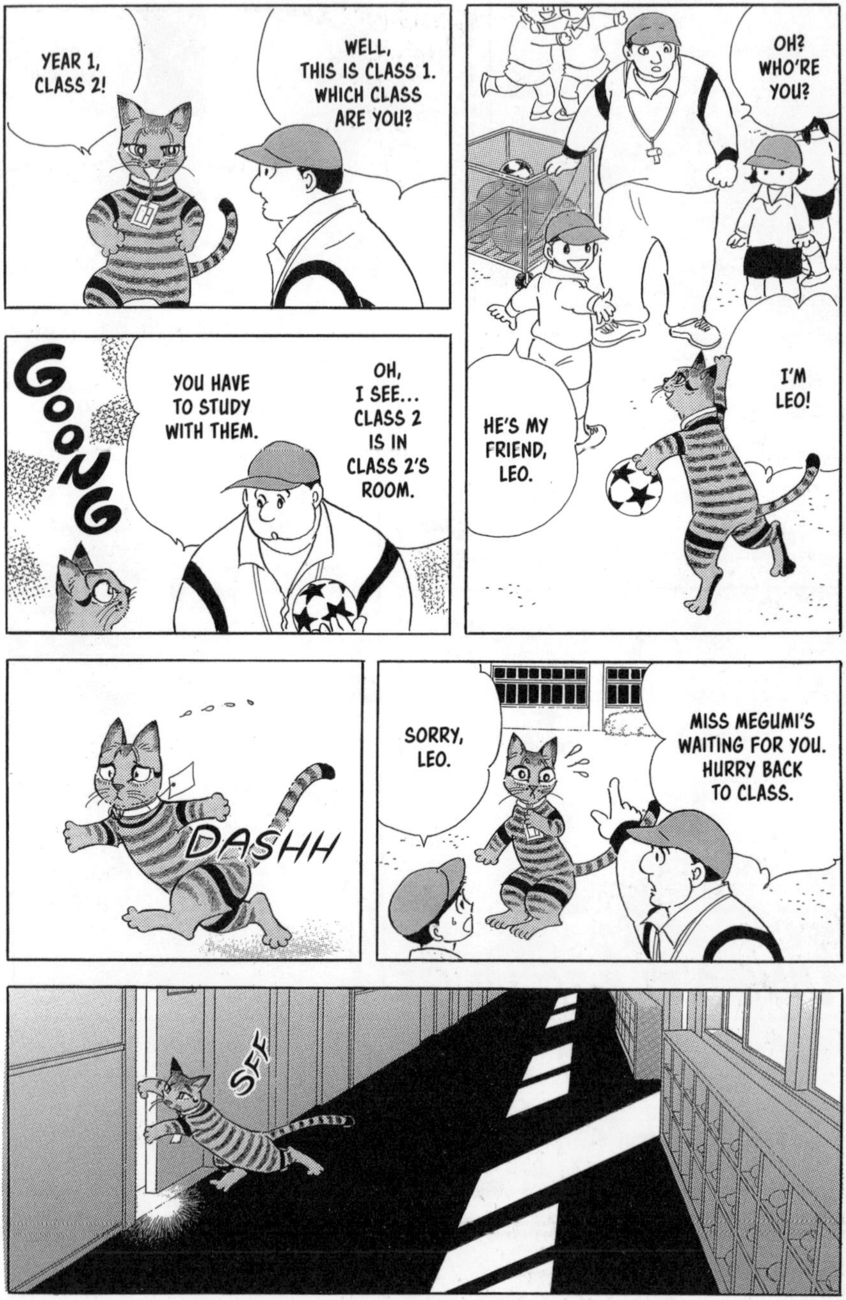
OH? WHO'RE YOU?
I'M LEO!
HE'S MY FRIEND, LEO.
WELL, THIS IS CLASS 1. WHICH CLASS ARE YOU?
YEAR 1, CLASS 2!
OH, I SEE... CLASS 2 IS IN CLASS 2'S ROOM.
YOU HAVE TO STUDY WITH THEM.
GOONG
MISS MEGUMI'S WAITING FOR YOU. HURRY BACK TO CLASS.
SORRY, LEO.
DASHH
SFF

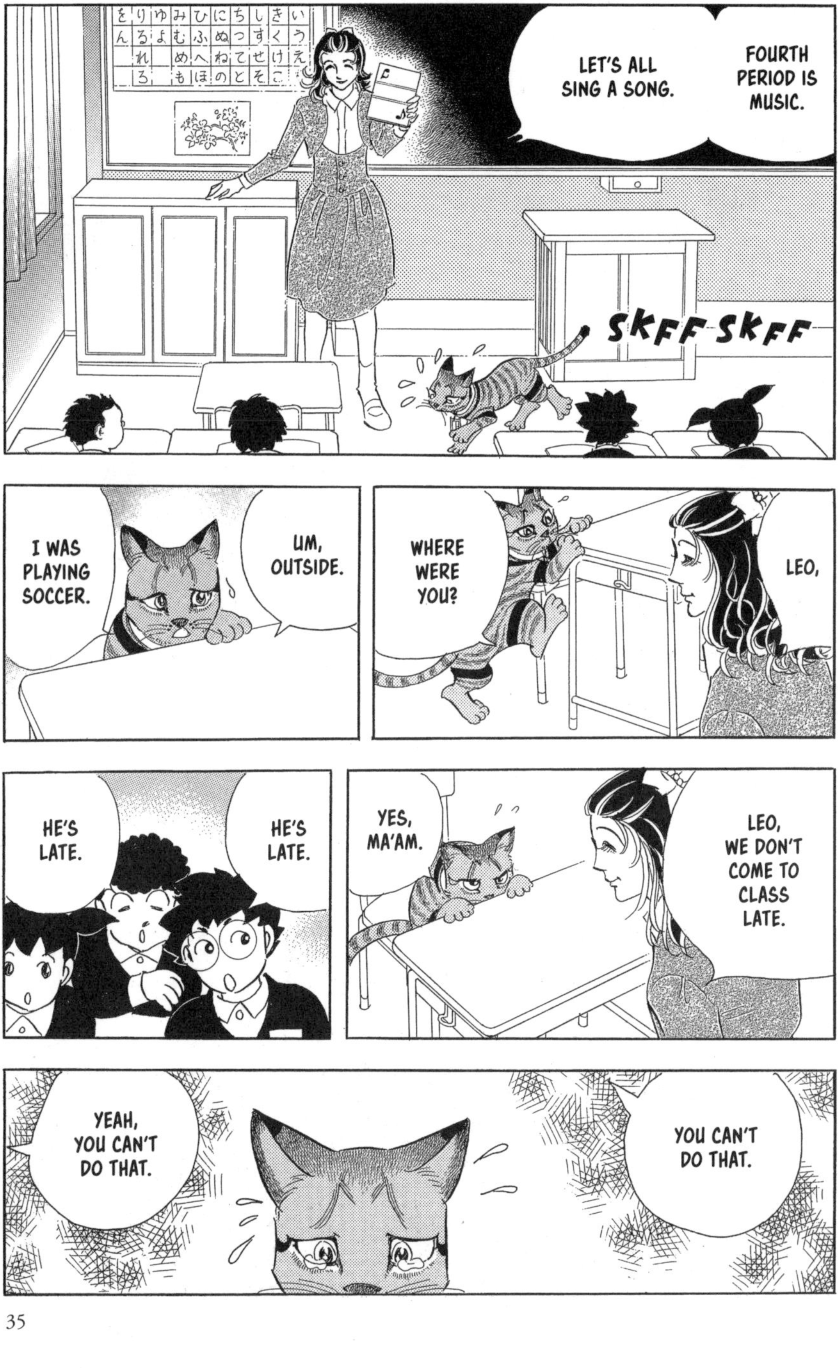

FOURTH PERIOD IS MUSIC.
LET'S ALL SING A SONG.
SKFF SKFF
LEO,
WHERE WERE YOU?
UM, OUTSIDE.
I WAS PLAYING SOCCER.
LEO, WE DON'T COME TO CLASS LATE.
YES, MA'AM.
HE'S LATE.
HE'S LATE.
YOU CAN'T DO THAT.
YEAH, YOU CAN'T DO THAT.

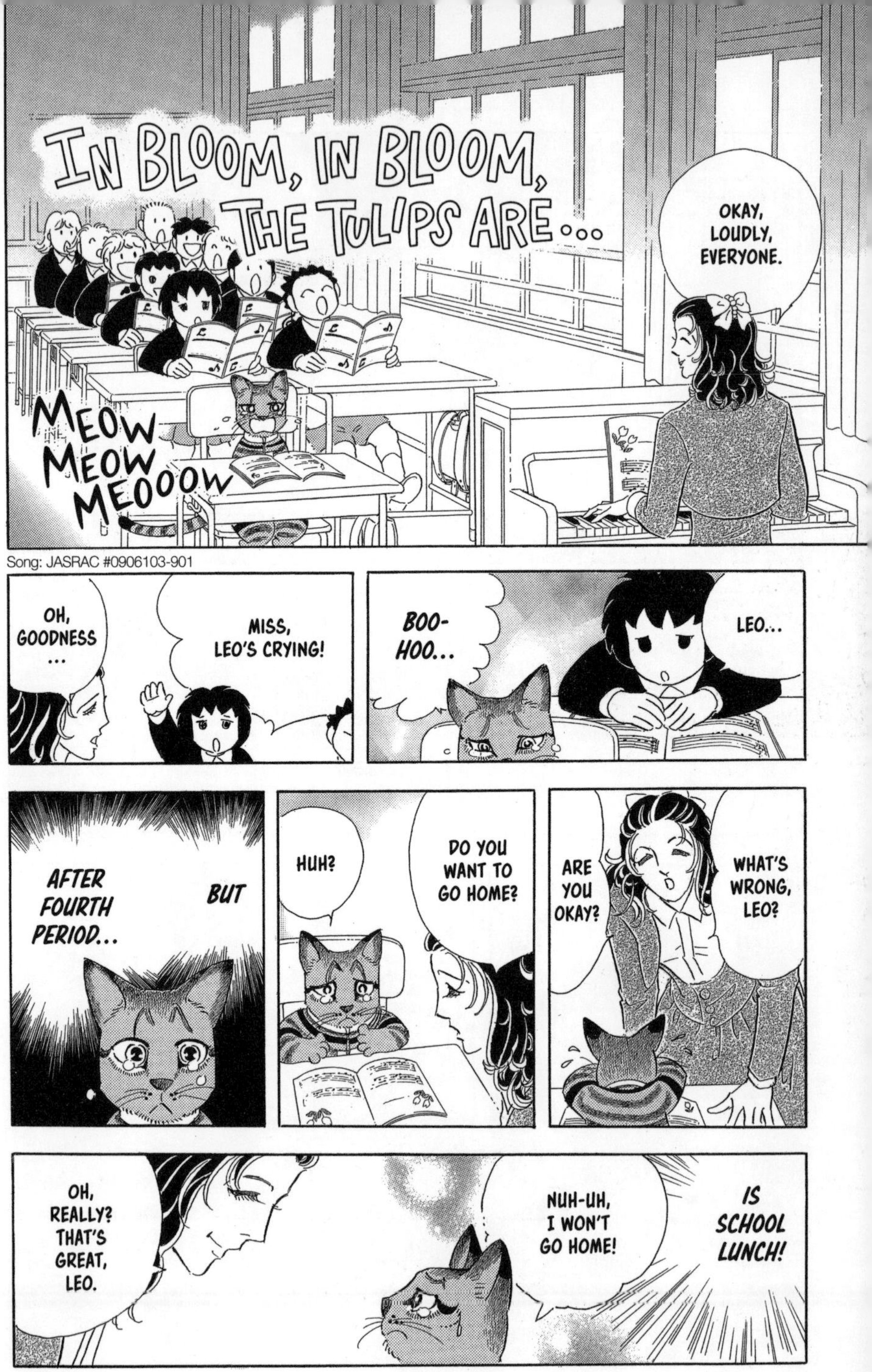
OKAY, LOUDLY, EVERYONE.
IN BLOOM, IN BLOOM, THE TULIPS ARE...
MEOW MEOW MEOOOW
LEO...
BOO-HOO...
MISS, LEO'S CRYING!
OH, GOODNESS...
WHAT'S WRONG, LEO?
ARE YOU OKAY?
DO YOU WANT TO GO HOME?
HUH?
BUT
AFTER FOURTH PERIOD...
IS SCHOOL LUNCH!
NUH-UH, I WON'T GO HOME!
OH, REALLY? THAT'S GREAT, LEO.

Song: JASRAC #0906103-901

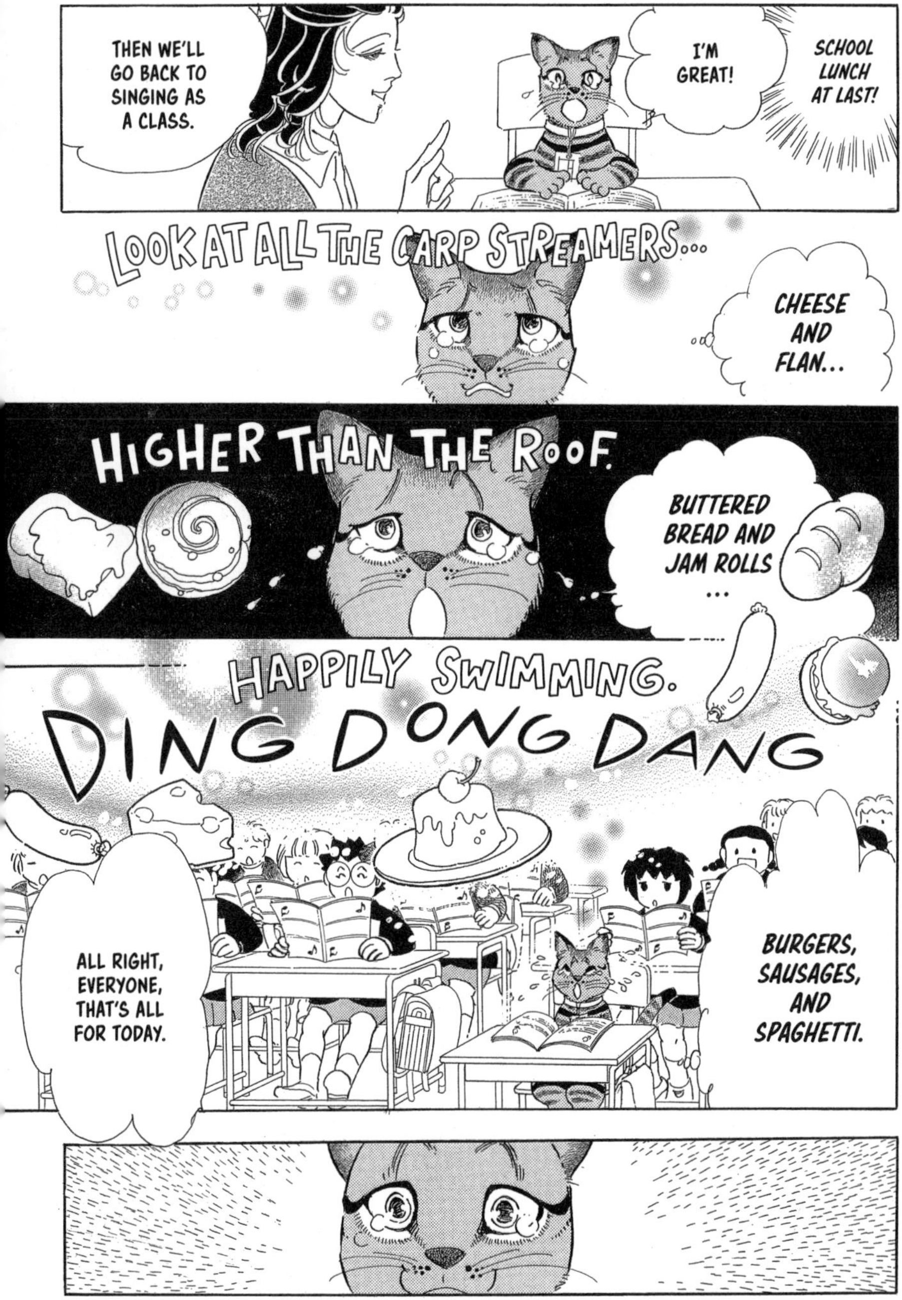
SCHOOL LUNCH AT LAST!
I'M GREAT!
THEN WE'LL GO BACK TO SINGING AS A CLASS.
CHEESE AND FLAN...
LOOK AT ALL THE CARP STREAMERS...
BUTTERED BREAD AND JAM ROLLS ...
HIGHER THAN THE ROOF.
BURGERS, SAUSAGES, AND SPAGHETTI.
HAPPILY SWIMMING.
DING DONG DANG
ALL RIGHT, EVERYONE, THAT'S ALL FOR TODAY.

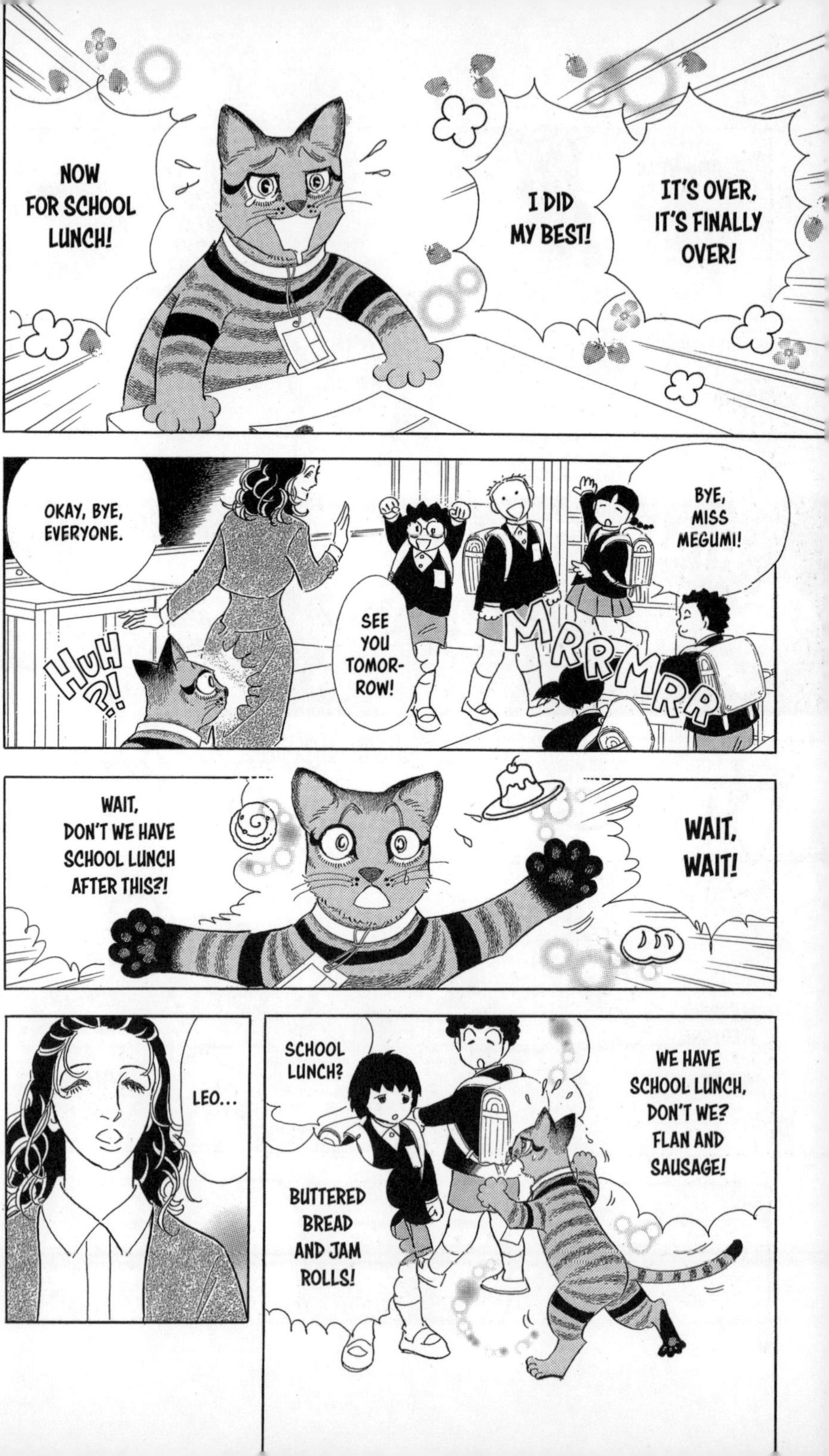
IT'S OVER, IT'S FINALLY OVER!
I DID MY BEST!
NOW FOR SCHOOL LUNCH!
BYE, MISS MEGUMI!
MRRMRR
SEE YOU TOMOR-ROW!
OKAY, BYE, EVERYONE.
HUH?!
WAIT, WAIT!
WAIT, DON'T WE HAVE SCHOOL LUNCH AFTER THIS?!
WE HAVE SCHOOL LUNCH, DON'T WE? FLAN AND SAUSAGE!
SCHOOL LUNCH?
BUTTERED BREAD AND JAM ROLLS!
LEO...

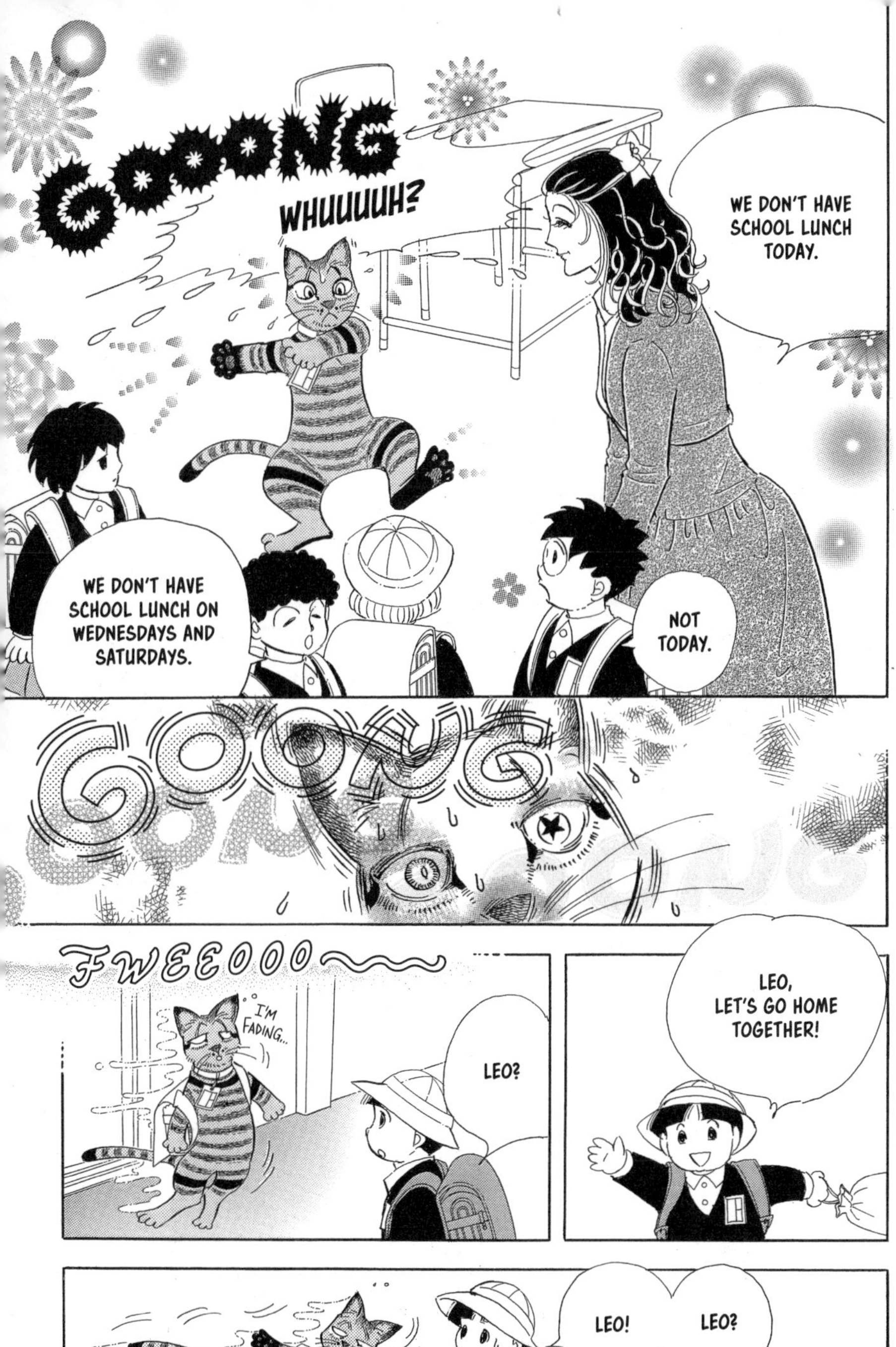
WE DON'T HAVE SCHOOL LUNCH TODAY.
GOOONG
WHUUUUH?
NOT TODAY.
WE DON'T HAVE SCHOOL LUNCH ON WEDNESDAYS AND SATURDAYS.
GOOONG
LEO, LET'S GO HOME TOGETHER!
FWEEOOO
I'M FADING...
LEO?
LEO?
LEO!

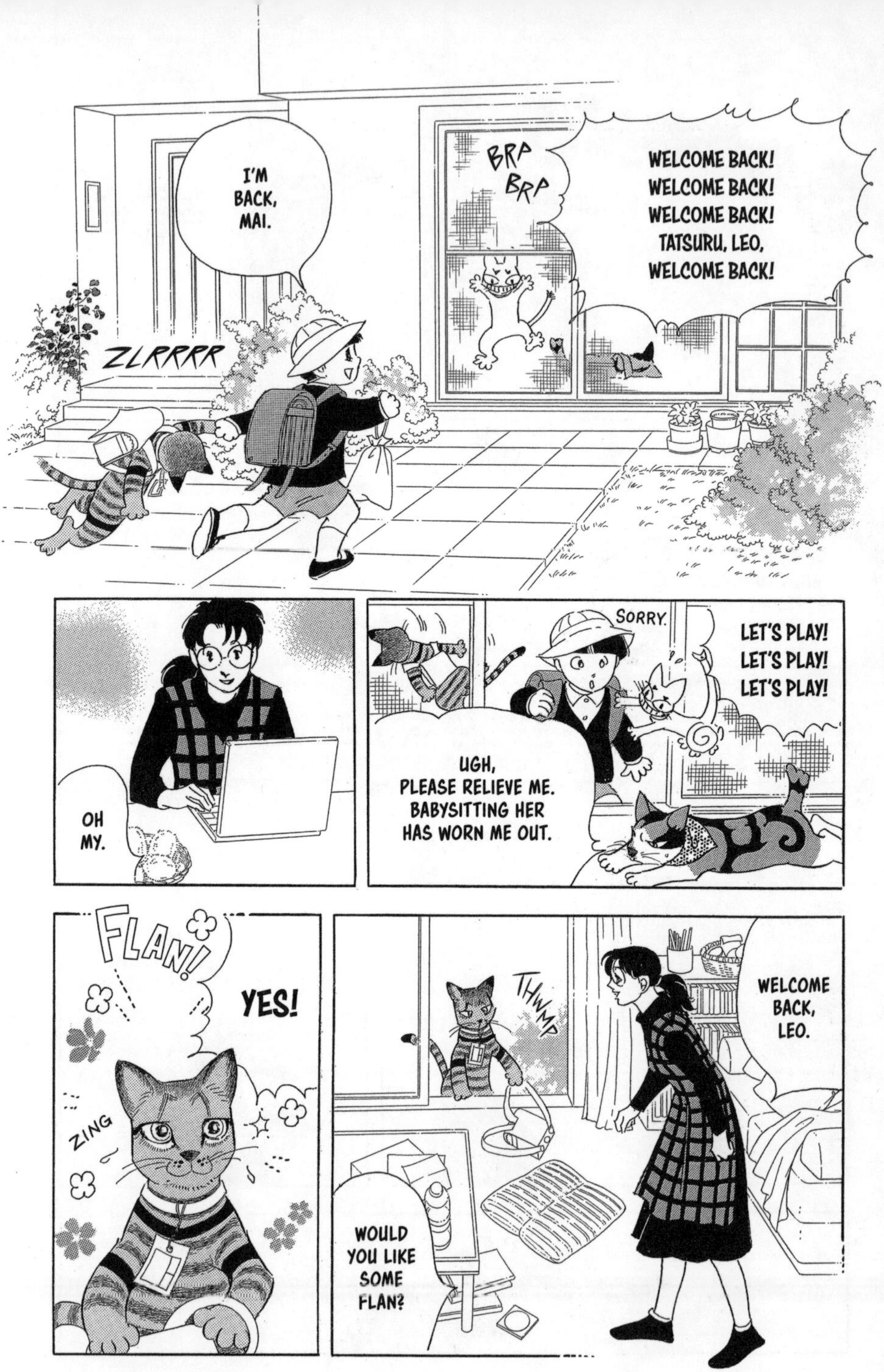
WELCOME BACK! WELCOME BACK! WELCOME BACK! TATSURU, LEO, WELCOME BACK!
BRP BRP
I'M BACK, MAI.
ZLRRRR
LET'S PLAY! LET'S PLAY! LET'S PLAY!
SORRY.
UGH, PLEASE RELIEVE ME. BABYSITTING HER HAS WORN ME OUT.
OH MY.
WELCOME BACK, LEO.
THWMP
WOULD YOU LIKE SOME FLAN?
YES!
FLAN!
ZING

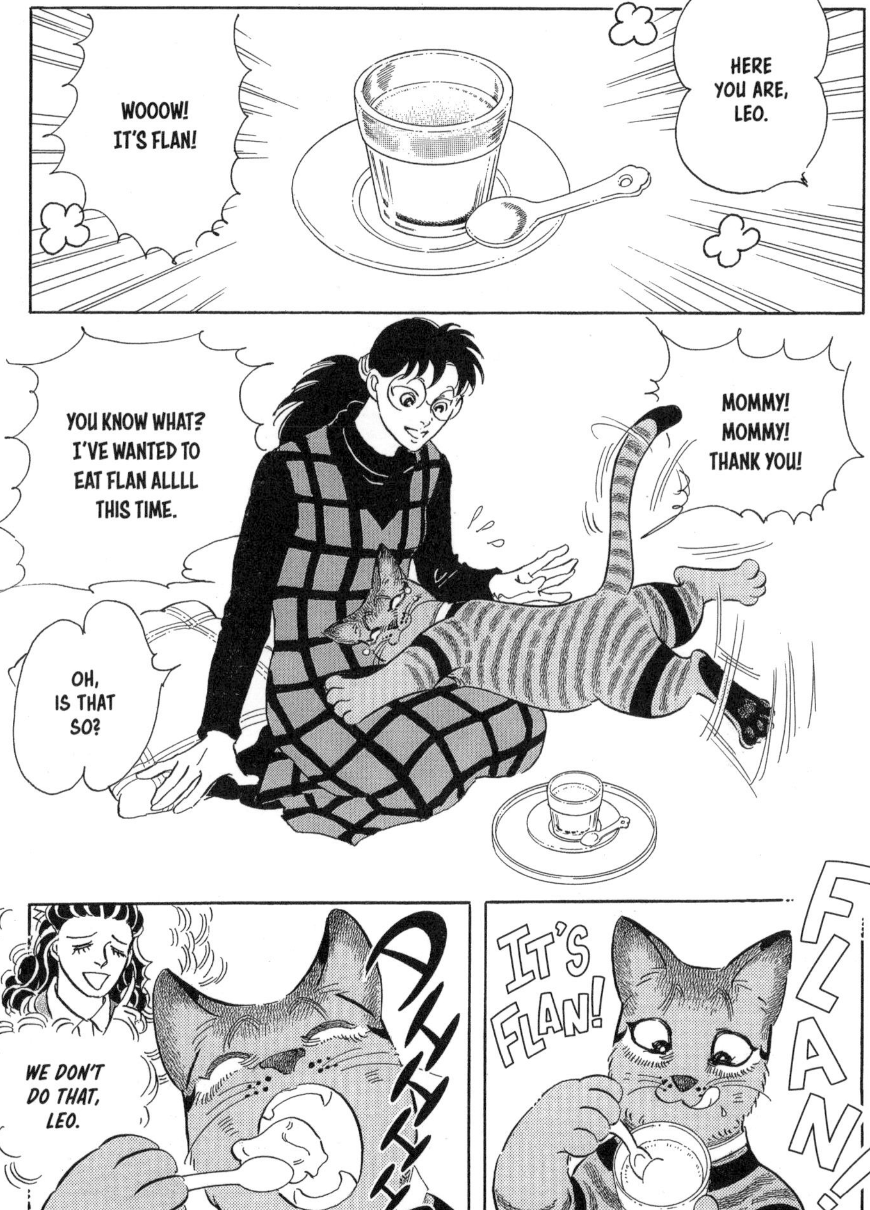
HERE YOU ARE, LEO.
WOOOW! IT'S FLAN!
MOMMY! MOMMY! THANK YOU!
YOU KNOW WHAT? I'VE WANTED TO EAT FLAN ALLLL THIS TIME.
OH, IS THAT SO?
FLAN!
IT'S FLAN!
AHHHH!
WE DON'T DO THAT, LEO.

HAMPH
EEK!
BA-BOOM
AHH!!
THAT'S BAD!
YOU CAN'T DO THAT, LEO!
BOOM
BOOM
HAMPH
OM NOM OM NOM
HOW WAS SCHOOL, LEO? WAS IT FUN?
MM-MMM.
HMM?
HMM?
WILL YOU GO AGAIN TOMOR-ROW?
WHUMP WHUMP

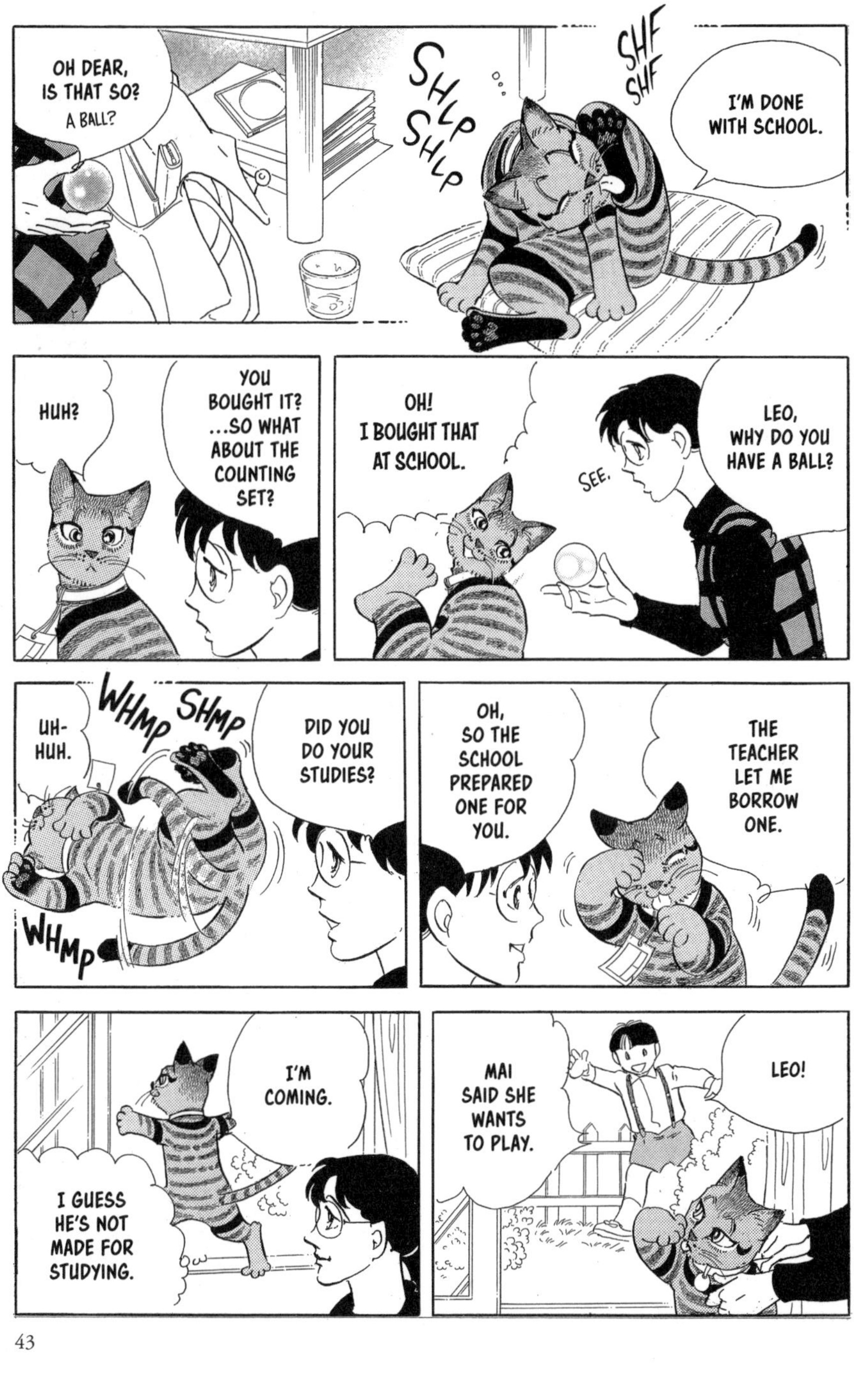
SHF SHF
I'M DONE WITH SCHOOL.
SHLP SHLP SHLP
OH DEAR, IS THAT SO?
A BALL?
LEO, WHY DO YOU HAVE A BALL?
SEE.
OH! I BOUGHT THAT AT SCHOOL.
YOU BOUGHT IT? ...SO WHAT ABOUT THE COUNTING SET?
HUH?
THE TEACHER LET ME BORROW ONE.
OH, SO THE SCHOOL PREPARED ONE FOR YOU.
DID YOU DO YOUR STUDIES?
SHMP
WHMP
UH-HUH.
WHMP
LEO!
MAI SAID SHE WANTS TO PLAY.
I'M COMING.
I GUESS HE'S NOT MADE FOR STUDYING.

OH, WELL...
HE IS A CAT.
CHIRP
MAI'S ESCAPED!
AAGH!
CATCH HER, LEO!

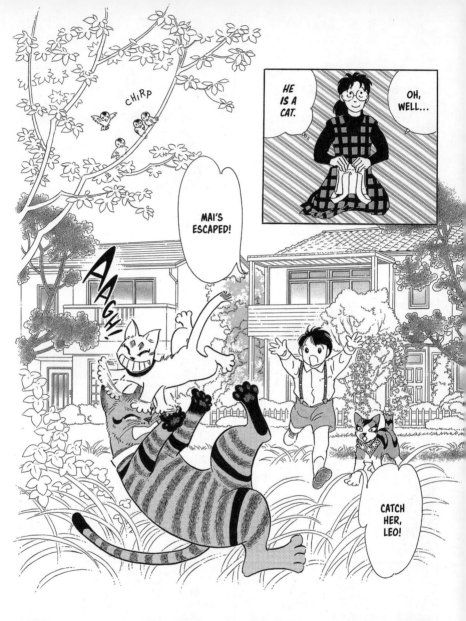

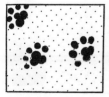

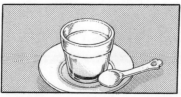

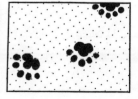

2 Let Me Out

ZASHHH
ZASHHH

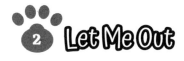

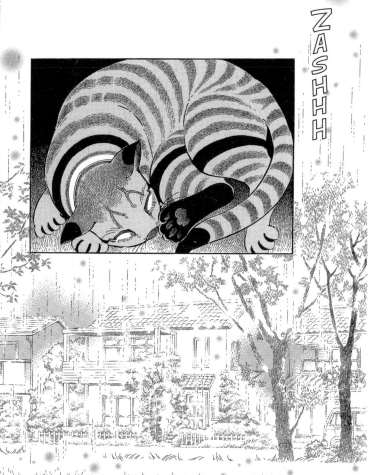

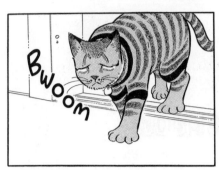

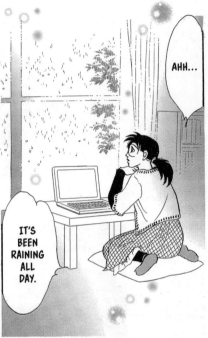

AHH...
IT'S BEEN RAINING ALL DAY.
BWOOM
MMNH
OH, MORNING, LEO.
I SEE YOU'RE FINALLY UP.
KRNCH KRNCH
YOU WERE SLEEPY TODAY, HUH.
LAP LAP LAP LAP
TMP TMP TMP TMP
TAK TAK TAK

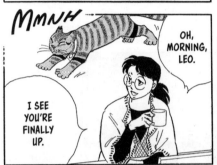

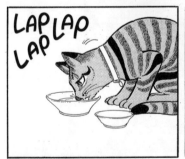

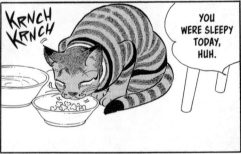

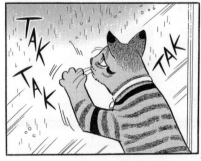

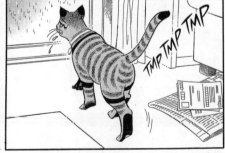

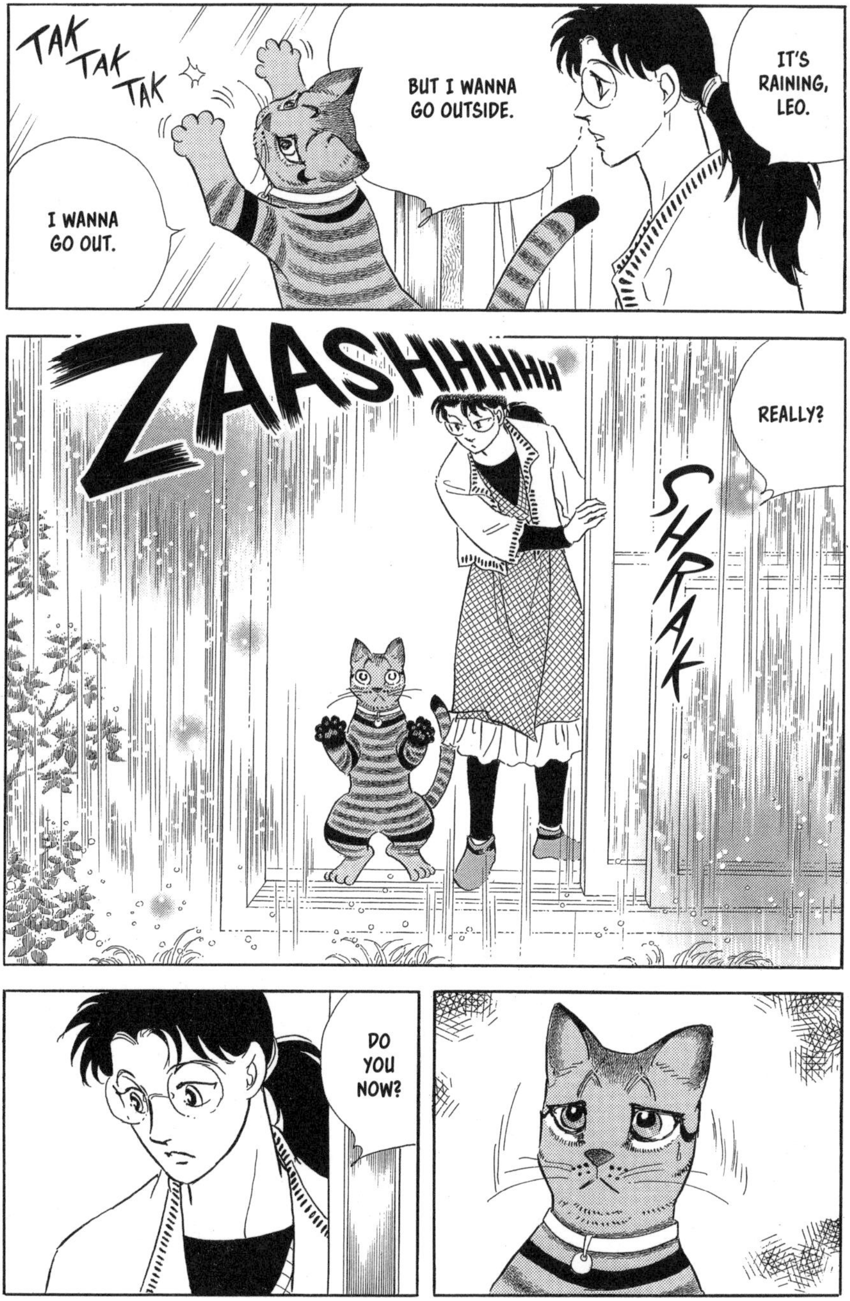
IT'S RAINING, LEO.
BUT I WANNA GO OUTSIDE.
TAK TAK TAK
I WANNA GO OUT.
REALLY?
SHRAK
ZAASHHHHH
DO YOU NOW?

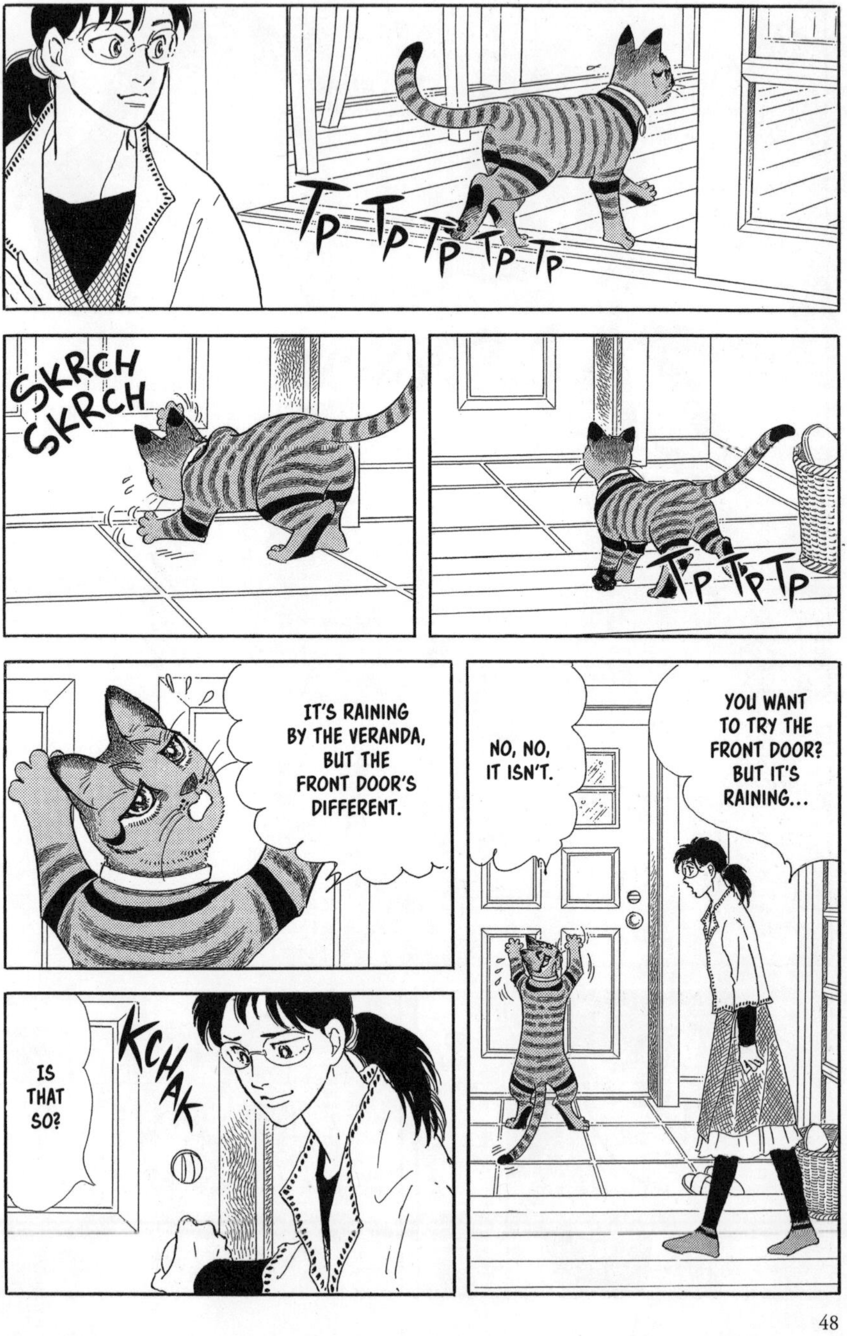
Tp Tp Tp Tp Tp
Tp Tp Tp
SKRCH SKRCH
YOU WANT TO TRY THE FRONT DOOR? BUT IT'S RAINING...
NO, NO, IT ISN'T.
IT'S RAINING BY THE VERANDA, BUT THE FRONT DOOR'S DIFFERENT.
KCHAK
IS THAT SO?

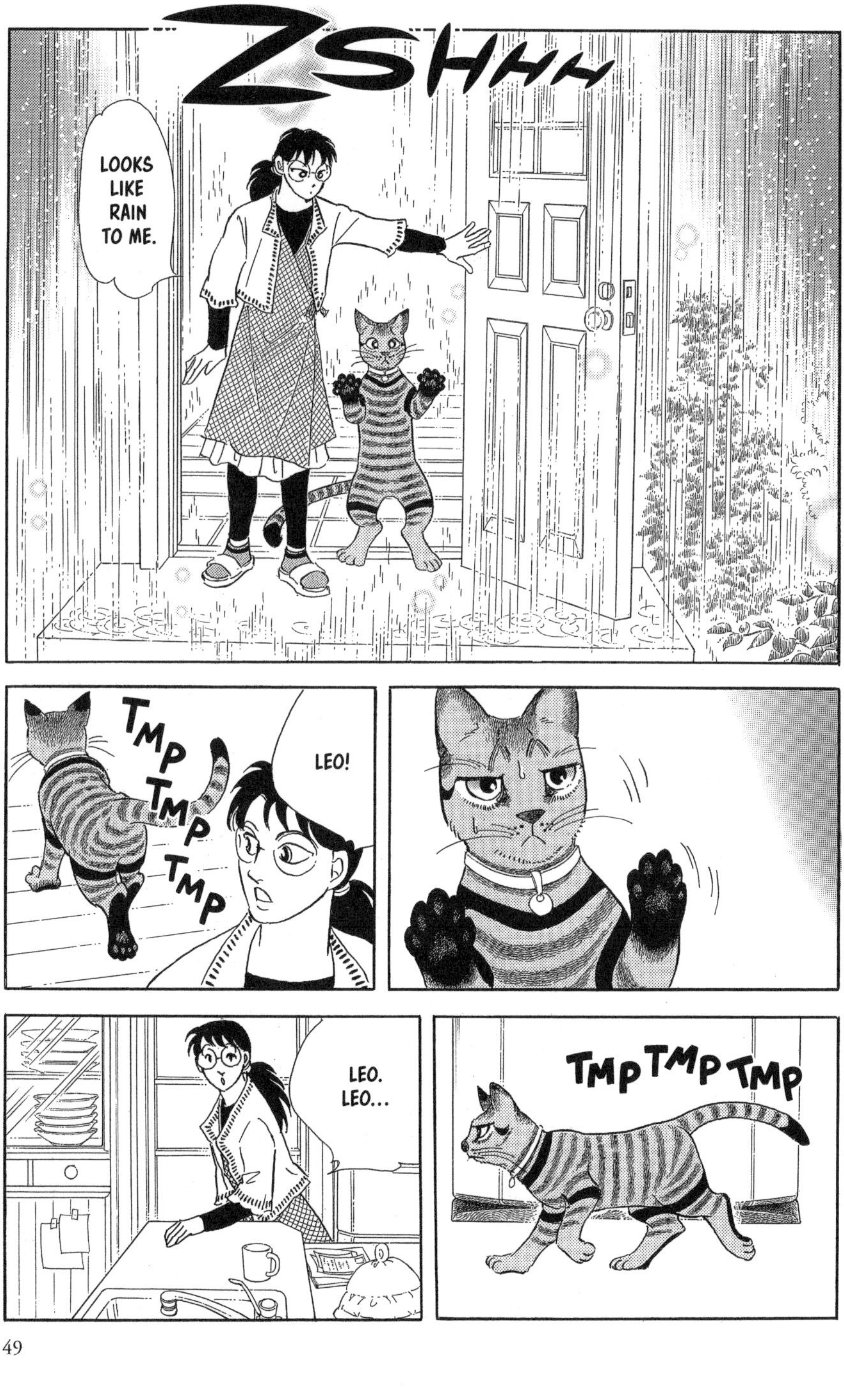
ZSHHH
LOOKS LIKE RAIN TO ME.
TMP TMP TMP TMP
LEO!
TMP TMP TMP
LEO. LEO...

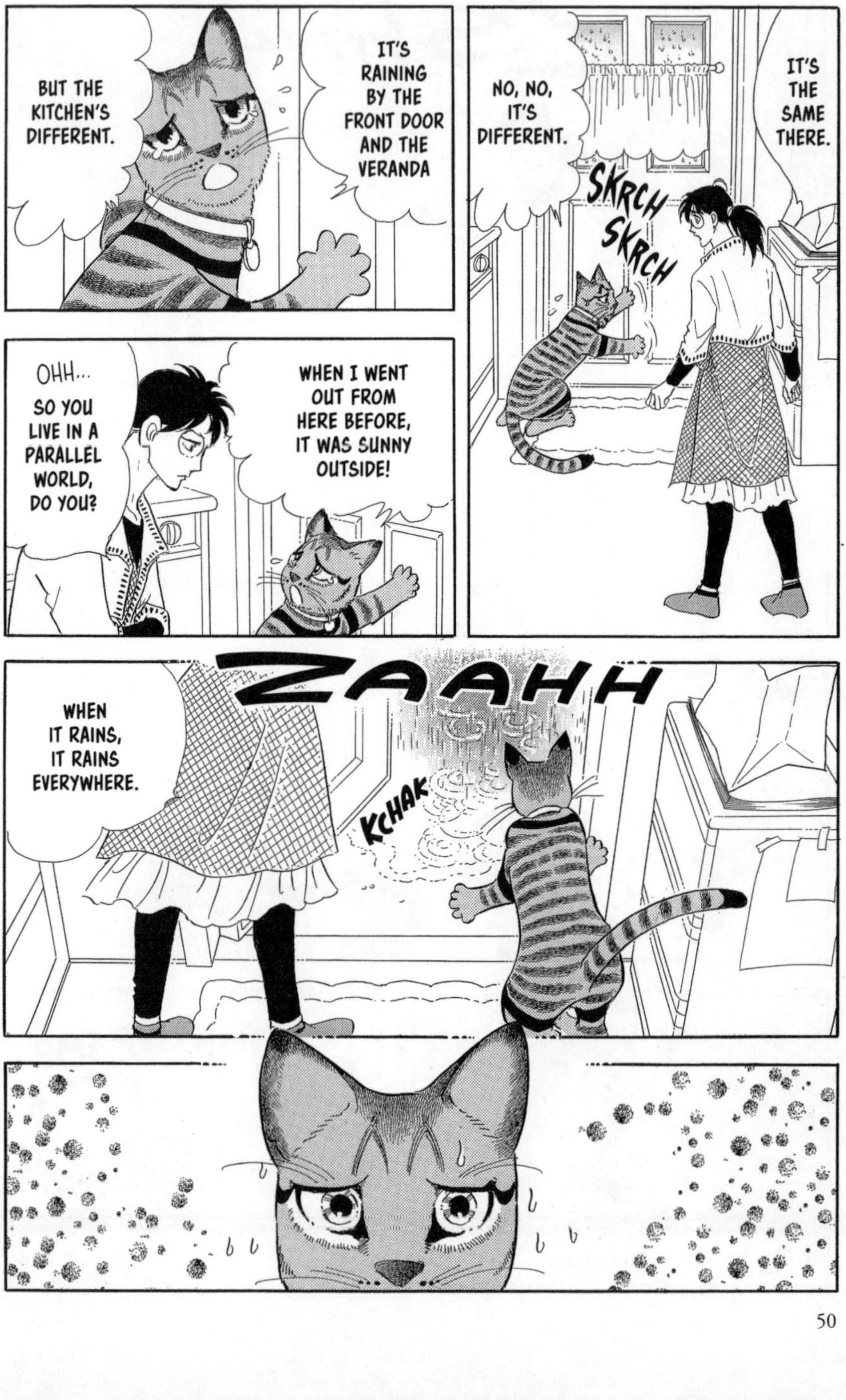
IT'S THE SAME THERE.
NO, NO, IT'S DIFFERENT.
SKRCH SKRCH
IT'S RAINING BY THE FRONT DOOR AND THE VERANDA
BUT THE KITCHEN'S DIFFERENT.
WHEN I WENT OUT FROM HERE BEFORE, IT WAS SUNNY OUTSIDE!
OHH... SO YOU LIVE IN A PARALLEL WORLD, DO YOU?
ZAAHH
WHEN IT RAINS, IT RAINS EVERYWHERE.
KCHAK

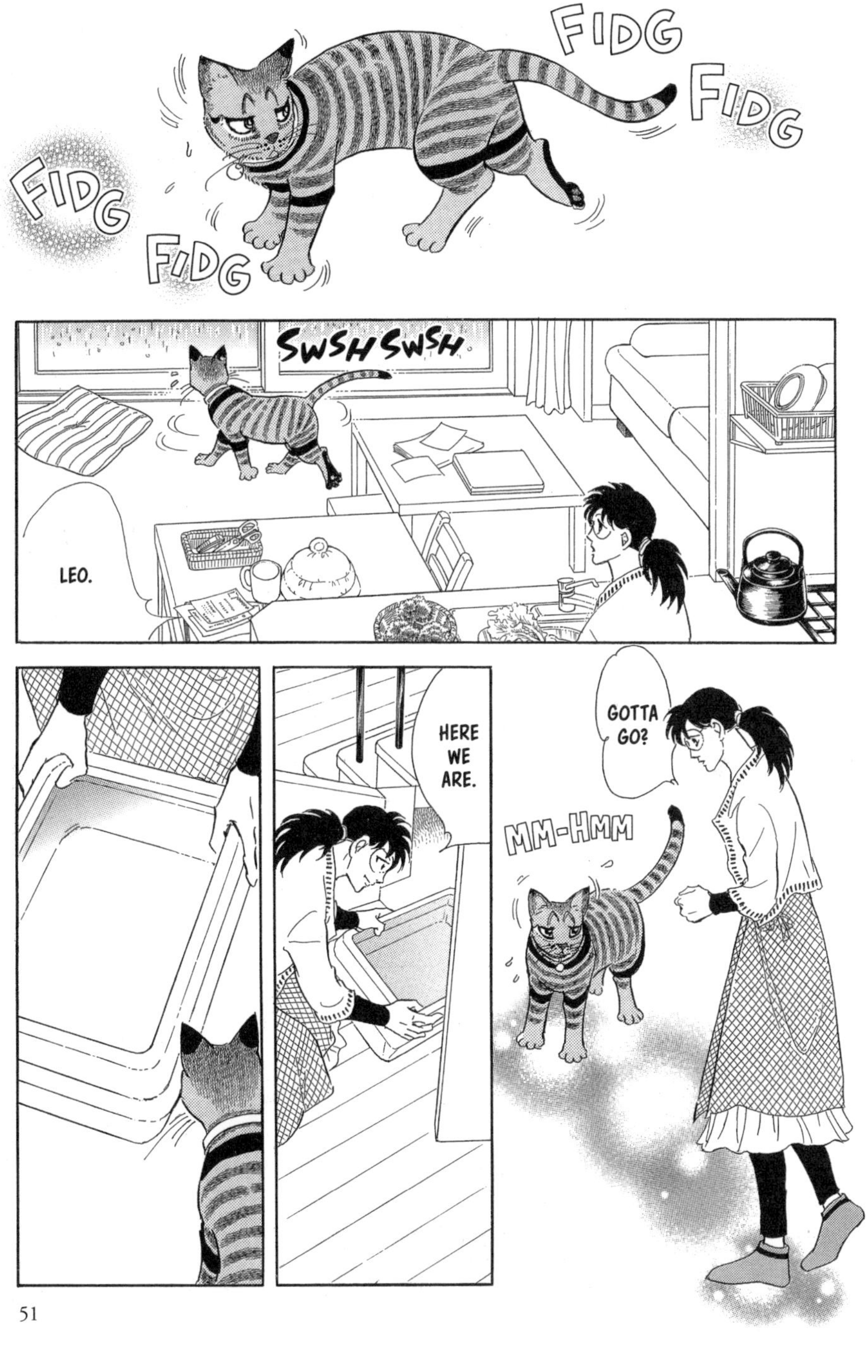
FIDG
FIDG
FIDG
FIDG
SWSH SWSH
LEO.
GOTTA GO?
MM-HMM
HERE WE ARE.

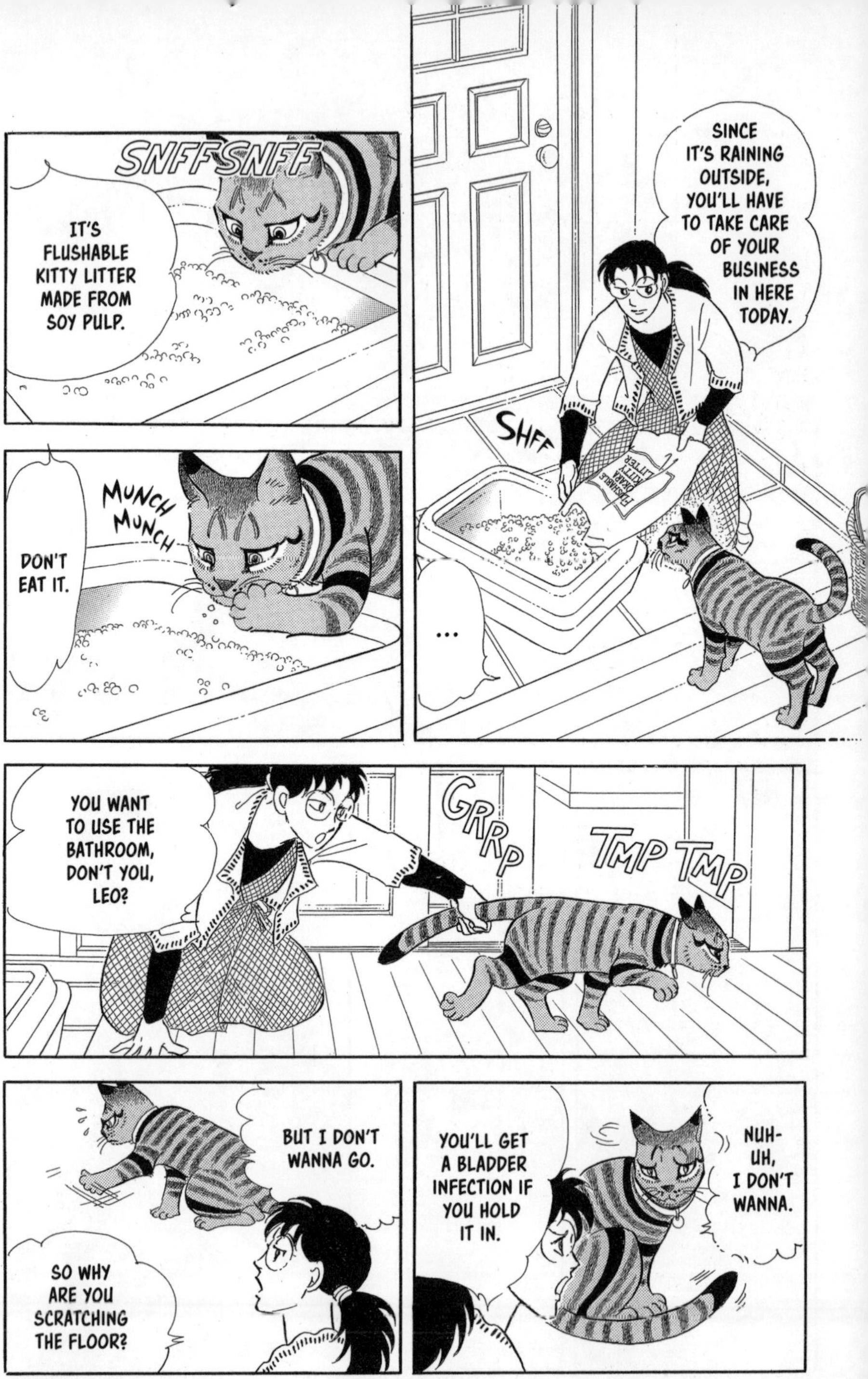
SINCE IT'S RAINING OUTSIDE, YOU'LL HAVE TO TAKE CARE OF YOUR BUSINESS IN HERE TODAY.
SHFF
...
SNFFSNFF
IT'S FLUSHABLE KITTY LITTER MADE FROM SOY PULP.
MUNCH MUNCH
DON'T EAT IT.
TMP TMP
GRRP
YOU WANT TO USE THE BATHROOM, DON'T YOU, LEO?
NUH-UH, I DON'T WANNA.
YOU'LL GET A BLADDER INFECTION IF YOU HOLD IT IN.
BUT I DON'T WANNA GO.
SO WHY ARE YOU SCRATCHING THE FLOOR?

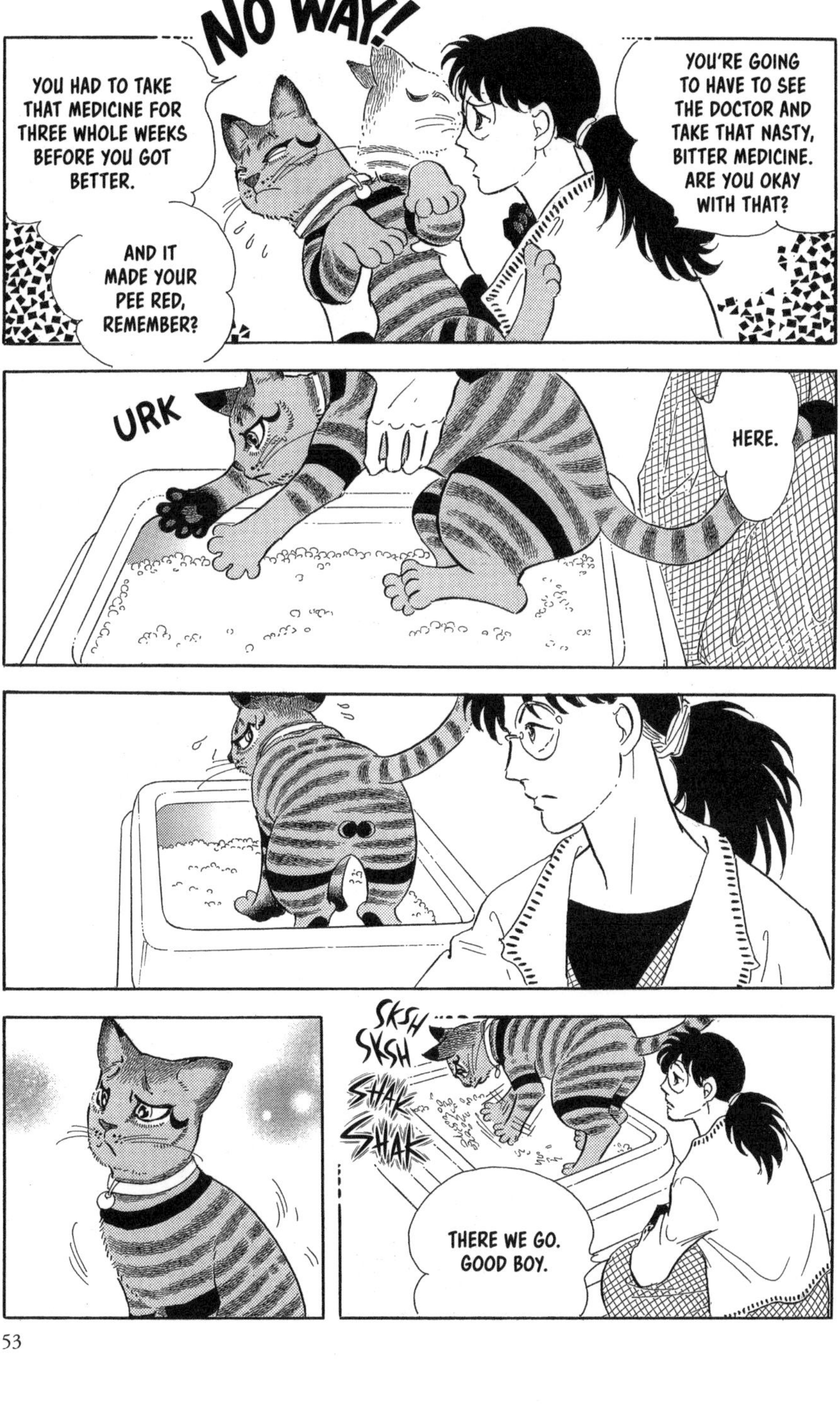
YOU'RE GOING TO HAVE TO SEE THE DOCTOR AND TAKE THAT NASTY, BITTER MEDICINE. ARE YOU OKAY WITH THAT?
NO WAY!
YOU HAD TO TAKE THAT MEDICINE FOR THREE WHOLE WEEKS BEFORE YOU GOT BETTER.
AND IT MADE YOUR PEE RED, REMEMBER?
HERE.
URK
SKSH SKSH
SHAK SHAK
THERE WE GO. GOOD BOY.

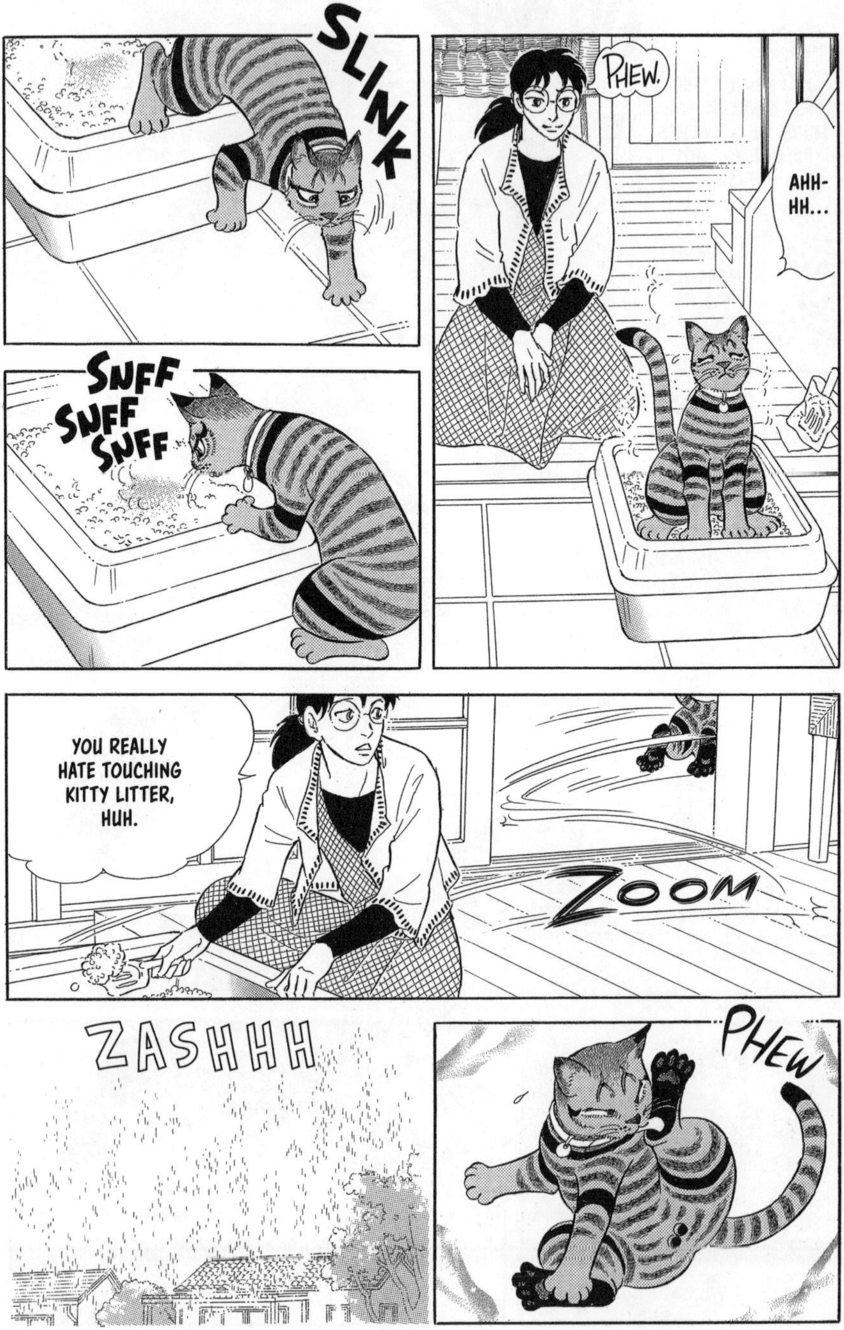
PHEW.
AHH-HH...
SLINK
SNFF SNFF SNFF
YOU REALLY HATE TOUCHING KITTY LITTER, HUH.
ZOOM
PHEW
ZASHHH

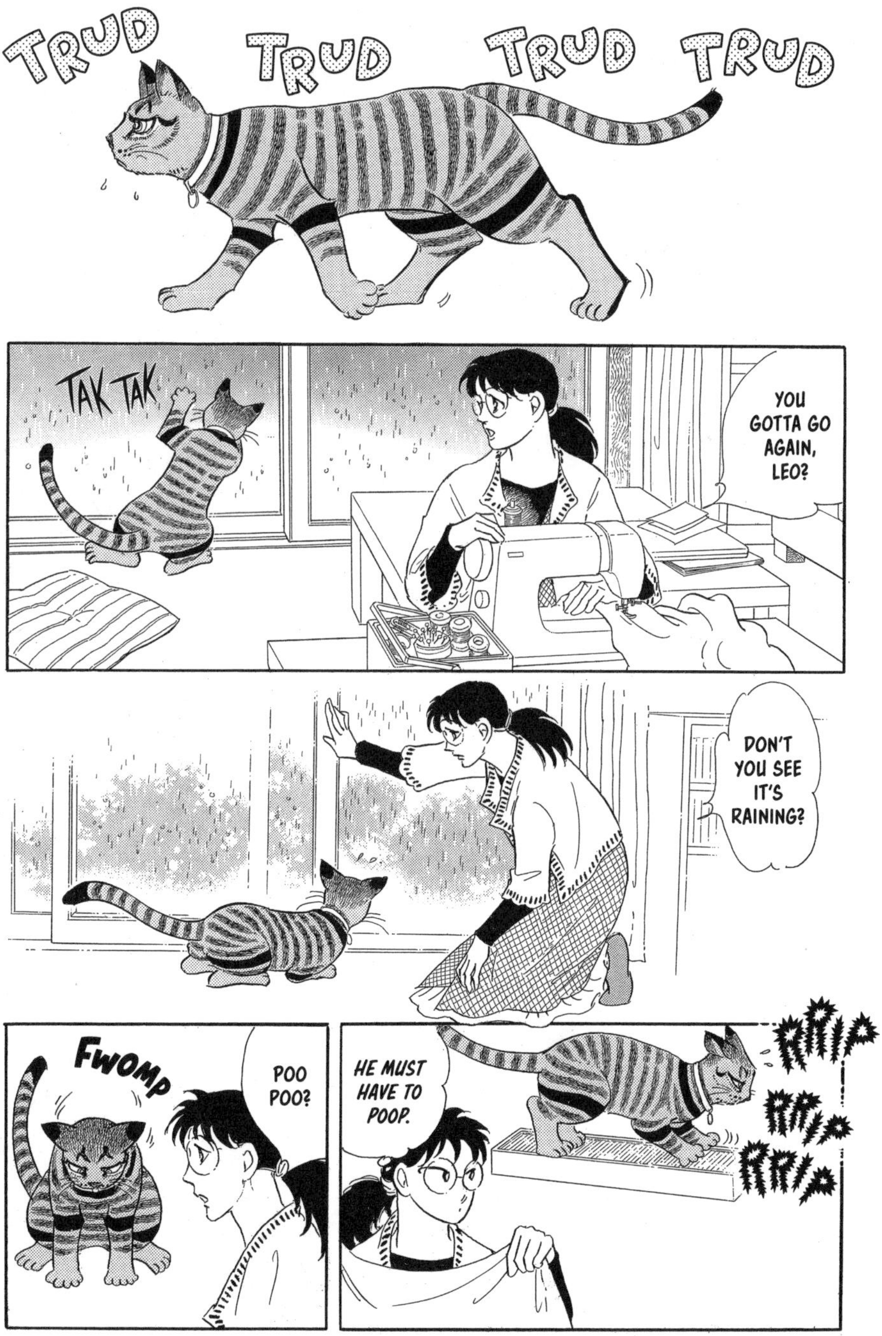
TRUD TRUD TRUD TRUD
TAK TAK
YOU GOTTA GO AGAIN, LEO?
DON'T YOU SEE IT'S RAINING?
RRIP RRIP RRIP
HE MUST HAVE TO POOP.
FWOMP
POO POO?

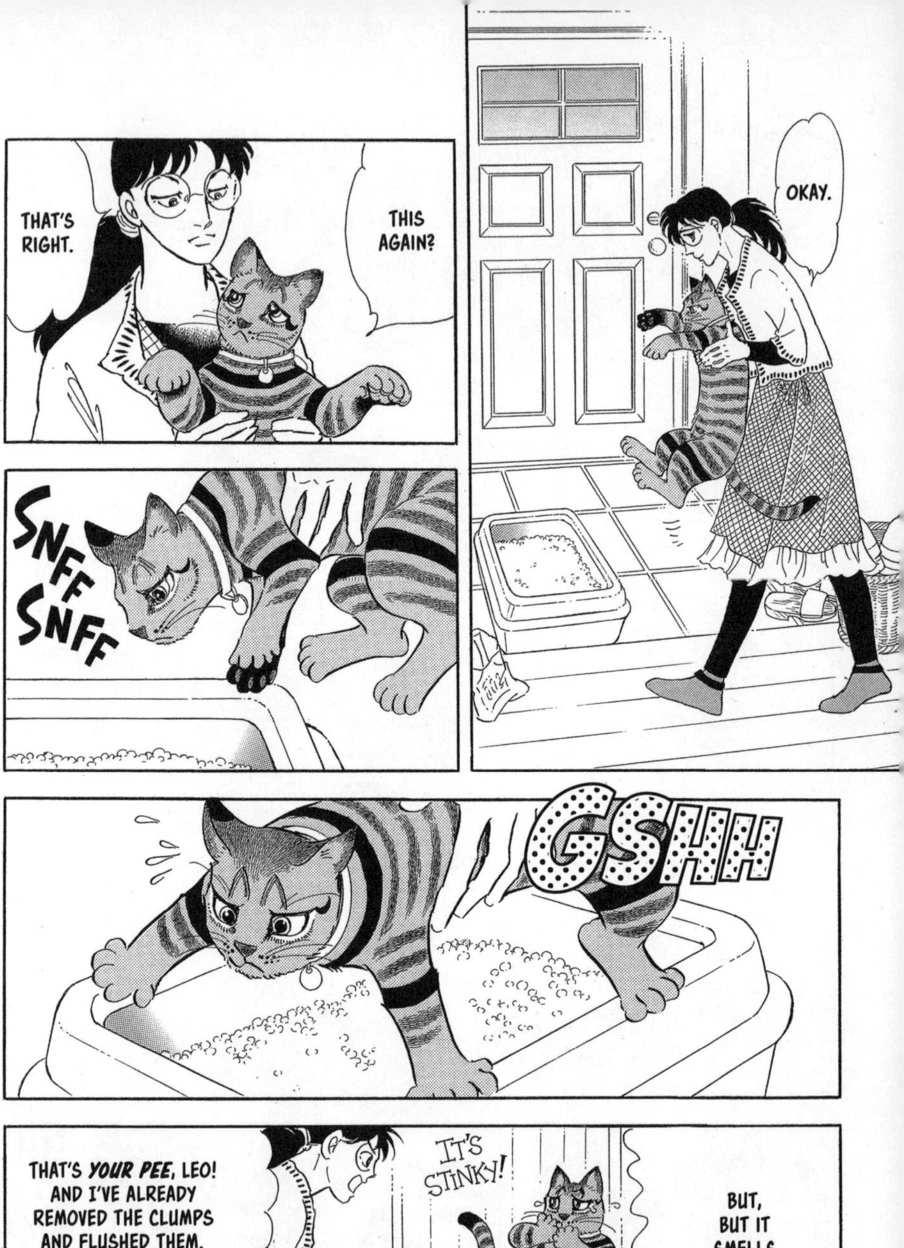
OKAY.
THIS AGAIN?
THAT'S RIGHT.
SNFF SNFF
GSHH
BUT, BUT IT SMELLS LIKE PEE!
IT'S STINKY!
THAT'S *YOUR PEE*, LEO! AND I'VE ALREADY REMOVED THE CLUMPS AND FLUSHED THEM. IT'S ALL GONE ALREADY!

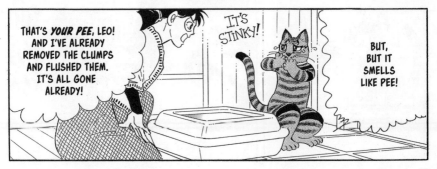

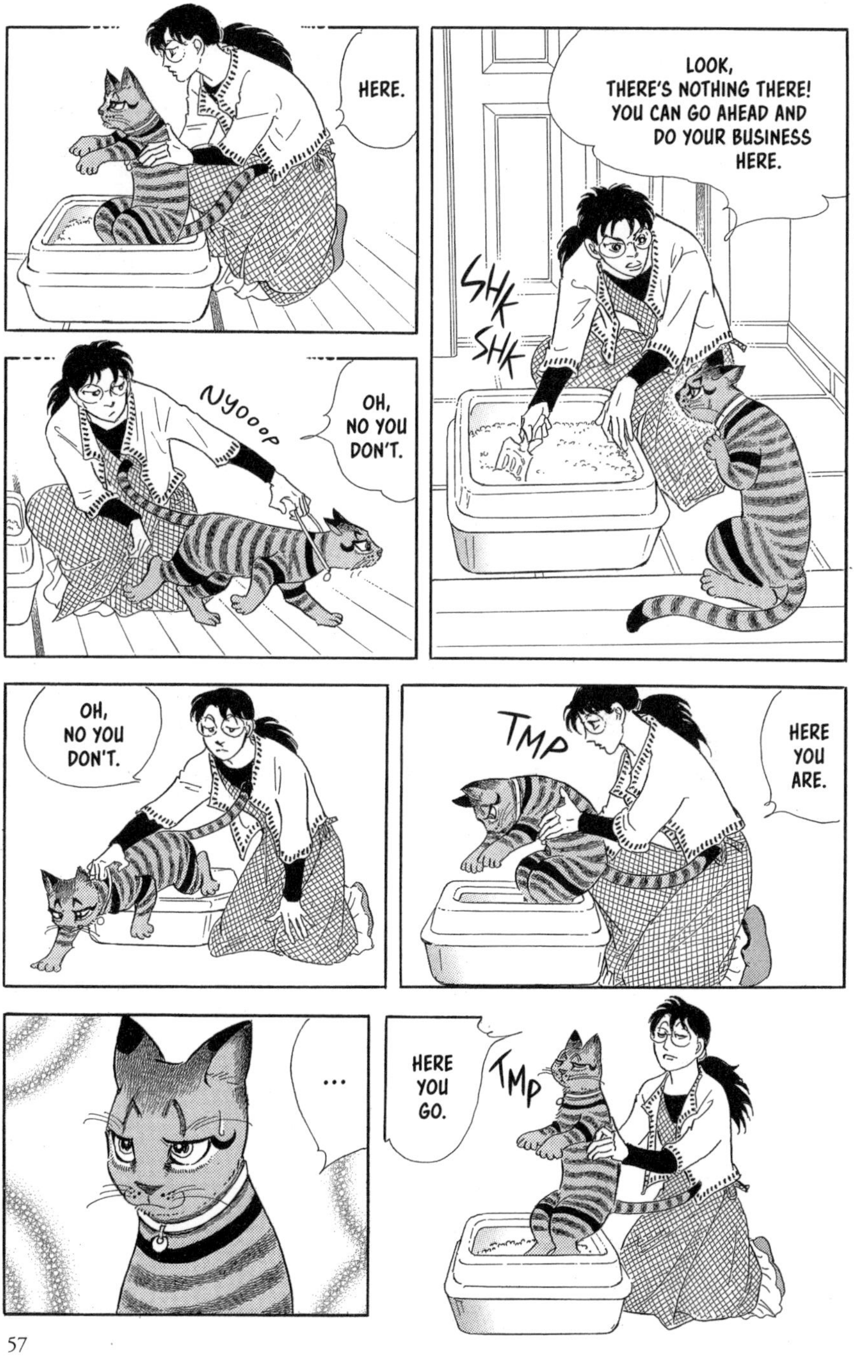
LOOK, THERE'S NOTHING THERE! YOU CAN GO AHEAD AND DO YOUR BUSINESS HERE.
SHK SHK
HERE.
OH, NO YOU DON'T.
NYOOOP
HERE YOU ARE.
TMP
OH, NO YOU DON'T.
TMP
HERE YOU GO.
...

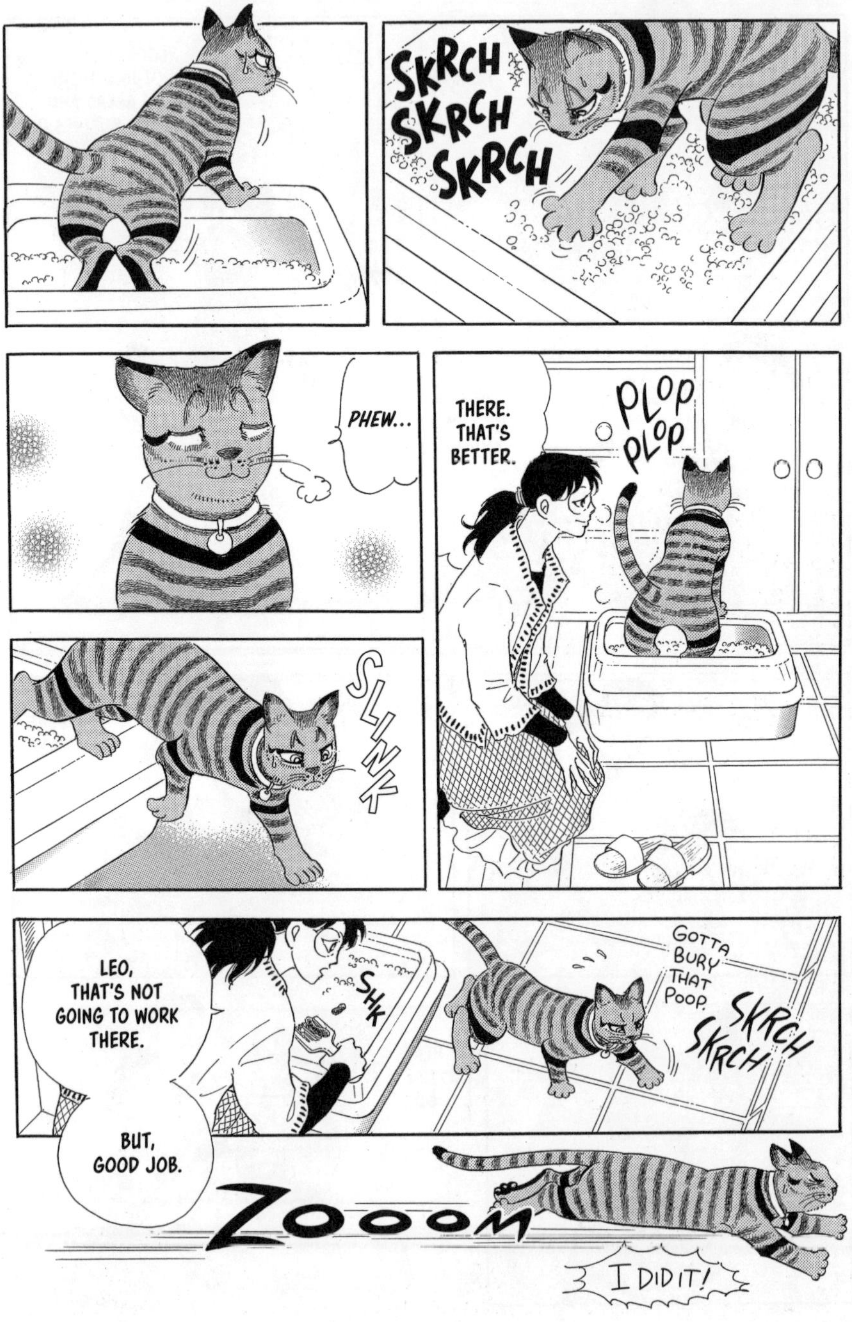
SKRCH SKRCH SKRCH
THERE. THAT'S BETTER.
PLOP PLOP
PHEW...
SLINK
GOTTA BURY THAT POOP.
SKRCH SKRCH
SHK
LEO, THAT'S NOT GOING TO WORK THERE.
BUT, GOOD JOB.
ZOOOM
I DID IT!

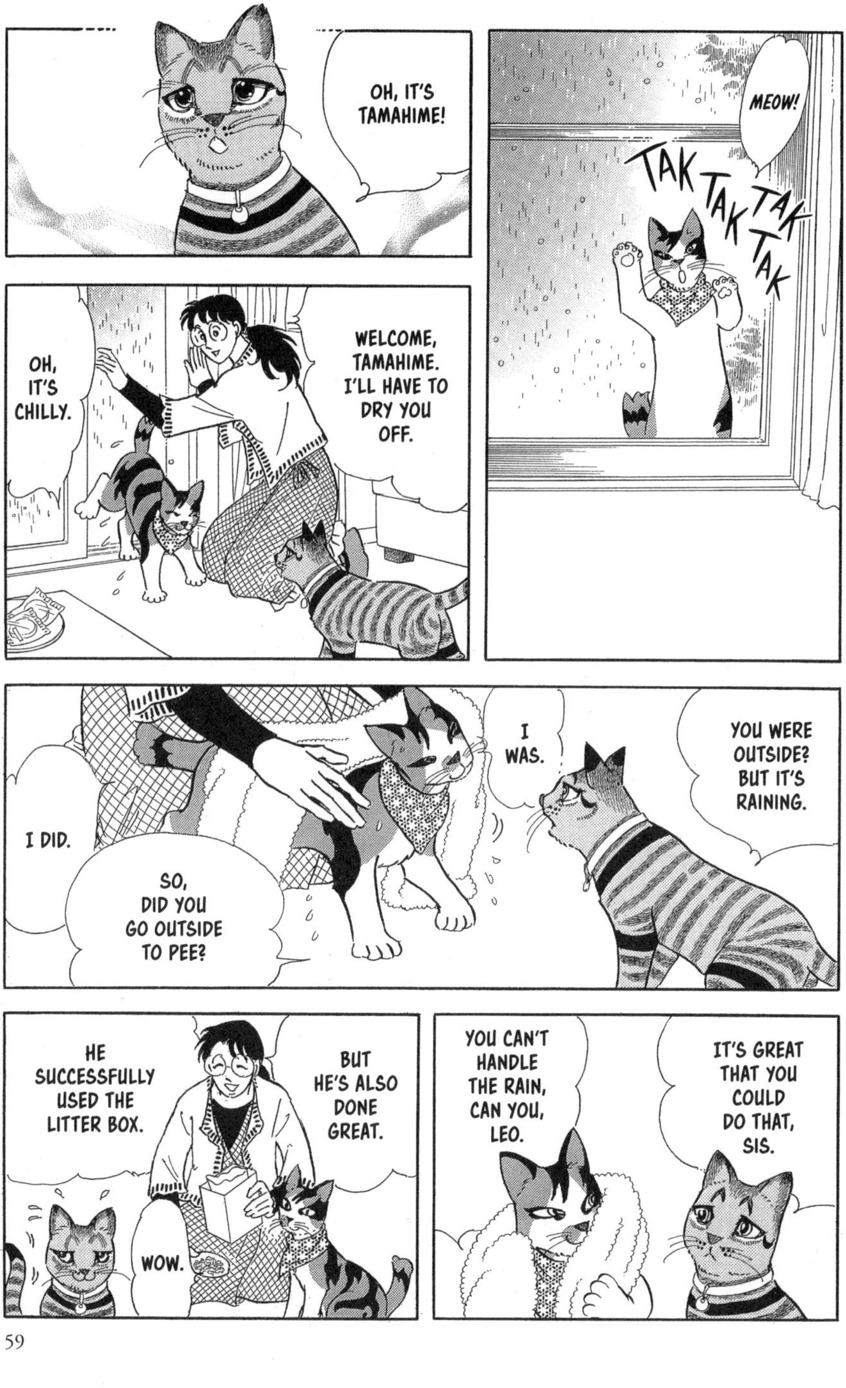
MEOW!
TAK TAK TAK TAK
OH, IT'S TAMAHIME!
WELCOME, TAMAHIME. I'LL HAVE TO DRY YOU OFF.
OH, IT'S CHILLY.
YOU WERE OUTSIDE? BUT IT'S RAINING.
I WAS.
SO, DID YOU GO OUTSIDE TO PEE?
I DID.
IT'S GREAT THAT YOU COULD DO THAT, SIS.
YOU CAN'T HANDLE THE RAIN, CAN YOU, LEO.
BUT HE'S ALSO DONE GREAT.
HE SUCCESSFULLY USED THE LITTER BOX.
WOW.

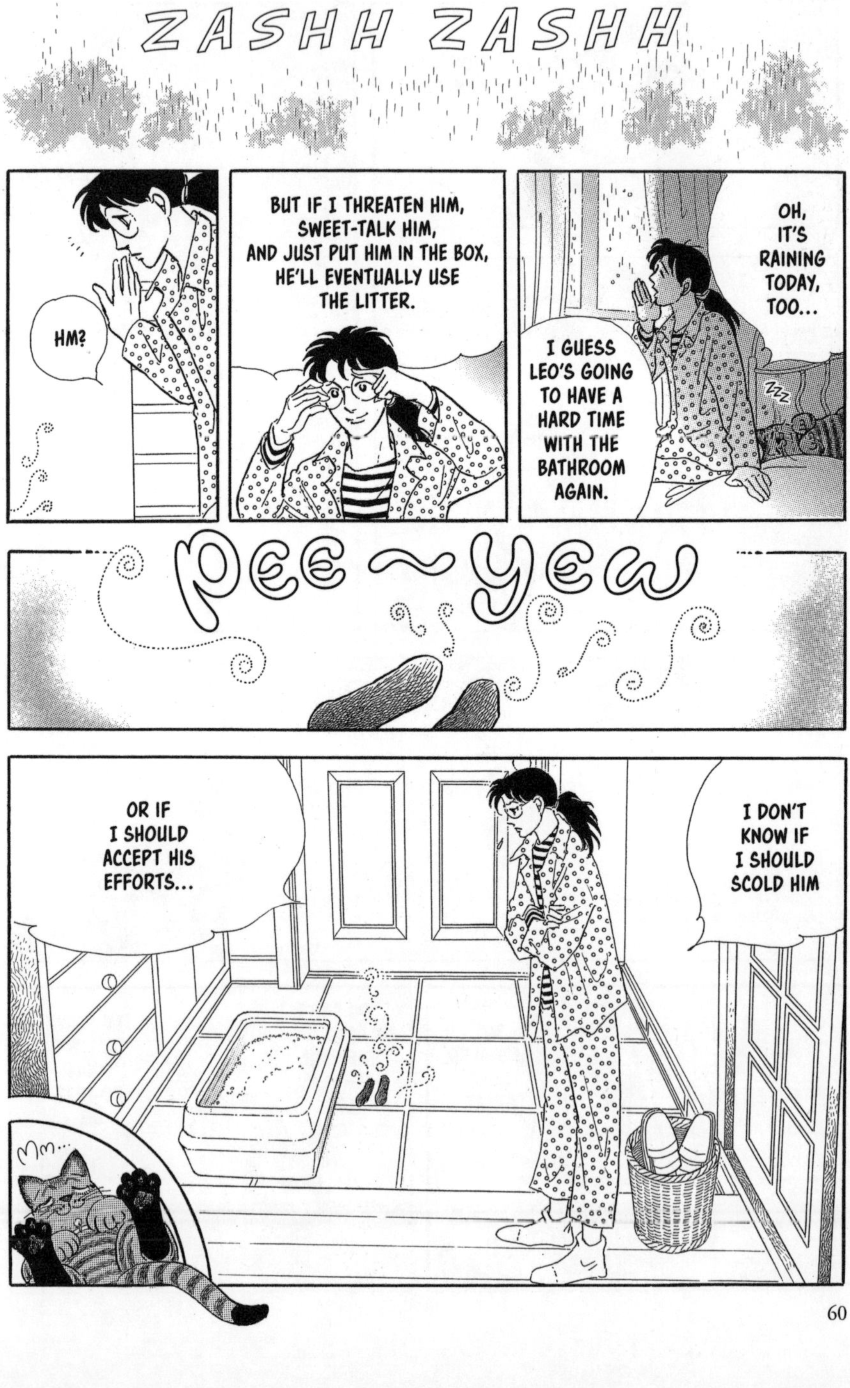
ZASHH ZASHH
OH, IT'S RAINING TODAY, TOO...
I GUESS LEO'S GOING TO HAVE A HARD TIME WITH THE BATHROOM AGAIN.
BUT IF I THREATEN HIM, SWEET-TALK HIM, AND JUST PUT HIM IN THE BOX, HE'LL EVENTUALLY USE THE LITTER.
HM?
PEE~YEW
I DON'T KNOW IF I SHOULD SCOLD HIM
OR IF I SHOULD ACCEPT HIS EFFORTS...
Mm...

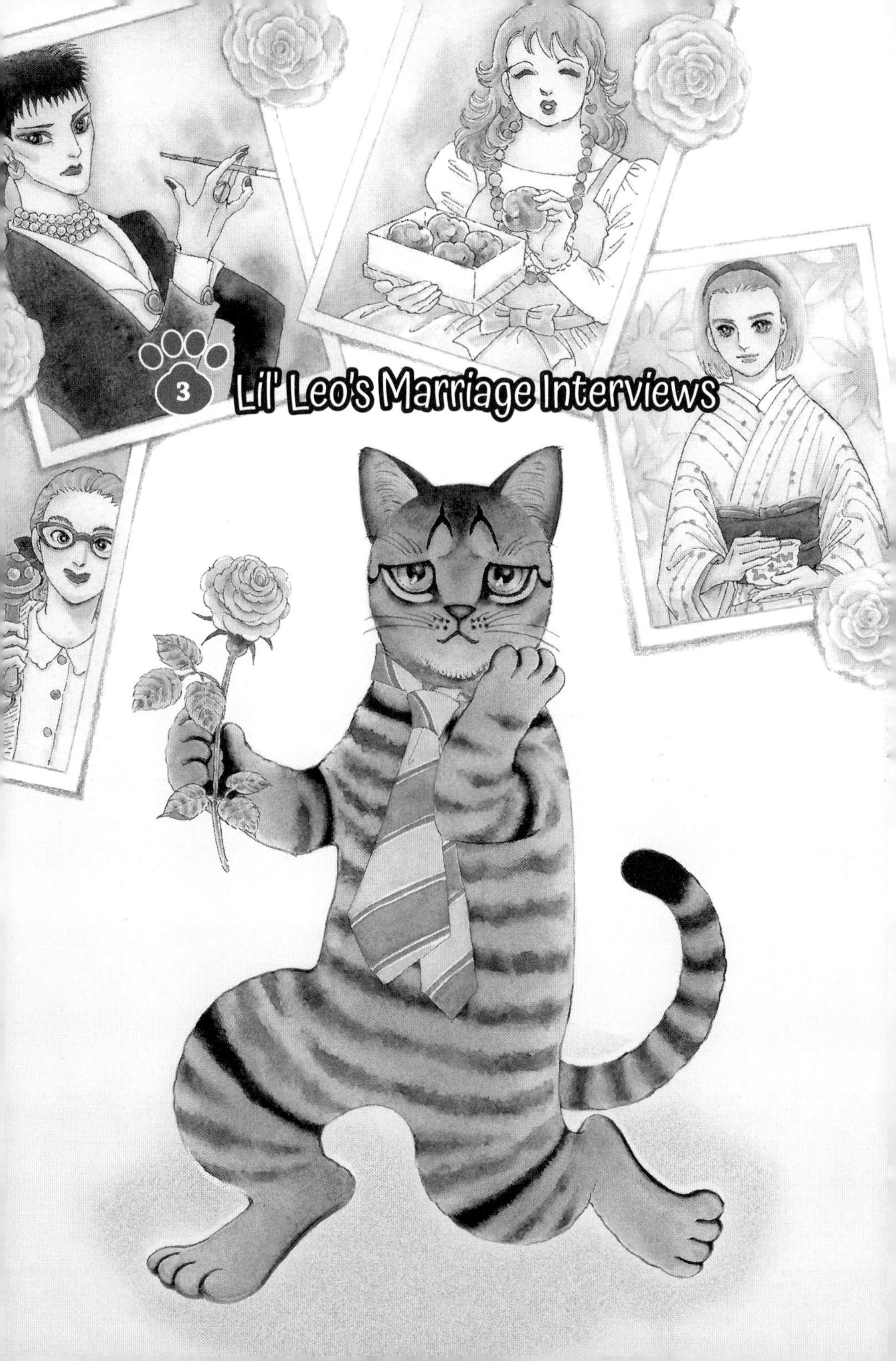
3
Lil' Leo's Marriage Interviews

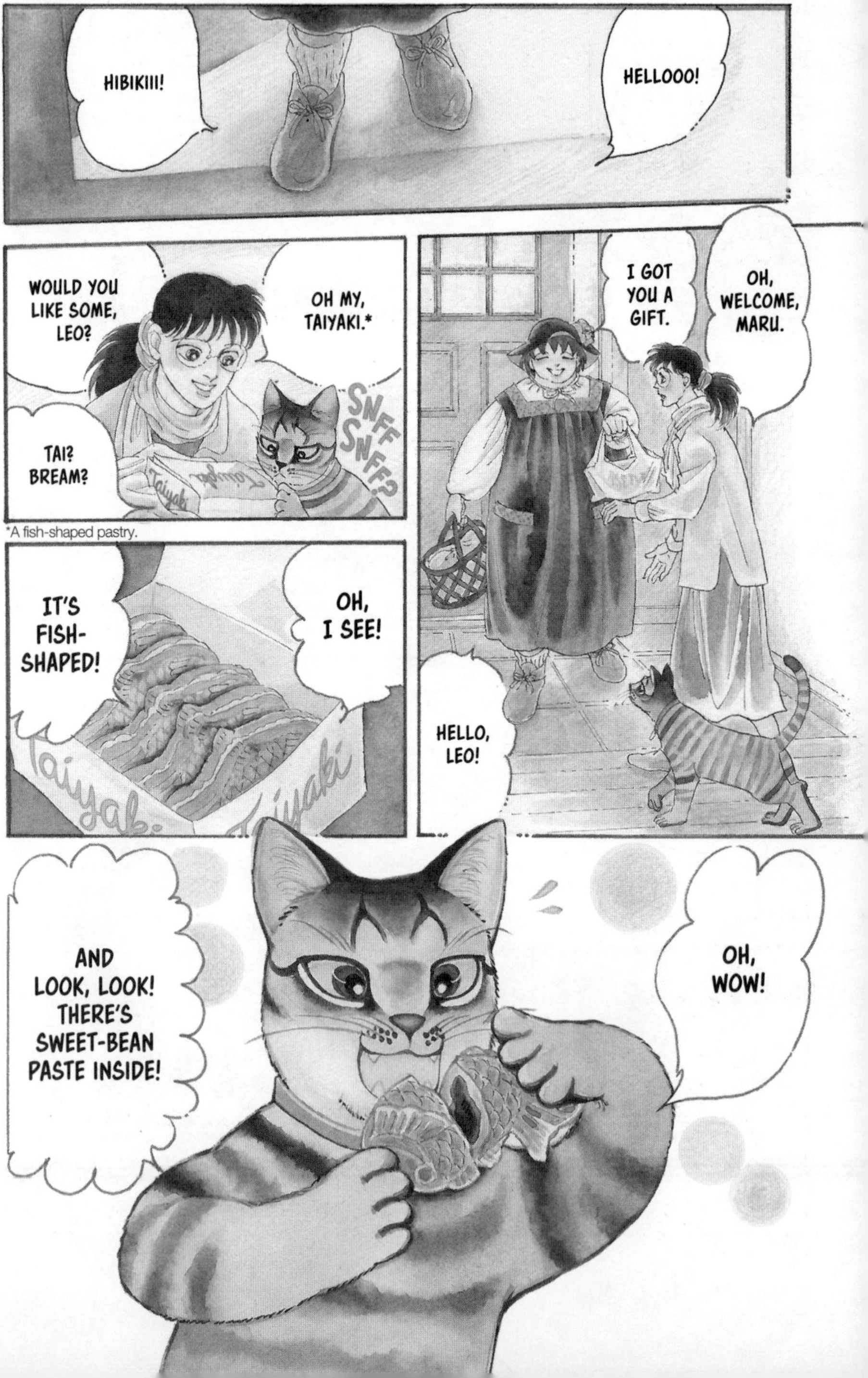
HELLOOO!
HIBIKIII!
OH, WELCOME, MARU.
I GOT YOU A GIFT.
HELLO, LEO!
OH MY, TAIYAKI.*
WOULD YOU LIKE SOME, LEO?
SNFF SNFF?
TAI? BREAM?
Taiyaki
OH, I SEE!
IT'S FISH-SHAPED!
Taiyaki
OH, WOW!
AND LOOK, LOOK! THERE'S SWEET-BEAN PASTE INSIDE!

*A fish-shaped pastry.

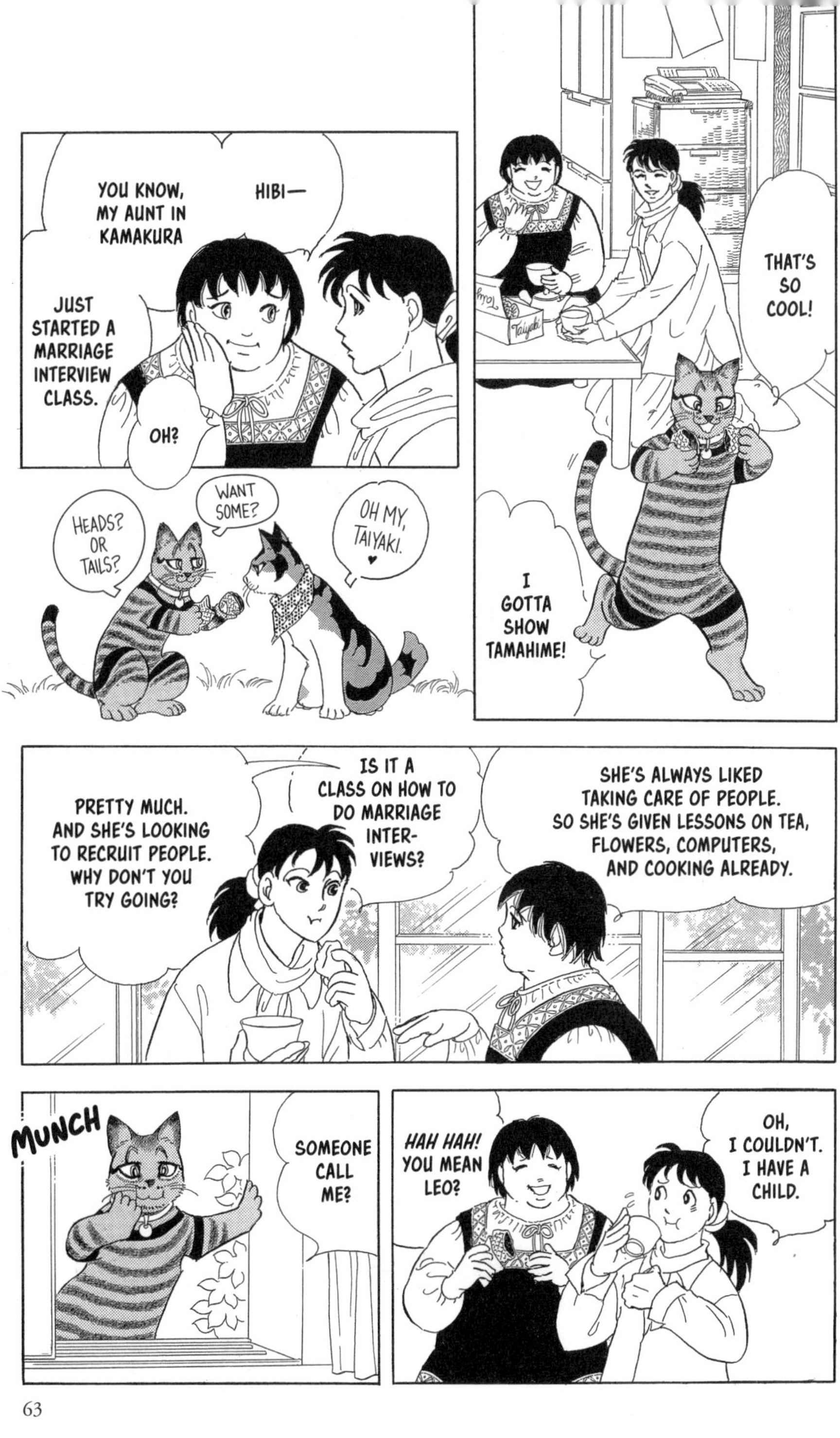
THAT'S SO COOL!
I GOTTA SHOW TAMAHIME!
HIBI—
YOU KNOW, MY AUNT IN KAMAKURA
JUST STARTED A MARRIAGE INTERVIEW CLASS.
OH?
OH MY, TAIYAKI. ♥
WANT SOME?
HEADS? OR TAILS?
SHE'S ALWAYS LIKED TAKING CARE OF PEOPLE. SO SHE'S GIVEN LESSONS ON TEA, FLOWERS, COMPUTERS, AND COOKING ALREADY.
IS IT A CLASS ON HOW TO DO MARRIAGE INTER-VIEWS?
PRETTY MUCH. AND SHE'S LOOKING TO RECRUIT PEOPLE. WHY DON'T YOU TRY GOING?
OH, I COULDN'T. I HAVE A CHILD.
HAH HAH! YOU MEAN LEO?
SOMEONE CALL ME?
MUNCH

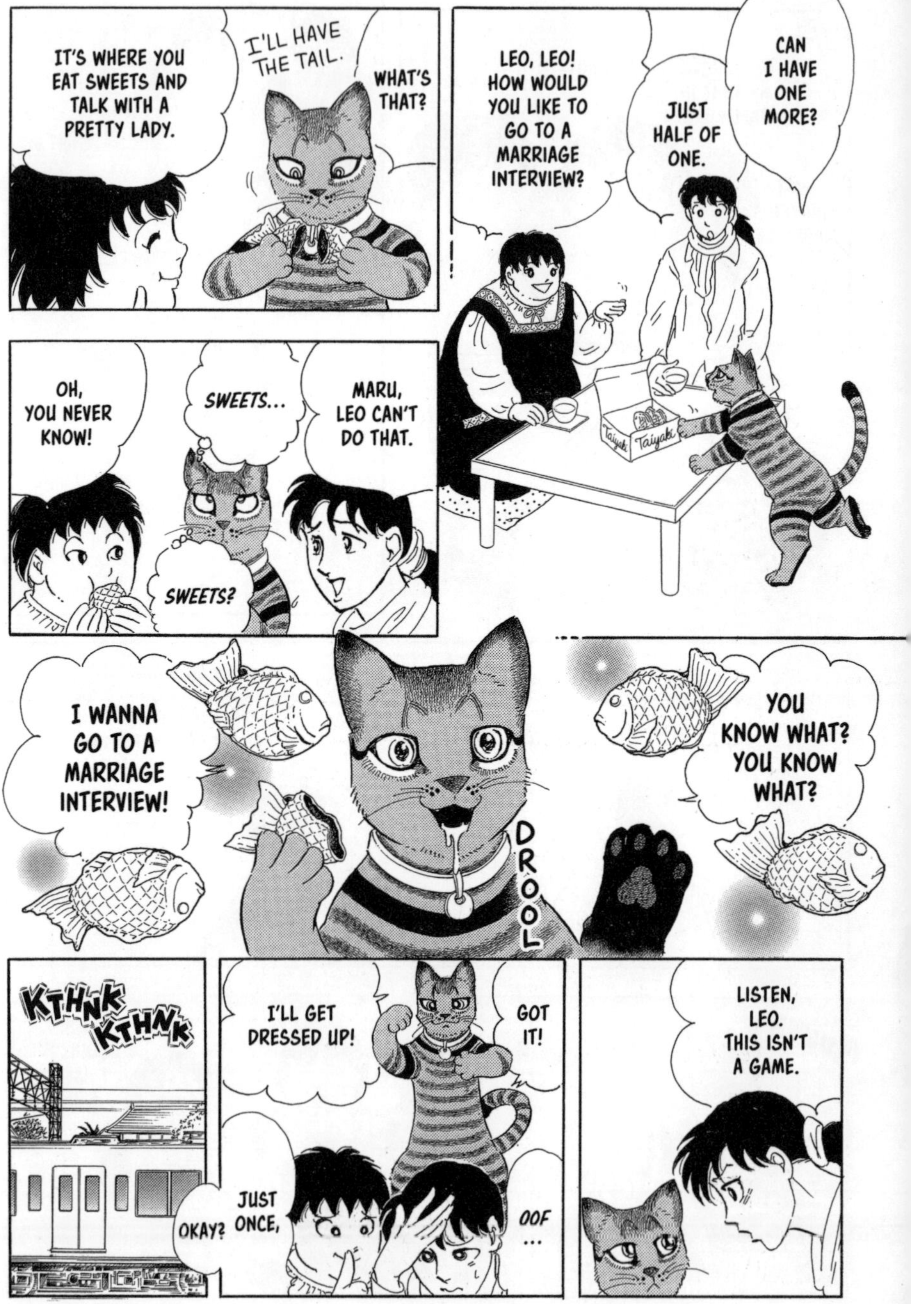
CAN I HAVE ONE MORE?
JUST HALF OF ONE.
LEO, LEO! HOW WOULD YOU LIKE TO GO TO A MARRIAGE INTERVIEW?
Taiyaki
Taiyaki
WHAT'S THAT?
I'LL HAVE THE TAIL.
IT'S WHERE YOU EAT SWEETS AND TALK WITH A PRETTY LADY.
MARU, LEO CAN'T DO THAT.
SWEETS...
OH, YOU NEVER KNOW!
SWEETS?
YOU KNOW WHAT? YOU KNOW WHAT?
DROOL
I WANNA GO TO A MARRIAGE INTERVIEW!
LISTEN, LEO. THIS ISN'T A GAME.
GOT IT!
I'LL GET DRESSED UP!
OOF...
JUST ONCE,
OKAY?
KTHNK KTHNK

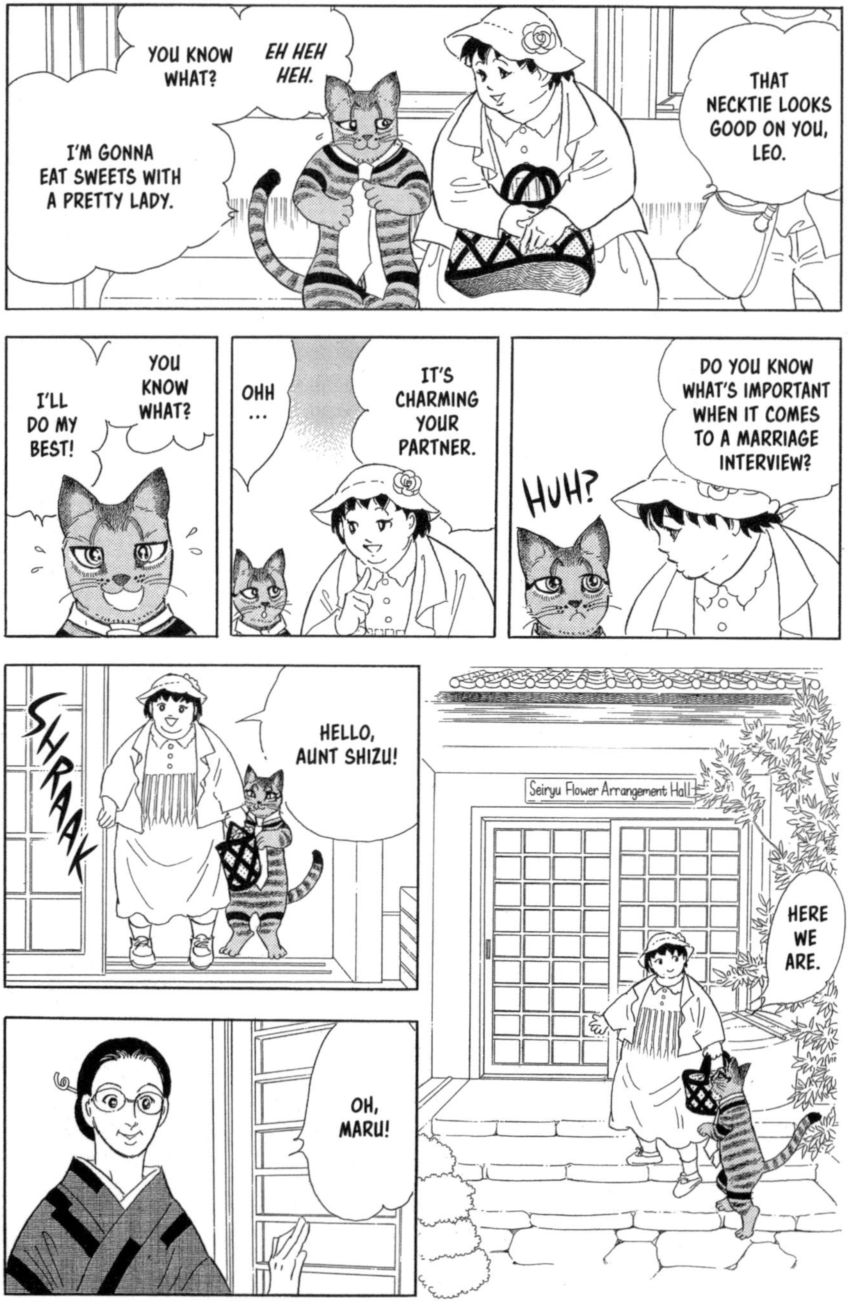
THAT NECKTIE LOOKS GOOD ON YOU, LEO.
EH HEH HEH.
YOU KNOW WHAT?
I'M GONNA EAT SWEETS WITH A PRETTY LADY.
DO YOU KNOW WHAT'S IMPORTANT WHEN IT COMES TO A MARRIAGE INTERVIEW?
HUH?
IT'S CHARMING YOUR PARTNER.
OHH ...
YOU KNOW WHAT?
I'LL DO MY BEST!
Seiryu Flower Arrangement Hall
HERE WE ARE.
HELLO, AUNT SHIZU!
SHRAAK
OH, MARU!

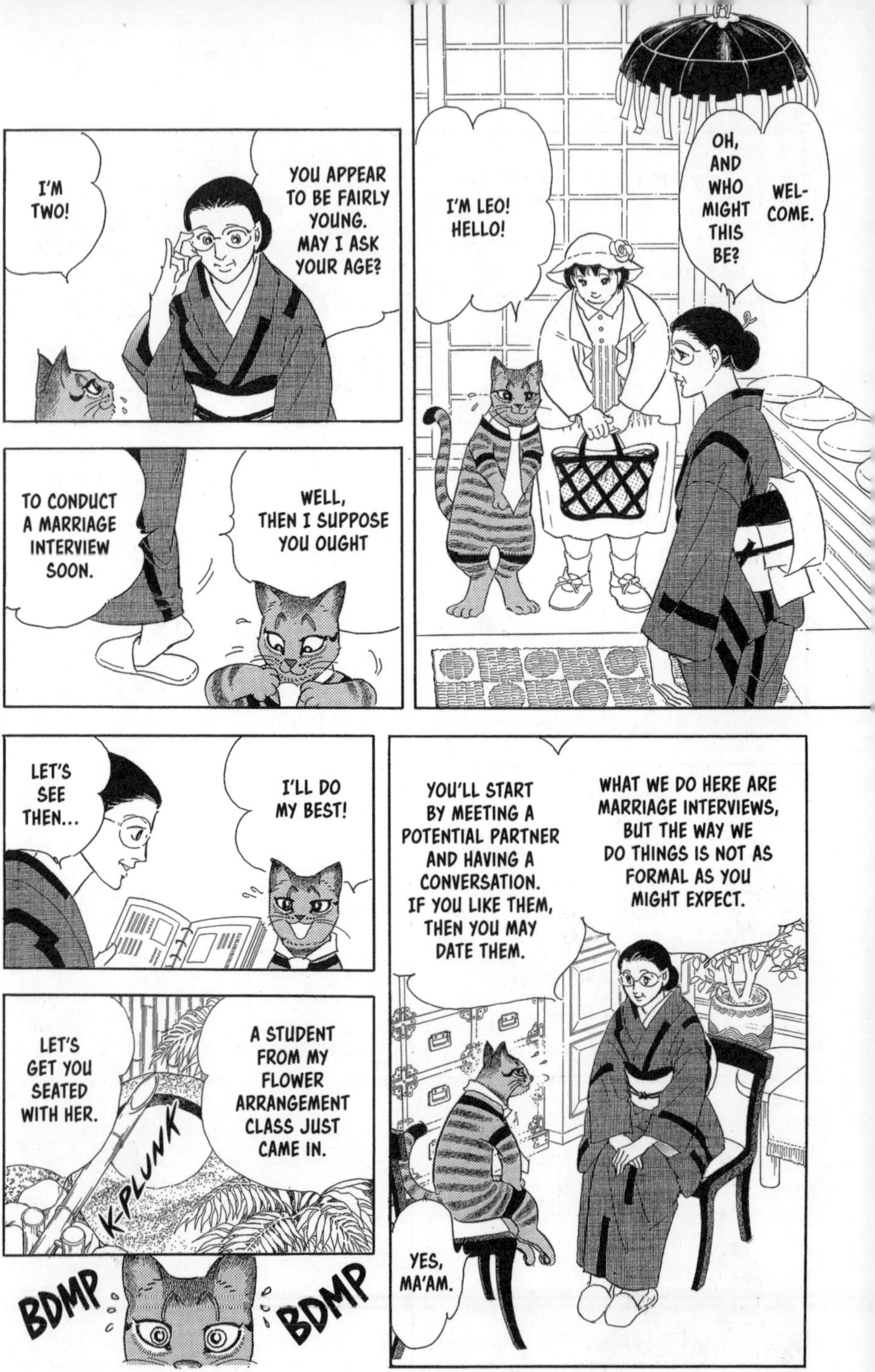
WEL-COME.
OH, AND WHO MIGHT THIS BE?
I'M LEO! HELLO!
YOU APPEAR TO BE FAIRLY YOUNG. MAY I ASK YOUR AGE?
I'M TWO!
WELL, THEN I SUPPOSE YOU OUGHT
TO CONDUCT A MARRIAGE INTERVIEW SOON.
WHAT WE DO HERE ARE MARRIAGE INTERVIEWS, BUT THE WAY WE DO THINGS IS NOT AS FORMAL AS YOU MIGHT EXPECT.
YOU'LL START BY MEETING A POTENTIAL PARTNER AND HAVING A CONVERSATION. IF YOU LIKE THEM, THEN YOU MAY DATE THEM.
YES, MA'AM.
I'LL DO MY BEST!
LET'S SEE THEN...
A STUDENT FROM MY FLOWER ARRANGEMENT CLASS JUST CAME IN.
LET'S GET YOU SEATED WITH HER.
K-PLUNK
BDMP
BDMP

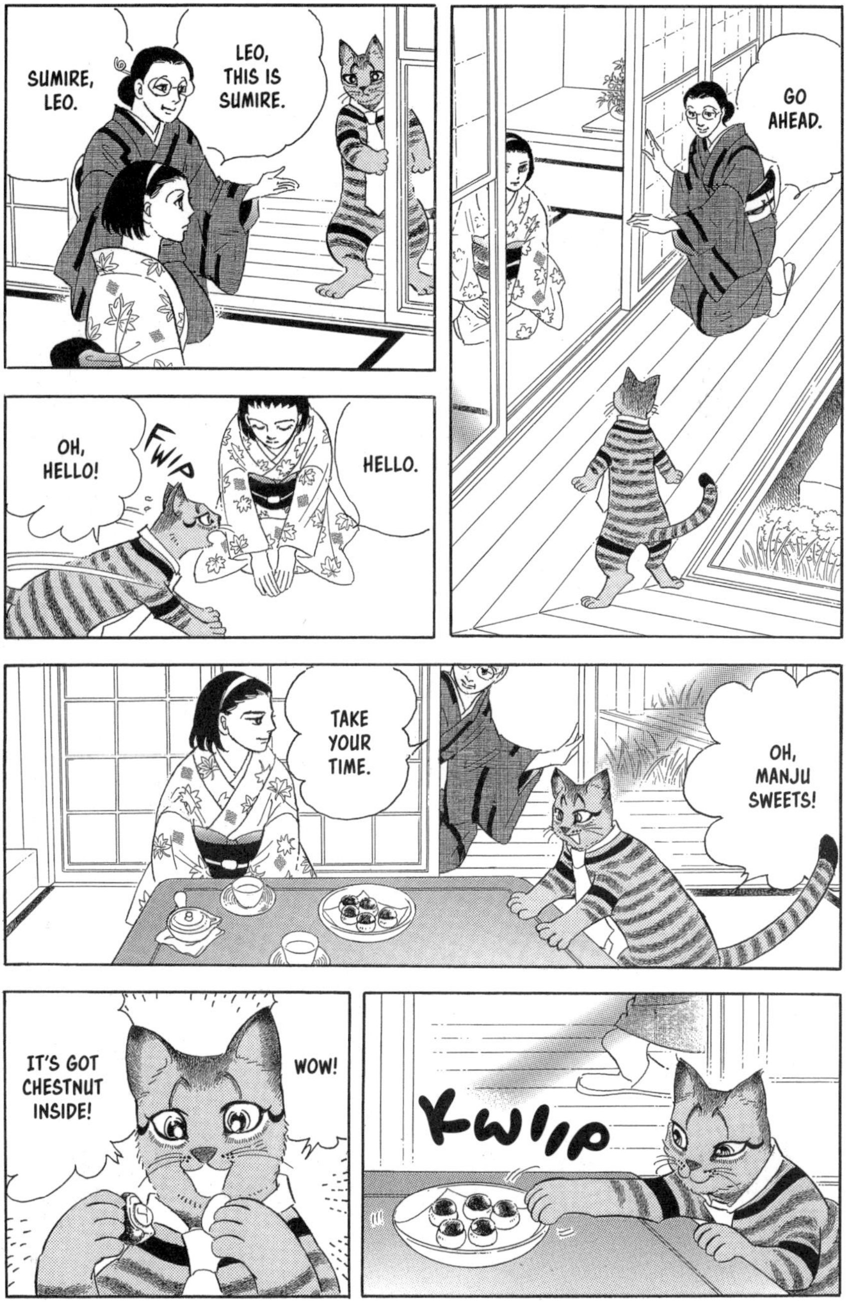
GO AHEAD.
LEO, THIS IS SUMIRE.
SUMIRE, LEO.
HELLO.
FWIP
OH, HELLO!
OH, MANJU SWEETS!
TAKE YOUR TIME.
KWIIP
WOW!
IT'S GOT CHESTNUT INSIDE!

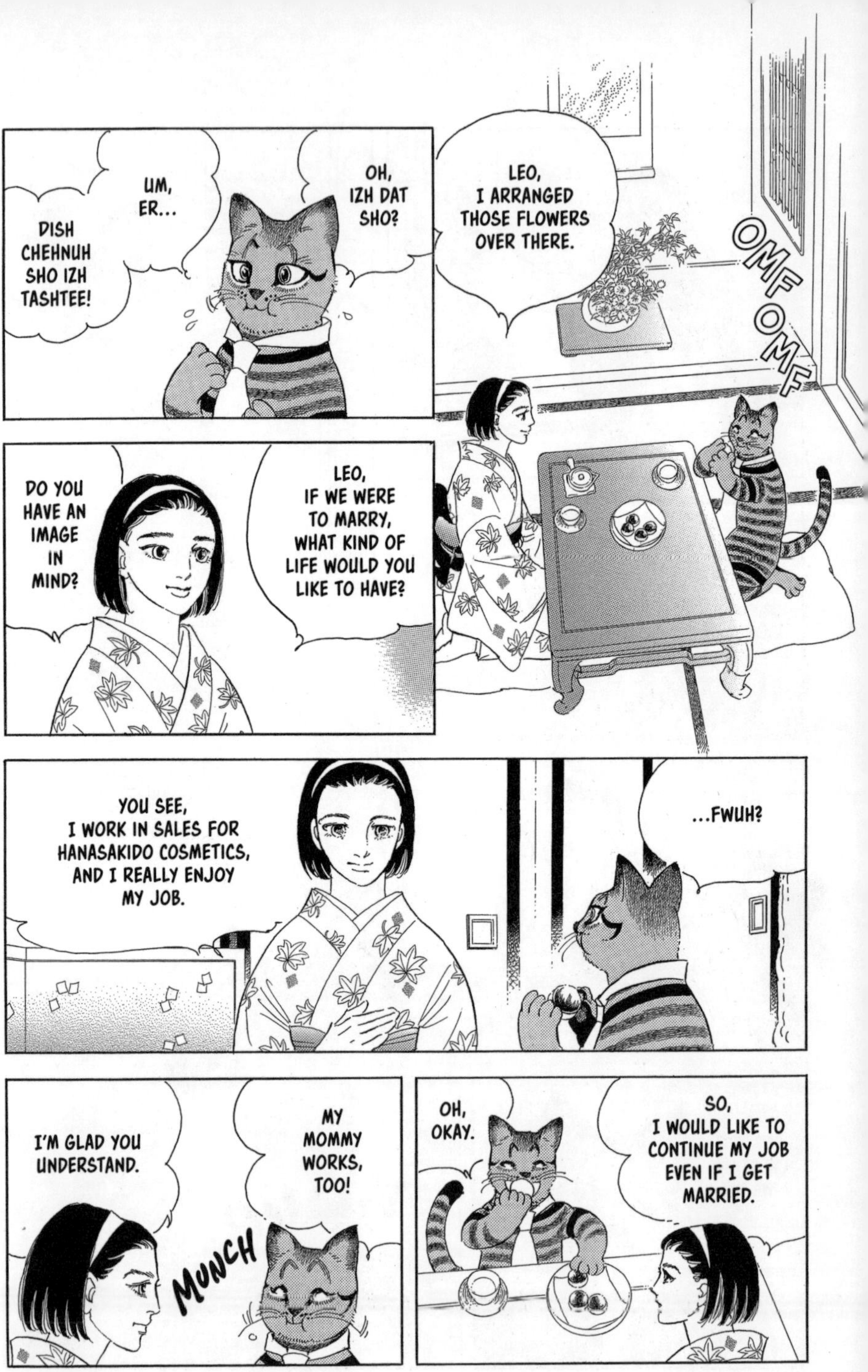
LEO, I ARRANGED THOSE FLOWERS OVER THERE.
OMF OMF
OH, IZH DAT SHO?
UM, ER...
DISH CHEHNUH SHO IZH TASHTEE!
LEO, IF WE WERE TO MARRY, WHAT KIND OF LIFE WOULD YOU LIKE TO HAVE?
DO YOU HAVE AN IMAGE IN MIND?
...FWUH?
YOU SEE, I WORK IN SALES FOR HANASAKIDO COSMETICS, AND I REALLY ENJOY MY JOB.
SO, I WOULD LIKE TO CONTINUE MY JOB EVEN IF I GET MARRIED.
OH, OKAY.
MY MOMMY WORKS, TOO!
MUNCH
I'M GLAD YOU UNDERSTAND.

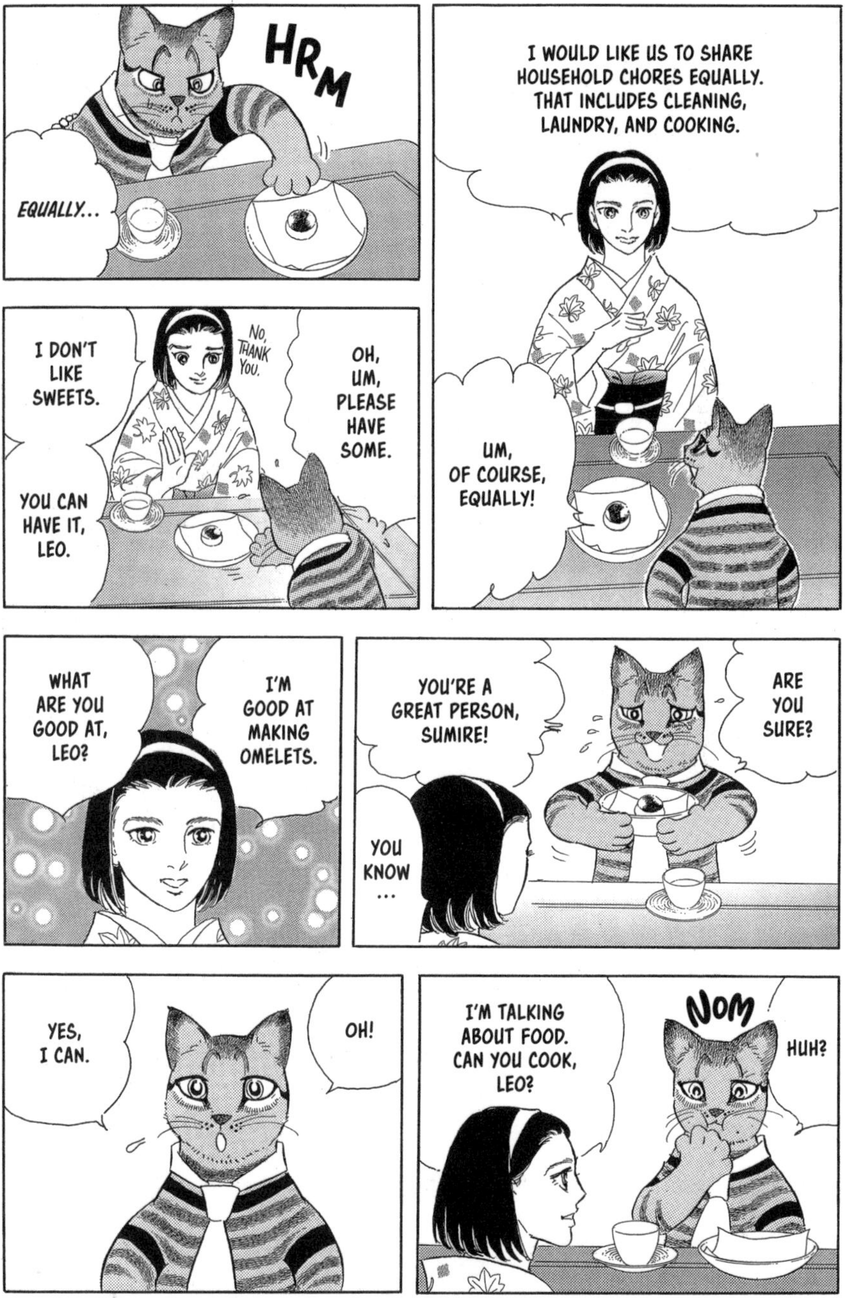
I WOULD LIKE US TO SHARE HOUSEHOLD CHORES EQUALLY. THAT INCLUDES CLEANING, LAUNDRY, AND COOKING.
UM, OF COURSE, EQUALLY!
HRM
EQUALLY...
OH, UM, PLEASE HAVE SOME.
NO, THANK YOU.
I DON'T LIKE SWEETS.
YOU CAN HAVE IT, LEO.
ARE YOU SURE?
YOU'RE A GREAT PERSON, SUMIRE!
YOU KNOW ...
I'M GOOD AT MAKING OMELETS.
WHAT ARE YOU GOOD AT, LEO?
HUH?
NOM
I'M TALKING ABOUT FOOD. CAN YOU COOK, LEO?
OH!
YES, I CAN.

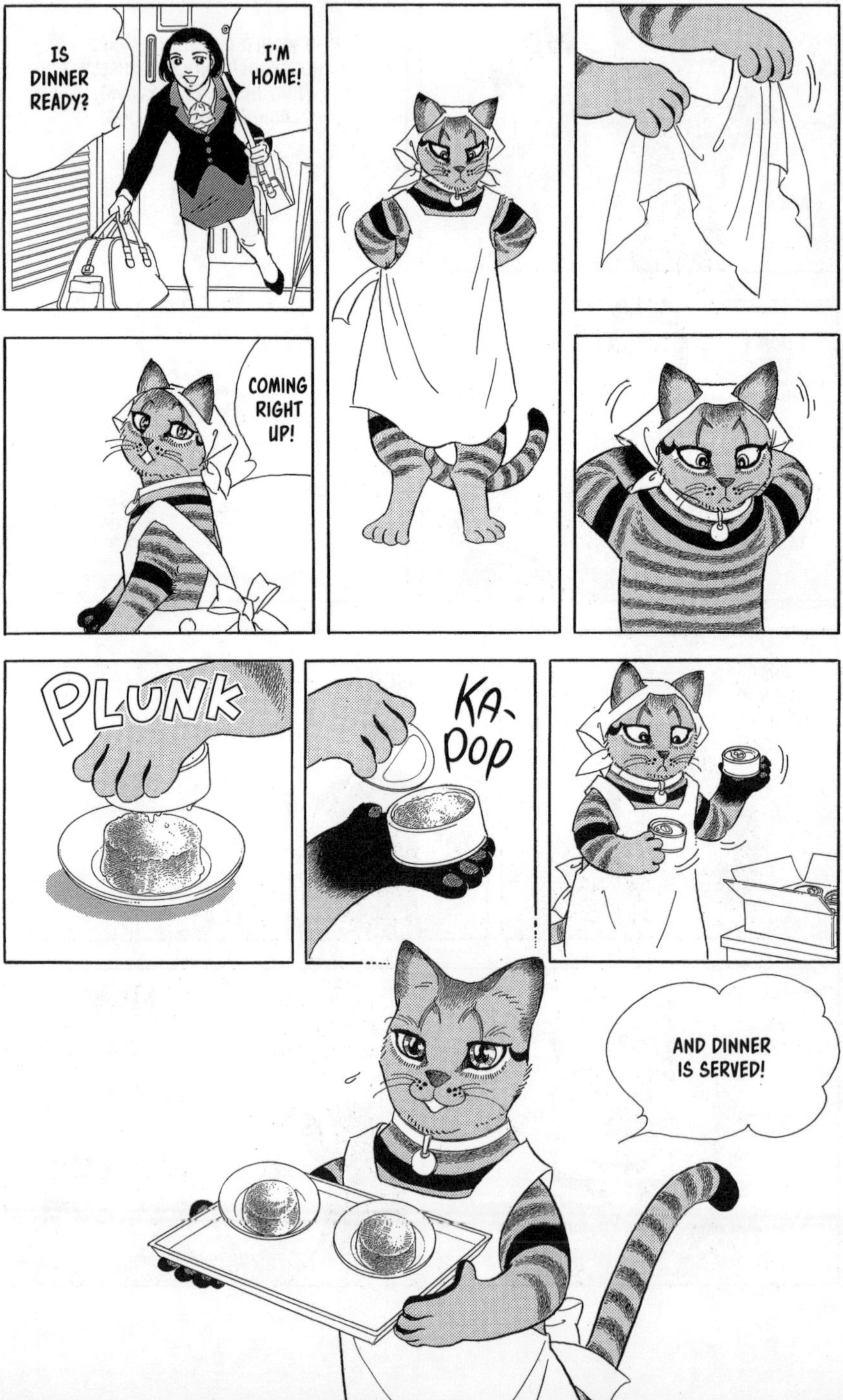
I'M HOME!
IS DINNER READY?
COMING RIGHT UP!
KA-POP
PLUNK
AND DINNER IS SERVED!

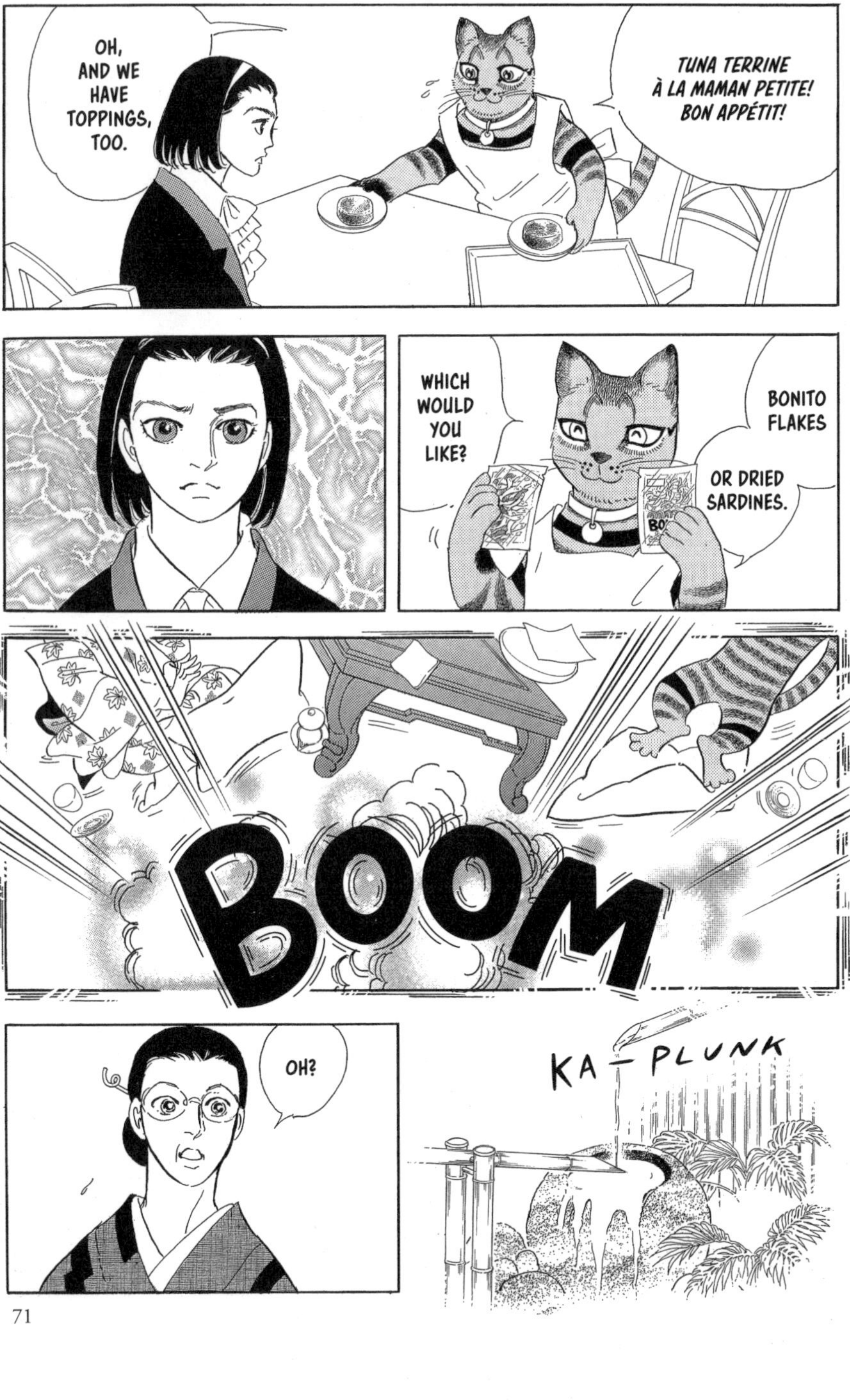
TUNA TERRINE À LA MAMAN PETITE! BON APPÉTIT!
OH, AND WE HAVE TOPPINGS, TOO.
BONITO FLAKES
OR DRIED SARDINES.
WHICH WOULD YOU LIKE?
BOOM
KA-PLUNK
OH?

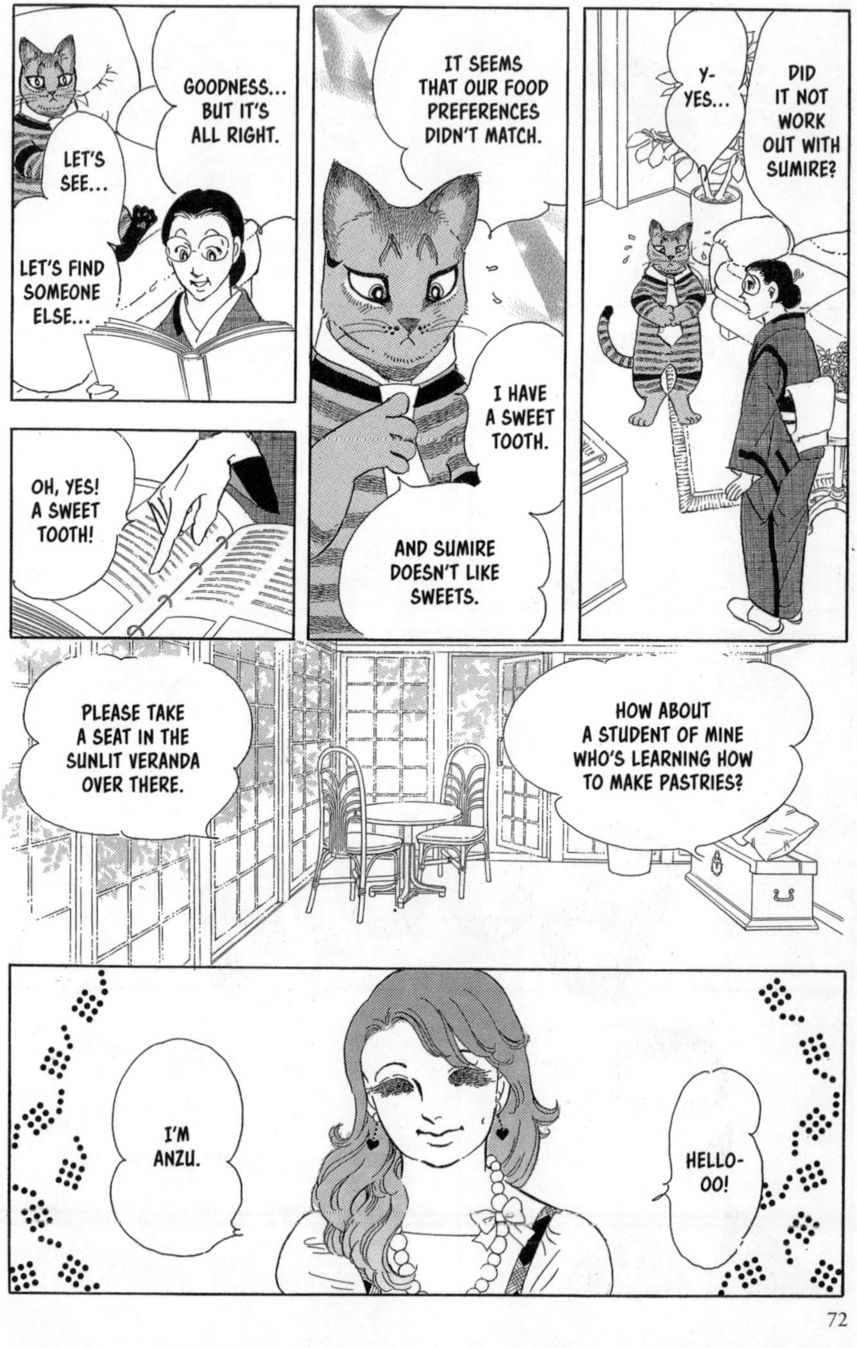
DID IT NOT WORK OUT WITH SUMIRE?
Y-YES...
IT SEEMS THAT OUR FOOD PREFERENCES DIDN'T MATCH.
I HAVE A SWEET TOOTH.
AND SUMIRE DOESN'T LIKE SWEETS.
GOODNESS... BUT IT'S ALL RIGHT.
LET'S SEE...
LET'S FIND SOMEONE ELSE...
OH, YES! A SWEET TOOTH!
HOW ABOUT A STUDENT OF MINE WHO'S LEARNING HOW TO MAKE PASTRIES?
PLEASE TAKE A SEAT IN THE SUNLIT VERANDA OVER THERE.
HELLO-OO!
I'M ANZU.

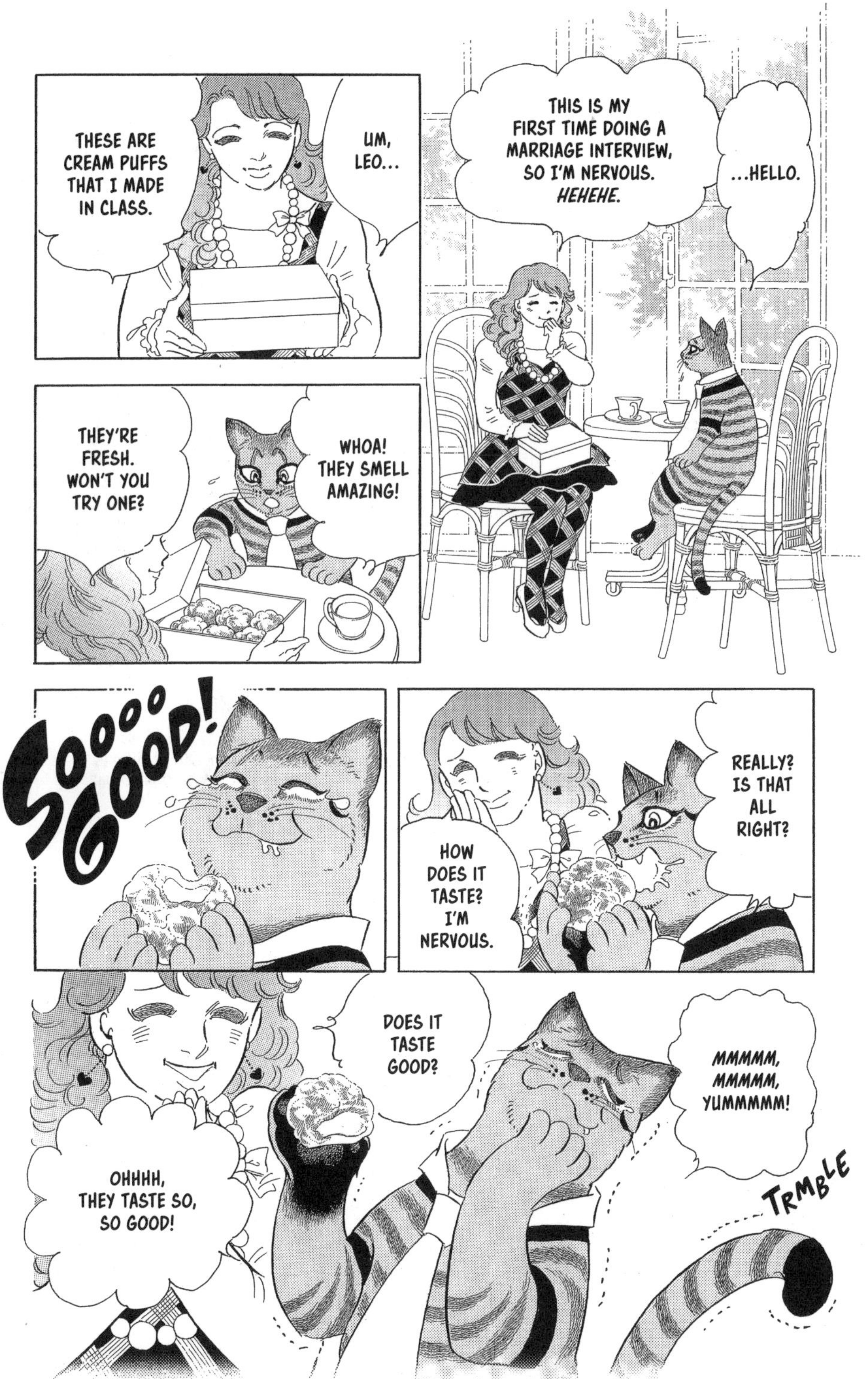
...HELLO.
THIS IS MY FIRST TIME DOING A MARRIAGE INTERVIEW, SO I'M NERVOUS. *HEHEHE.*
UM, LEO...
THESE ARE CREAM PUFFS THAT I MADE IN CLASS.
WHOA! THEY SMELL AMAZING!
THEY'RE FRESH. WON'T YOU TRY ONE?
REALLY? IS THAT ALL RIGHT?
HOW DOES IT TASTE? I'M NERVOUS.
SOOOO GOOD!
MMMMM, MMMMM, YUMMMMM!
TRMBLE
DOES IT TASTE GOOD?
OHHHH, THEY TASTE SO, SO GOOD!

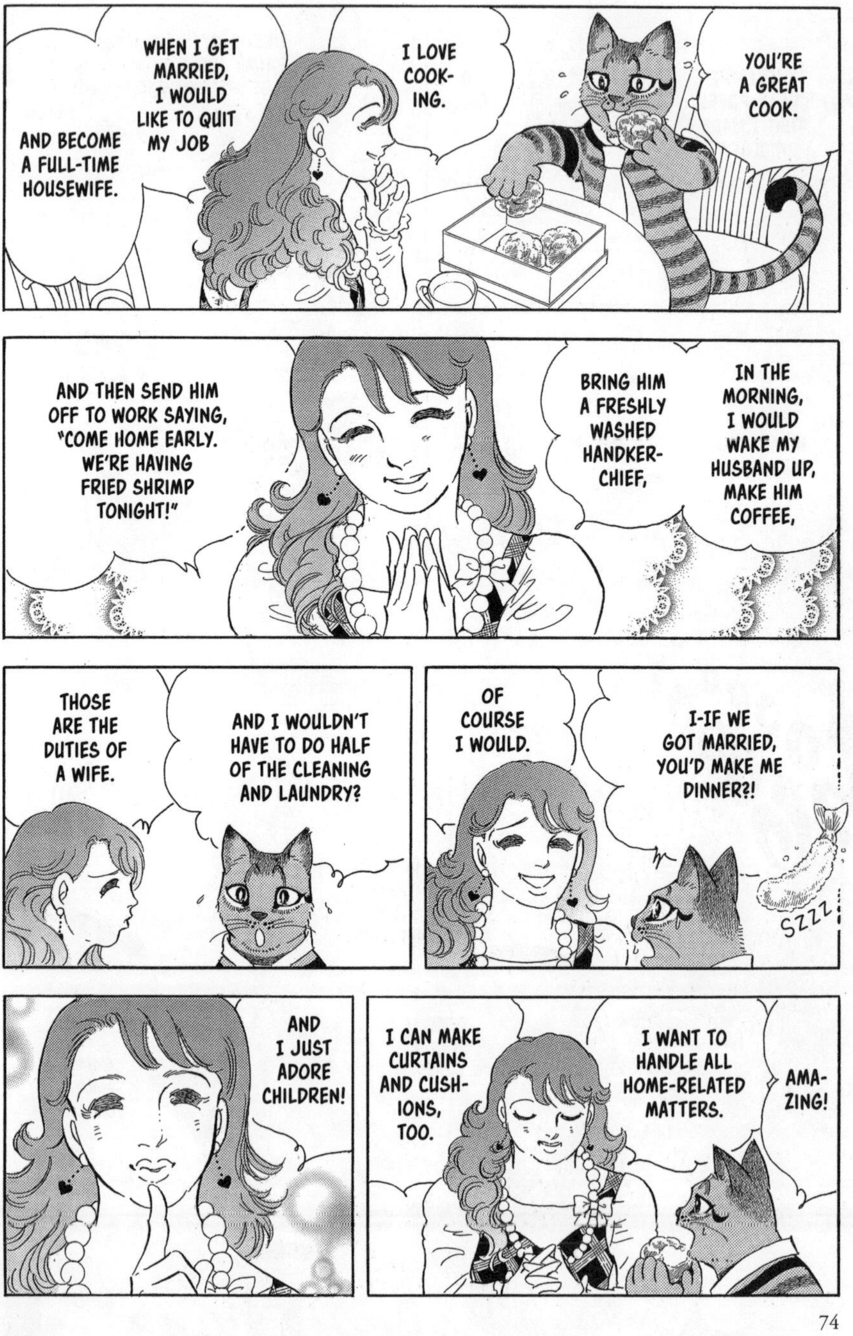
YOU'RE A GREAT COOK.
I LOVE COOK-ING.
WHEN I GET MARRIED, I WOULD LIKE TO QUIT MY JOB
AND BECOME A FULL-TIME HOUSEWIFE.
IN THE MORNING, I WOULD WAKE MY HUSBAND UP, MAKE HIM COFFEE,
BRING HIM A FRESHLY WASHED HANDKER-CHIEF,
AND THEN SEND HIM OFF TO WORK SAYING, "COME HOME EARLY. WE'RE HAVING FRIED SHRIMP TONIGHT!"
I-IF WE GOT MARRIED, YOU'D MAKE ME DINNER?!
OF COURSE I WOULD.
SZZZ
AND I WOULDN'T HAVE TO DO HALF OF THE CLEANING AND LAUNDRY?
THOSE ARE THE DUTIES OF A WIFE.
AMA-ZING!
I WANT TO HANDLE ALL HOME-RELATED MATTERS.
I CAN MAKE CURTAINS AND CUSH-IONS, TOO.
AND I JUST ADORE CHILDREN!

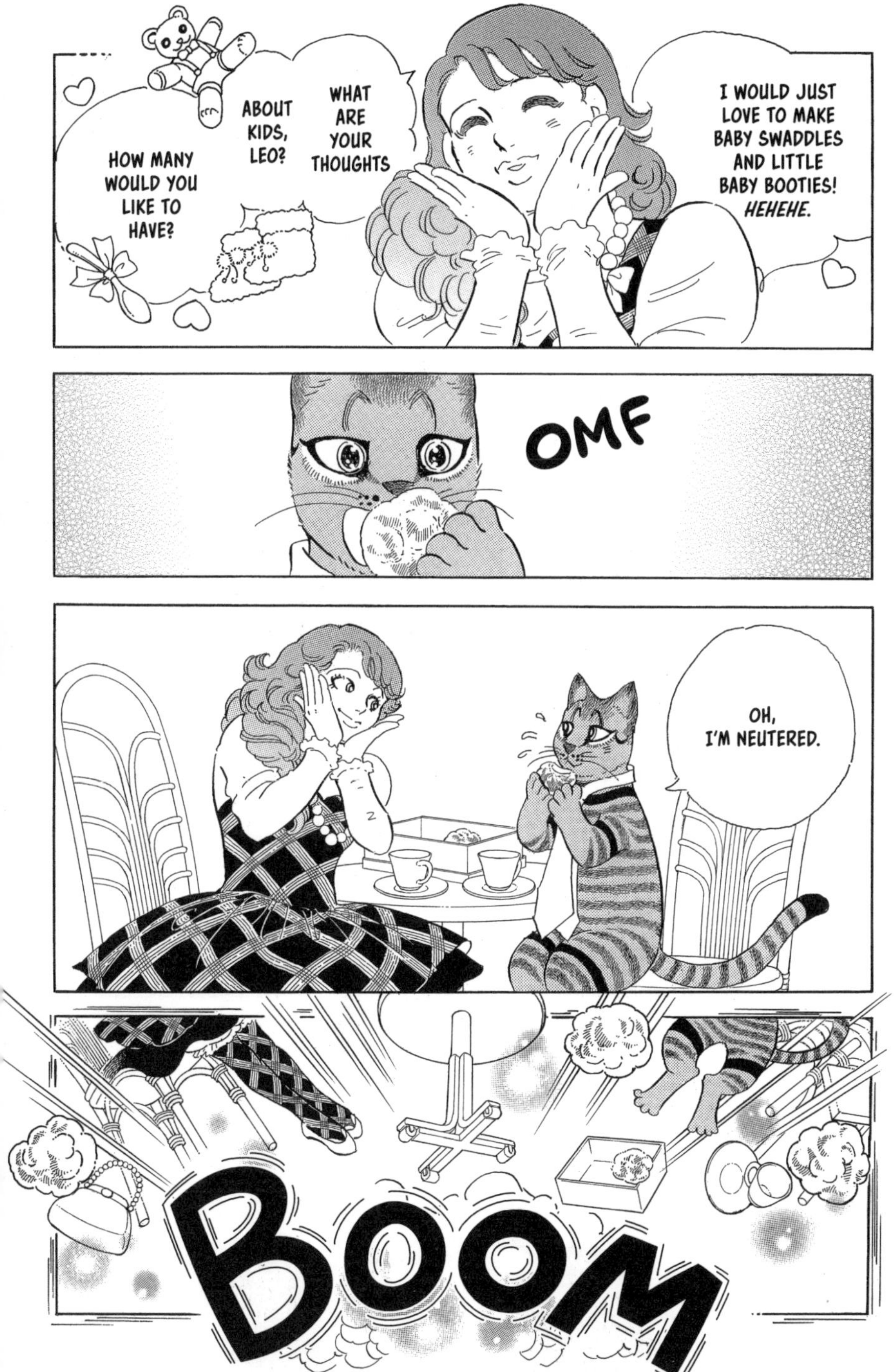
I WOULD JUST LOVE TO MAKE BABY SWADDLES AND LITTLE BABY BOOTIES! *HEHEHE.*
WHAT ARE YOUR THOUGHTS
ABOUT KIDS, LEO?
HOW MANY WOULD YOU LIKE TO HAVE?
OMF
OH, I'M NEUTERED.
BOOM

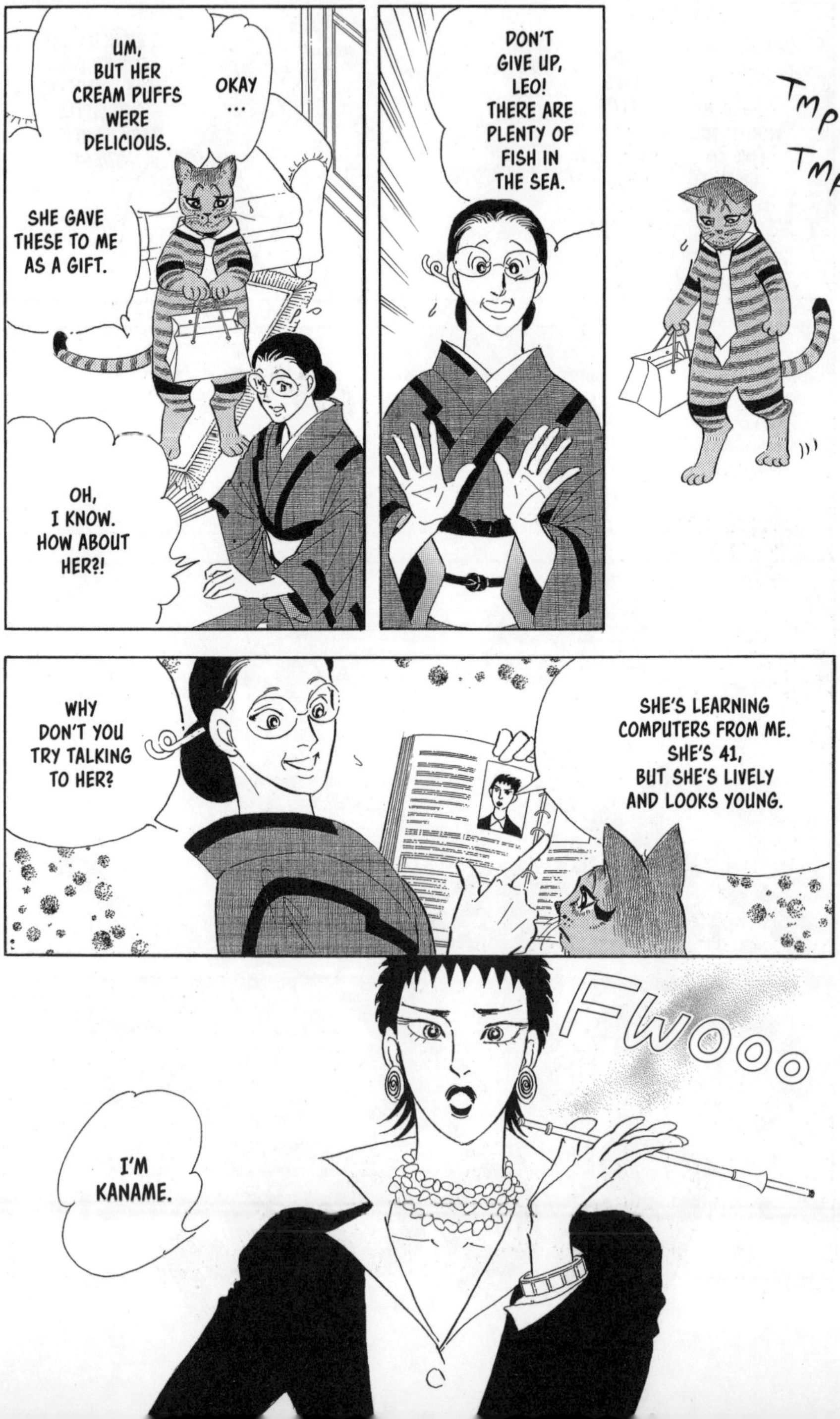
TMP
TMP
DON'T GIVE UP, LEO! THERE ARE PLENTY OF FISH IN THE SEA.
OKAY ...
UM, BUT HER CREAM PUFFS WERE DELICIOUS.
SHE GAVE THESE TO ME AS A GIFT.
OH, I KNOW. HOW ABOUT HER?!
SHE'S LEARNING COMPUTERS FROM ME. SHE'S 41, BUT SHE'S LIVELY AND LOOKS YOUNG.
WHY DON'T YOU TRY TALKING TO HER?
FWOOO
I'M KANAME.

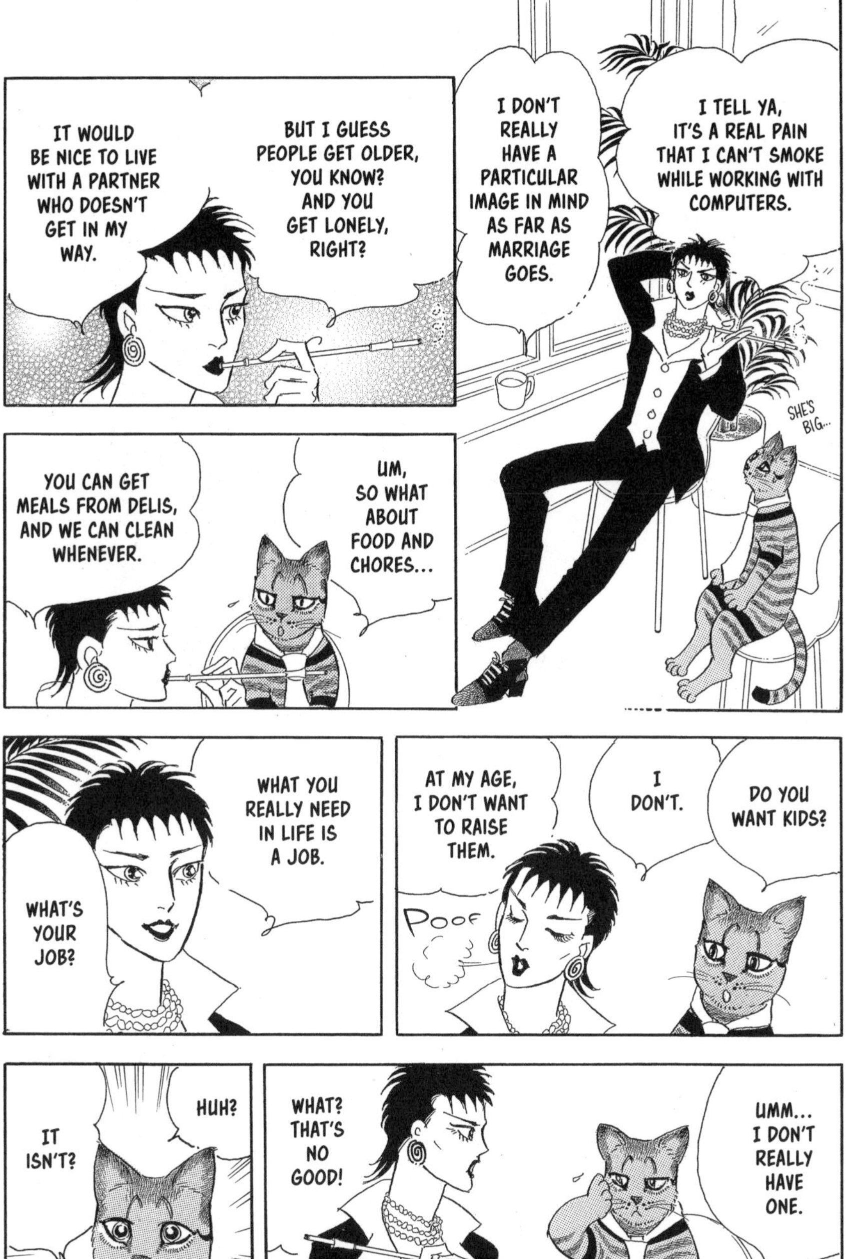
I TELL YA, IT'S A REAL PAIN THAT I CAN'T SMOKE WHILE WORKING WITH COMPUTERS.
I DON'T REALLY HAVE A PARTICULAR IMAGE IN MIND AS FAR AS MARRIAGE GOES.
SHE'S BIG...
BUT I GUESS PEOPLE GET OLDER, YOU KNOW? AND YOU GET LONELY, RIGHT?
IT WOULD BE NICE TO LIVE WITH A PARTNER WHO DOESN'T GET IN MY WAY.
UM, SO WHAT ABOUT FOOD AND CHORES...
YOU CAN GET MEALS FROM DELIS, AND WE CAN CLEAN WHENEVER.
DO YOU WANT KIDS?
I DON'T.
AT MY AGE, I DON'T WANT TO RAISE THEM.
POOF
WHAT YOU REALLY NEED IN LIFE IS A JOB.
WHAT'S YOUR JOB?
UMM... I DON'T REALLY HAVE ONE.
WHAT? THAT'S NO GOOD!
HUH?
IT ISN'T?

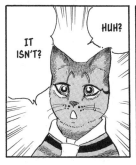

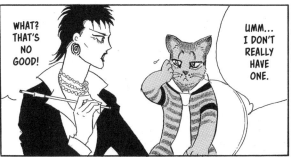

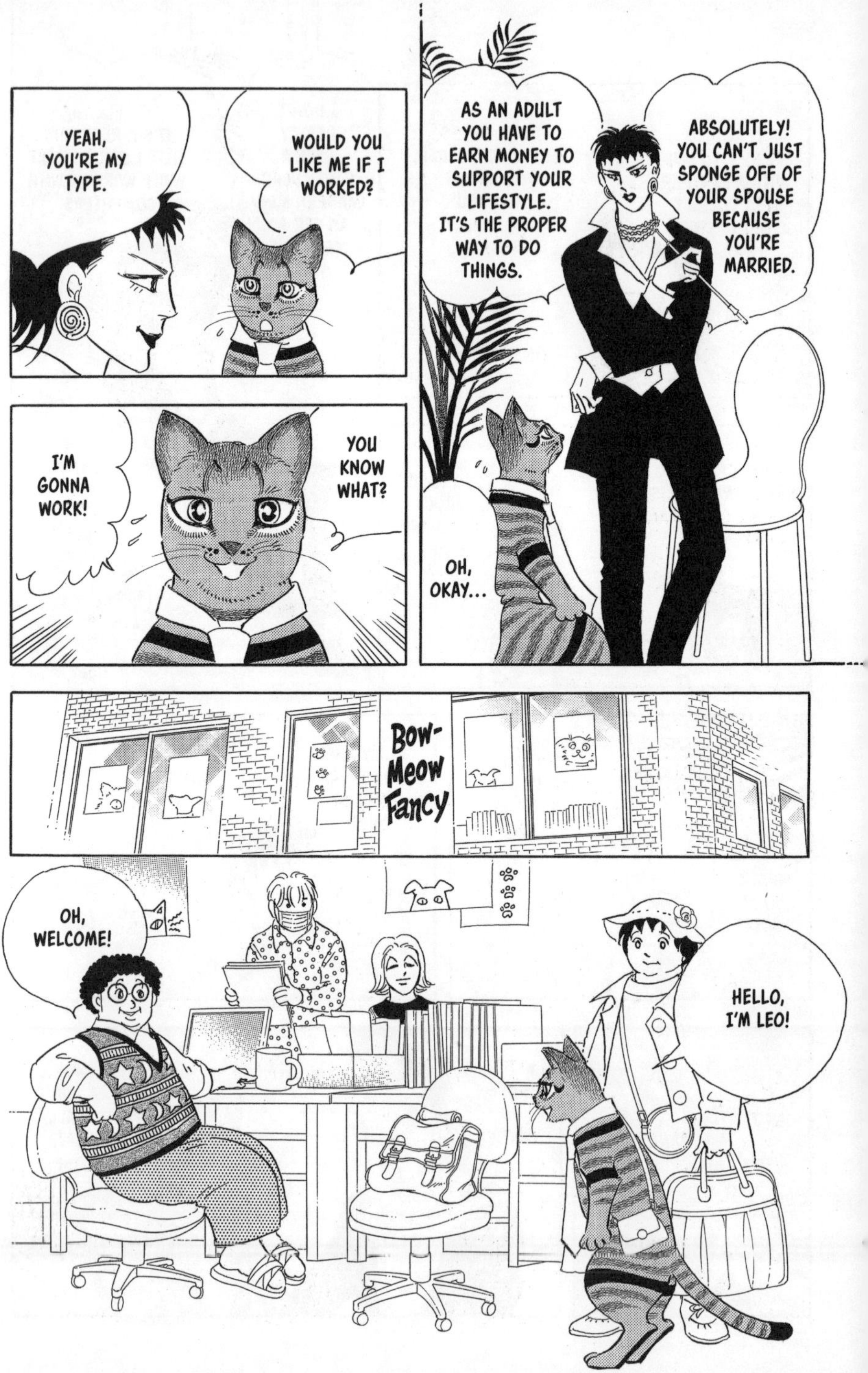
ABSOLUTELY! YOU CAN'T JUST SPONGE OFF OF YOUR SPOUSE BECAUSE YOU'RE MARRIED.
AS AN ADULT YOU HAVE TO EARN MONEY TO SUPPORT YOUR LIFESTYLE. IT'S THE PROPER WAY TO DO THINGS.
OH, OKAY...
WOULD YOU LIKE ME IF I WORKED?
YEAH, YOU'RE MY TYPE.
YOU KNOW WHAT?
I'M GONNA WORK!
Bow-Meow Fancy
HELLO, I'M LEO!
OH, WELCOME!

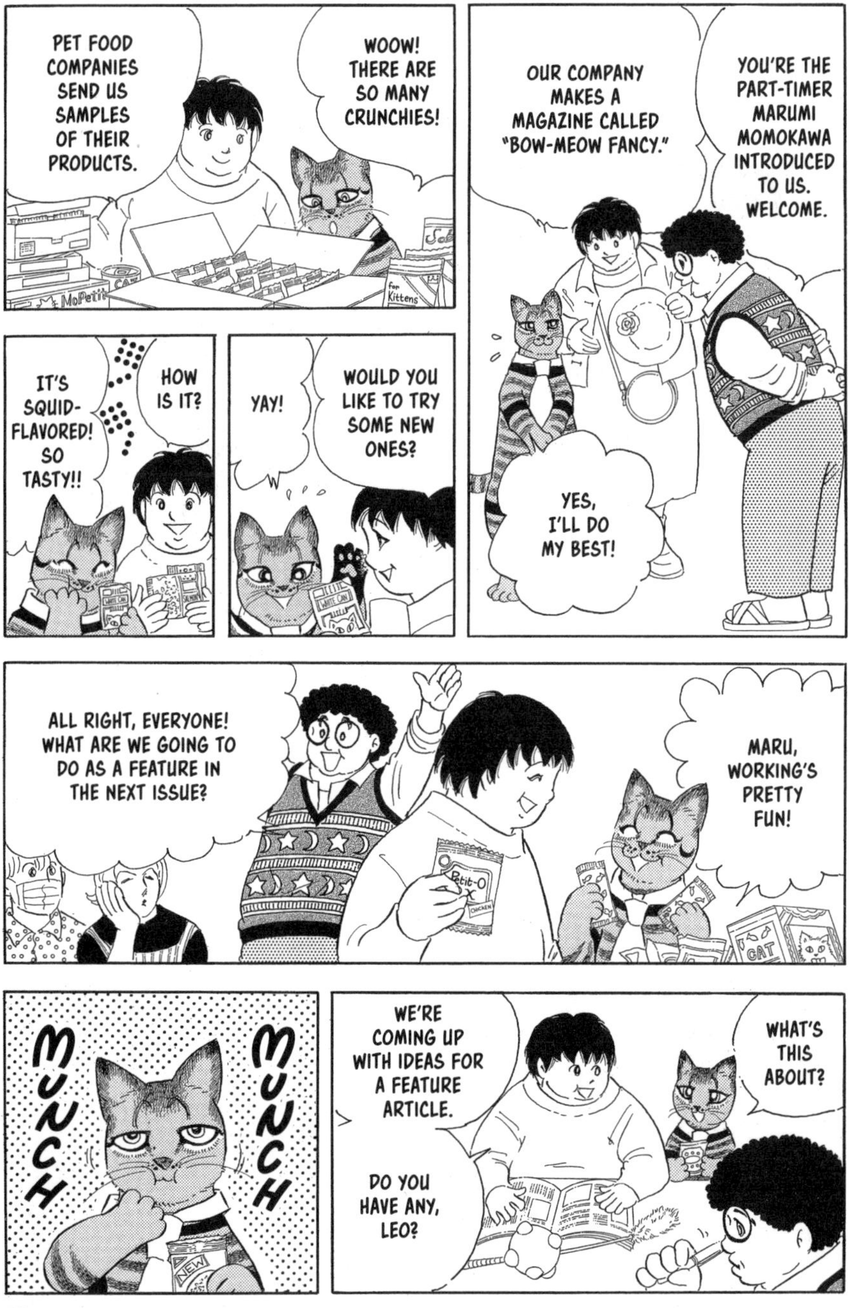
YOU'RE THE PART-TIMER MARUMI MOMOKAWA INTRODUCED TO US. WELCOME.
OUR COMPANY MAKES A MAGAZINE CALLED "BOW-MEOW FANCY."
YES, I'LL DO MY BEST!
WOOW! THERE ARE SO MANY CRUNCHIES!
PET FOOD COMPANIES SEND US SAMPLES OF THEIR PRODUCTS.
WOULD YOU LIKE TO TRY SOME NEW ONES?
YAY!
HOW IS IT?
IT'S SQUID-FLAVORED! SO TASTY!!
MARU, WORKING'S PRETTY FUN!
ALL RIGHT, EVERYONE! WHAT ARE WE GOING TO DO AS A FEATURE IN THE NEXT ISSUE?
WHAT'S THIS ABOUT?
WE'RE COMING UP WITH IDEAS FOR A FEATURE ARTICLE.
DO YOU HAVE ANY, LEO?
MUNCH
MUNCH

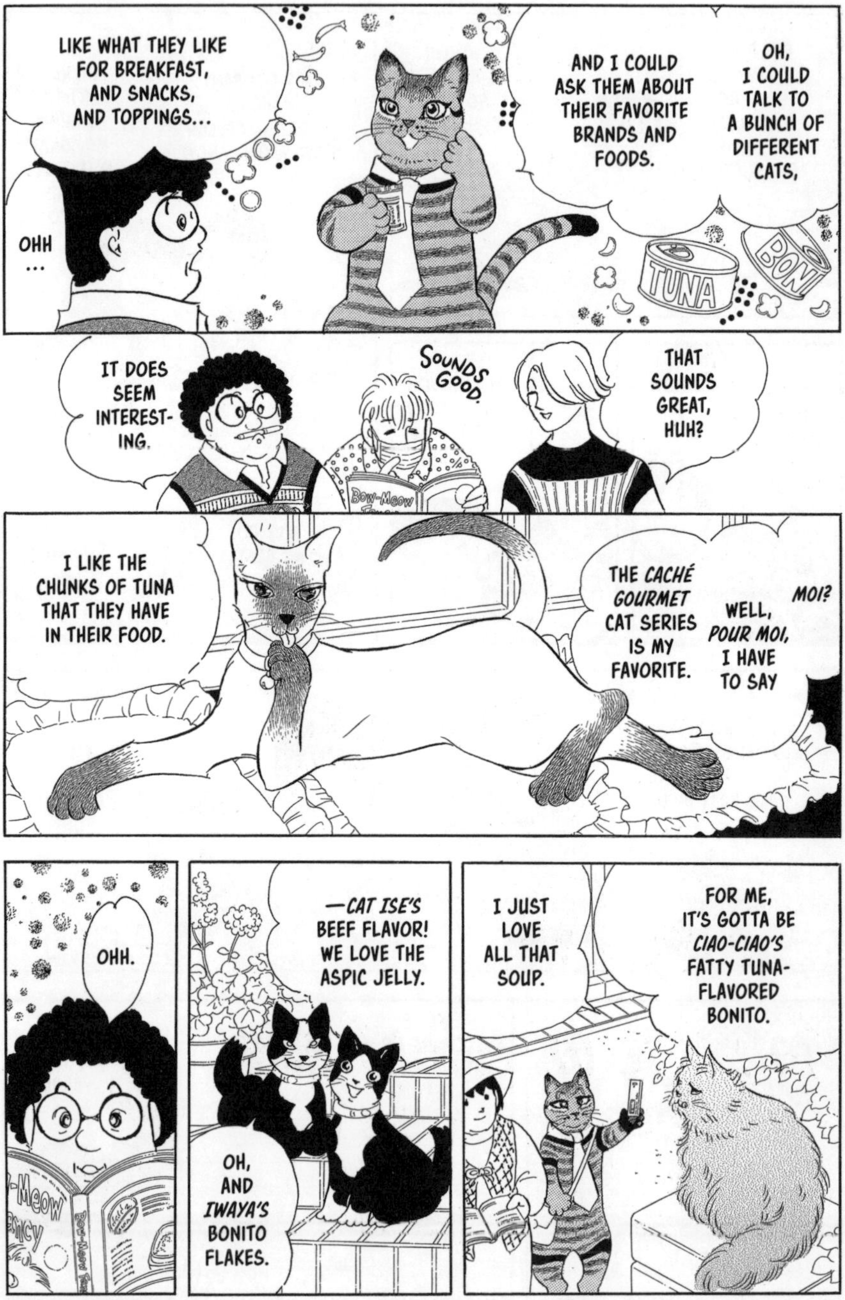
OH, I COULD TALK TO A BUNCH OF DIFFERENT CATS,
AND I COULD ASK THEM ABOUT THEIR FAVORITE BRANDS AND FOODS.
LIKE WHAT THEY LIKE FOR BREAKFAST, AND SNACKS, AND TOPPINGS...
OHH ...
BON
TUNA
THAT SOUNDS GREAT, HUH?
SOUNDS GOOD.
IT DOES SEEM INTEREST-ING.
MOI?
WELL, *POUR MOI,* I HAVE TO SAY
THE *CACHÉ GOURMET* CAT SERIES IS MY FAVORITE.
I LIKE THE CHUNKS OF TUNA THAT THEY HAVE IN THEIR FOOD.
FOR ME, IT'S GOTTA BE *CIAO-CIAO'S* FATTY TUNA-FLAVORED BONITO.
I JUST LOVE ALL THAT SOUP.
—*CAT ISE'S* BEEF FLAVOR! WE LOVE THE ASPIC JELLY.
OH, AND *IWAYA'S* BONITO FLAKES.
OHH.

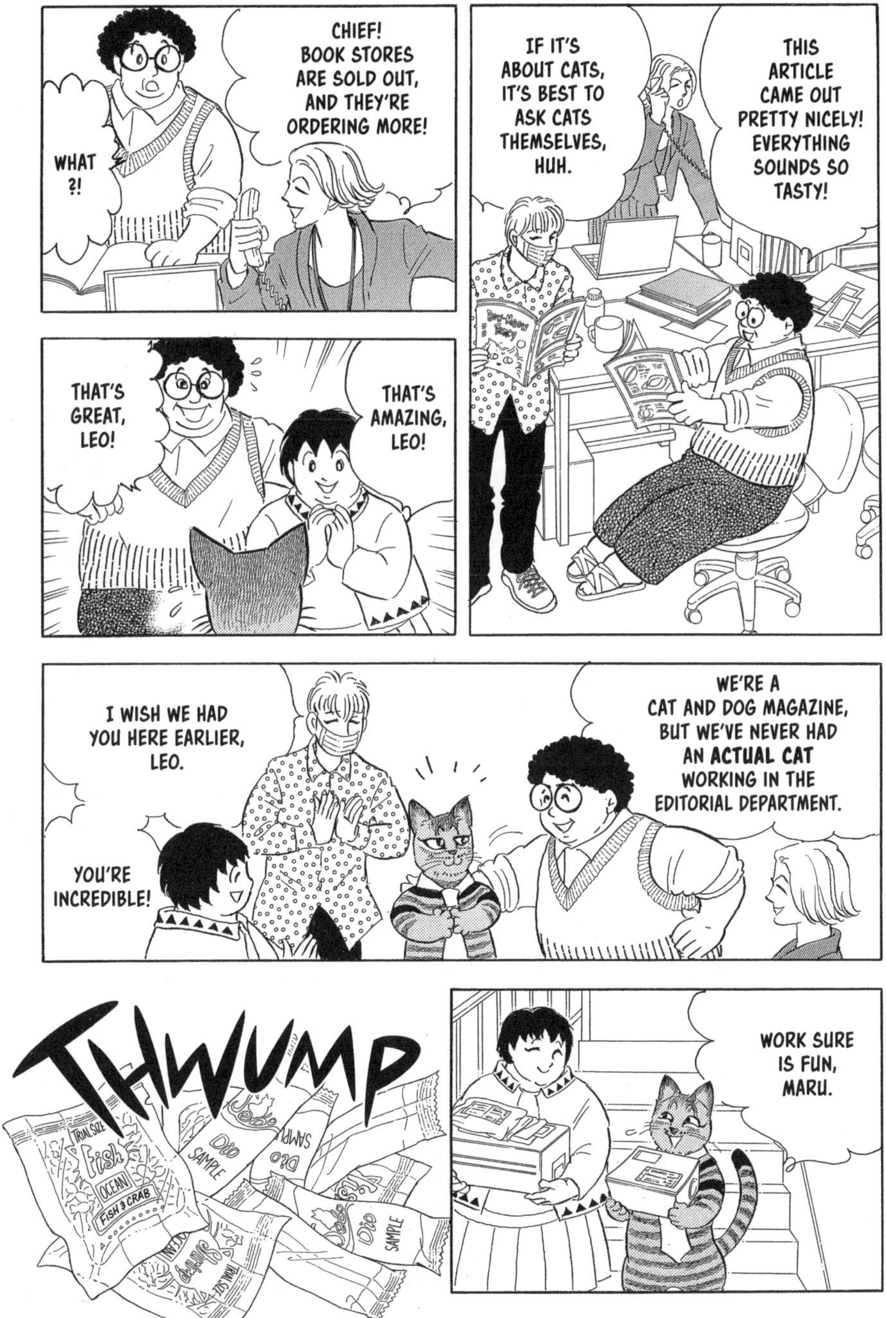
THIS ARTICLE CAME OUT PRETTY NICELY! EVERYTHING SOUNDS SO TASTY!
IF IT'S ABOUT CATS, IT'S BEST TO ASK CATS THEMSELVES, HUH.
CHIEF! BOOK STORES ARE SOLD OUT, AND THEY'RE ORDERING MORE!
WHAT ?!
THAT'S AMAZING, LEO!
THAT'S GREAT, LEO!
WE'RE A CAT AND DOG MAGAZINE, BUT WE'VE NEVER HAD AN **ACTUAL CAT** WORKING IN THE EDITORIAL DEPARTMENT.
I WISH WE HAD YOU HERE EARLIER, LEO.
YOU'RE INCREDIBLE!
WORK SURE IS FUN, MARU.
THWUMP

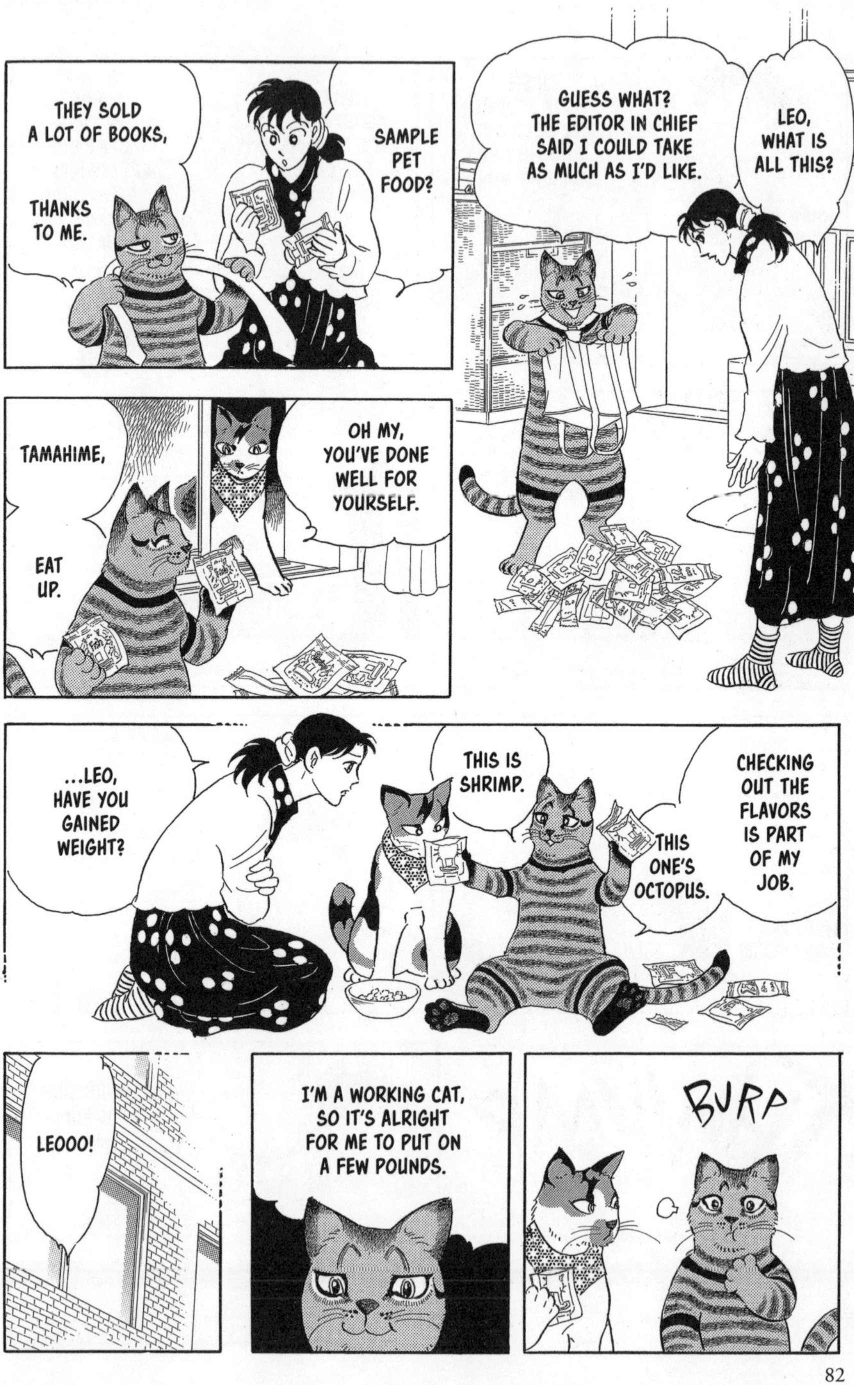
LEO, WHAT IS ALL THIS?
GUESS WHAT? THE EDITOR IN CHIEF SAID I COULD TAKE AS MUCH AS I'D LIKE.
SAMPLE PET FOOD?
THEY SOLD A LOT OF BOOKS,
THANKS TO ME.
OH MY, YOU'VE DONE WELL FOR YOURSELF.
TAMAHIME,
EAT UP.
CHECKING OUT THE FLAVORS IS PART OF MY JOB.
THIS ONE'S OCTOPUS.
THIS IS SHRIMP.
...LEO, HAVE YOU GAINED WEIGHT?
BURP
I'M A WORKING CAT, SO IT'S ALRIGHT FOR ME TO PUT ON A FEW POUNDS.
LEOOO!

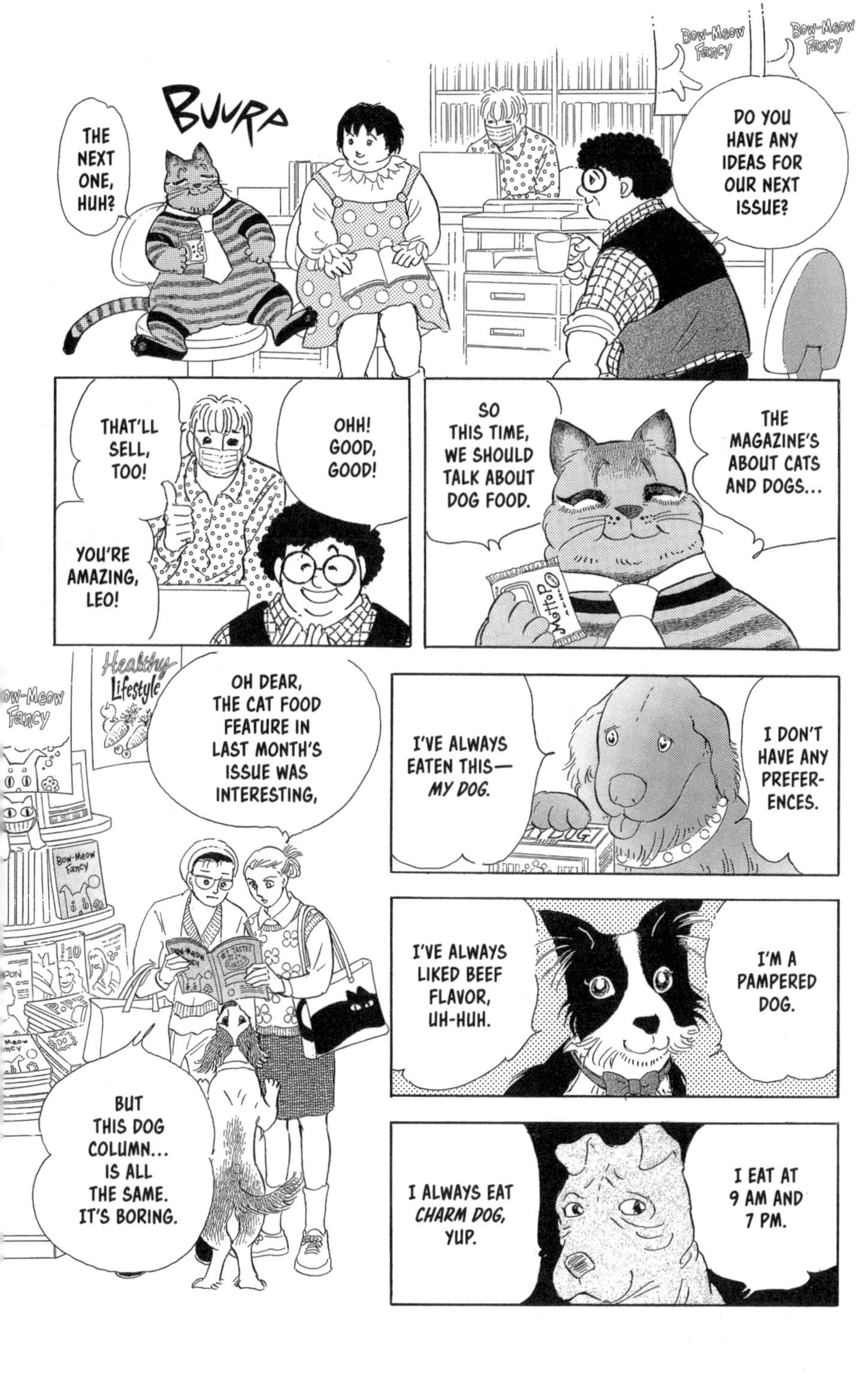
Bow-Meow Fancy
Bow-Meow Fancy
DO YOU HAVE ANY IDEAS FOR OUR NEXT ISSUE?
BUURP
THE NEXT ONE, HUH?
THE MAGAZINE'S ABOUT CATS AND DOGS...
SO THIS TIME, WE SHOULD TALK ABOUT DOG FOOD.
OHH! GOOD, GOOD!
THAT'LL SELL, TOO!
YOU'RE AMAZING, LEO!
I DON'T HAVE ANY PREFER-ENCES.
I'VE ALWAYS EATEN THIS— *MY DOG.*
I'M A PAMPERED DOG.
I'VE ALWAYS LIKED BEEF FLAVOR, UH-HUH.
I EAT AT 9 AM AND 7 PM.
I ALWAYS EAT *CHARM DOG,* YUP.
Healthy Lifestyle
Bow-Meow Fancy
OH DEAR, THE CAT FOOD FEATURE IN LAST MONTH'S ISSUE WAS INTERESTING,
BUT THIS DOG COLUMN... IS ALL THE SAME. IT'S BORING.

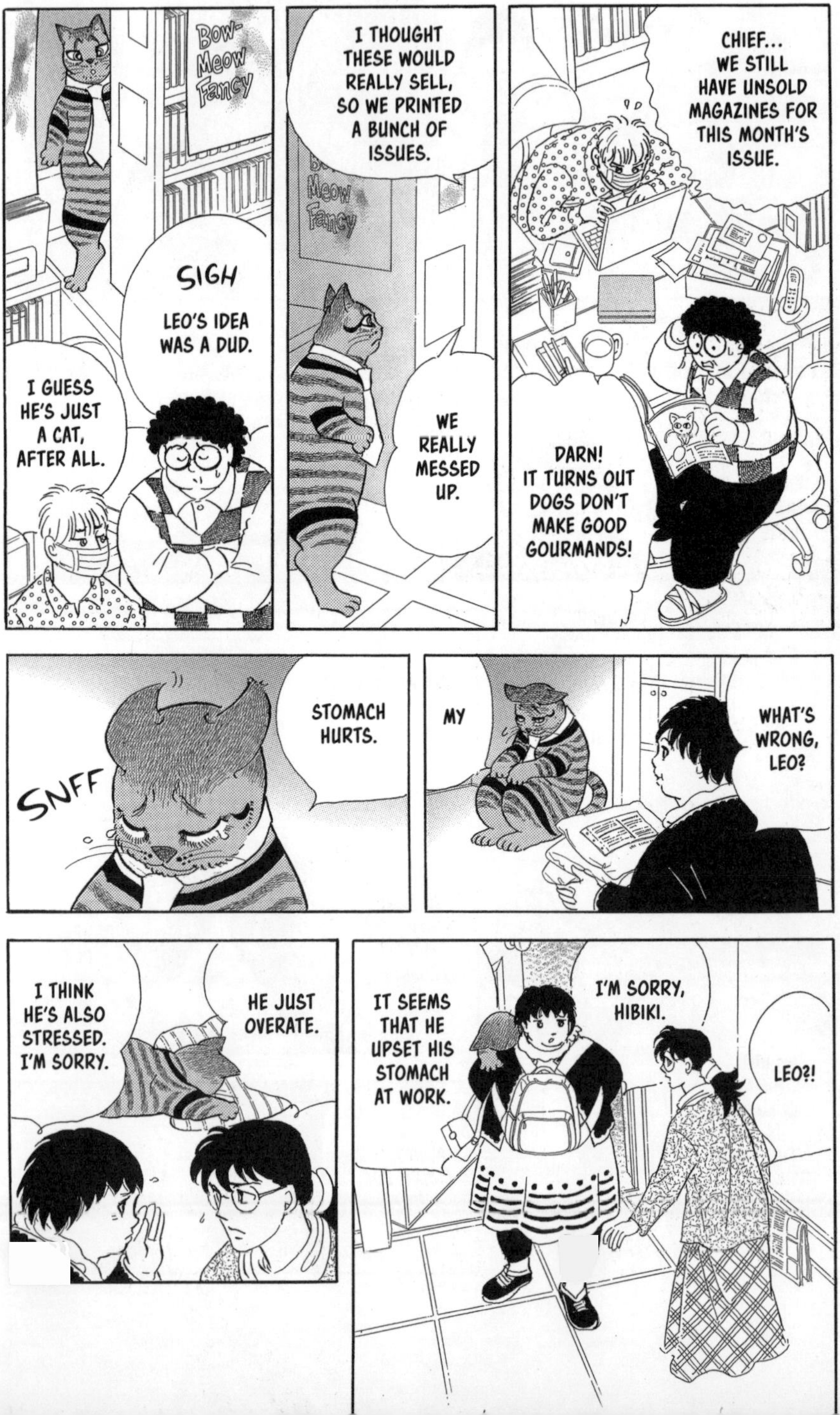
CHIEF... WE STILL HAVE UNSOLD MAGAZINES FOR THIS MONTH'S ISSUE.
DARN! IT TURNS OUT DOGS DON'T MAKE GOOD GOURMANDS!
I THOUGHT THESE WOULD REALLY SELL, SO WE PRINTED A BUNCH OF ISSUES.
WE REALLY MESSED UP.
Bow-Meow Fancy
SIGH
LEO'S IDEA WAS A DUD.
I GUESS HE'S JUST A CAT, AFTER ALL.
WHAT'S WRONG, LEO?
MY
STOMACH HURTS.
SNFF
LEO?!
I'M SORRY, HIBIKI.
IT SEEMS THAT HE UPSET HIS STOMACH AT WORK.
HE JUST OVERATE.
I THINK HE'S ALSO STRESSED. I'M SORRY.

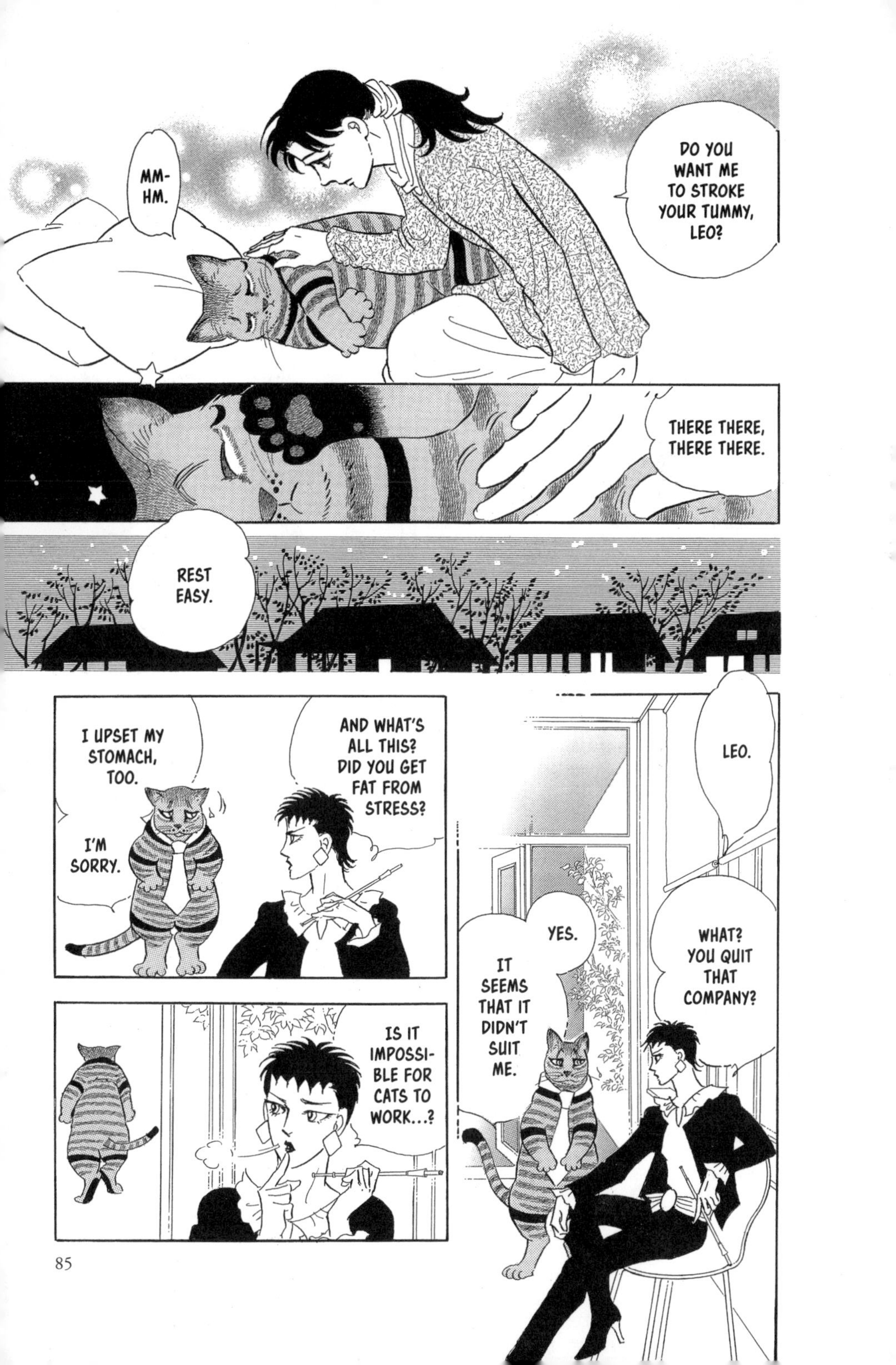
DO YOU WANT ME TO STROKE YOUR TUMMY, LEO?
MM-HM.
THERE THERE, THERE THERE.
REST EASY.
LEO.
WHAT? YOU QUIT THAT COMPANY?
YES.
IT SEEMS THAT IT DIDN'T SUIT ME.
AND WHAT'S ALL THIS? DID YOU GET FAT FROM STRESS?
I UPSET MY STOMACH, TOO.
I'M SORRY.
IS IT IMPOSSIBLE FOR CATS TO WORK...?

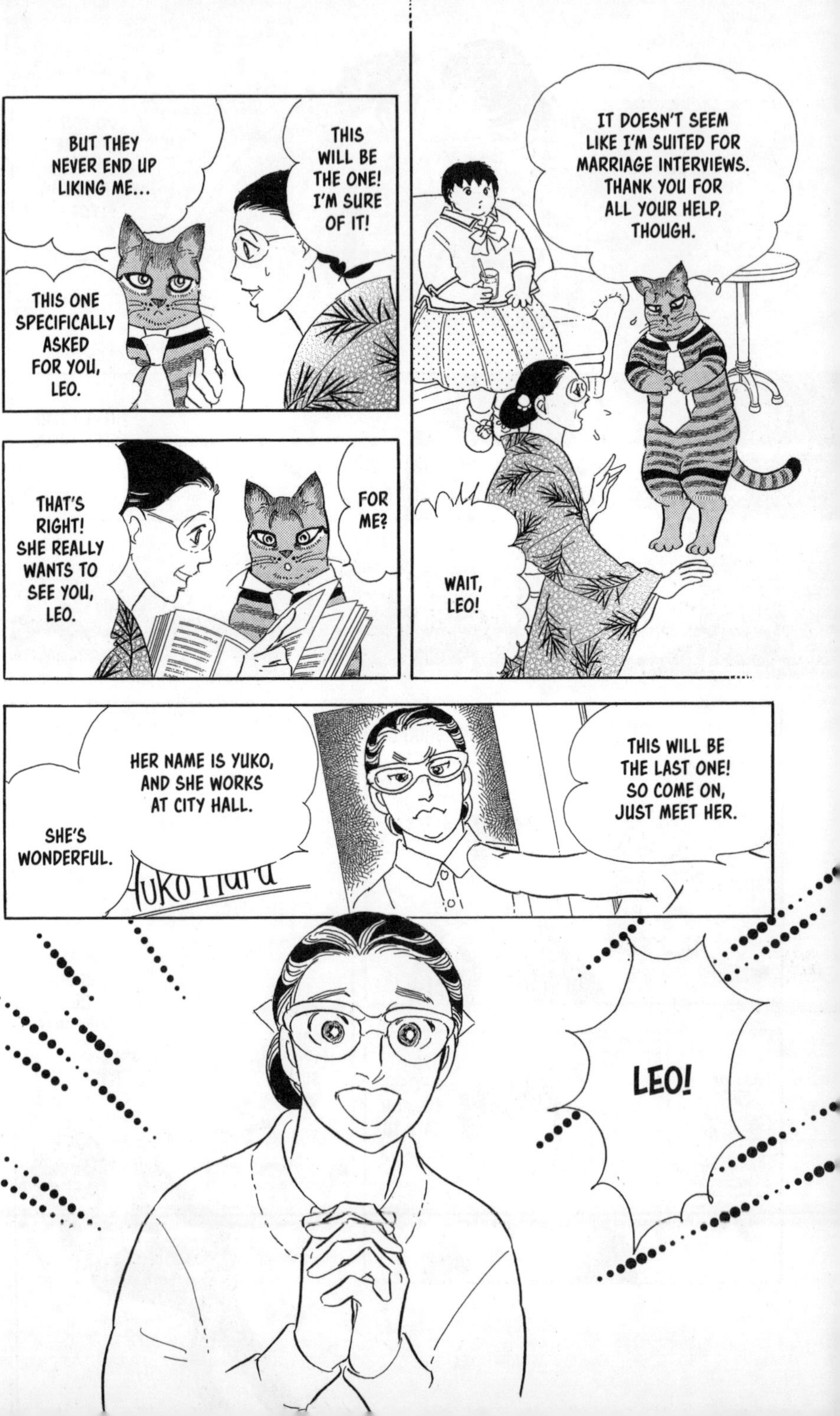

IT DOESN'T SEEM LIKE I'M SUITED FOR MARRIAGE INTERVIEWS. THANK YOU FOR ALL YOUR HELP, THOUGH.
WAIT, LEO!
THIS WILL BE THE ONE! I'M SURE OF IT!
BUT THEY NEVER END UP LIKING ME...
THIS ONE SPECIFICALLY ASKED FOR YOU, LEO.
FOR ME?
THAT'S RIGHT! SHE REALLY WANTS TO SEE YOU, LEO.
THIS WILL BE THE LAST ONE! SO COME ON, JUST MEET HER.
HER NAME IS YUKO, AND SHE WORKS AT CITY HALL.
SHE'S WONDERFUL.
LEO!

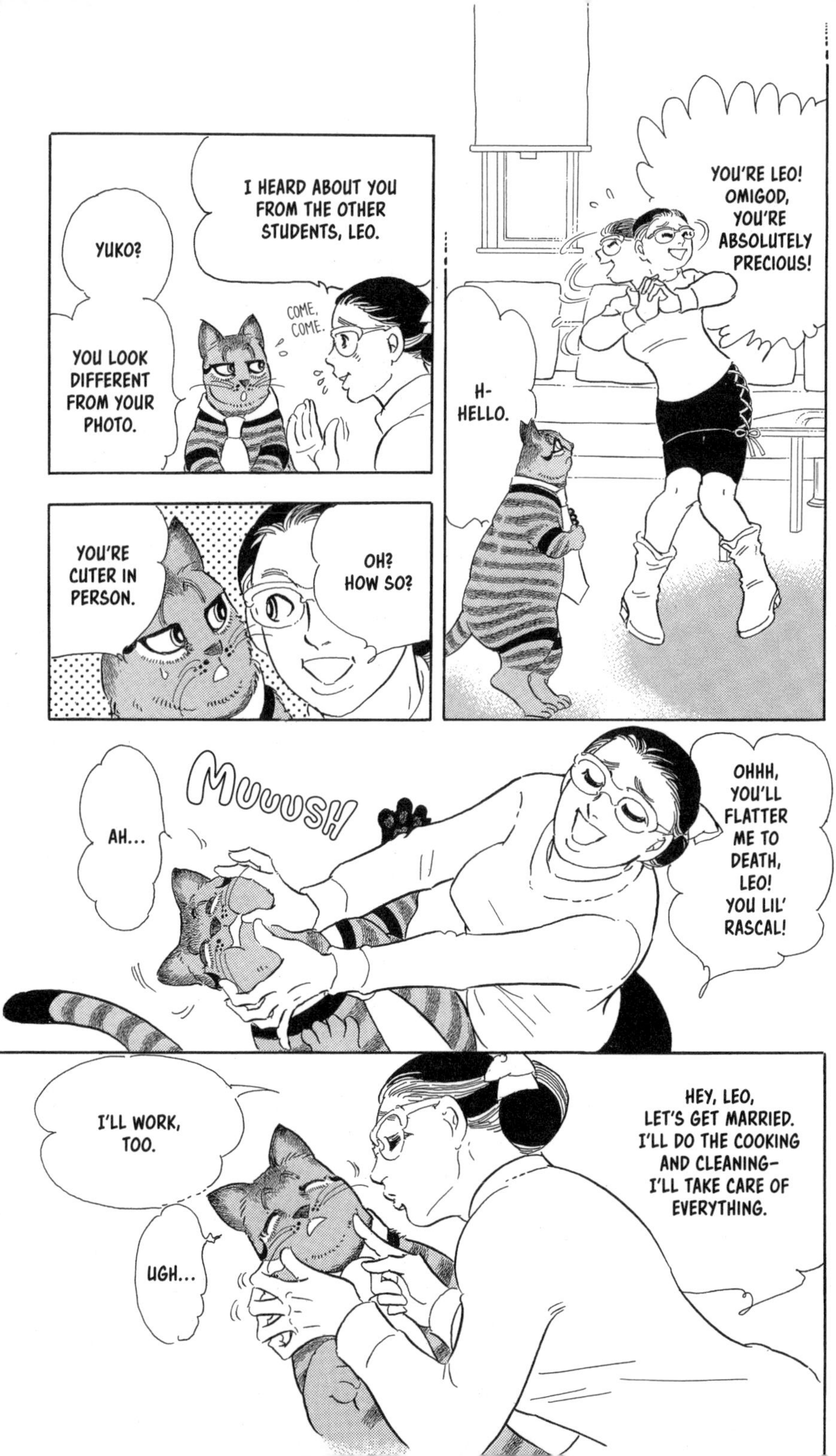

YOU'RE LEO! OMIGOD, YOU'RE ABSOLUTELY PRECIOUS!
H-HELLO.
I HEARD ABOUT YOU FROM THE OTHER STUDENTS, LEO.
COME, COME.
YUKO?
YOU LOOK DIFFERENT FROM YOUR PHOTO.
OH? HOW SO?
YOU'RE CUTER IN PERSON.
OHHH, YOU'LL FLATTER ME TO DEATH, LEO! YOU LIL' RASCAL!
MUUUSH
AH...
HEY, LEO, LET'S GET MARRIED. I'LL DO THE COOKING AND CLEANING– I'LL TAKE CARE OF EVERYTHING.
I'LL WORK, TOO.
UGH...

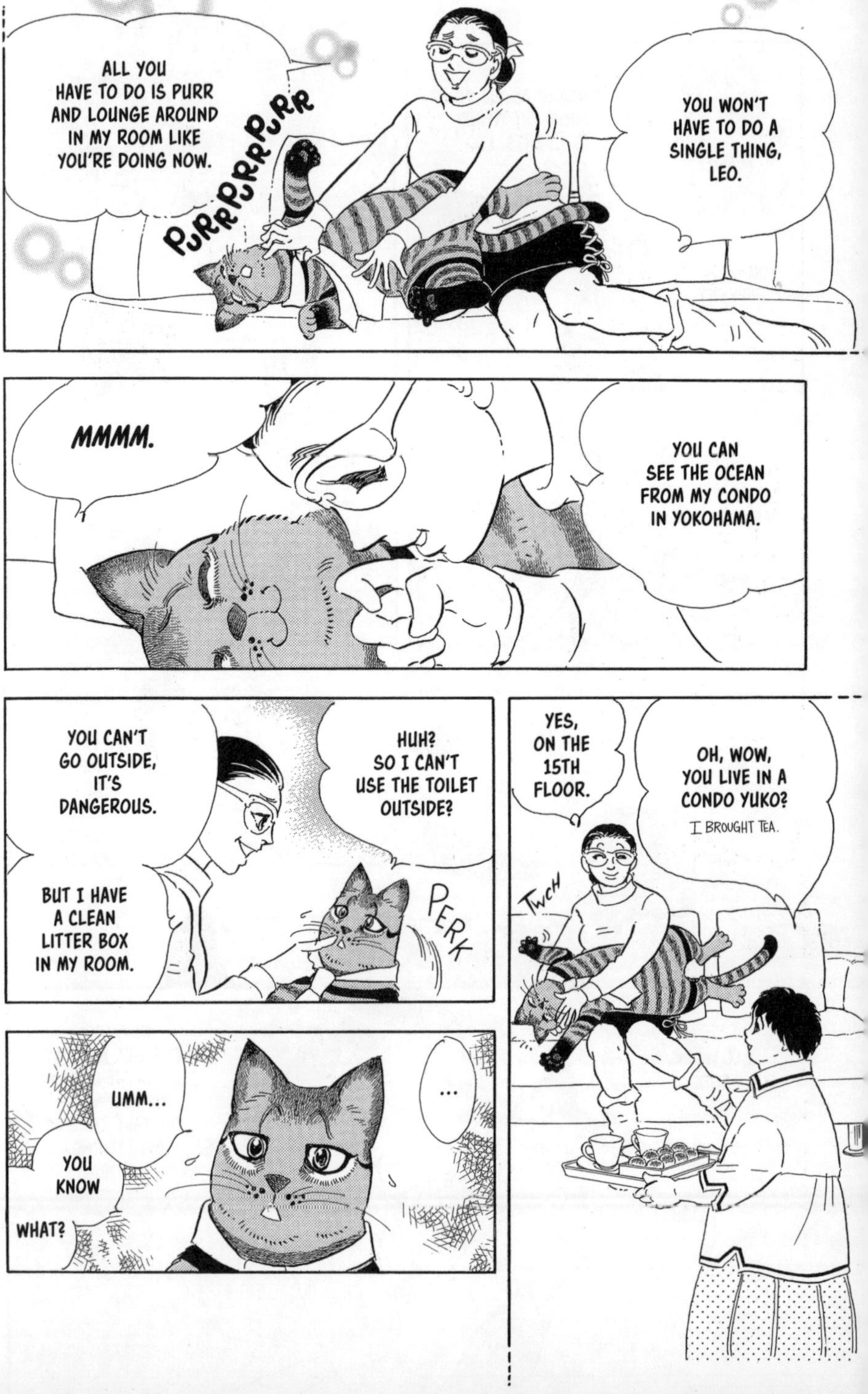
YOU WON'T HAVE TO DO A SINGLE THING, LEO.
ALL YOU HAVE TO DO IS PURR AND LOUNGE AROUND IN MY ROOM LIKE YOU'RE DOING NOW.
PURRPURRPURR
YOU CAN SEE THE OCEAN FROM MY CONDO IN YOKOHAMA.
MMMM.
OH, WOW, YOU LIVE IN A CONDO YUKO?
I BROUGHT TEA.
YES, ON THE 15TH FLOOR.
TWCH
HUH? SO I CAN'T USE THE TOILET OUTSIDE?
PERK
YOU CAN'T GO OUTSIDE, IT'S DANGEROUS.
BUT I HAVE A CLEAN LITTER BOX IN MY ROOM.
...
UMM...
YOU KNOW WHAT?

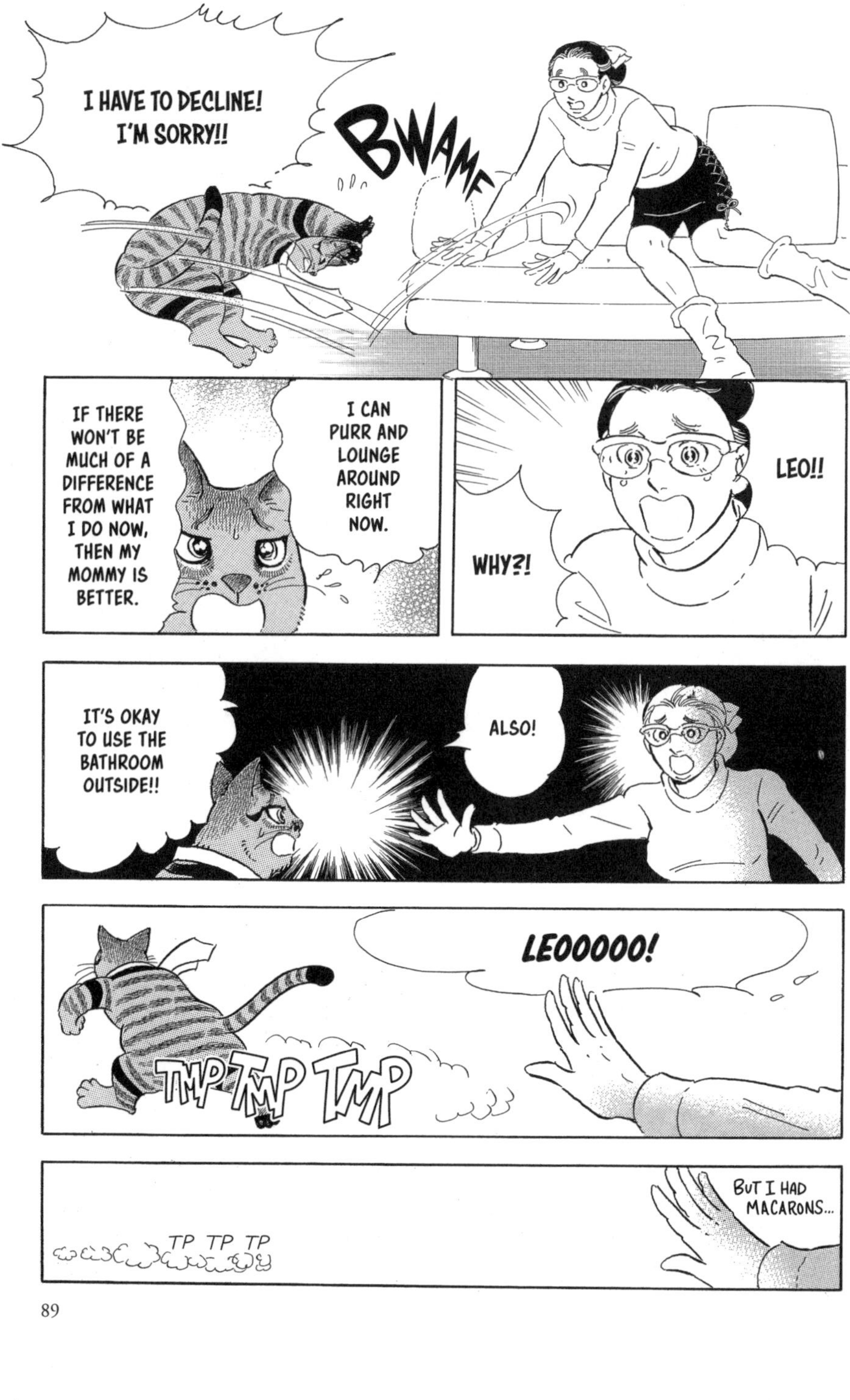

I HAVE TO DECLINE! I'M SORRY!!
BWAMF
LEO!!
WHY?!
I CAN PURR AND LOUNGE AROUND RIGHT NOW.
IF THERE WON'T BE MUCH OF A DIFFERENCE FROM WHAT I DO NOW, THEN MY MOMMY IS BETTER.
ALSO!
IT'S OKAY TO USE THE BATHROOM OUTSIDE!!
LEOOOOO!
TMP TMP TMP
BUT I HAD MACARONS...
TP TP TP

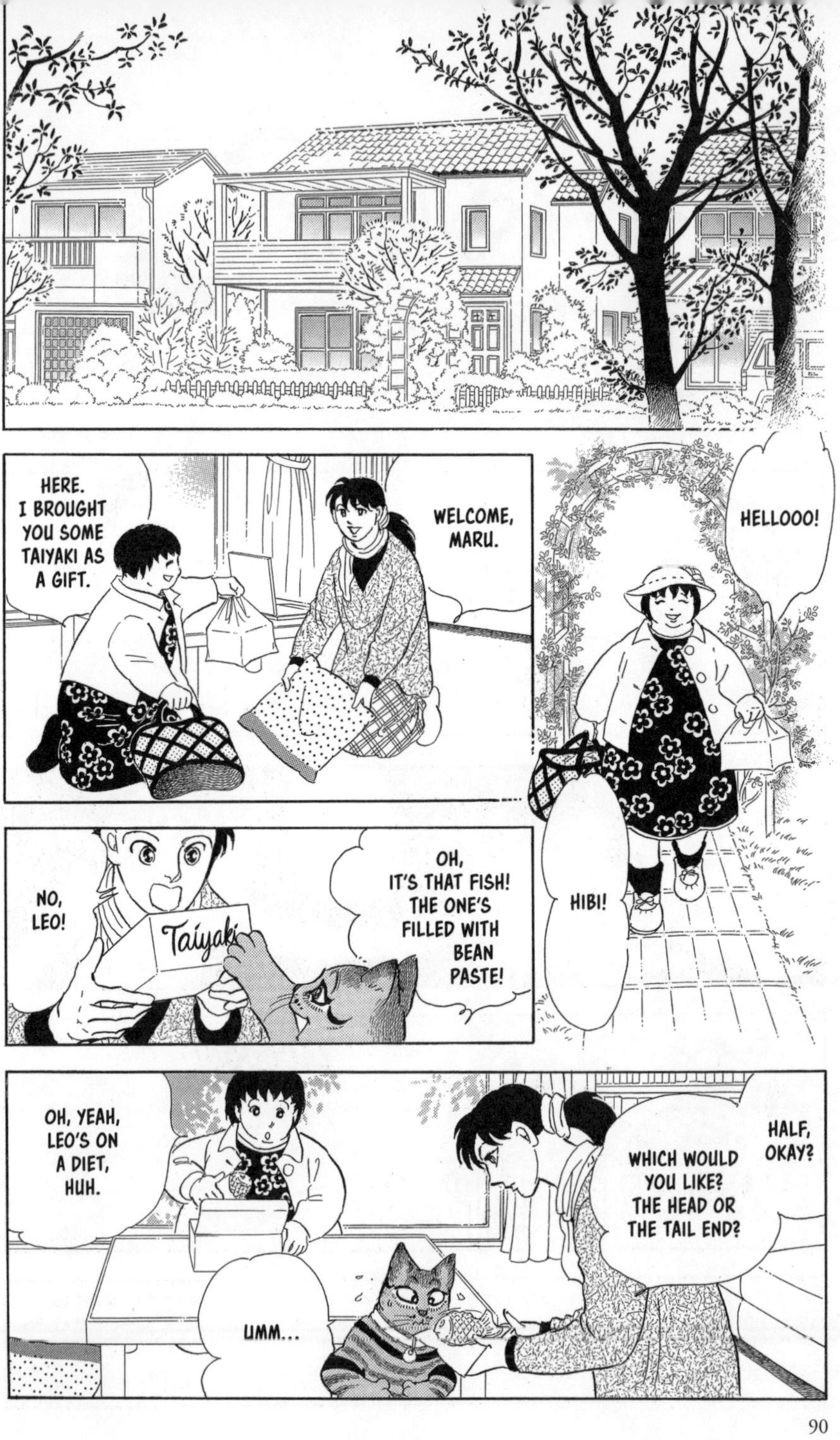
HELLOOO!
HIBI!
WELCOME, MARU.
HERE. I BROUGHT YOU SOME TAIYAKI AS A GIFT.
OH, IT'S THAT FISH! THE ONE'S FILLED WITH BEAN PASTE!
Taiyaki
NO, LEO!
HALF, OKAY?
WHICH WOULD YOU LIKE? THE HEAD OR THE TAIL END?
OH, YEAH, LEO'S ON A DIET, HUH.
UMM...

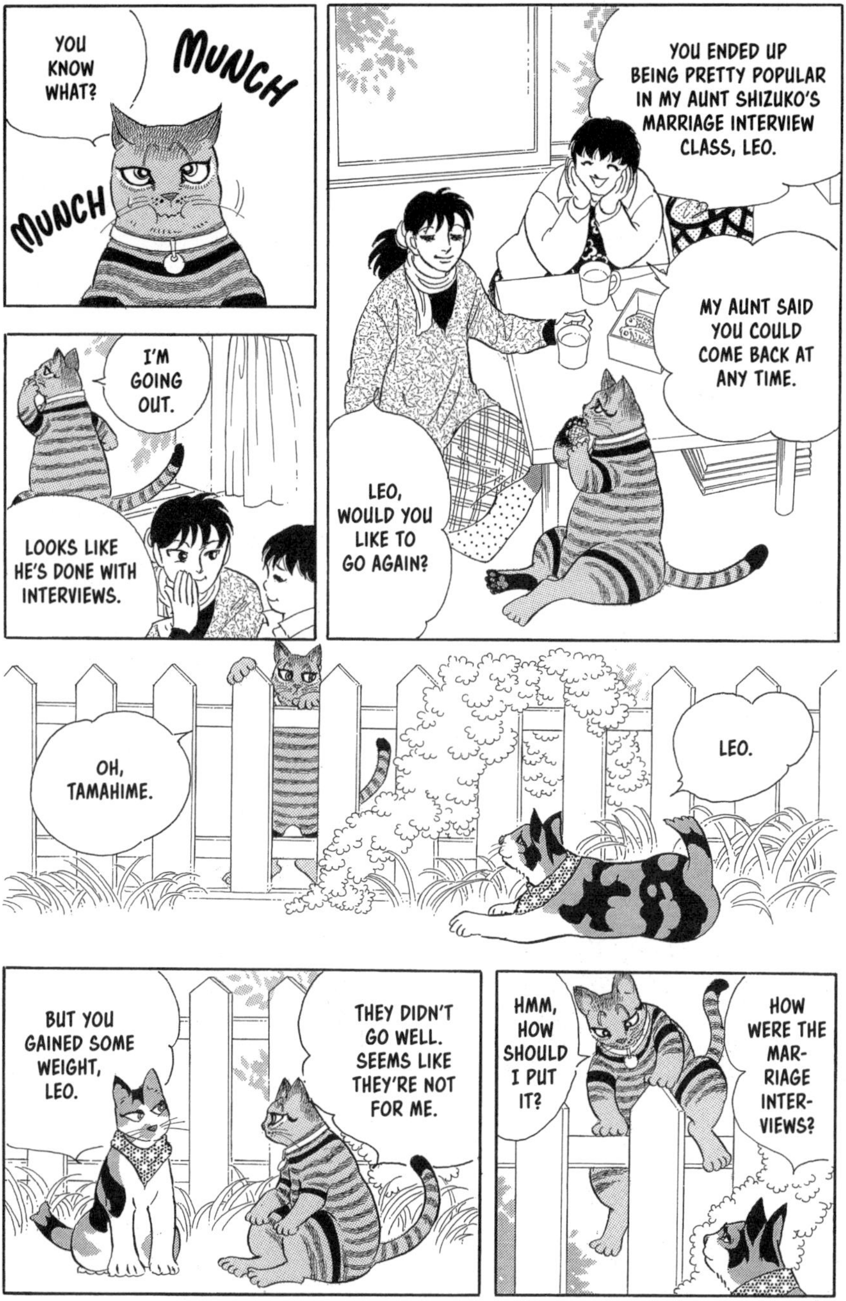
YOU ENDED UP BEING PRETTY POPULAR IN MY AUNT SHIZUKO'S MARRIAGE INTERVIEW CLASS, LEO.
MY AUNT SAID YOU COULD COME BACK AT ANY TIME.
LEO, WOULD YOU LIKE TO GO AGAIN?
YOU KNOW WHAT?
MUNCH
MUNCH
I'M GOING OUT.
LOOKS LIKE HE'S DONE WITH INTERVIEWS.
LEO.
OH, TAMAHIME.
HOW WERE THE MAR-RIAGE INTER-VIEWS?
HMM, HOW SHOULD I PUT IT?
THEY DIDN'T GO WELL. SEEMS LIKE THEY'RE NOT FOR ME.
BUT YOU GAINED SOME WEIGHT, LEO.

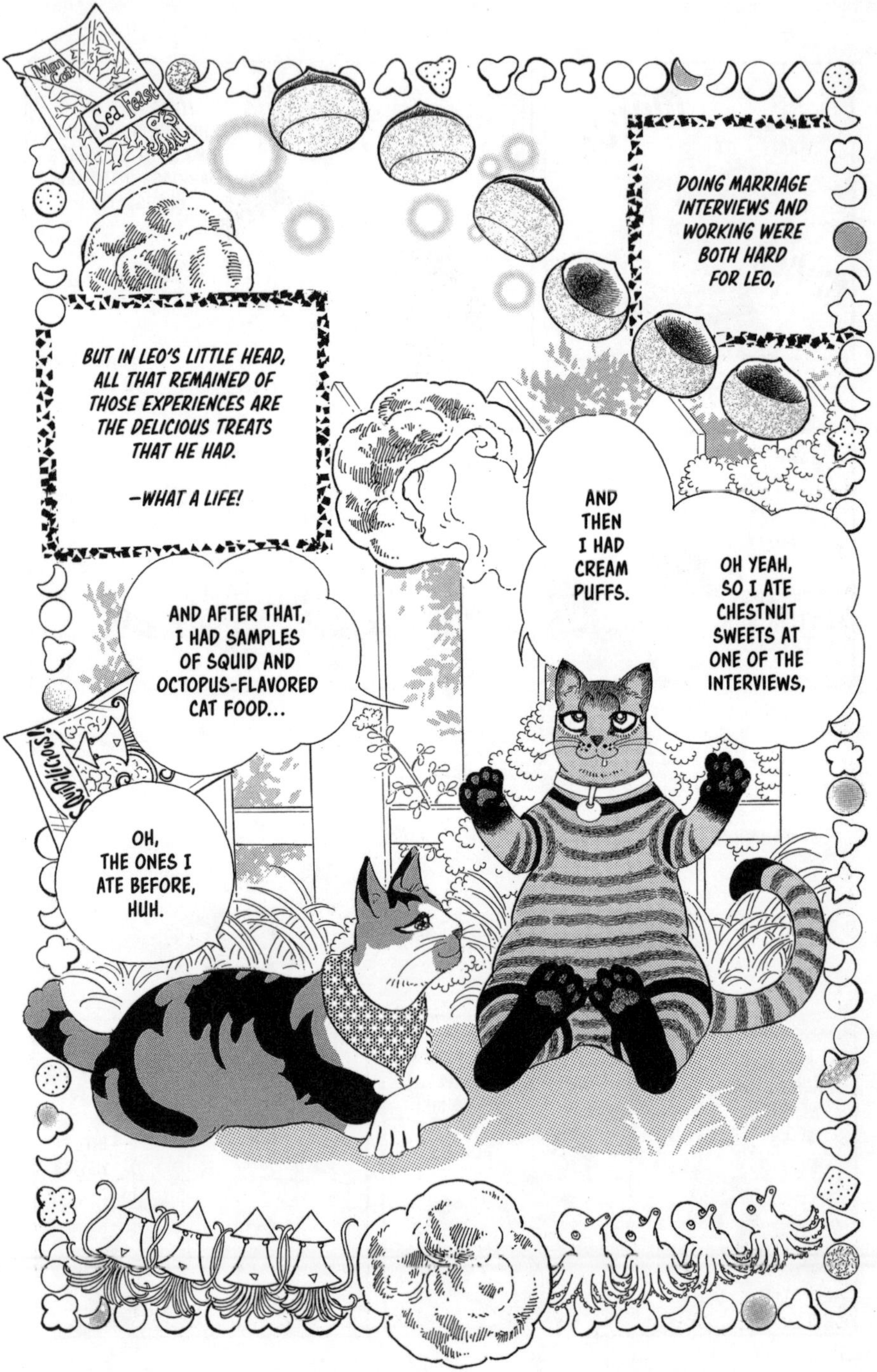
DOING MARRIAGE INTERVIEWS AND WORKING WERE BOTH HARD FOR LEO,
OH YEAH, SO I ATE CHESTNUT SWEETS AT ONE OF THE INTERVIEWS,
AND THEN I HAD CREAM PUFFS.
AND AFTER THAT, I HAD SAMPLES OF SQUID AND OCTOPUS-FLAVORED CAT FOOD...
OH, THE ONES I ATE BEFORE, HUH.
BUT IN LEO'S LITTLE HEAD, ALL THAT REMAINED OF THOSE EXPERIENCES ARE THE DELICIOUS TREATS THAT HE HAD.
—WHAT A LIFE!
Sea Feast

4 Lil' Yamato in Love

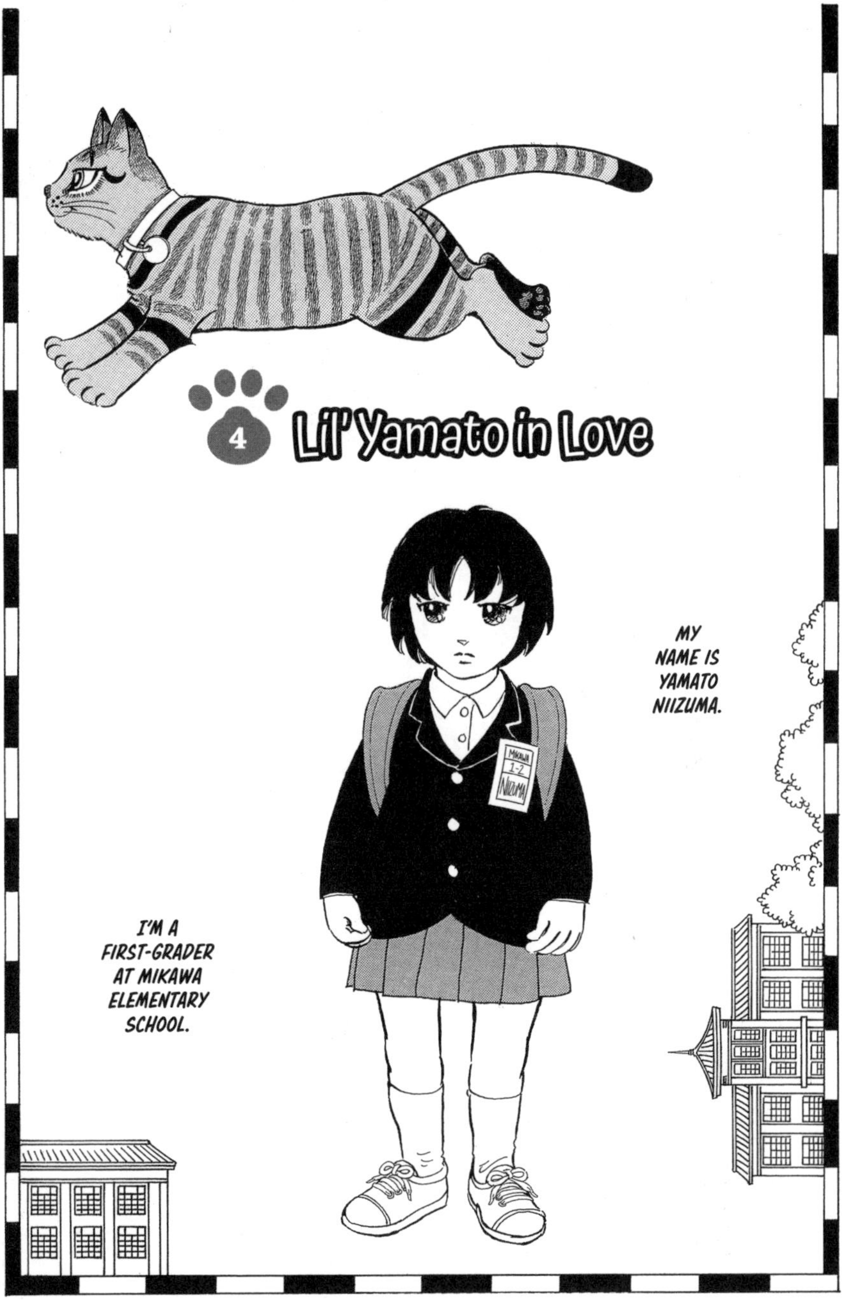
MY NAME IS YAMATO NIIZUMA.
MIKAWA 1-2 NIIZUMA
I'M A FIRST-GRADER AT MIKAWA ELEMENTARY SCHOOL.

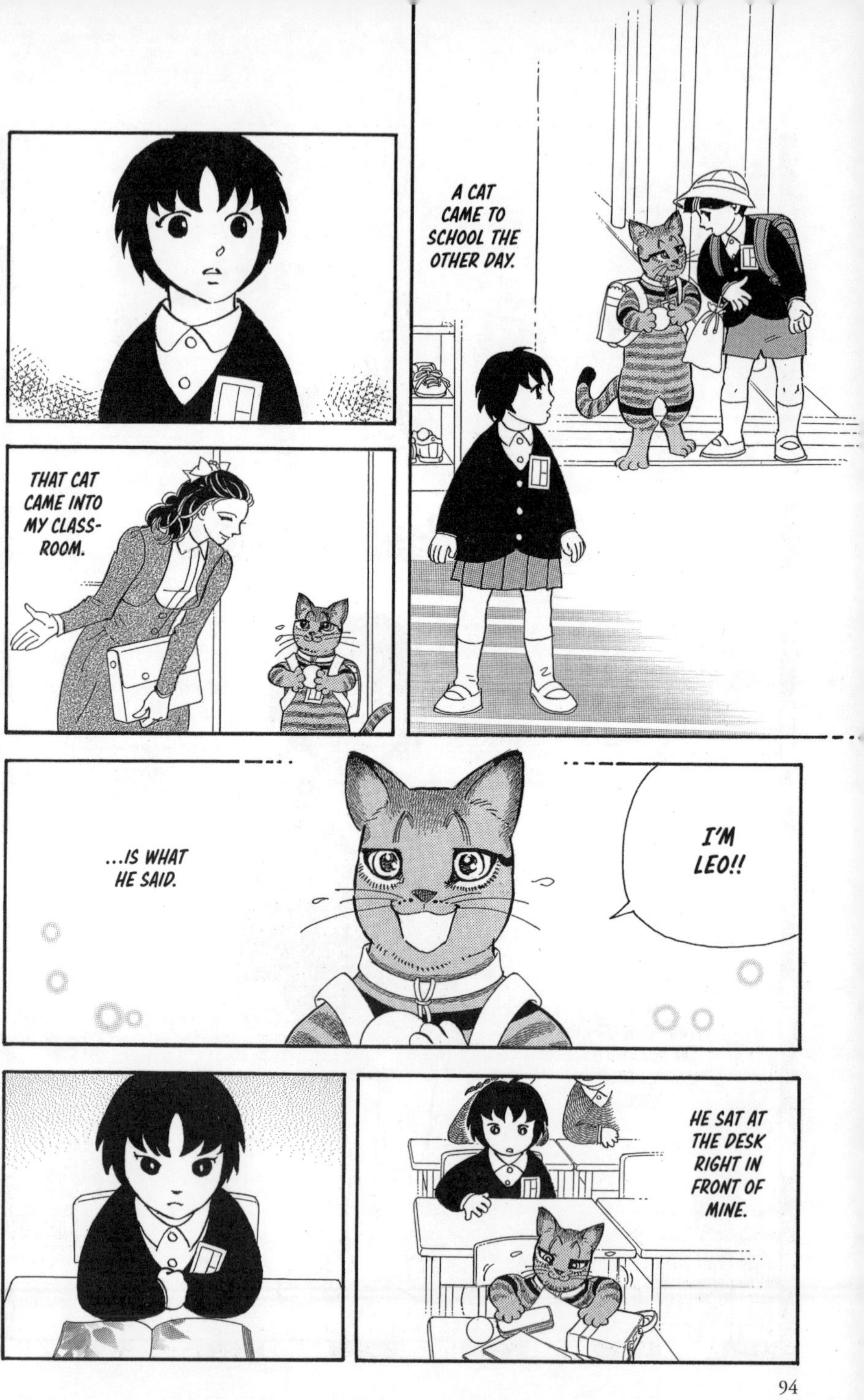
A CAT CAME TO SCHOOL THE OTHER DAY.
THAT CAT CAME INTO MY CLASS-ROOM.
I'M LEO!!
...IS WHAT HE SAID.
HE SAT AT THE DESK RIGHT IN FRONT OF MINE.

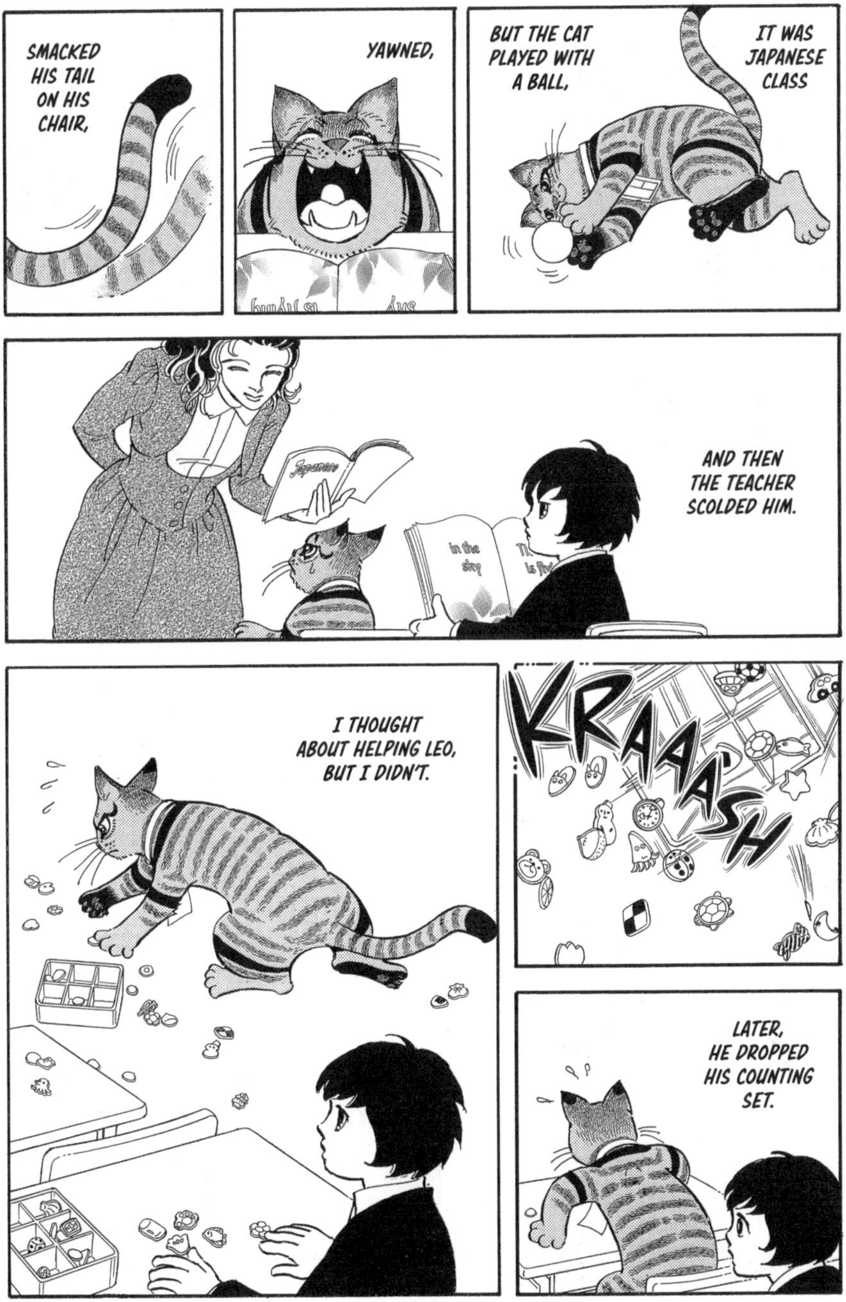
IT WAS JAPANESE CLASS
BUT THE CAT PLAYED WITH A BALL,
YAWNED,
SMACKED HIS TAIL ON HIS CHAIR,
AND THEN THE TEACHER SCOLDED HIM.
Japanese
in the sky
KRAAASH
LATER, HE DROPPED HIS COUNTING SET.
I THOUGHT ABOUT HELPING LEO, BUT I DIDN'T.

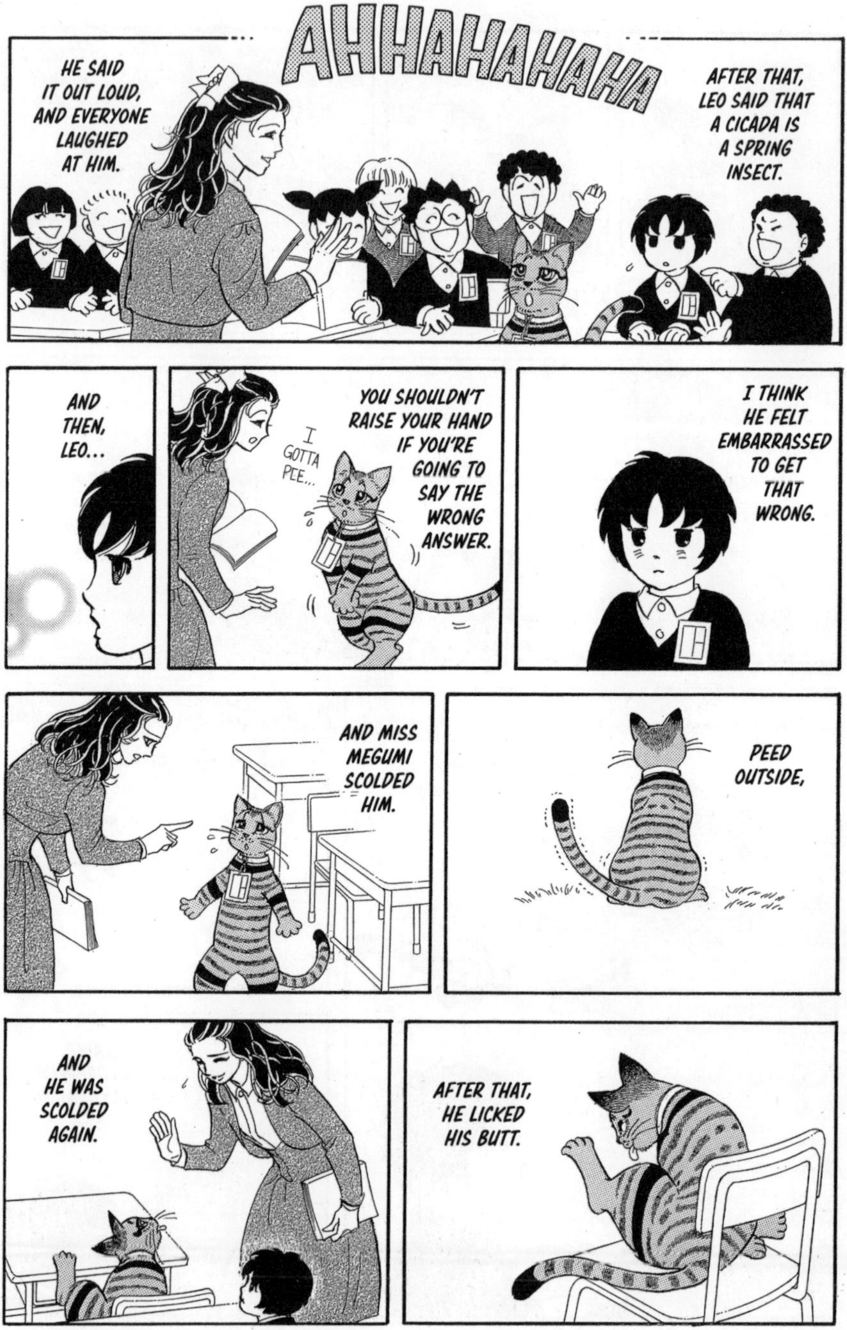
AFTER THAT, LEO SAID THAT A CICADA IS A SPRING INSECT.
AHHAHAHAHAHA
HE SAID IT OUT LOUD, AND EVERYONE LAUGHED AT HIM.
I THINK HE FELT EMBARRASSED TO GET THAT WRONG.
YOU SHOULDN'T RAISE YOUR HAND IF YOU'RE GOING TO SAY THE WRONG ANSWER.
I GOTTA PEE...
AND THEN, LEO...
PEED OUTSIDE,
AND MISS MEGUMI SCOLDED HIM.
AFTER THAT, HE LICKED HIS BUTT.
AND HE WAS SCOLDED AGAIN.

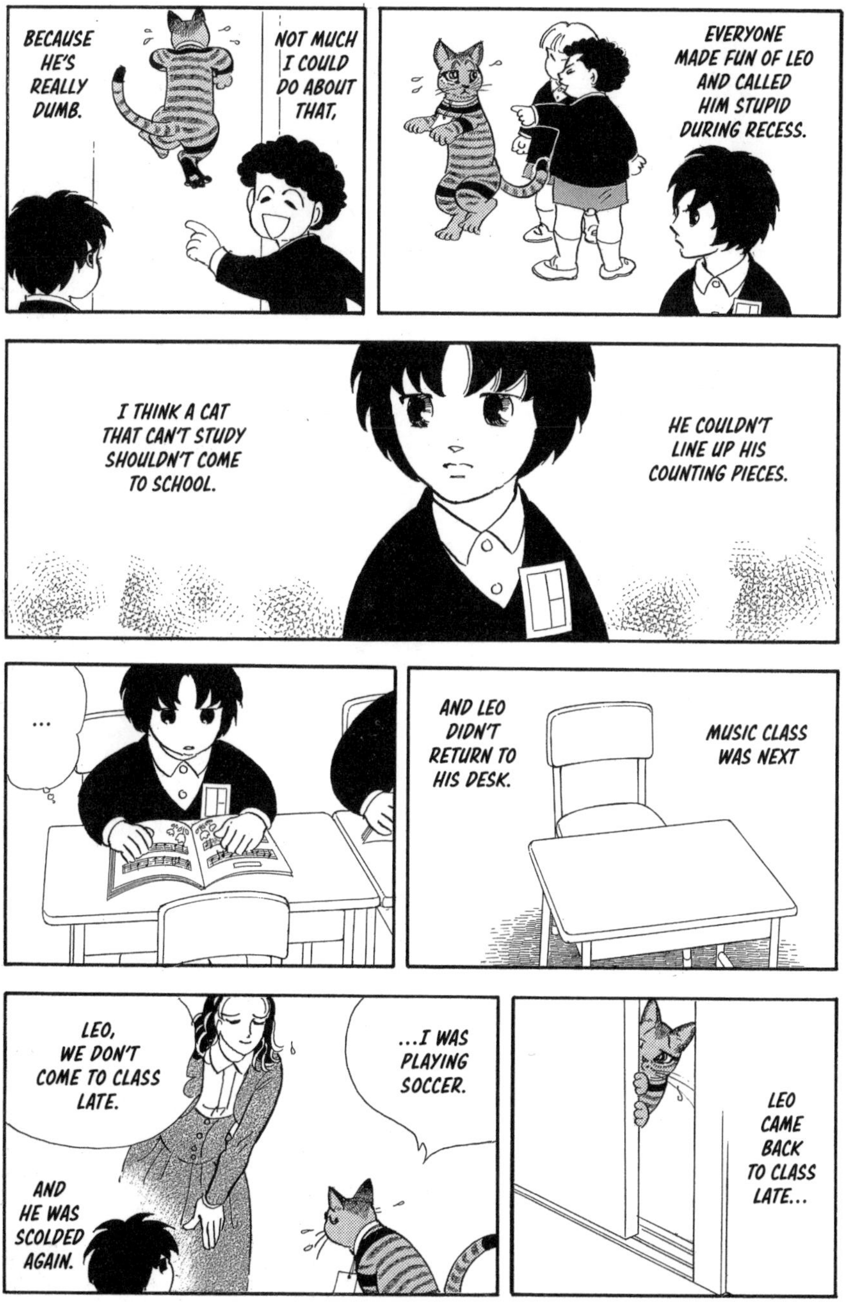
EVERYONE MADE FUN OF LEO AND CALLED HIM STUPID DURING RECESS.
NOT MUCH I COULD DO ABOUT THAT,
BECAUSE HE'S REALLY DUMB.
HE COULDN'T LINE UP HIS COUNTING PIECES.
I THINK A CAT THAT CAN'T STUDY SHOULDN'T COME TO SCHOOL.
MUSIC CLASS WAS NEXT
AND LEO DIDN'T RETURN TO HIS DESK.
...
LEO CAME BACK TO CLASS LATE...
...I WAS PLAYING SOCCER.
LEO, WE DON'T COME TO CLASS LATE.
AND HE WAS SCOLDED AGAIN.

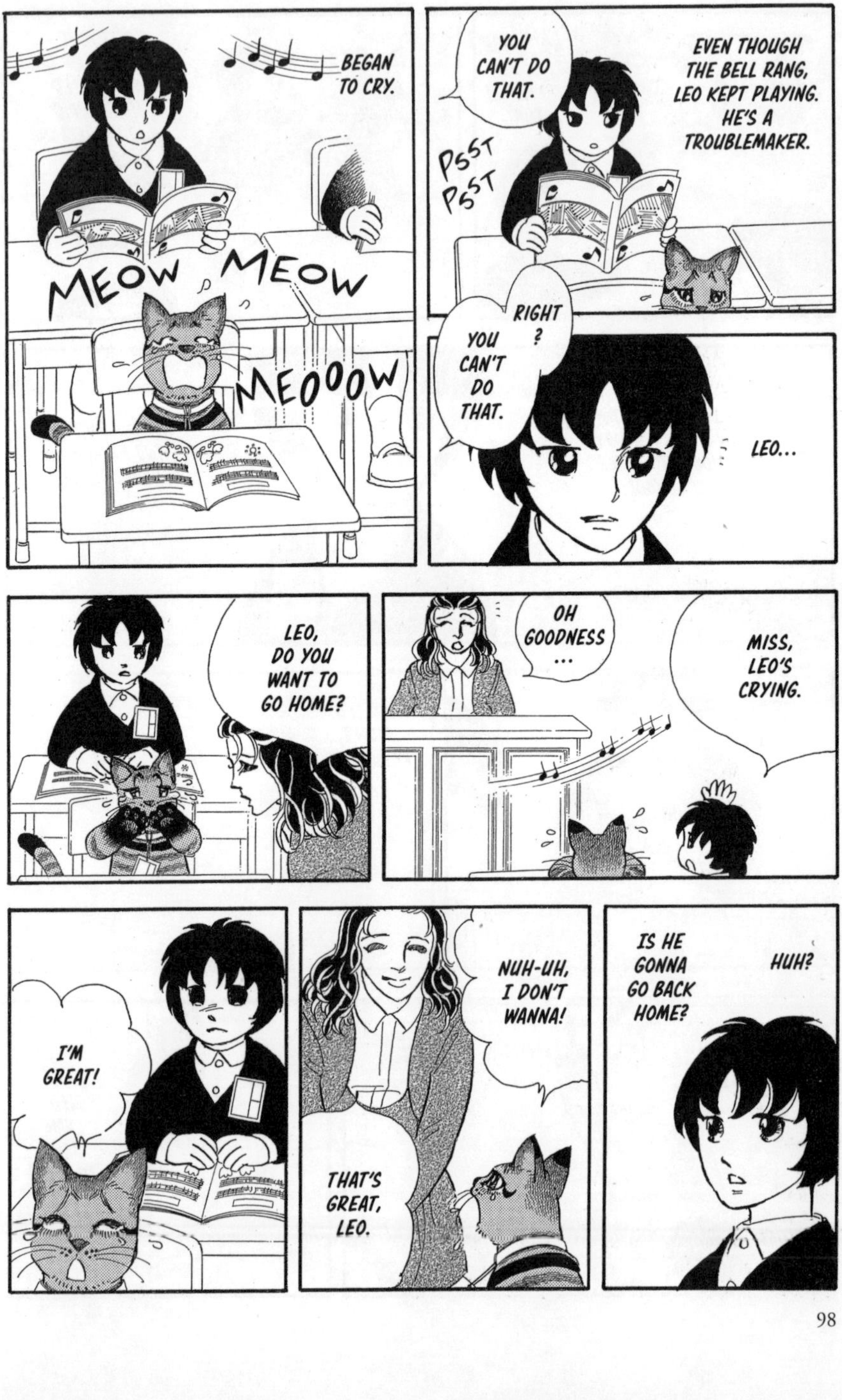
EVEN THOUGH THE BELL RANG, LEO KEPT PLAYING. HE'S A TROUBLEMAKER.
YOU CAN'T DO THAT.
PSST PSST
LEO...
RIGHT? YOU CAN'T DO THAT.
BEGAN TO CRY.
MEOW MEOW
MEOOOW
MISS, LEO'S CRYING.
OH GOODNESS ...
LEO, DO YOU WANT TO GO HOME?
HUH?
IS HE GONNA GO BACK HOME?
NUH-UH, I DON'T WANNA!
THAT'S GREAT, LEO.
I'M GREAT!

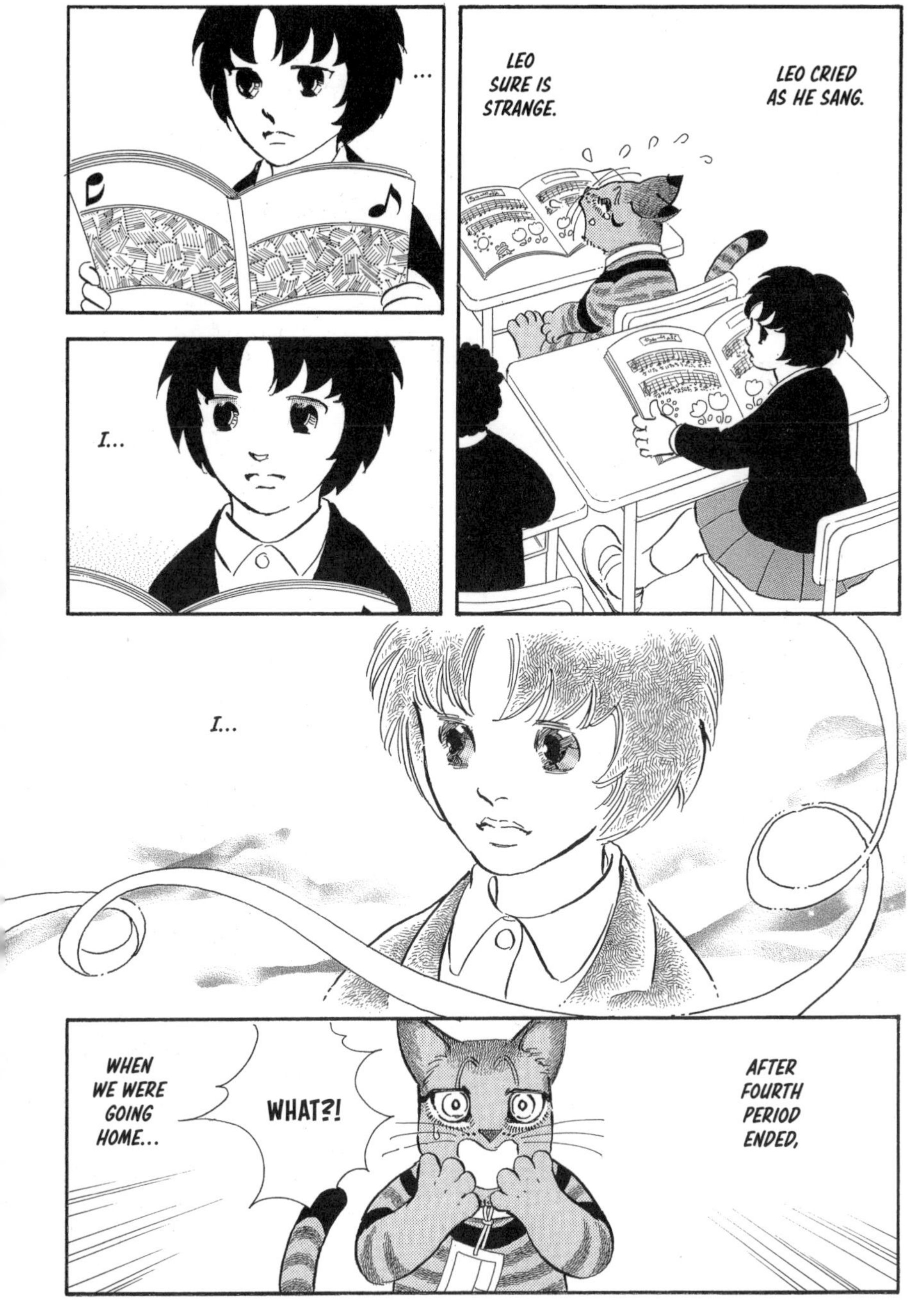
LEO CRIED AS HE SANG.
LEO SURE IS STRANGE.
...
I...
I...
AFTER FOURTH PERIOD ENDED,
WHAT?!
WHEN WE WERE GOING HOME...

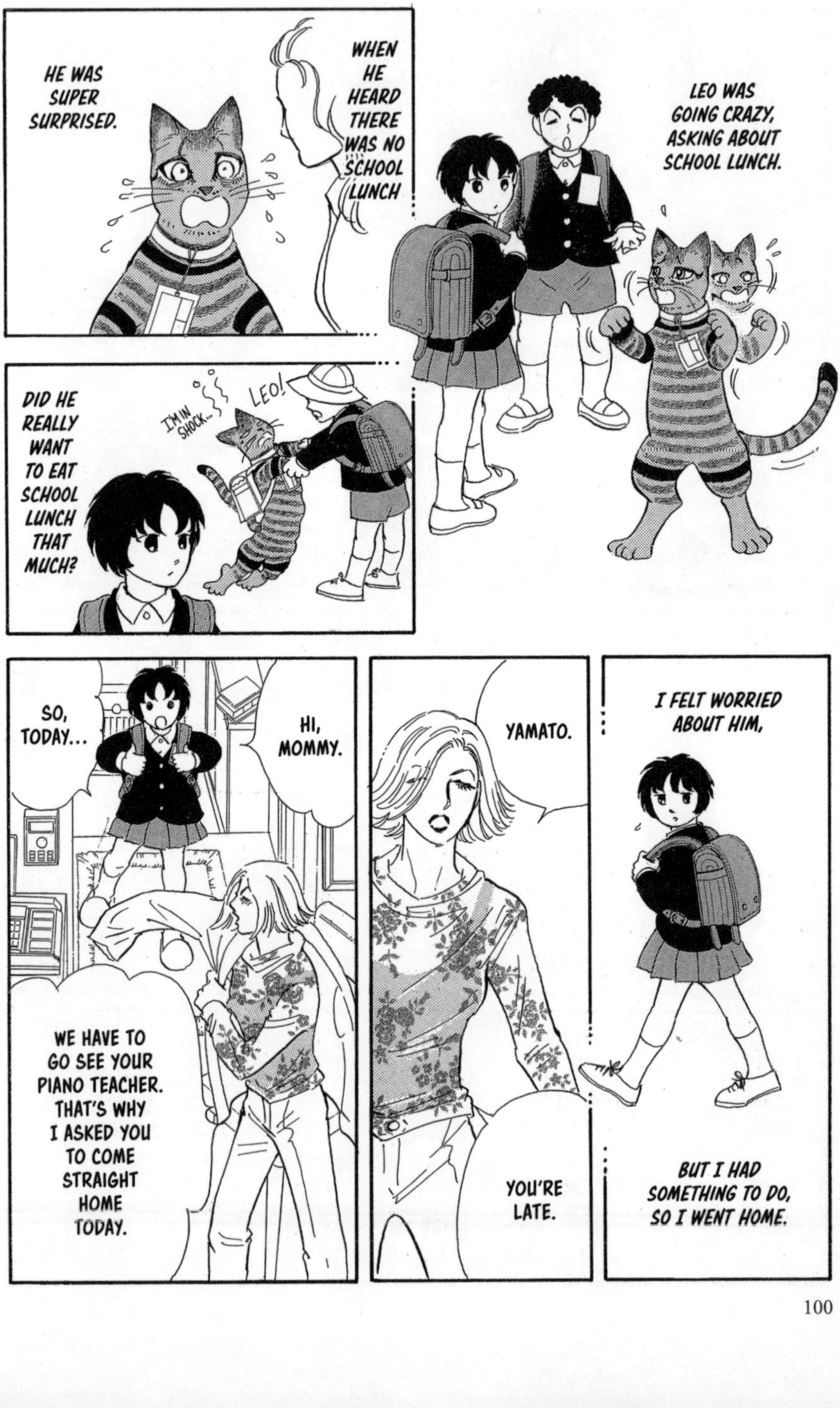
LEO WAS GOING CRAZY, ASKING ABOUT SCHOOL LUNCH.
WHEN HE HEARD THERE WAS NO SCHOOL LUNCH
HE WAS SUPER SURPRISED.
LEO!
I'M IN SHOCK...
DID HE REALLY WANT TO EAT SCHOOL LUNCH THAT MUCH?
I FELT WORRIED ABOUT HIM,
BUT I HAD SOMETHING TO DO, SO I WENT HOME.
YAMATO.
YOU'RE LATE.
HI, MOMMY.
SO, TODAY...
WE HAVE TO GO SEE YOUR PIANO TEACHER. THAT'S WHY I ASKED YOU TO COME STRAIGHT HOME TODAY.

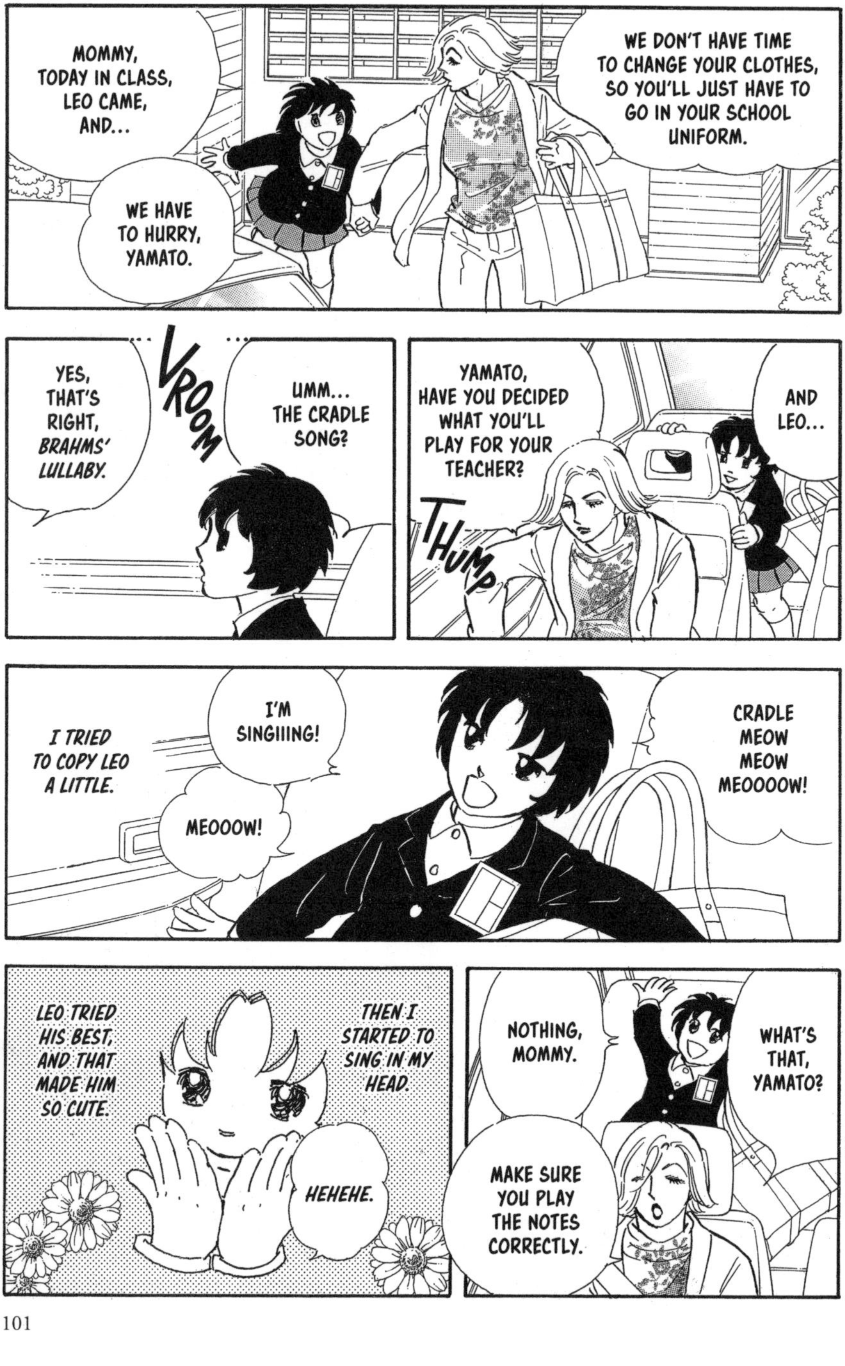
MOMMY, TODAY IN CLASS, LEO CAME, AND...
WE HAVE TO HURRY, YAMATO.
WE DON'T HAVE TIME TO CHANGE YOUR CLOTHES, SO YOU'LL JUST HAVE TO GO IN YOUR SCHOOL UNIFORM.
AND LEO...
YAMATO, HAVE YOU DECIDED WHAT YOU'LL PLAY FOR YOUR TEACHER?
THUMP
UMM... THE CRADLE SONG?
VROOM
YES, THAT'S RIGHT, *BRAHMS' LULLABY.*
CRADLE MEOW MEOW MEOOOOW!
I'M SINGIIING!
MEOOOW!
I TRIED TO COPY LEO A LITTLE.
WHAT'S THAT, YAMATO?
NOTHING, MOMMY.
MAKE SURE YOU PLAY THE NOTES CORRECTLY.
THEN I STARTED TO SING IN MY HEAD.
LEO TRIED HIS BEST, AND THAT MADE HIM SO CUTE.
HEHEHE.

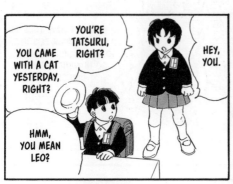

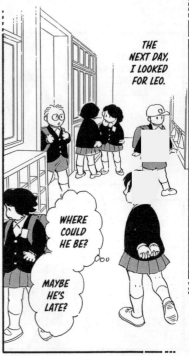

THE NEXT DAY, I LOOKED FOR LEO.
WHERE COULD HE BE?
MAYBE HE'S LATE?
HEY, YOU.
YOU'RE TATSURU, RIGHT?
YOU CAME WITH A CAT YESTERDAY, RIGHT?
HMM, YOU MEAN LEO?
WHERE IS LEO TODAY?
OH, LEO'S NOT COMING.
...HE'S NOT?
HE SAID HE'S DONE WITH SCHOOL.
HUH?
HE'S PLAYING AT HOME.
EHH?
WHAT?
THAT'S NO FAIR!
I CAME TO SCHOOL
BUT LEO DIDN'T COME.

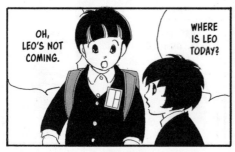

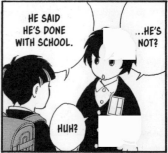

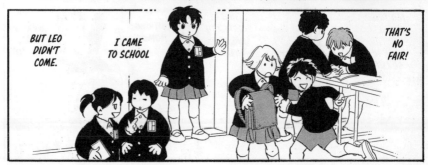

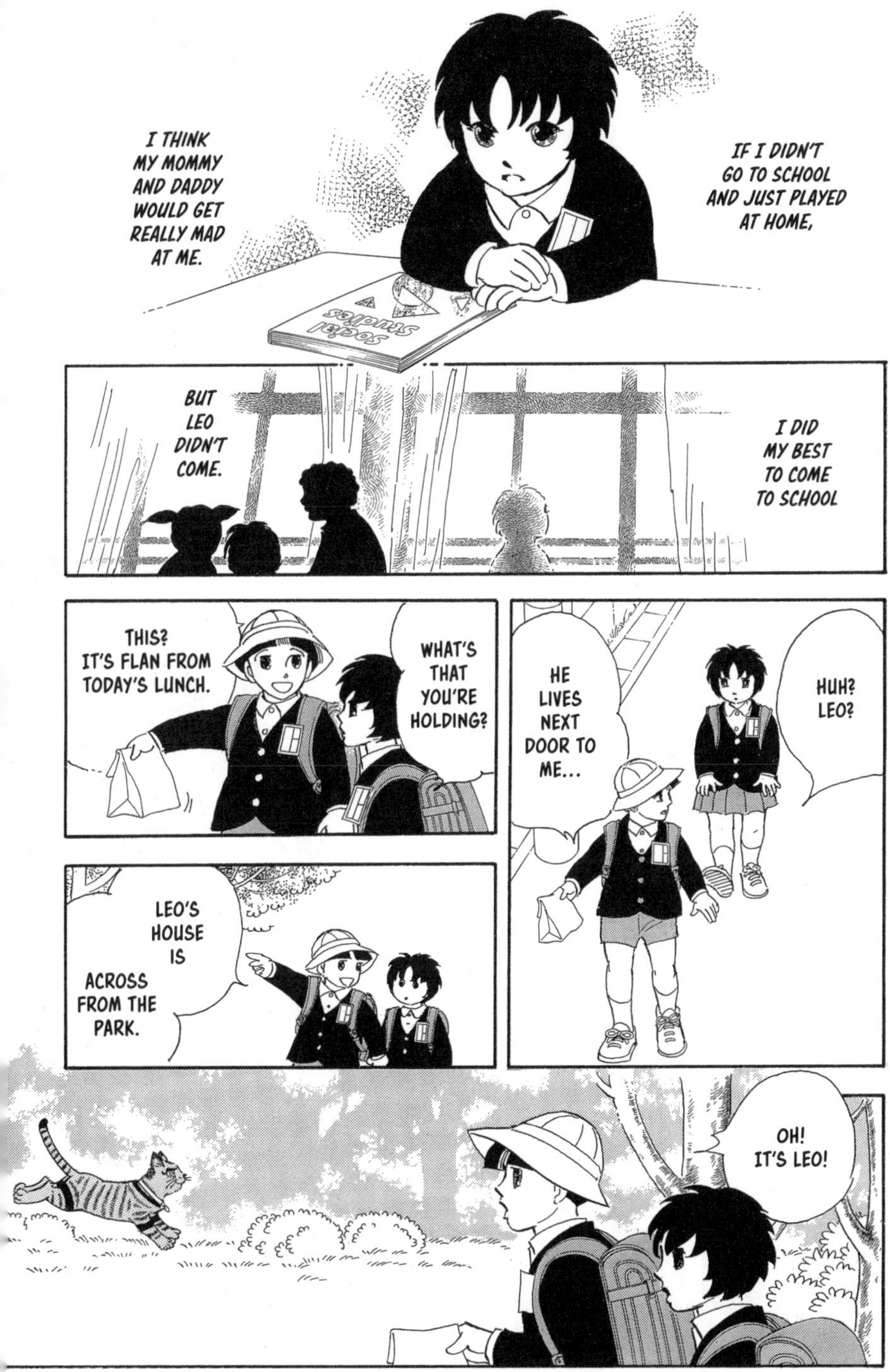
IF I DIDN'T GO TO SCHOOL AND JUST PLAYED AT HOME,
I THINK MY MOMMY AND DADDY WOULD GET REALLY MAD AT ME.
Social Studies
I DID MY BEST TO COME TO SCHOOL
BUT LEO DIDN'T COME.
HUH? LEO?
HE LIVES NEXT DOOR TO ME...
WHAT'S THAT YOU'RE HOLDING?
THIS? IT'S FLAN FROM TODAY'S LUNCH.
LEO'S HOUSE IS
ACROSS FROM THE PARK.
OH! IT'S LEO!

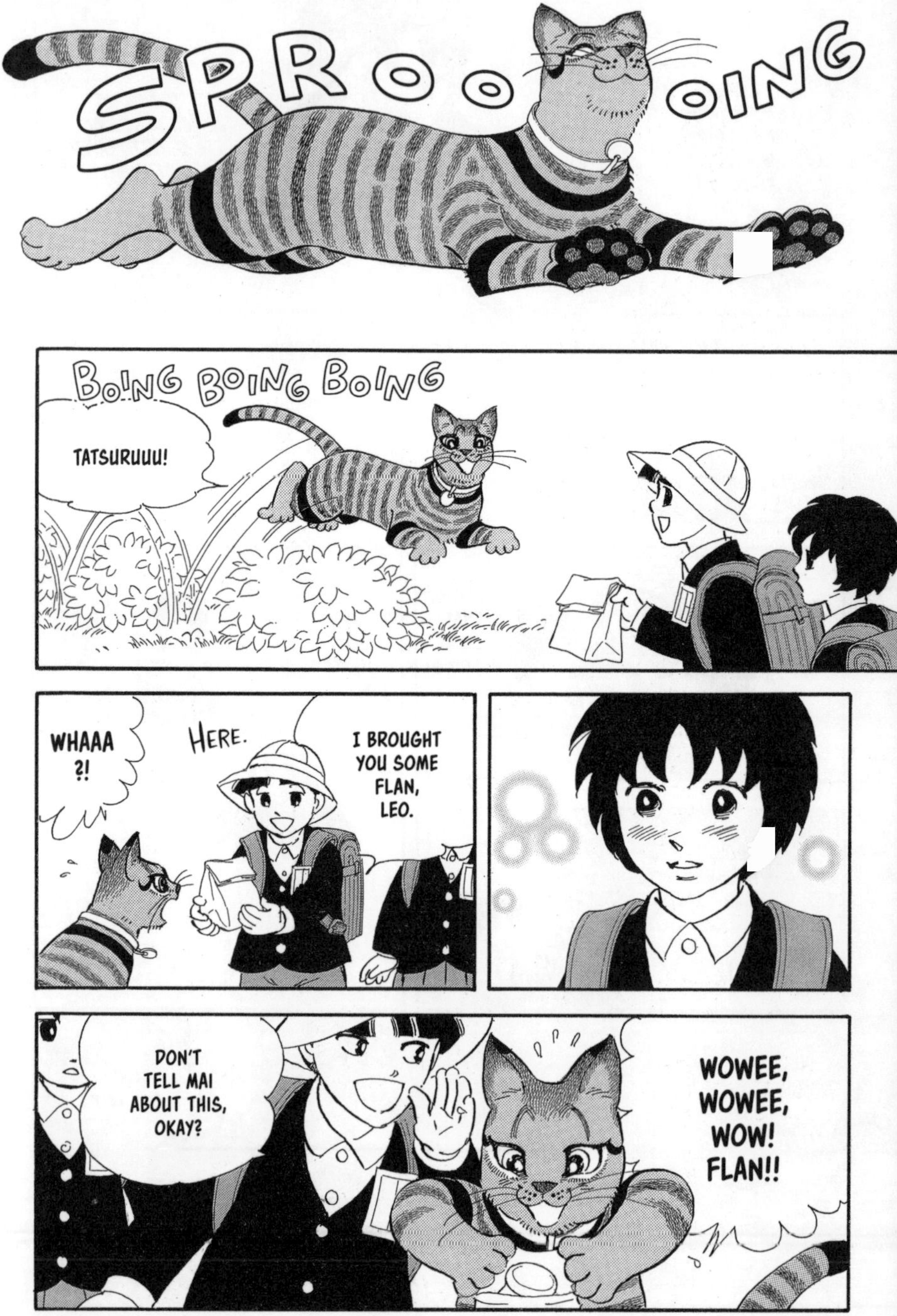
SPROOOOING
BOING BOING BOING
TATSURUUU!
I BROUGHT YOU SOME FLAN, LEO.
HERE.
WHAAA ?!
WOWEE, WOWEE, WOW! FLAN!!
DON'T TELL MAI ABOUT THIS, OKAY?

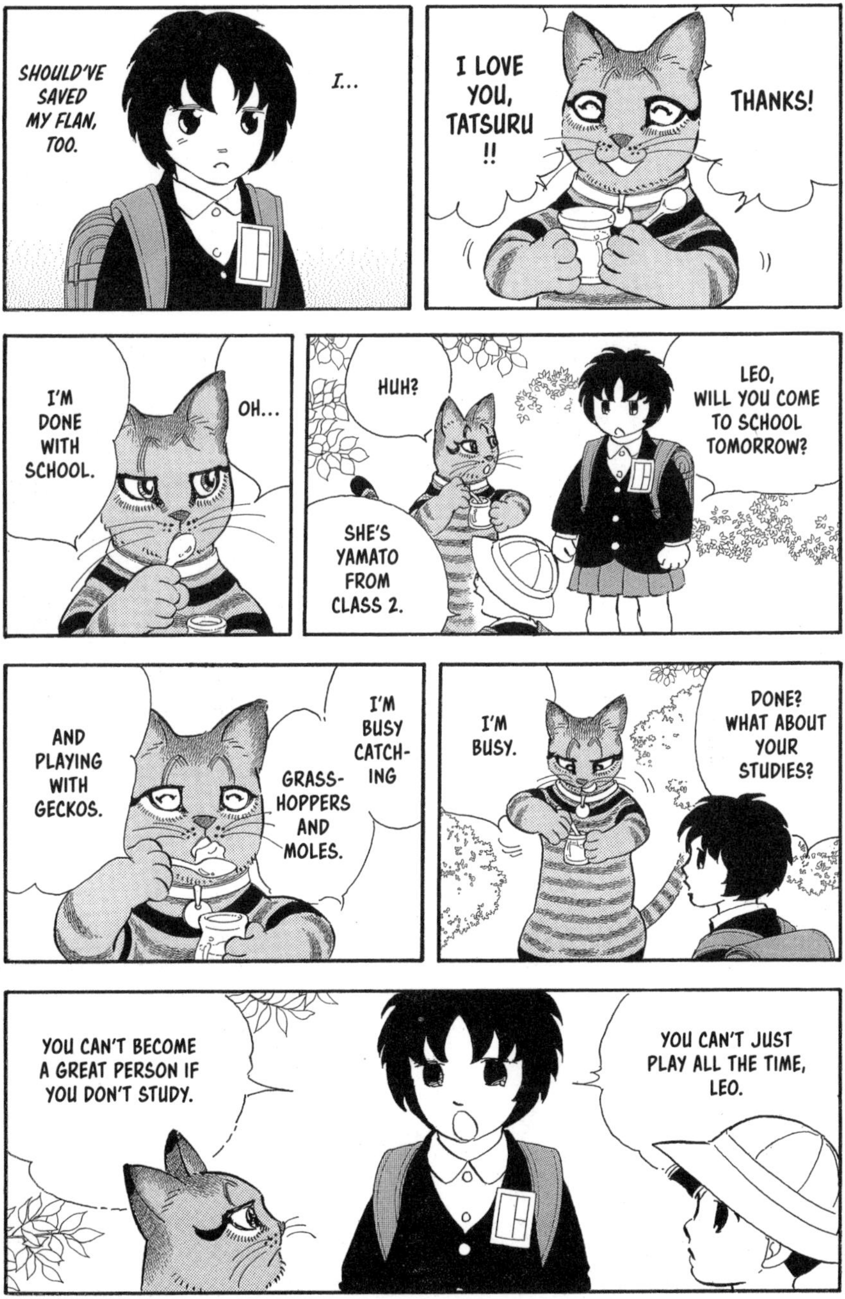
THANKS!
I LOVE YOU, TATSURU!!
I...
SHOULD'VE SAVED MY FLAN, TOO.
LEO, WILL YOU COME TO SCHOOL TOMORROW?
HUH?
SHE'S YAMATO FROM CLASS 2.
OH...
I'M DONE WITH SCHOOL.
DONE? WHAT ABOUT YOUR STUDIES?
I'M BUSY.
I'M BUSY CATCHING
GRASSHOPPERS AND MOLES.
AND PLAYING WITH GECKOS.
YOU CAN'T JUST PLAY ALL THE TIME, LEO.
YOU CAN'T BECOME A GREAT PERSON IF YOU DON'T STUDY.

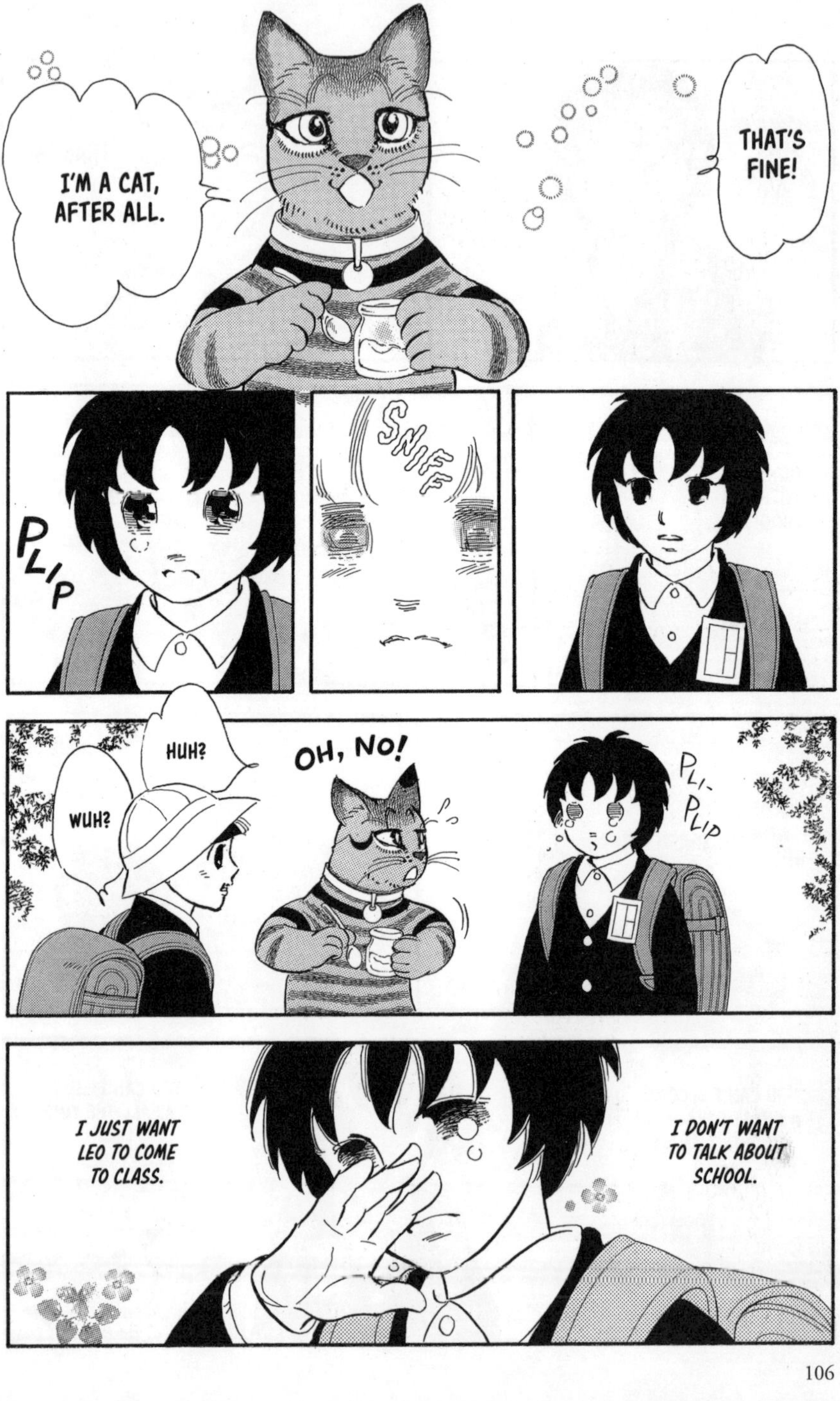
THAT'S FINE!
I'M A CAT, AFTER ALL.
SNIFF
PLIP
PLI-PLIP
OH, NO!
HUH?
WUH?
I DON'T WANT TO TALK ABOUT SCHOOL.
I JUST WANT LEO TO COME TO CLASS.

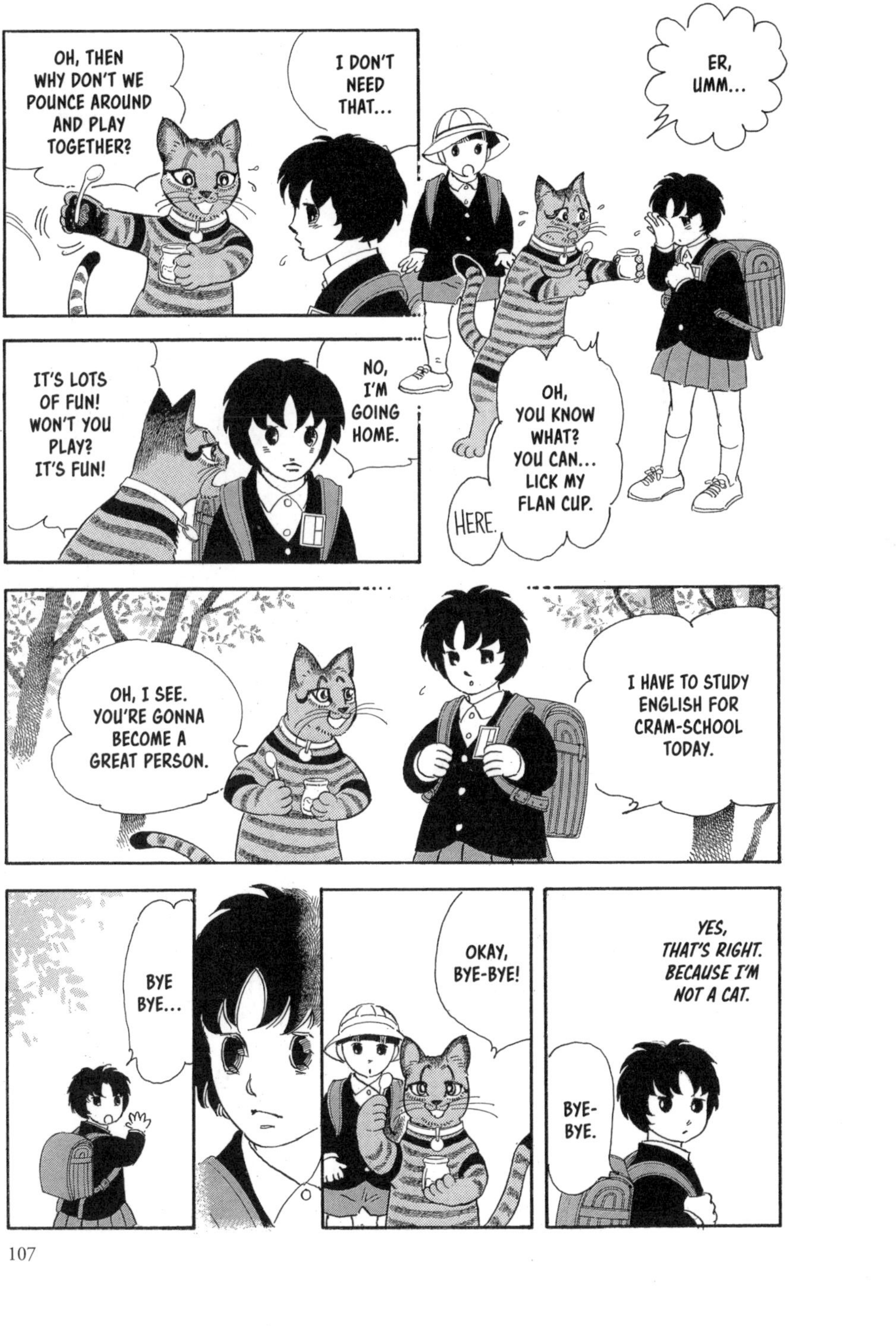
ER, UMM...
OH, YOU KNOW WHAT? YOU CAN... LICK MY FLAN CUP.
HERE.
I DON'T NEED THAT...
OH, THEN WHY DON'T WE POUNCE AROUND AND PLAY TOGETHER?
NO, I'M GOING HOME.
IT'S LOTS OF FUN! WON'T YOU PLAY? IT'S FUN!
I HAVE TO STUDY ENGLISH FOR CRAM-SCHOOL TODAY.
OH, I SEE. YOU'RE GONNA BECOME A GREAT PERSON.
YES, THAT'S RIGHT. BECAUSE I'M NOT A CAT.
BYE-BYE.
OKAY, BYE-BYE!
BYE BYE...

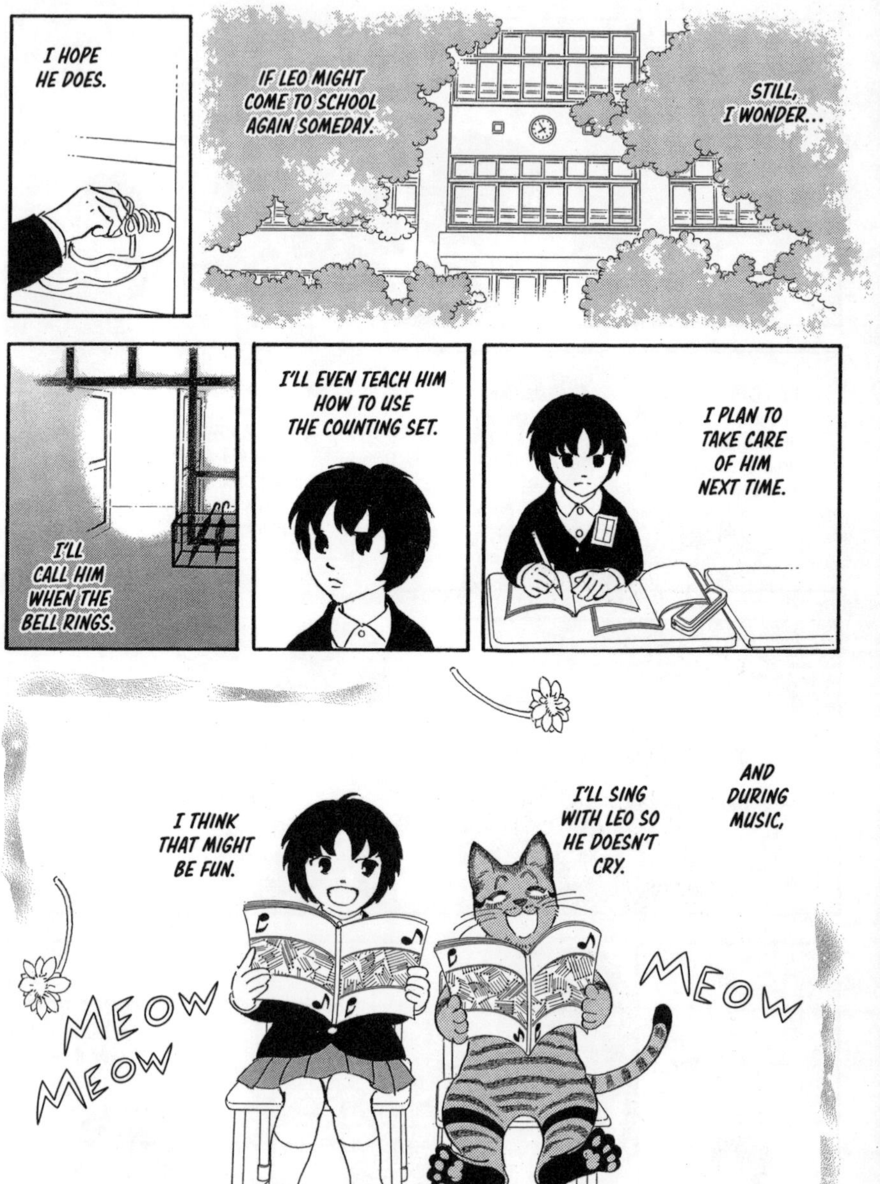
STILL, I WONDER...
IF LEO MIGHT COME TO SCHOOL AGAIN SOMEDAY.
I HOPE HE DOES.
I PLAN TO TAKE CARE OF HIM NEXT TIME.
I'LL EVEN TEACH HIM HOW TO USE THE COUNTING SET.
I'LL CALL HIM WHEN THE BELL RINGS.
AND DURING MUSIC,
I'LL SING WITH LEO SO HE DOESN'T CRY.
MEOW
I THINK THAT MIGHT BE FUN.
MEOW
MEOW

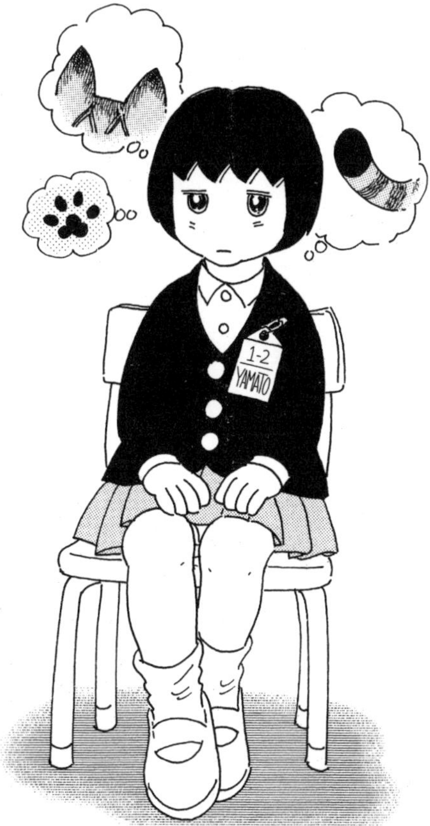
1-2
YAMATO

5 Lil' Leo the Assistant

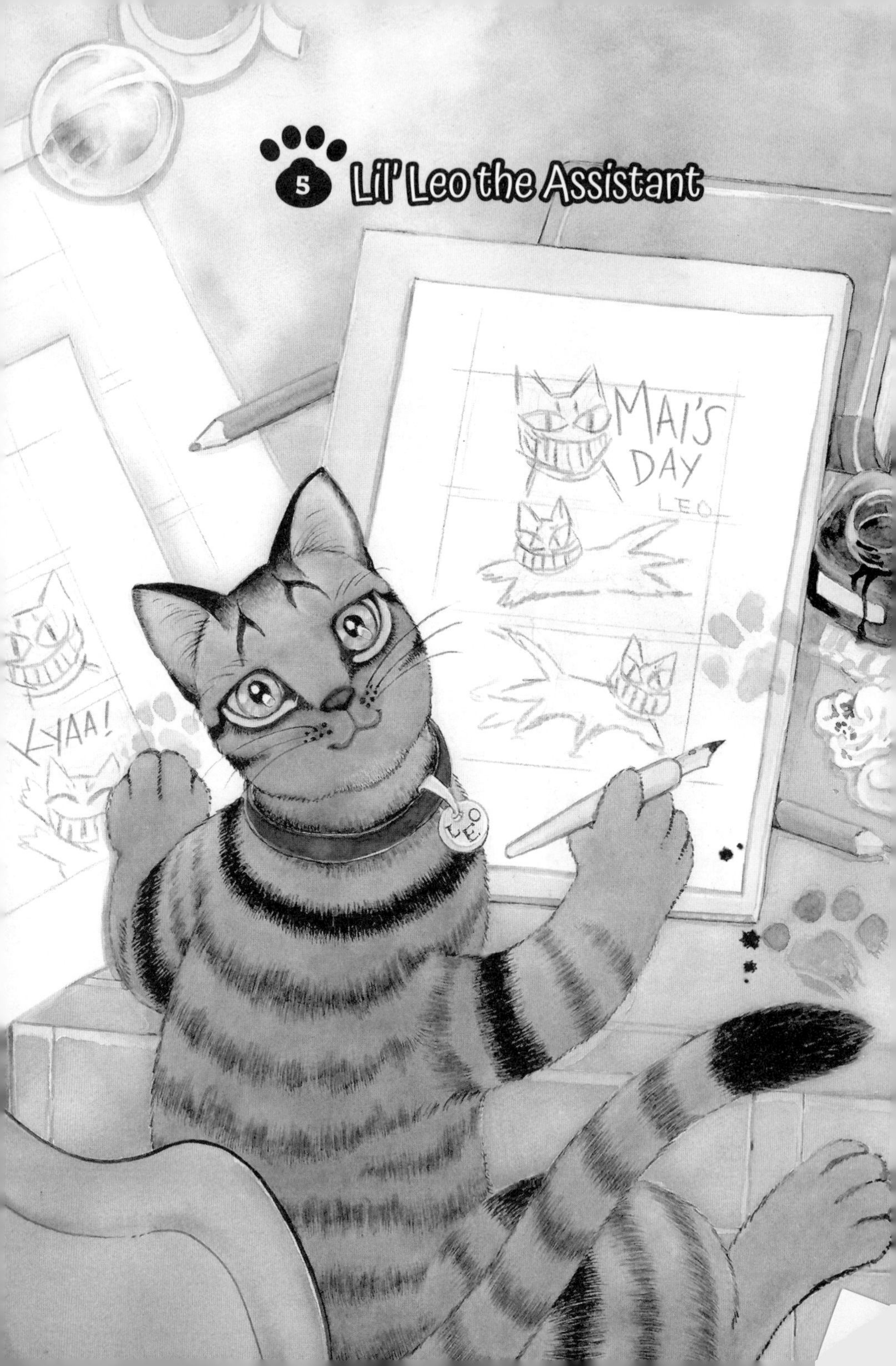
MAI'S DAY
LEO
KYAA!
LEO

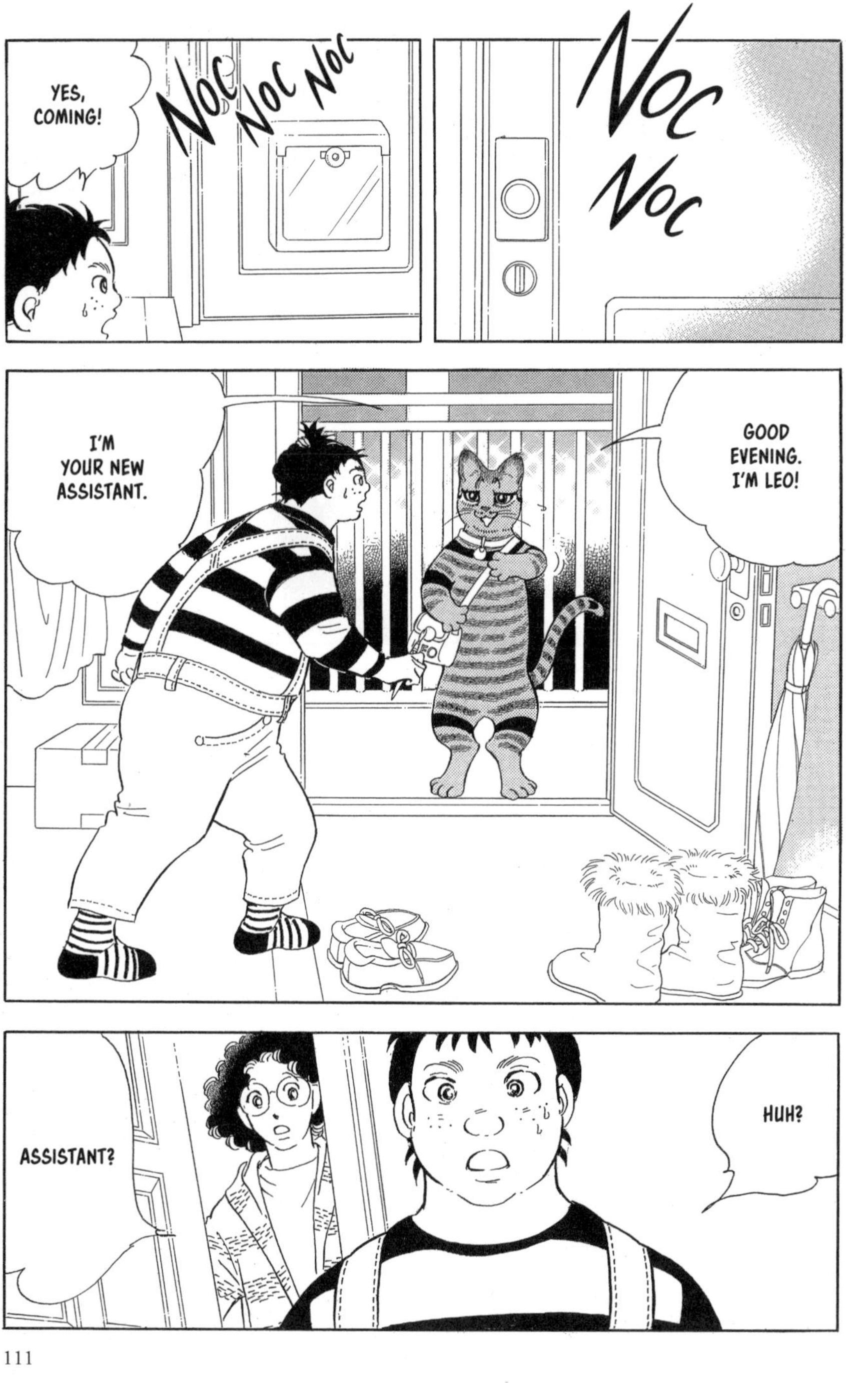
NOC NOC
NOC NOC NOC
YES, COMING!
GOOD EVENING. I'M LEO!
I'M YOUR NEW ASSISTANT.
HUH?
ASSISTANT?

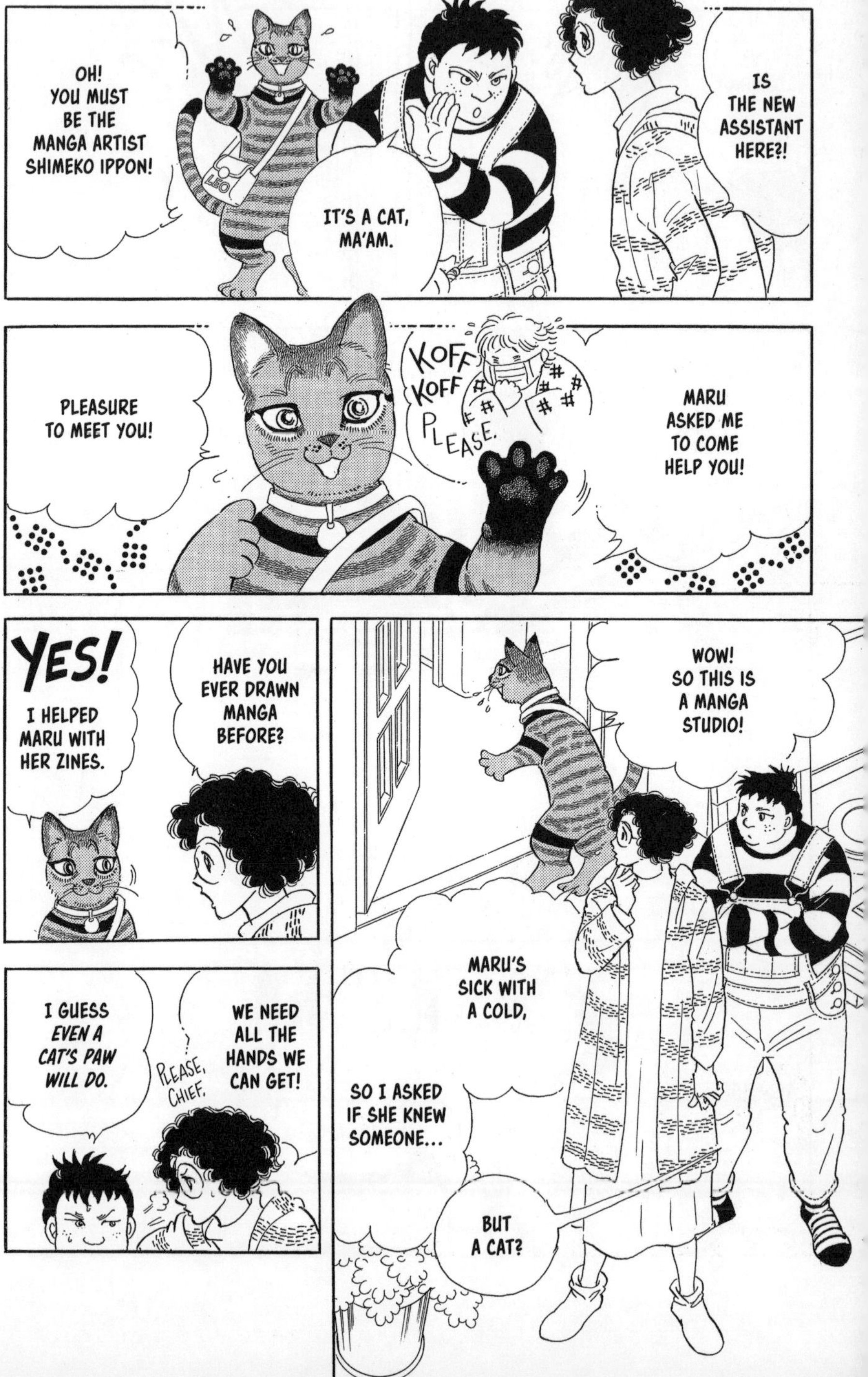
IS THE NEW ASSISTANT HERE?!
OH! YOU MUST BE THE MANGA ARTIST SHIMEKO IPPON!
IT'S A CAT, MA'AM.
MARU ASKED ME TO COME HELP YOU!
KOFF KOFF
PLEASE.
PLEASURE TO MEET YOU!
WOW! SO THIS IS A MANGA STUDIO!
MARU'S SICK WITH A COLD,
SO I ASKED IF SHE KNEW SOMEONE...
BUT A CAT?
HAVE YOU EVER DRAWN MANGA BEFORE?
YES! I HELPED MARU WITH HER ZINES.
WE NEED ALL THE HANDS WE CAN GET!
PLEASE, CHIEF.
I GUESS *EVEN A CAT'S PAW* WILL DO.

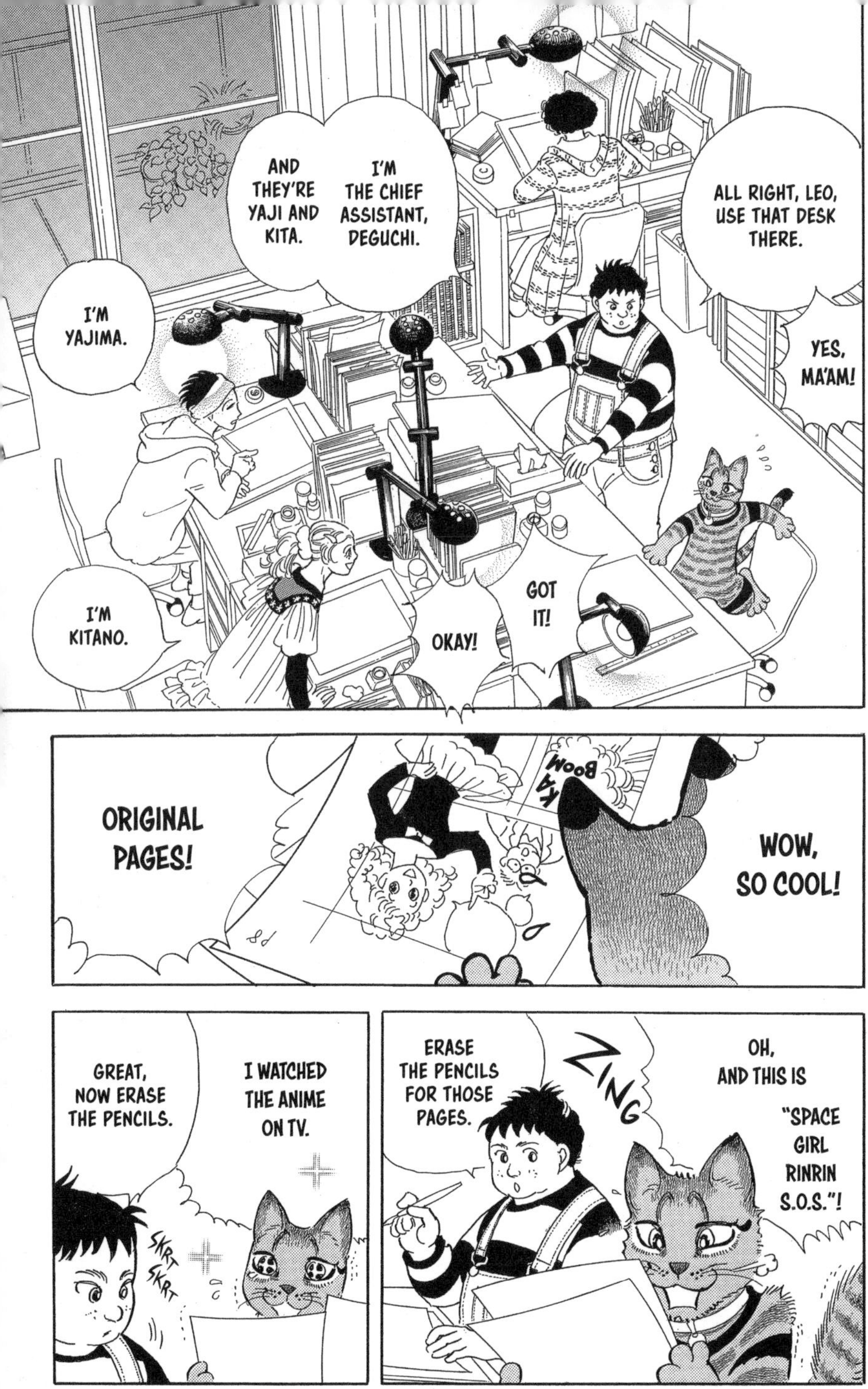
ALL RIGHT, LEO, USE THAT DESK THERE.
I'M THE CHIEF ASSISTANT, DEGUCHI.
AND THEY'RE YAJI AND KITA.
YES, MA'AM!
I'M YAJIMA.
GOT IT!
OKAY!
I'M KITANO.
WOW, SO COOL!
KA BOOM
ORIGINAL PAGES!
OH, AND THIS IS "SPACE GIRL RINRIN S.O.S."!
ZING
ERASE THE PENCILS FOR THOSE PAGES.
I WATCHED THE ANIME ON TV.
GREAT, NOW ERASE THE PENCILS.
SKRT SKRT

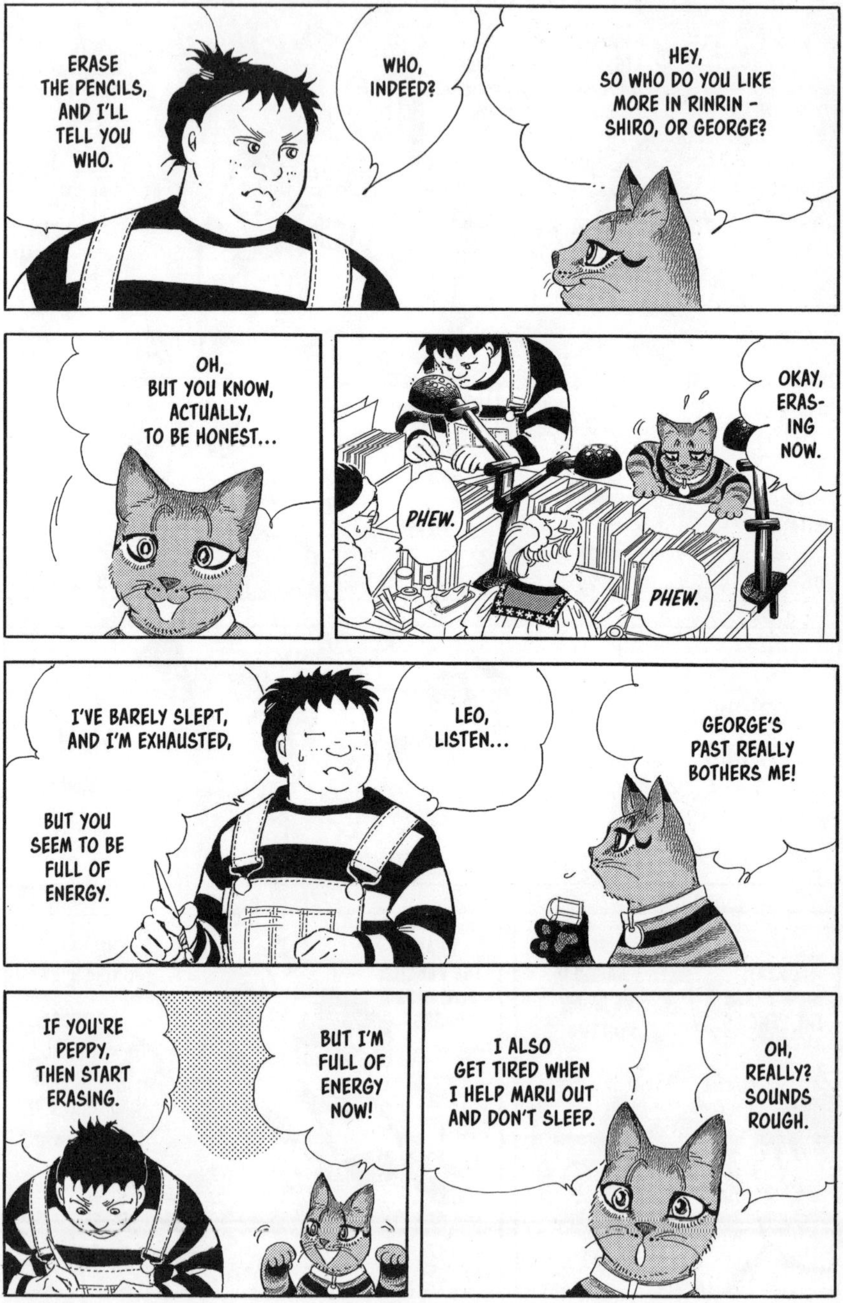
HEY, SO WHO DO YOU LIKE MORE IN RINRIN – SHIRO, OR GEORGE?
WHO, INDEED?
ERASE THE PENCILS, AND I'LL TELL YOU WHO.
OKAY, ERAS-ING NOW.
PHEW.
PHEW.
OH, BUT YOU KNOW, ACTUALLY, TO BE HONEST...
GEORGE'S PAST REALLY BOTHERS ME!
LEO, LISTEN...
I'VE BARELY SLEPT, AND I'M EXHAUSTED,
BUT YOU SEEM TO BE FULL OF ENERGY.
OH, REALLY? SOUNDS ROUGH.
I ALSO GET TIRED WHEN I HELP MARU OUT AND DON'T SLEEP.
BUT I'M FULL OF ENERGY NOW!
IF YOU'RE PEPPY, THEN START ERASING.

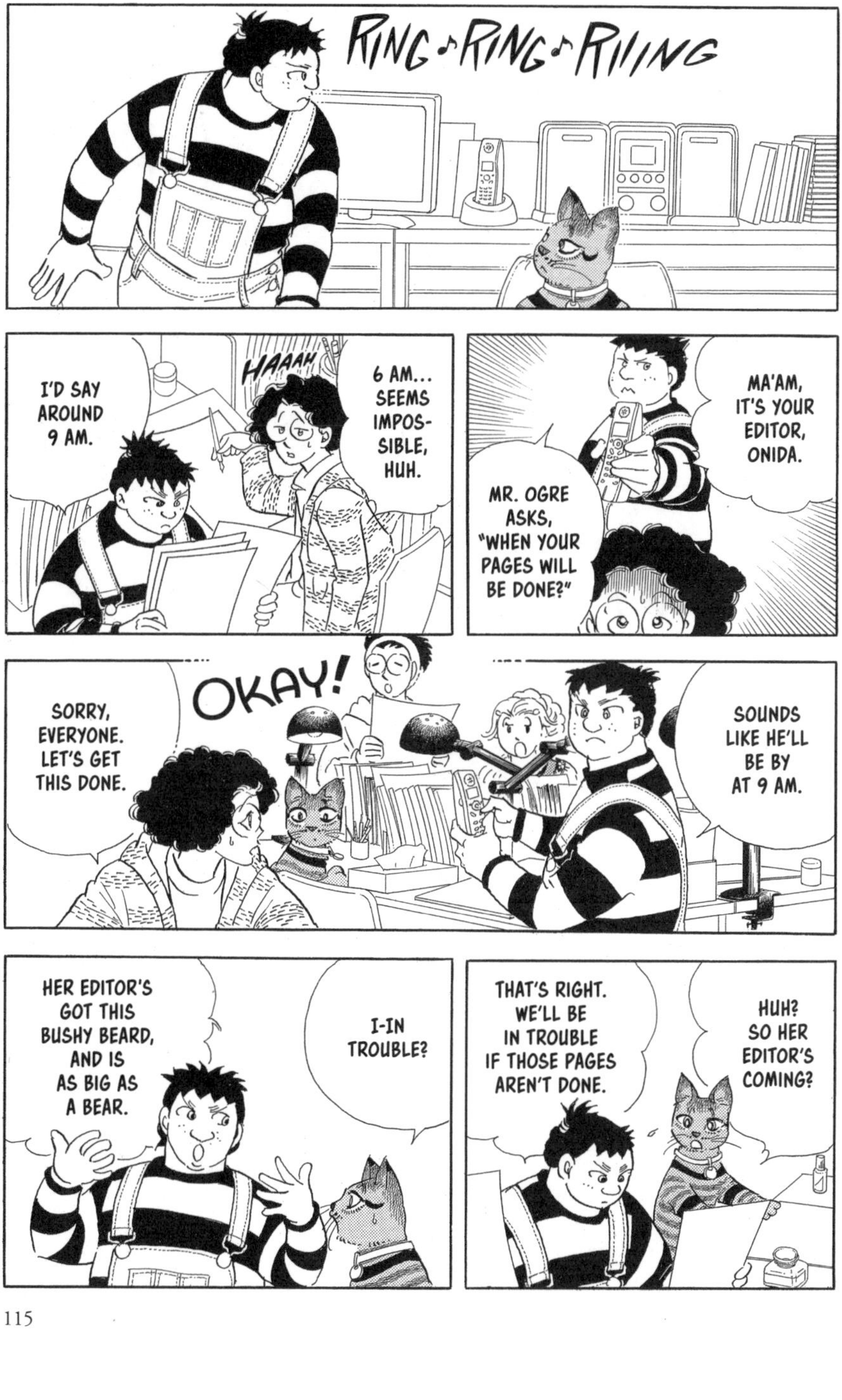
RING♪RING♪RIIING
MA'AM, IT'S YOUR EDITOR, ONIDA.
MR. OGRE ASKS, "WHEN YOUR PAGES WILL BE DONE?"
6 AM... SEEMS IMPOSSIBLE, HUH.
HAAAH
I'D SAY AROUND 9 AM.
SOUNDS LIKE HE'LL BE BY AT 9 AM.
OKAY!
SORRY, EVERYONE. LET'S GET THIS DONE.
HUH? SO HER EDITOR'S COMING?
THAT'S RIGHT. WE'LL BE IN TROUBLE IF THOSE PAGES AREN'T DONE.
I-IN TROUBLE?
HER EDITOR'S GOT THIS BUSHY BEARD, AND IS AS BIG AS A BEAR.

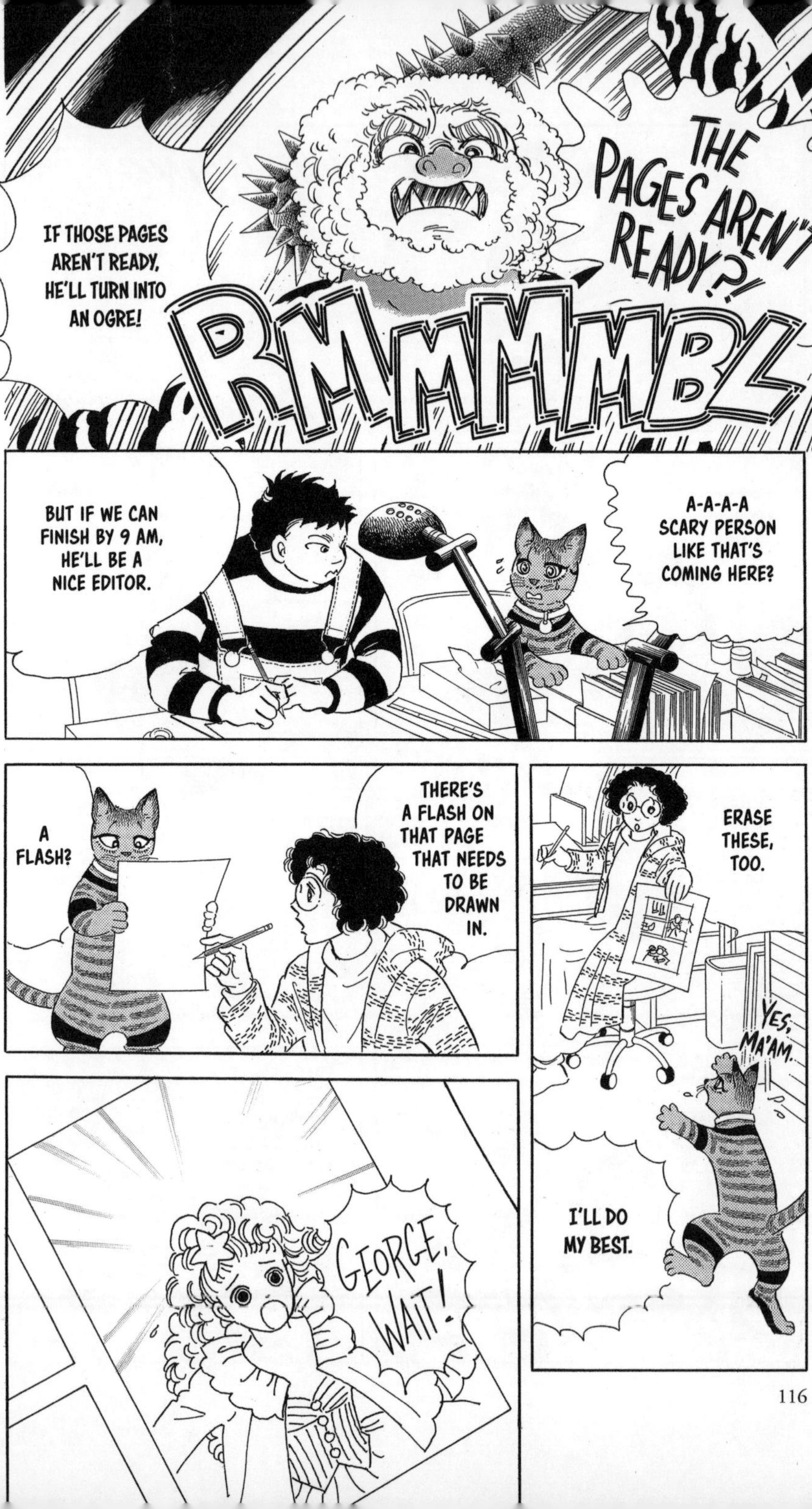

THE PAGES AREN'T READY?!
RMMMMBL
IF THOSE PAGES AREN'T READY, HE'LL TURN INTO AN OGRE!
A-A-A-A SCARY PERSON LIKE THAT'S COMING HERE?
BUT IF WE CAN FINISH BY 9 AM, HE'LL BE A NICE EDITOR.
ERASE THESE, TOO.
YES, MA'AM.
I'LL DO MY BEST.
THERE'S A FLASH ON THAT PAGE THAT NEEDS TO BE DRAWN IN.
A FLASH?
GEORGE, WAIT!

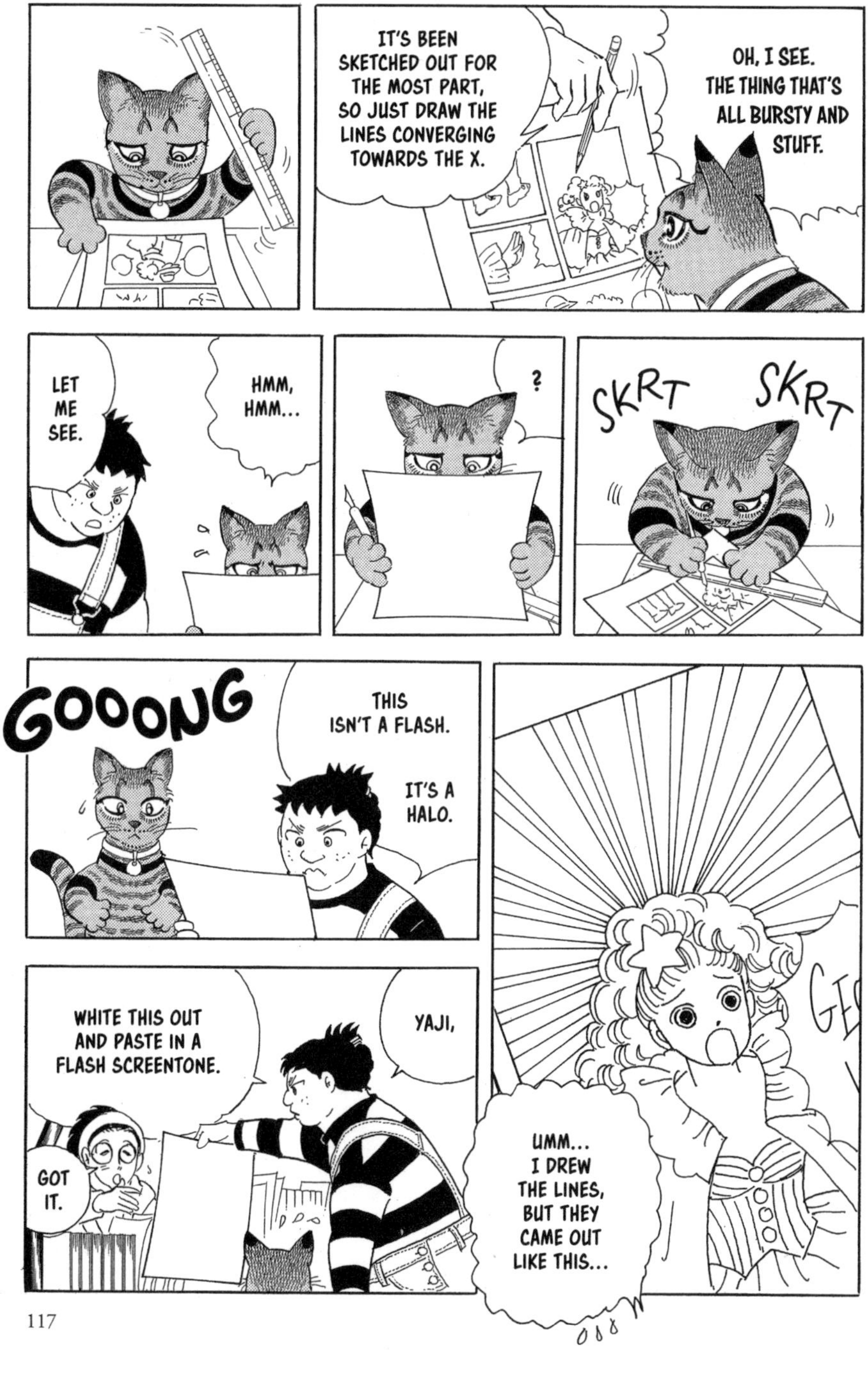
IT'S BEEN SKETCHED OUT FOR THE MOST PART, SO JUST DRAW THE LINES CONVERGING TOWARDS THE X.
OH, I SEE. THE THING THAT'S ALL BURSTY AND STUFF.
SKRT SKRT
?
HMM, HMM...
LET ME SEE.
UMM... I DREW THE LINES, BUT THEY CAME OUT LIKE THIS...
THIS ISN'T A FLASH.
IT'S A HALO.
GOOONG
YAJI,
WHITE THIS OUT AND PASTE IN A FLASH SCREENTONE.
GOT IT.

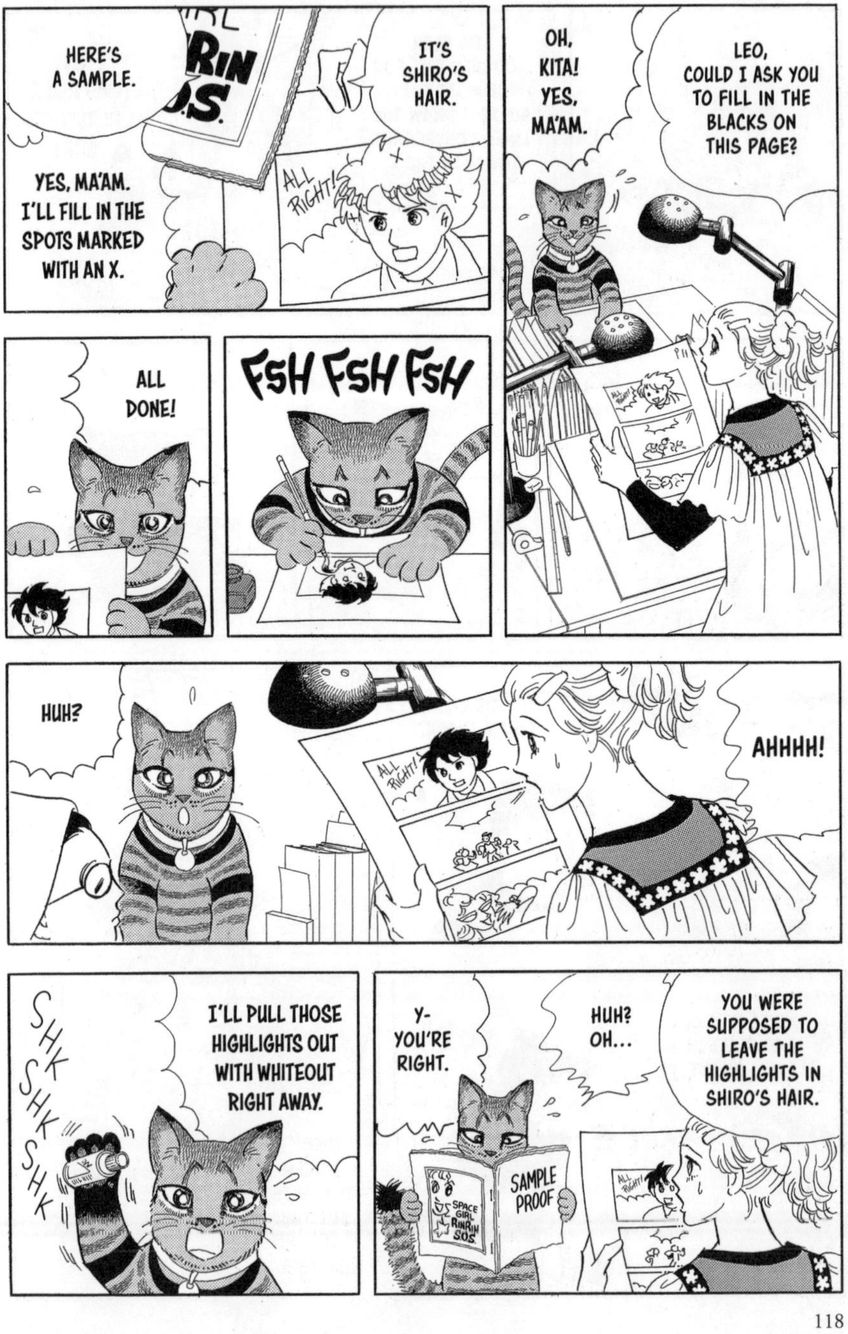
LEO, COULD I ASK YOU TO FILL IN THE BLACKS ON THIS PAGE?
OH, KITA! YES, MA'AM.
ALL RIGHT!
IT'S SHIRO'S HAIR.
HERE'S A SAMPLE.
ALL RIGHT!
YES, MA'AM. I'LL FILL IN THE SPOTS MARKED WITH AN X.
FSH FSH FSH
ALL DONE!
AHHHH!
ALL RIGHT!
HUH?
YOU WERE SUPPOSED TO LEAVE THE HIGHLIGHTS IN SHIRO'S HAIR.
HUH? OH...
Y- YOU'RE RIGHT.
SAMPLE PROOF
SPACE GIRL RINRIN S.O.S.
I'LL PULL THOSE HIGHLIGHTS OUT WITH WHITEOUT RIGHT AWAY.
SHK SHK SHK

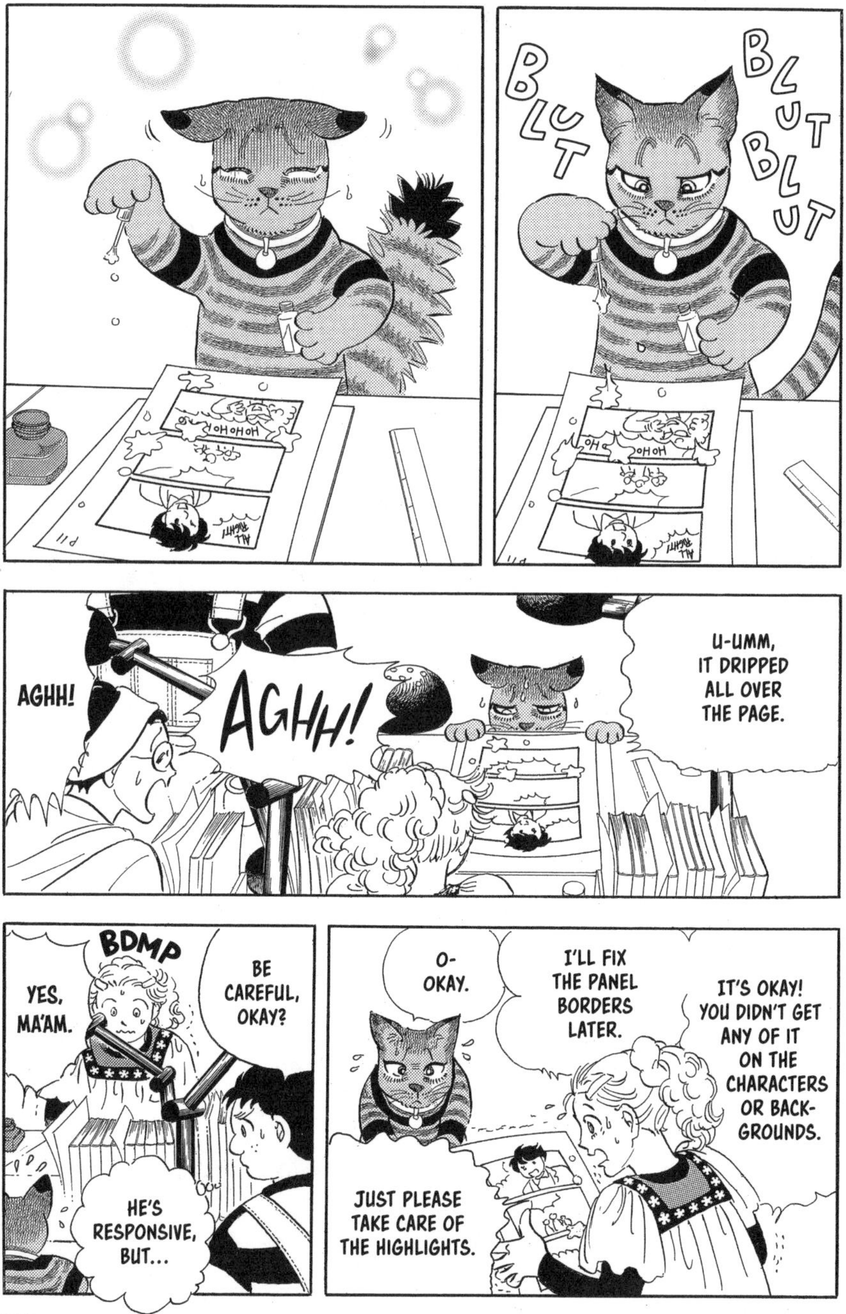
BLUT BLUT BLUT
U-UMM, IT DRIPPED ALL OVER THE PAGE.
AGHH!
AGHH!
IT'S OKAY! YOU DIDN'T GET ANY OF IT ON THE CHARACTERS OR BACK-GROUNDS.
I'LL FIX THE PANEL BORDERS LATER.
O- OKAY.
JUST PLEASE TAKE CARE OF THE HIGHLIGHTS.
BE CAREFUL, OKAY?
BDMP
YES, MA'AM.
HE'S RESPONSIVE, BUT...

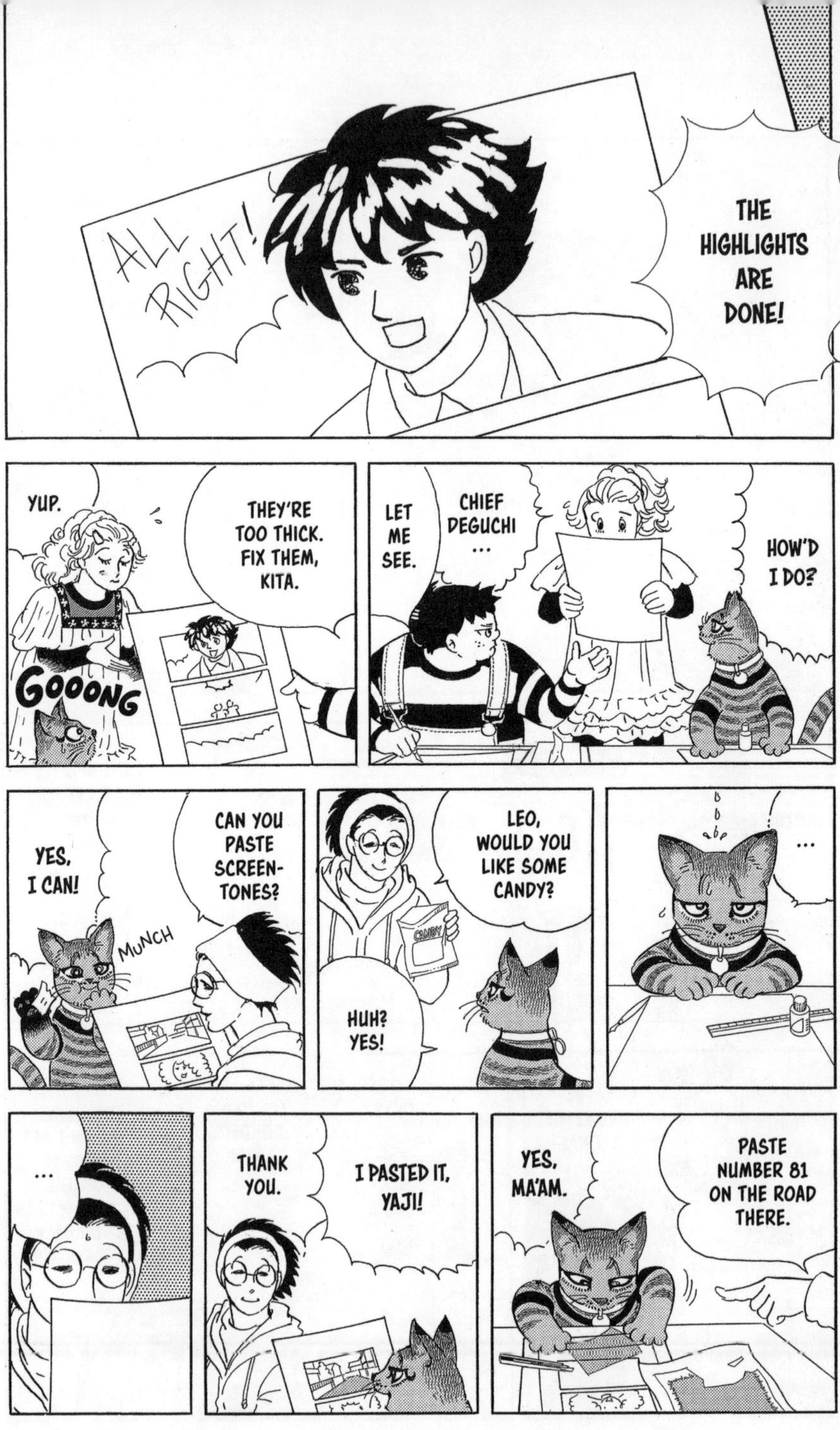
THE HIGHLIGHTS ARE DONE!
ALL RIGHT!
HOW'D I DO?
CHIEF DEGUCHI ...
LET ME SEE.
THEY'RE TOO THICK. FIX THEM, KITA.
YUP.
GOOONG
...
LEO, WOULD YOU LIKE SOME CANDY?
CANDY
HUH? YES!
CAN YOU PASTE SCREEN-TONES?
YES, I CAN!
MUNCH
PASTE NUMBER 81 ON THE ROAD THERE.
YES, MA'AM.
I PASTED IT, YAJI!
THANK YOU.
...

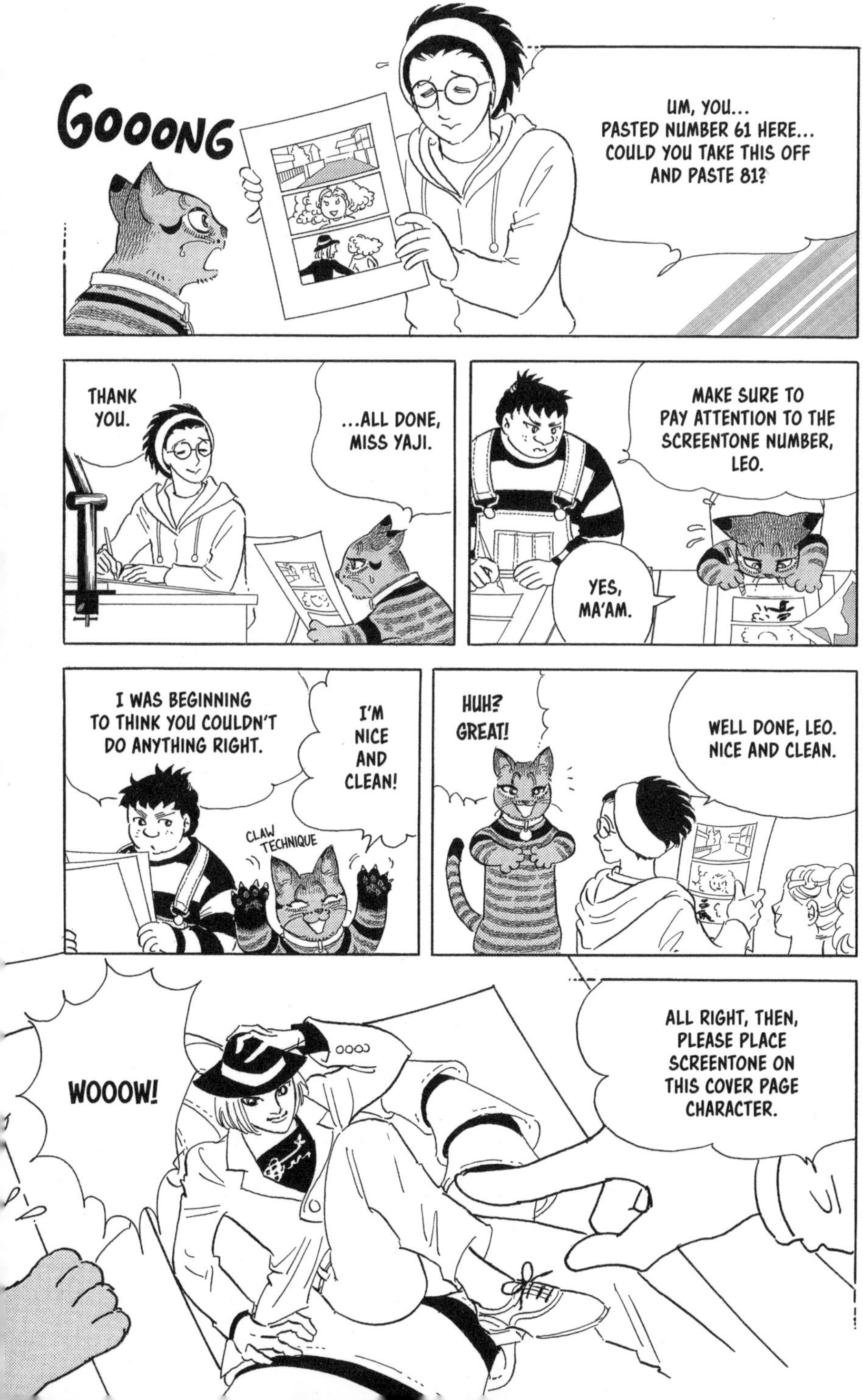
UM, YOU... PASTED NUMBER 61 HERE... COULD YOU TAKE THIS OFF AND PASTE 81?
GOOONG
MAKE SURE TO PAY ATTENTION TO THE SCREENTONE NUMBER, LEO.
YES, MA'AM.
...ALL DONE, MISS YAJI.
THANK YOU.
WELL DONE, LEO. NICE AND CLEAN.
HUH? GREAT!
I'M NICE AND CLEAN!
CLAW TECHNIQUE
I WAS BEGINNING TO THINK YOU COULDN'T DO ANYTHING RIGHT.
ALL RIGHT, THEN, PLEASE PLACE SCREENTONE ON THIS COVER PAGE CHARACTER.
WOOOW!

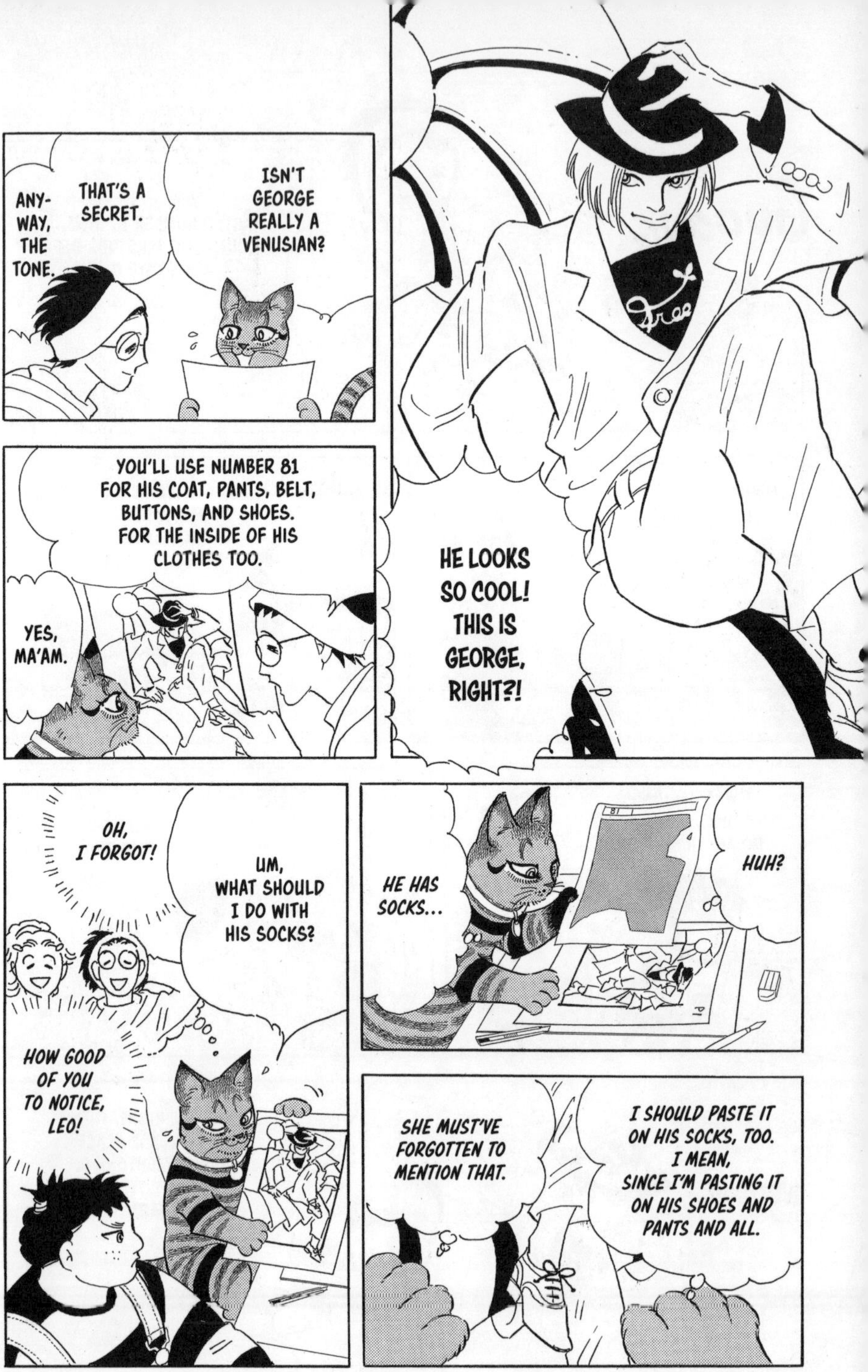
HE LOOKS SO COOL! THIS IS GEORGE, RIGHT?!
ISN'T GEORGE REALLY A VENUSIAN?
THAT'S A SECRET.
ANY-WAY, THE TONE.
YOU'LL USE NUMBER 81 FOR HIS COAT, PANTS, BELT, BUTTONS, AND SHOES. FOR THE INSIDE OF HIS CLOTHES TOO.
YES, MA'AM.
HUH?
HE HAS SOCKS...
I SHOULD PASTE IT ON HIS SOCKS, TOO. I MEAN, SINCE I'M PASTING IT ON HIS SHOES AND PANTS AND ALL.
SHE MUST'VE FORGOTTEN TO MENTION THAT.
UM, WHAT SHOULD I DO WITH HIS SOCKS?
OH, I FORGOT!
HOW GOOD OF YOU TO NOTICE, LEO!

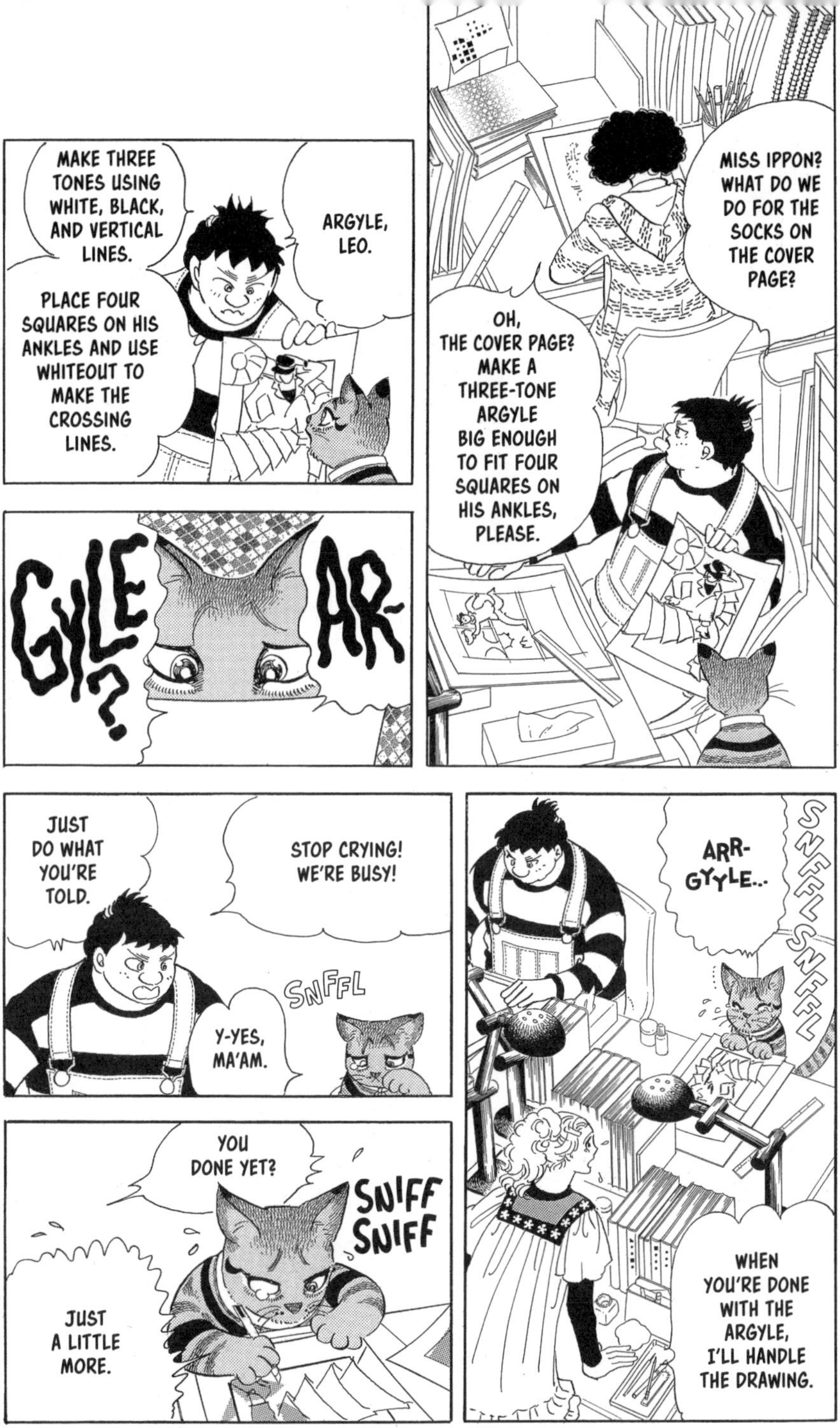
MISS IPPON? WHAT DO WE DO FOR THE SOCKS ON THE COVER PAGE?
OH, THE COVER PAGE? MAKE A THREE-TONE ARGYLE BIG ENOUGH TO FIT FOUR SQUARES ON HIS ANKLES, PLEASE.
ARGYLE, LEO.
MAKE THREE TONES USING WHITE, BLACK, AND VERTICAL LINES.
PLACE FOUR SQUARES ON HIS ANKLES AND USE WHITEOUT TO MAKE THE CROSSING LINES.
AR-
GYLE?
SNFFL SNFFL
ARR-GYYLE...
WHEN YOU'RE DONE WITH THE ARGYLE, I'LL HANDLE THE DRAWING.
STOP CRYING! WE'RE BUSY!
JUST DO WHAT YOU'RE TOLD.
SNFFL
Y-YES, MA'AM.
SNIFF SNIFF
YOU DONE YET?
JUST A LITTLE MORE.

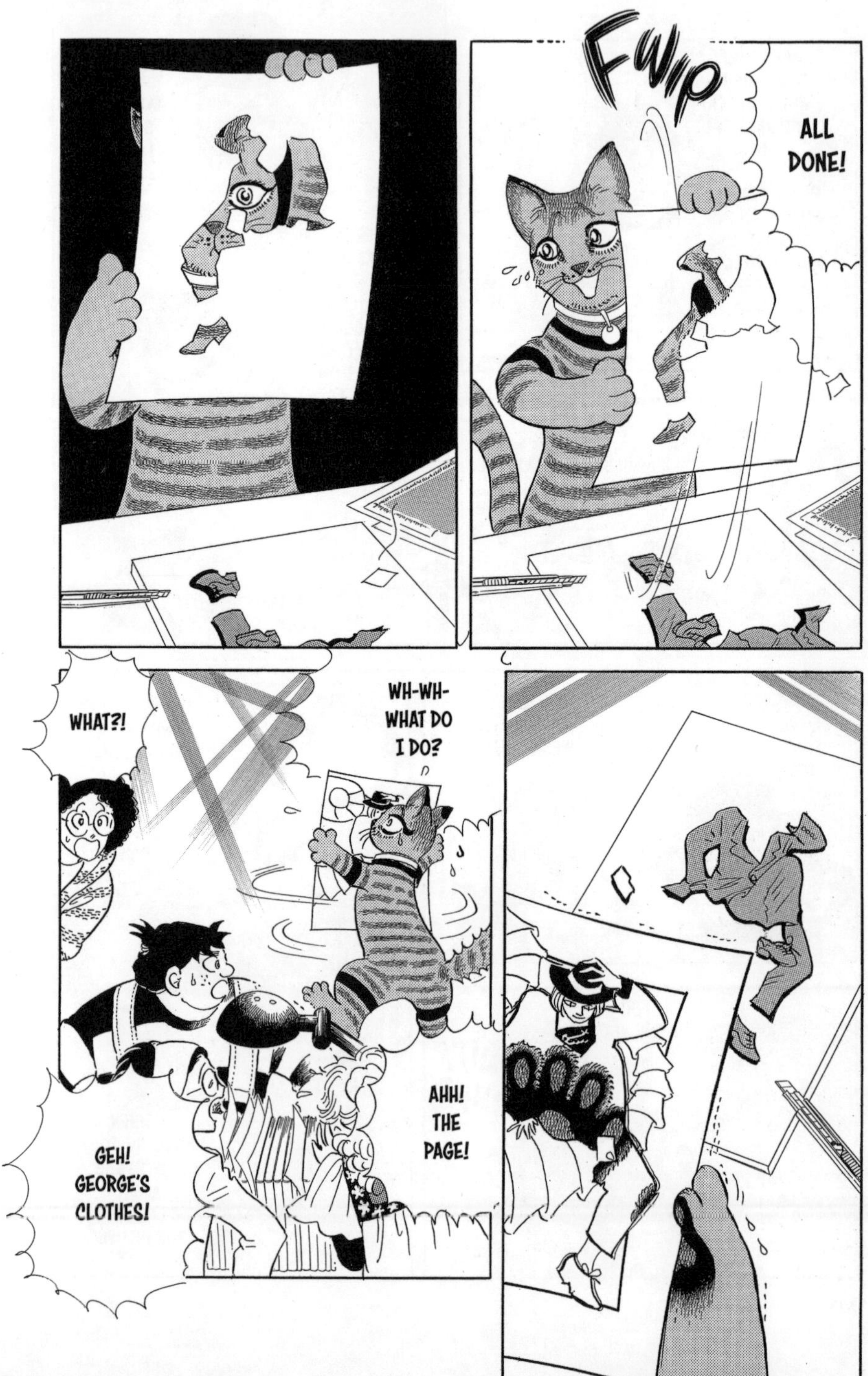
FWIP
ALL DONE!
WH-WH-WHAT DO I DO?
WHAT?!
AHH! THE PAGE!
GEH! GEORGE'S CLOTHES!

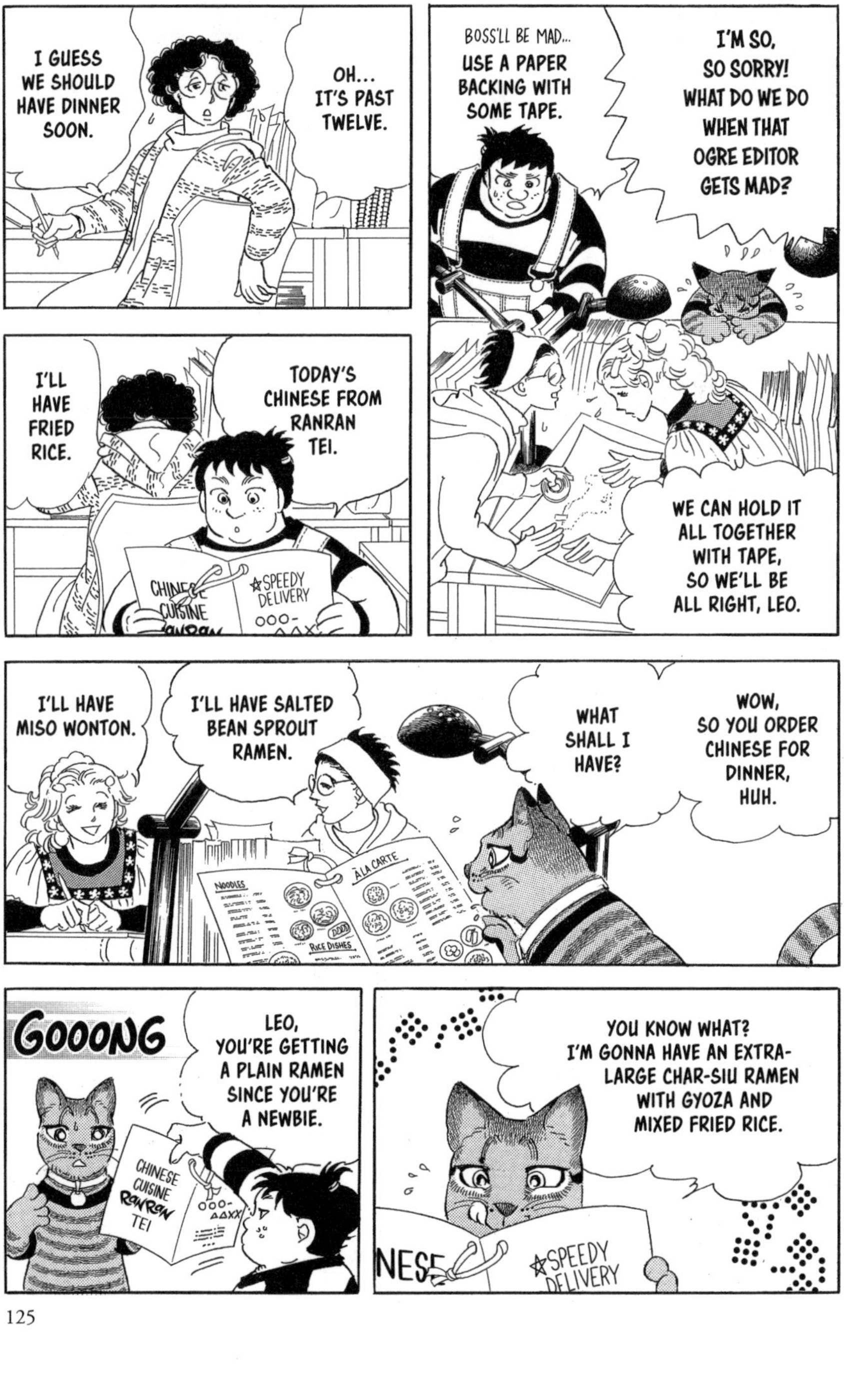
I'M SO, SO SORRY! WHAT DO WE DO WHEN THAT OGRE EDITOR GETS MAD?
BOSS'LL BE MAD...
USE A PAPER BACKING WITH SOME TAPE.
WE CAN HOLD IT ALL TOGETHER WITH TAPE, SO WE'LL BE ALL RIGHT, LEO.
OH... IT'S PAST TWELVE.
I GUESS WE SHOULD HAVE DINNER SOON.
TODAY'S CHINESE FROM RANRAN TEI.
I'LL HAVE FRIED RICE.
☆SPEEDY DELIVERY
WOW, SO YOU ORDER CHINESE FOR DINNER, HUH.
WHAT SHALL I HAVE?
I'LL HAVE SALTED BEAN SPROUT RAMEN.
I'LL HAVE MISO WONTON.
NOODLES
À LA CARTE
RICE DISHES
YOU KNOW WHAT? I'M GONNA HAVE AN EXTRA-LARGE CHAR-SIU RAMEN WITH GYOZA AND MIXED FRIED RICE.
☆SPEEDY DELIVERY
LEO, YOU'RE GETTING A PLAIN RAMEN SINCE YOU'RE A NEWBIE.
GOOONG
CHINESE CUISINE RANRAN TEI

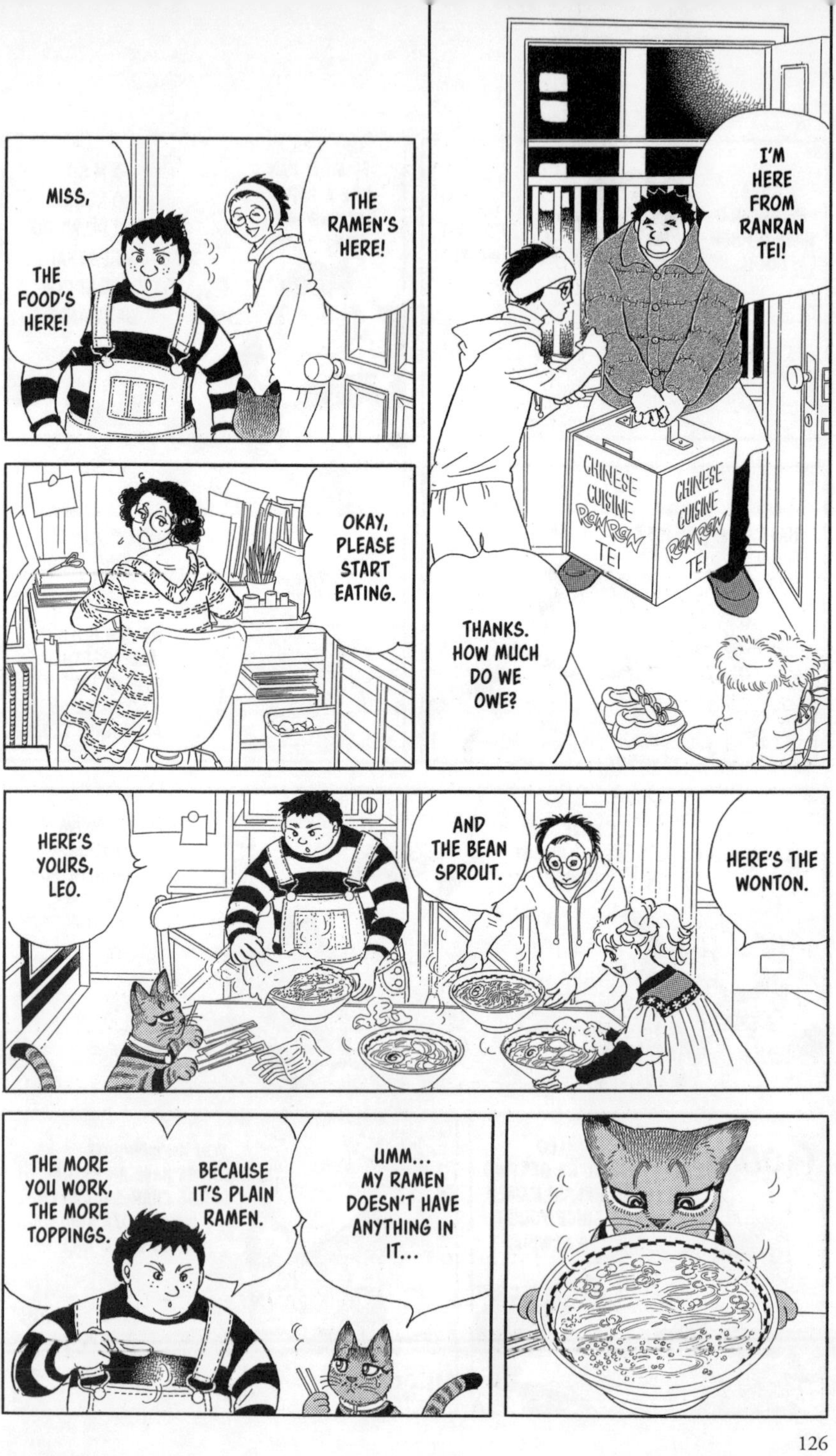
I'M HERE FROM RANRAN TEI!
CHINESE CUISINE RANRAN TEI
CHINESE CUISINE RANRAN TEI
THANKS. HOW MUCH DO WE OWE?
THE RAMEN'S HERE!
MISS,
THE FOOD'S HERE!
OKAY, PLEASE START EATING.
HERE'S THE WONTON.
AND THE BEAN SPROUT.
HERE'S YOURS, LEO.
UMM... MY RAMEN DOESN'T HAVE ANYTHING IN IT...
BECAUSE IT'S PLAIN RAMEN.
THE MORE YOU WORK, THE MORE TOPPINGS.

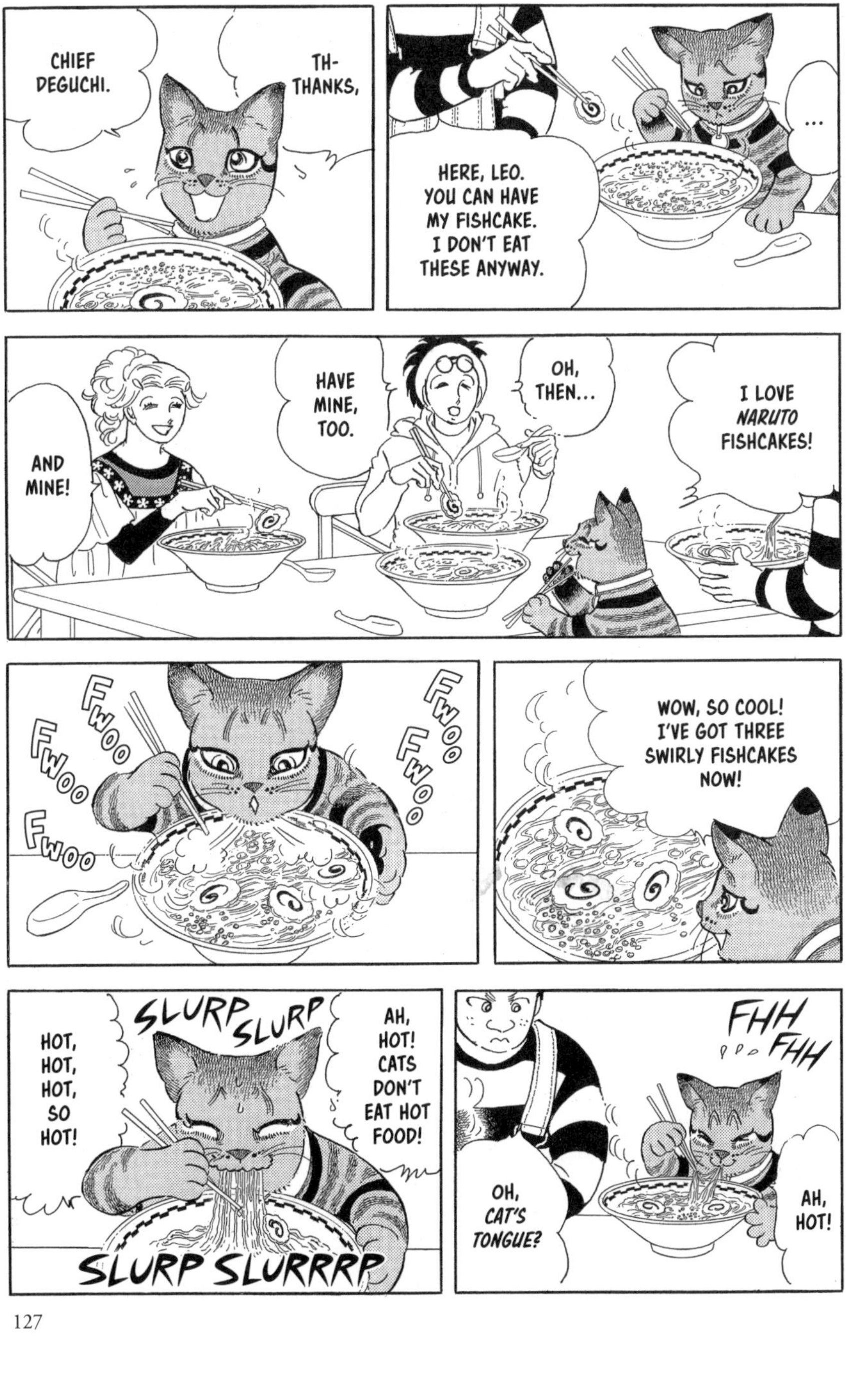

...
HERE, LEO. YOU CAN HAVE MY FISHCAKE. I DON'T EAT THESE ANYWAY.
TH- THANKS,
CHIEF DEGUCHI.
I LOVE *NARUTO* FISHCAKES!
OH, THEN...
HAVE MINE, TOO.
AND MINE!
WOW, SO COOL! I'VE GOT THREE SWIRLY FISHCAKES NOW!
FWOO FWOO FWOO
FWOO FWOO FWOO
FHH FHH
AH, HOT!
OH, CAT'S TONGUE?
AH, HOT! CATS DON'T EAT HOT FOOD!
SLURP SLURP
HOT, HOT, HOT, SO HOT!
SLURP SLURRRP

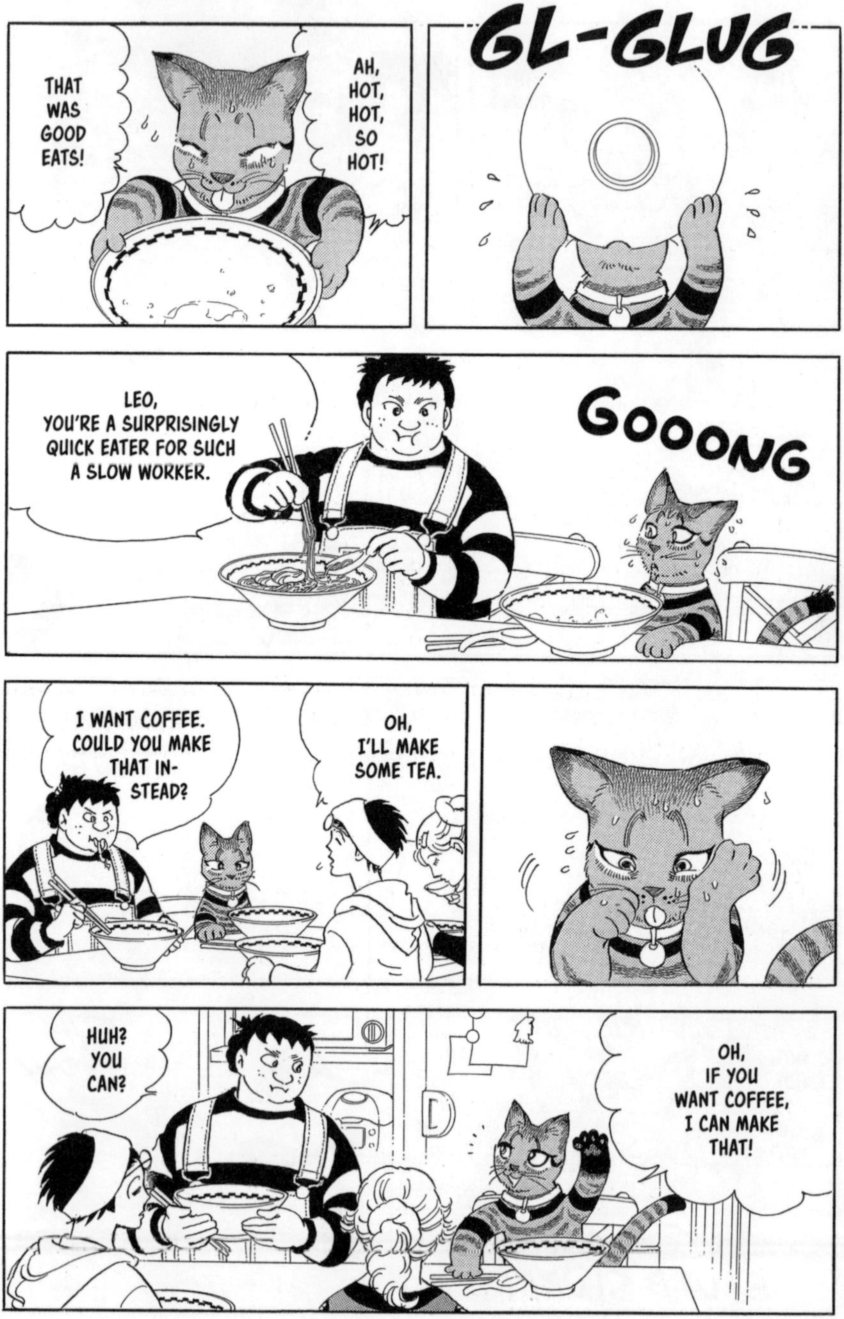
GL-GLUG
AH, HOT, HOT, SO HOT!
THAT WAS GOOD EATS!
GOOONG
LEO, YOU'RE A SURPRISINGLY QUICK EATER FOR SUCH A SLOW WORKER.
OH, I'LL MAKE SOME TEA.
I WANT COFFEE. COULD YOU MAKE THAT IN-STEAD?
OH, IF YOU WANT COFFEE, I CAN MAKE THAT!
HUH? YOU CAN?

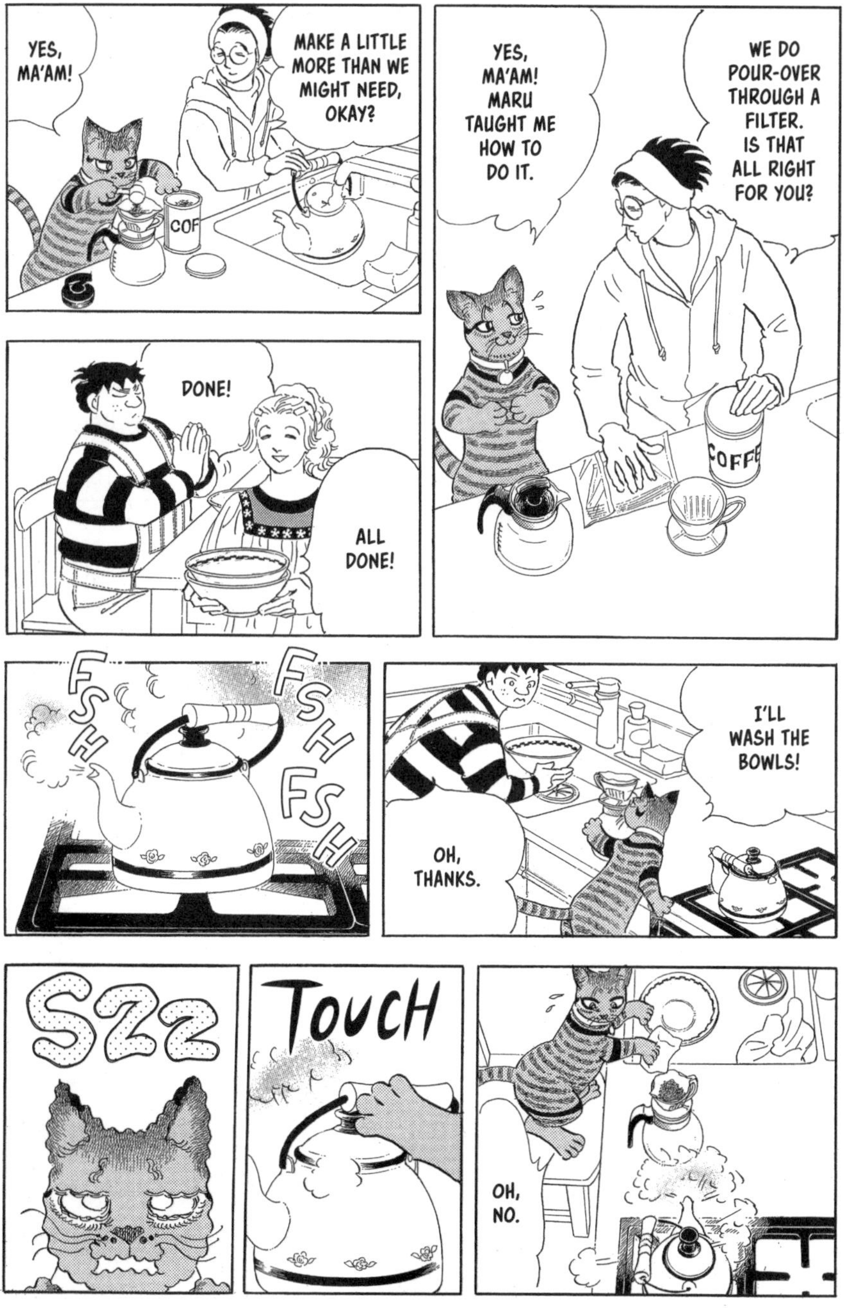
WE DO POUR-OVER THROUGH A FILTER. IS THAT ALL RIGHT FOR YOU?
YES, MA'AM! MARU TAUGHT ME HOW TO DO IT.
MAKE A LITTLE MORE THAN WE MIGHT NEED, OKAY?
YES, MA'AM!
COF
COFFE
DONE!
ALL DONE!
I'LL WASH THE BOWLS!
OH, THANKS.
FSH
FSH
FSH
OH, NO.
TOUCH
SZZ

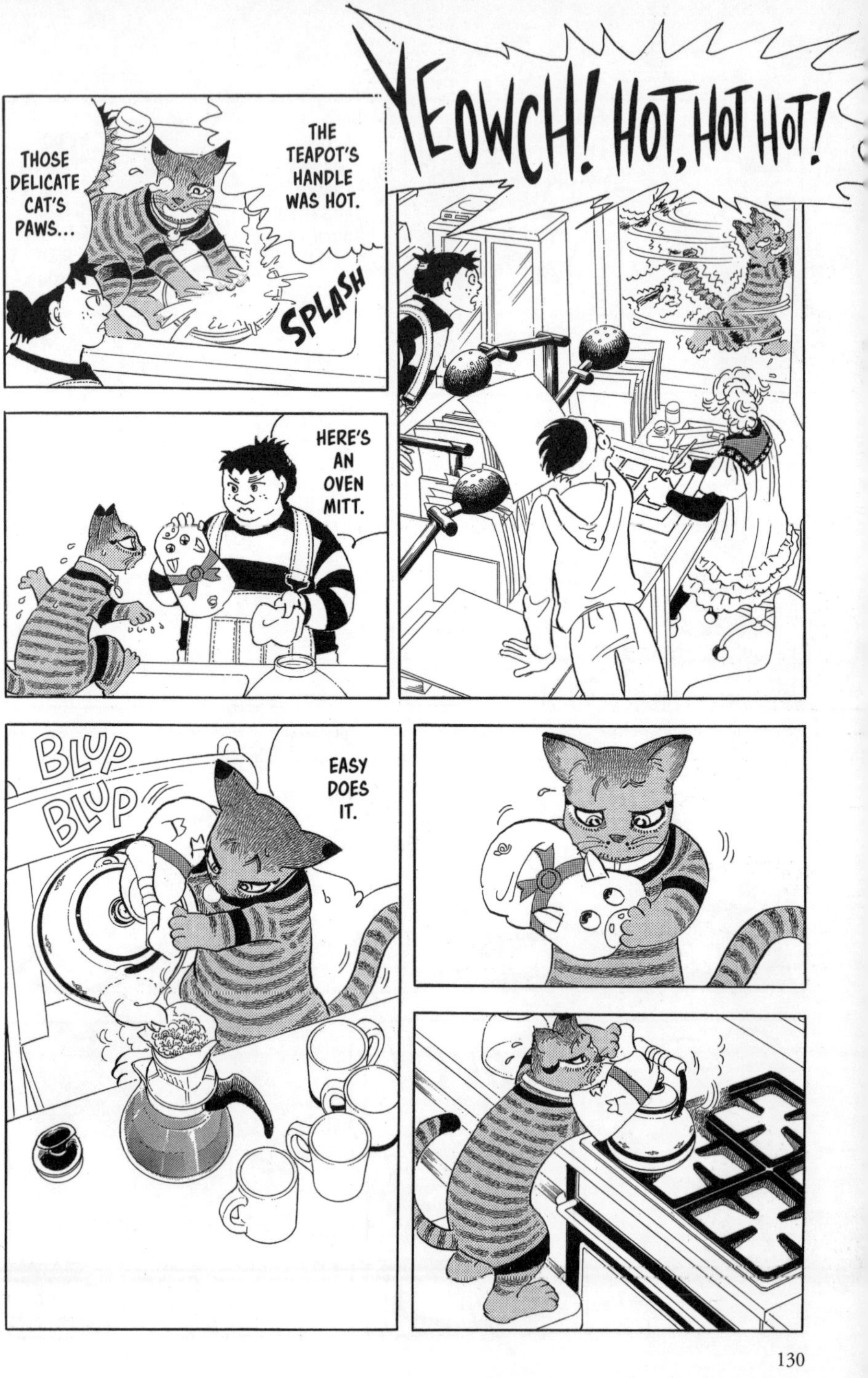
YEOWCH! HOT, HOT HOT!
THE TEAPOT'S HANDLE WAS HOT.
THOSE DELICATE CAT'S PAWS...
SPLASH
HERE'S AN OVEN MITT.
EASY DOES IT.
BLUP BLUP

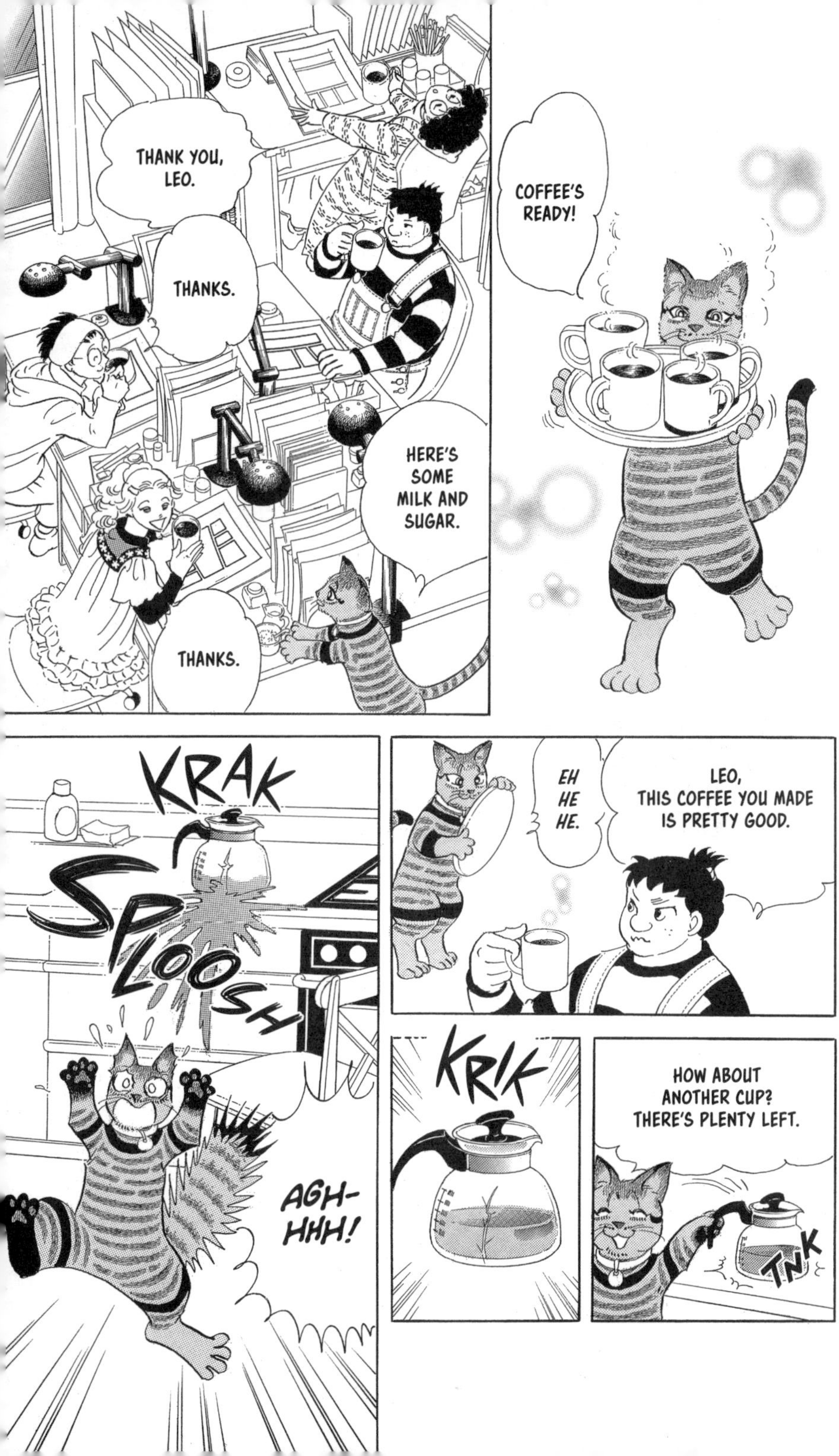
COFFEE'S READY!
THANK YOU, LEO.
THANKS.
HERE'S SOME MILK AND SUGAR.
THANKS.
LEO, THIS COFFEE YOU MADE IS PRETTY GOOD.
EH HE HE.
HOW ABOUT ANOTHER CUP? THERE'S PLENTY LEFT.
TNK
KRIK
KRAK
SPLOOSH
AGH-HHH!

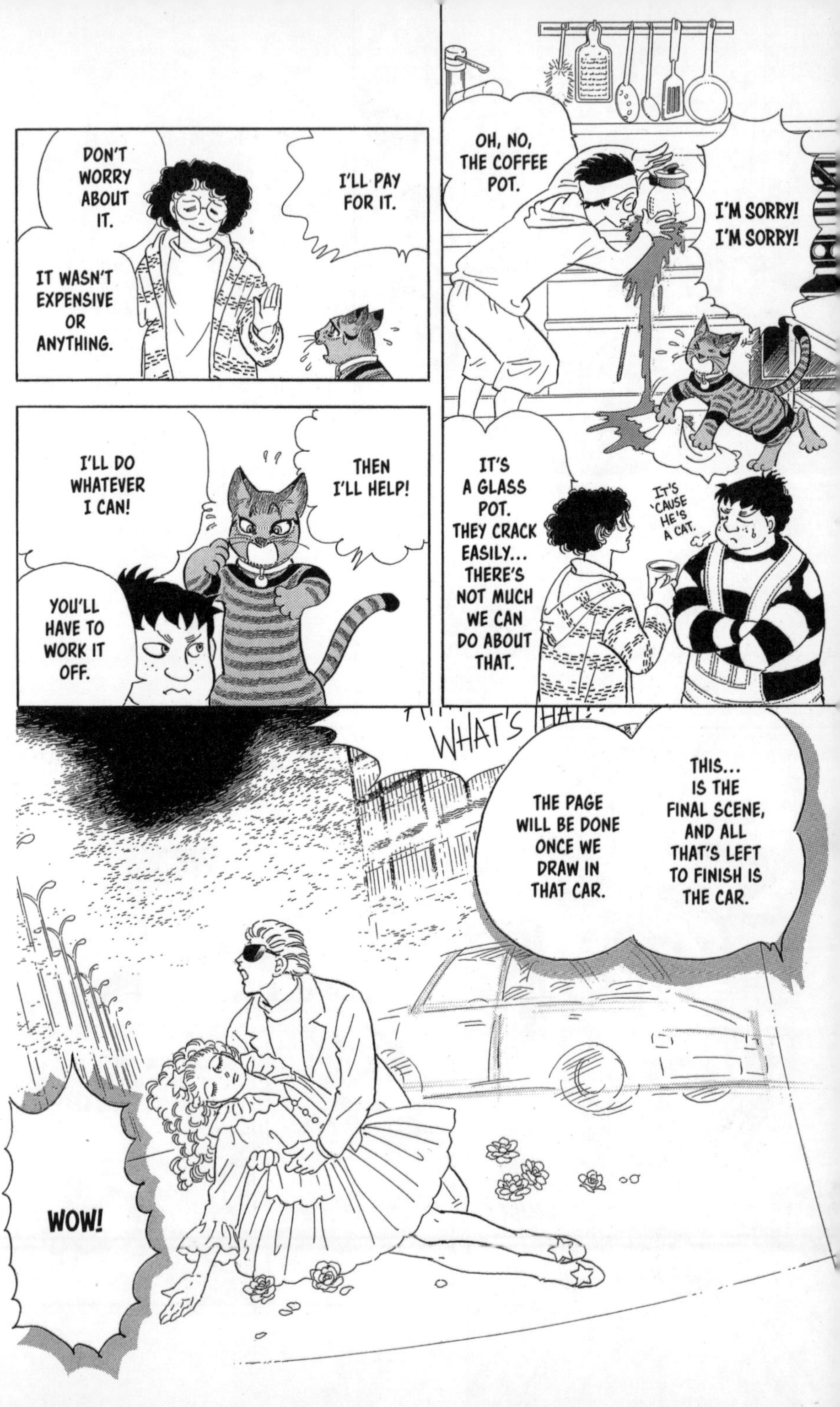
OH, NO, THE COFFEE POT.
I'M SORRY! I'M SORRY!
IT'S A GLASS POT. THEY CRACK EASILY... THERE'S NOT MUCH WE CAN DO ABOUT THAT.
IT'S 'CAUSE HE'S A CAT.
I'LL PAY FOR IT.
DON'T WORRY ABOUT IT.
IT WASN'T EXPENSIVE OR ANYTHING.
THEN I'LL HELP!
I'LL DO WHATEVER I CAN!
YOU'LL HAVE TO WORK IT OFF.
WHAT'S THAT
THIS... IS THE FINAL SCENE, AND ALL THAT'S LEFT TO FINISH IS THE CAR.
THE PAGE WILL BE DONE ONCE WE DRAW IN THAT CAR.
WOW!

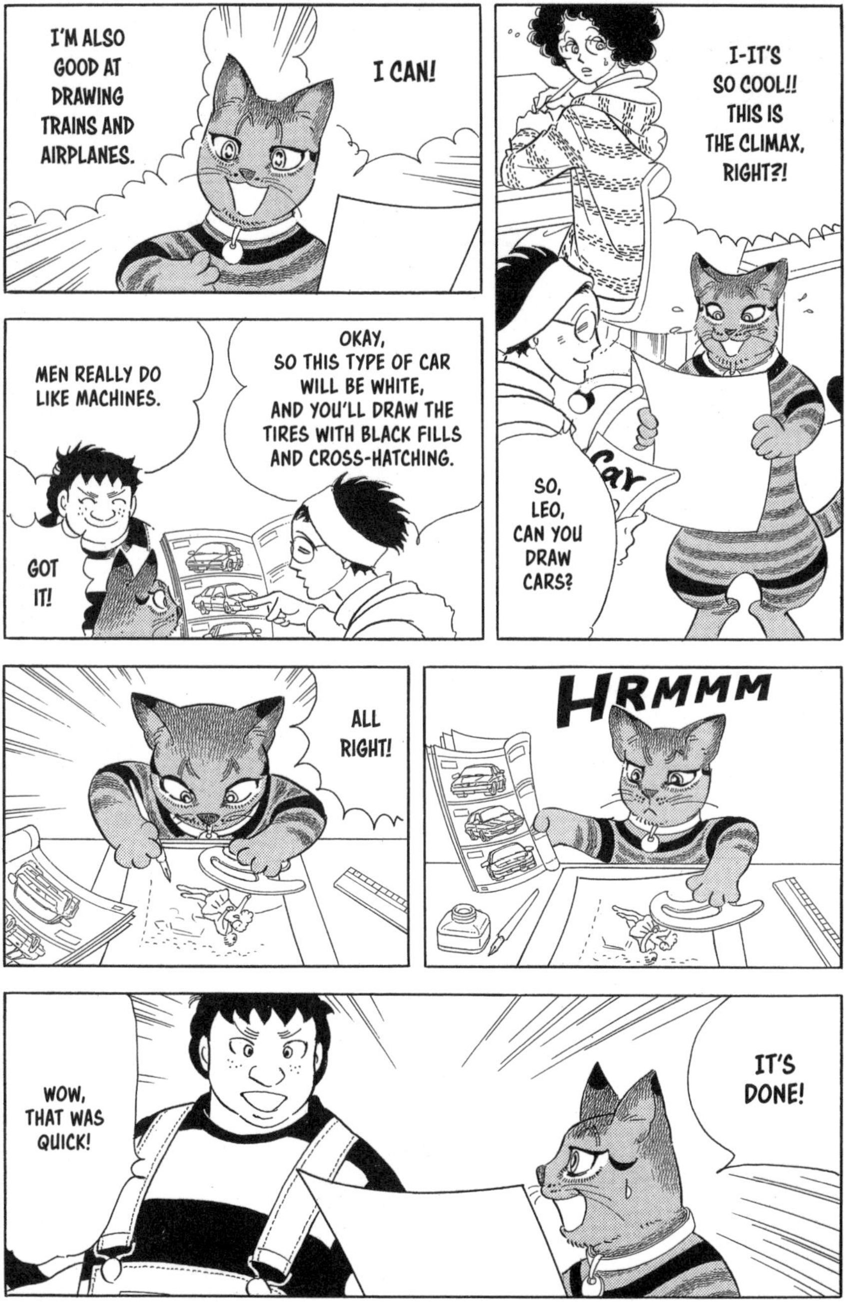
I-IT'S SO COOL!! THIS IS THE CLIMAX, RIGHT?!
SO, LEO, CAN YOU DRAW CARS?
I CAN!
I'M ALSO GOOD AT DRAWING TRAINS AND AIRPLANES.
OKAY, SO THIS TYPE OF CAR WILL BE WHITE, AND YOU'LL DRAW THE TIRES WITH BLACK FILLS AND CROSS-HATCHING.
MEN REALLY DO LIKE MACHINES.
GOT IT!
HRMMM
ALL RIGHT!
IT'S DONE!
WOW, THAT WAS QUICK!

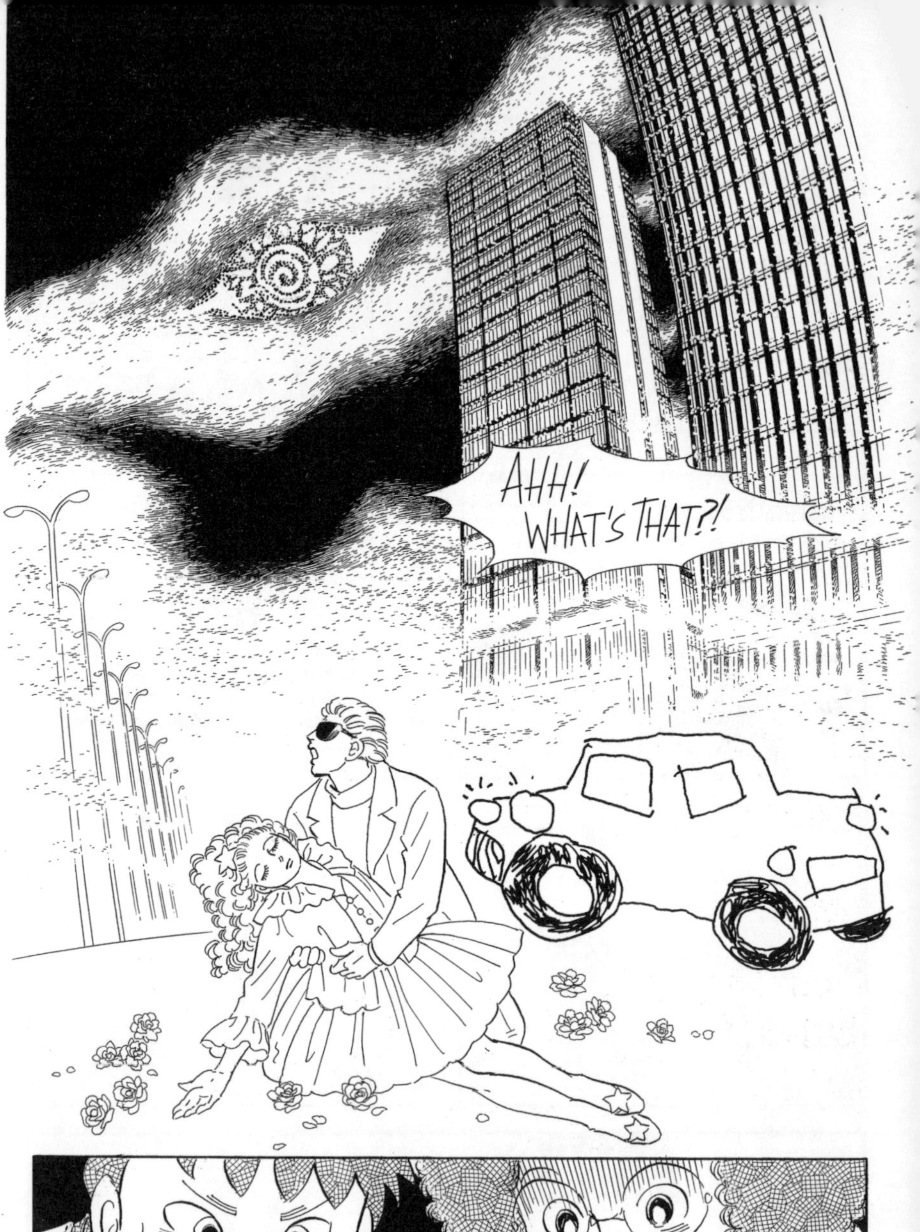
AHH! WHAT'S THAT?!
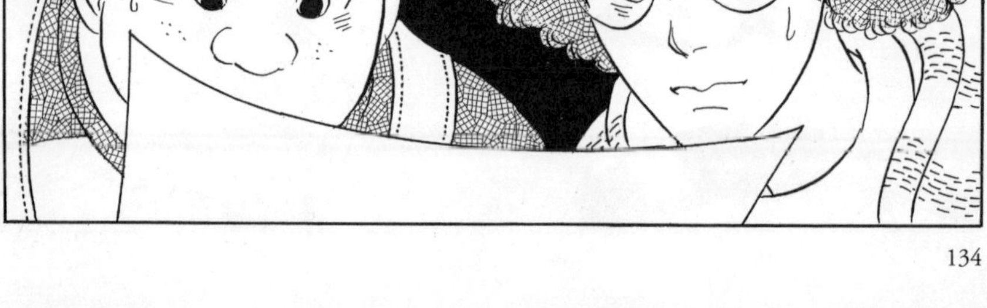

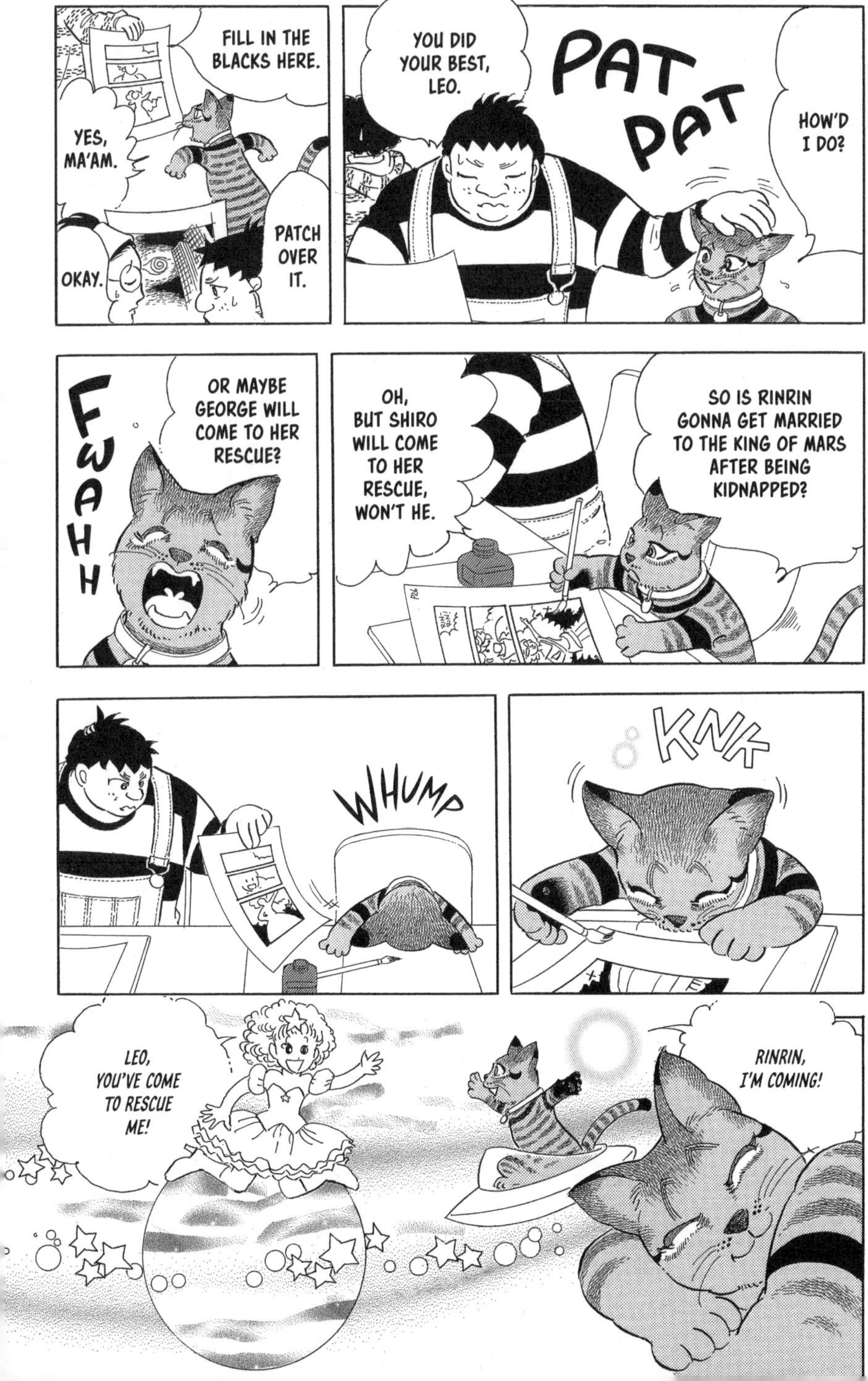
HOW'D I DO?
PAT PAT
YOU DID YOUR BEST, LEO.
FILL IN THE BLACKS HERE.
YES, MA'AM.
PATCH OVER IT.
OKAY.
SO IS RINRIN GONNA GET MARRIED TO THE KING OF MARS AFTER BEING KIDNAPPED?
OH, BUT SHIRO WILL COME TO HER RESCUE, WON'T HE.
OR MAYBE GEORGE WILL COME TO HER RESCUE?
FWAHH
KNK
WHUMP
RINRIN, I'M COMING!
LEO, YOU'VE COME TO RESCUE ME!

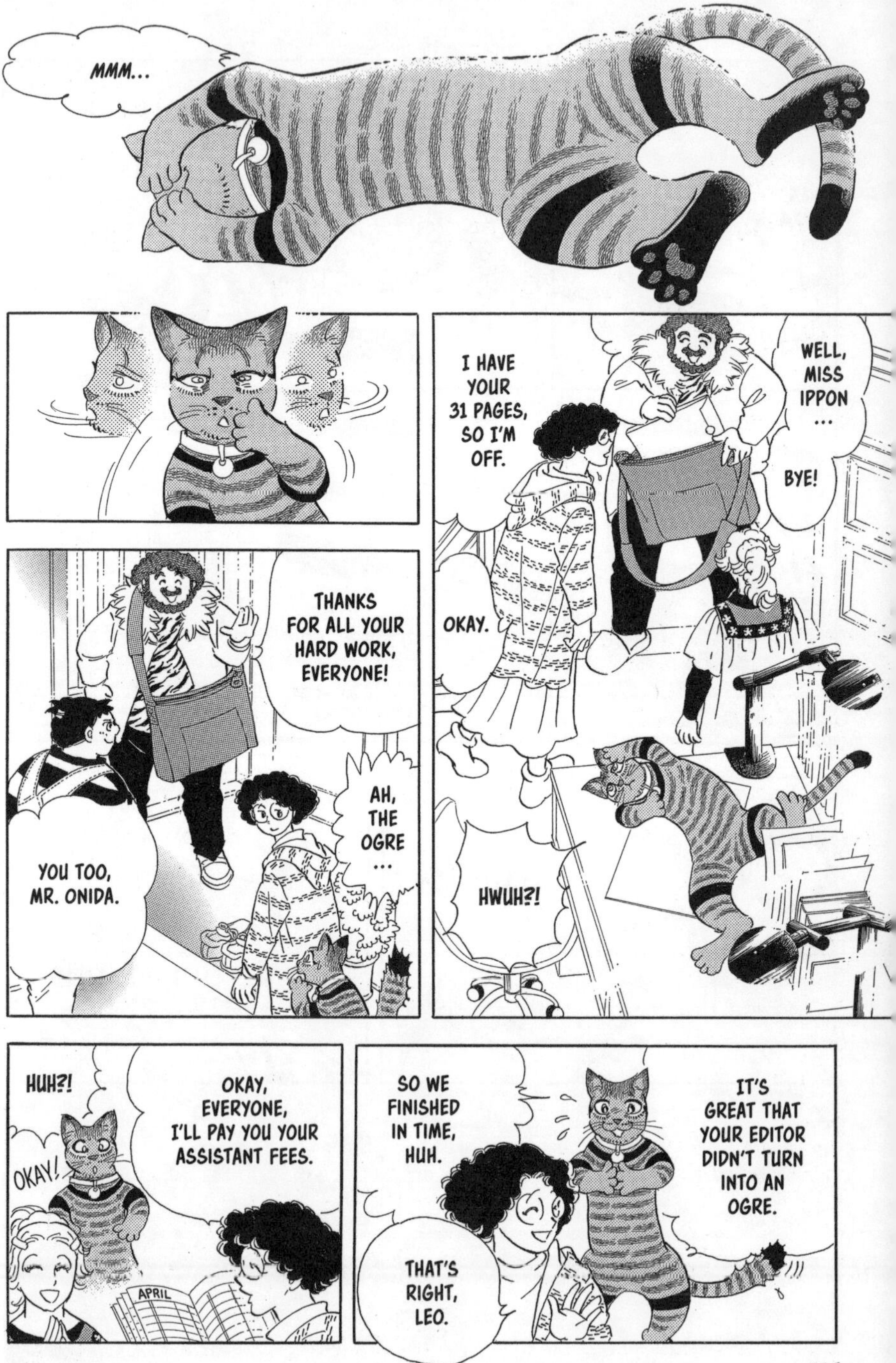
MMM...
WELL, MISS IPPON ...
BYE!
I HAVE YOUR 31 PAGES, SO I'M OFF.
OKAY.
HWUH?!
THANKS FOR ALL YOUR HARD WORK, EVERYONE!
AH, THE OGRE ...
YOU TOO, MR. ONIDA.
IT'S GREAT THAT YOUR EDITOR DIDN'T TURN INTO AN OGRE.
SO WE FINISHED IN TIME, HUH.
THAT'S RIGHT, LEO.
OKAY, EVERYONE, I'LL PAY YOU YOUR ASSISTANT FEES.
HUH?!
OKAY!
APRIL

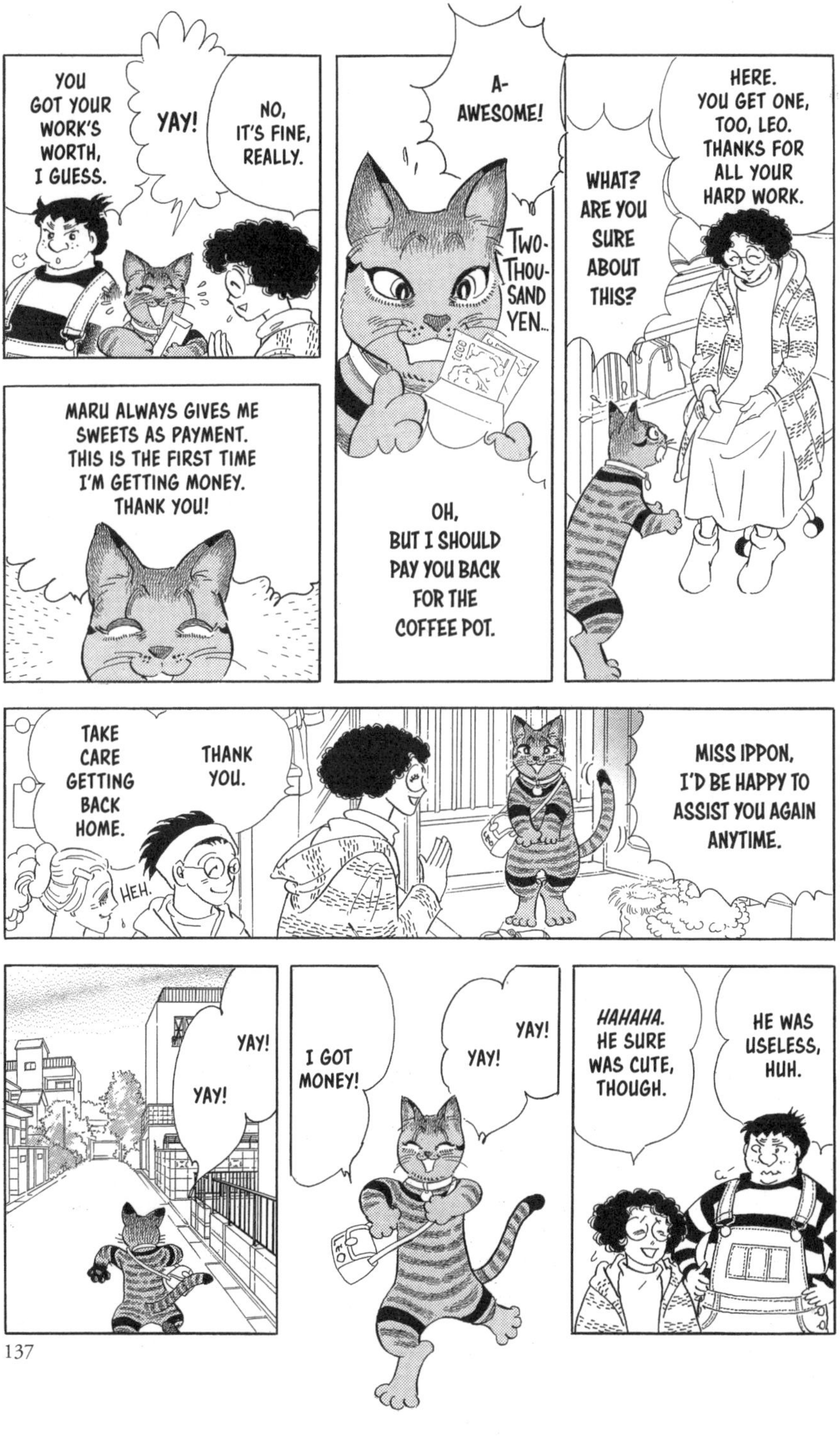
HERE. YOU GET ONE, TOO, LEO. THANKS FOR ALL YOUR HARD WORK.
WHAT? ARE YOU SURE ABOUT THIS?
A- AWESOME!
TWO-THOUSAND YEN...
OH, BUT I SHOULD PAY YOU BACK FOR THE COFFEE POT.
NO, IT'S FINE, REALLY.
YAY!
YOU GOT YOUR WORK'S WORTH, I GUESS.
MARU ALWAYS GIVES ME SWEETS AS PAYMENT. THIS IS THE FIRST TIME I'M GETTING MONEY. THANK YOU!
MISS IPPON, I'D BE HAPPY TO ASSIST YOU AGAIN ANYTIME.
THANK YOU.
TAKE CARE GETTING BACK HOME.
HEH.
HE WAS USELESS, HUH.
HAHAHA. HE SURE WAS CUTE, THOUGH.
YAY!
YAY!
I GOT MONEY!
YAY!
YAY!

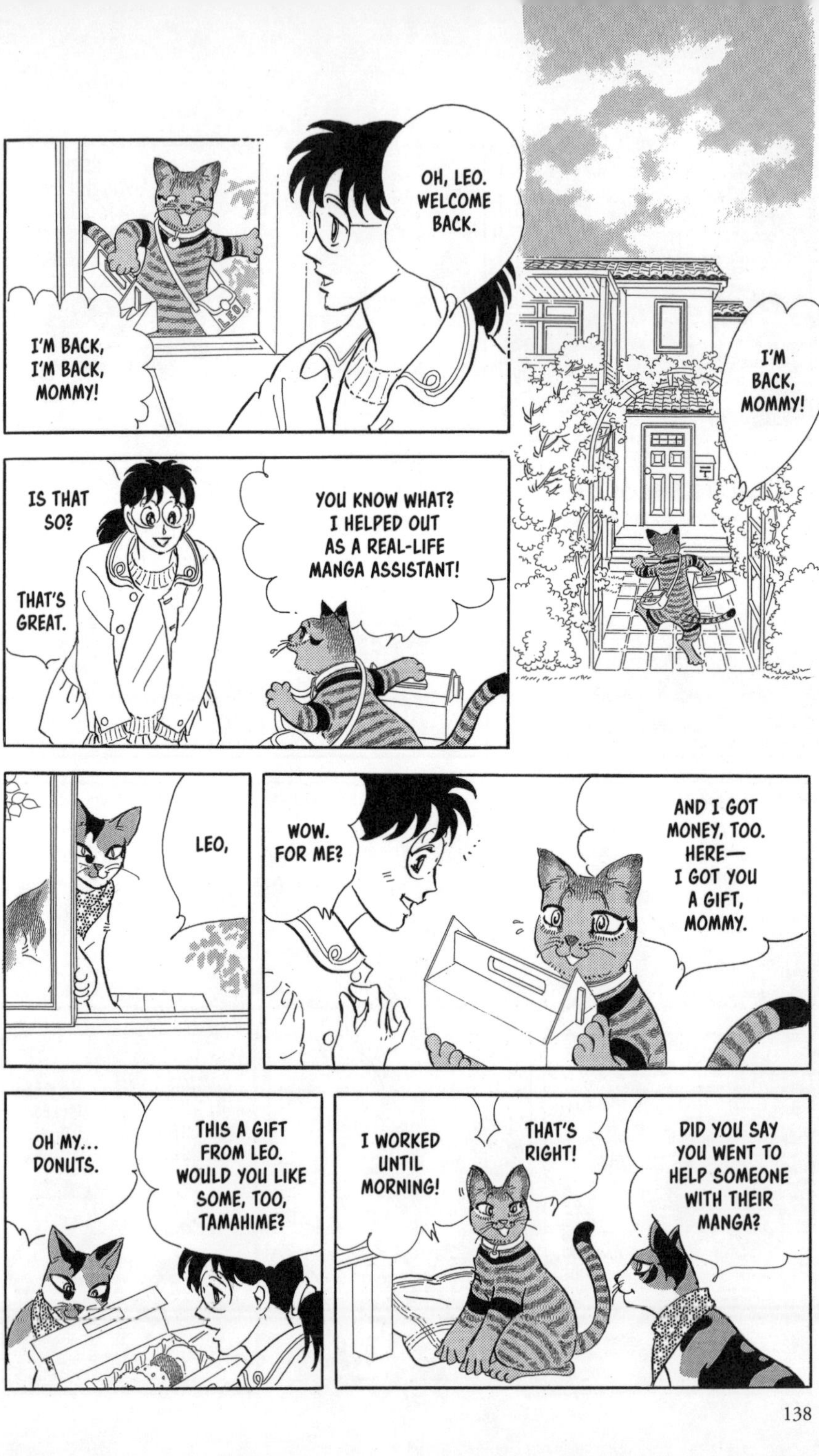
I'M BACK, MOMMY!
OH, LEO. WELCOME BACK.
I'M BACK, I'M BACK, MOMMY!
YOU KNOW WHAT? I HELPED OUT AS A REAL-LIFE MANGA ASSISTANT!
IS THAT SO?
THAT'S GREAT.
AND I GOT MONEY, TOO. HERE— I GOT YOU A GIFT, MOMMY.
WOW. FOR ME?
LEO,
DID YOU SAY YOU WENT TO HELP SOMEONE WITH THEIR MANGA?
THAT'S RIGHT!
I WORKED UNTIL MORNING!
THIS A GIFT FROM LEO. WOULD YOU LIKE SOME, TOO, TAMAHIME?
OH MY... DONUTS.

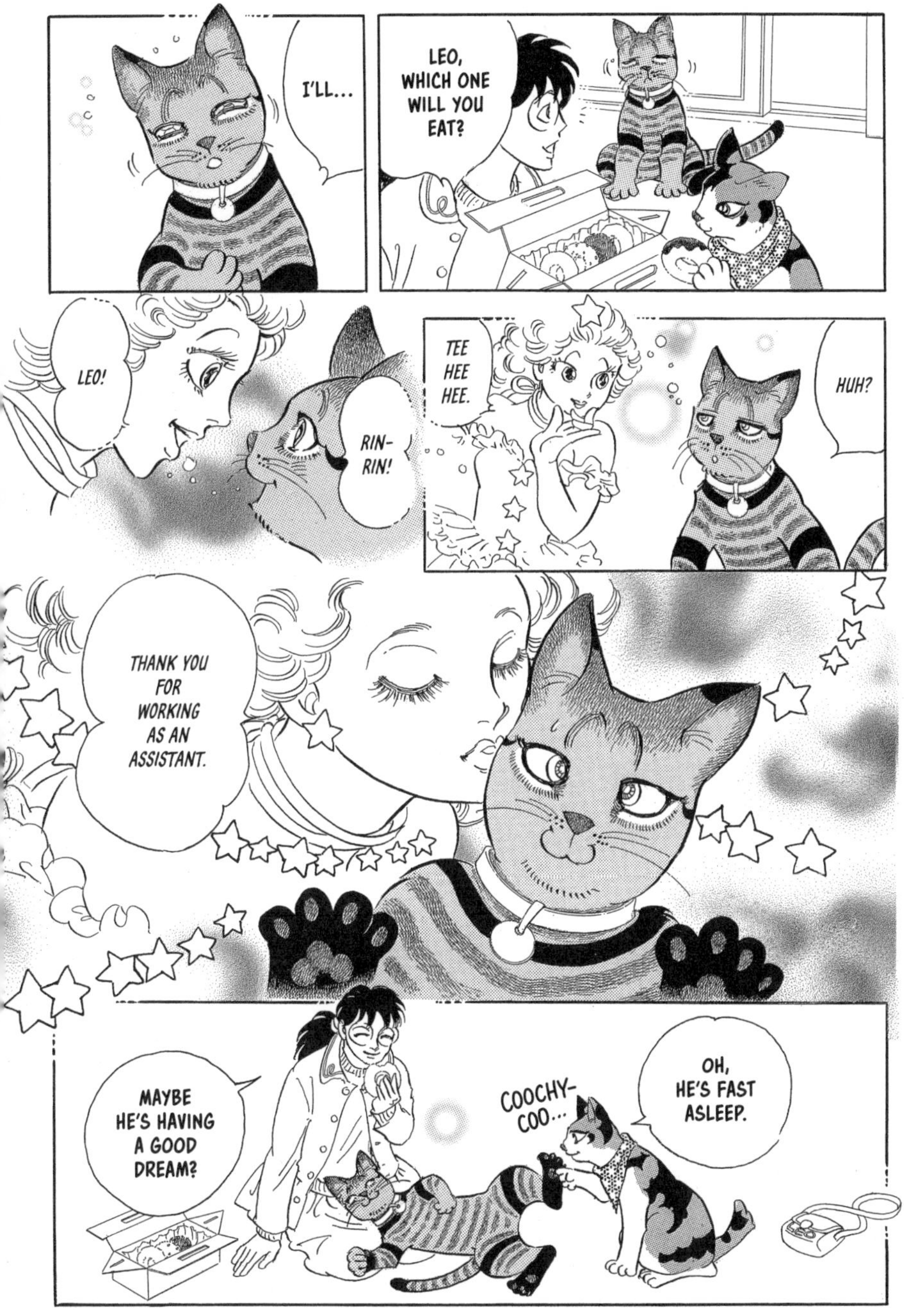
LEO, WHICH ONE WILL YOU EAT?
I'LL...
HUH?
TEE HEE HEE.
LEO!
RIN-RIN!
THANK YOU FOR WORKING AS AN ASSISTANT.
OH, HE'S FAST ASLEEP.
COOCHY-COO...
MAYBE HE'S HAVING A GOOD DREAM?

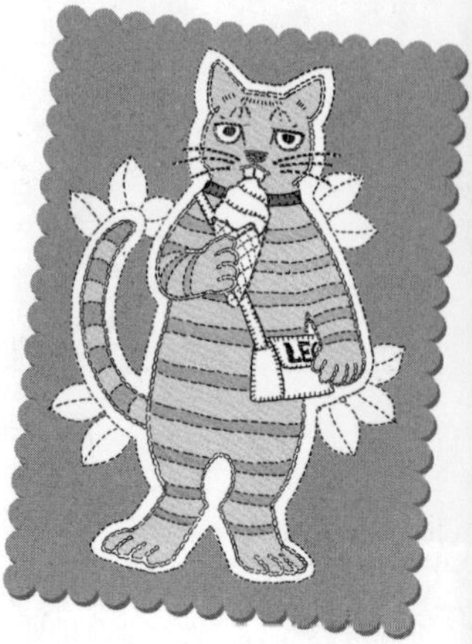

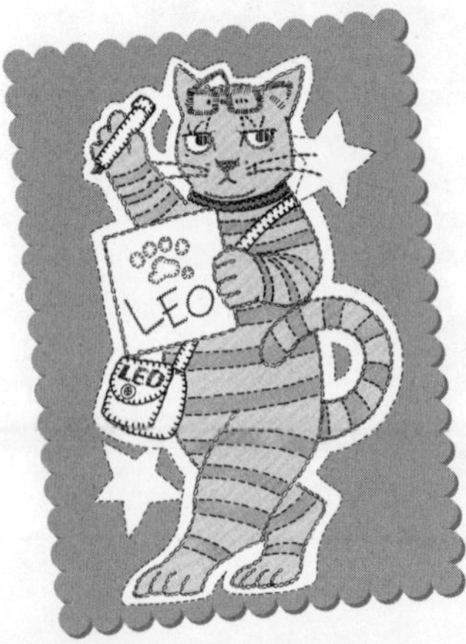
LEO
LEO

6 Lil' Leo's Gourmet Diary

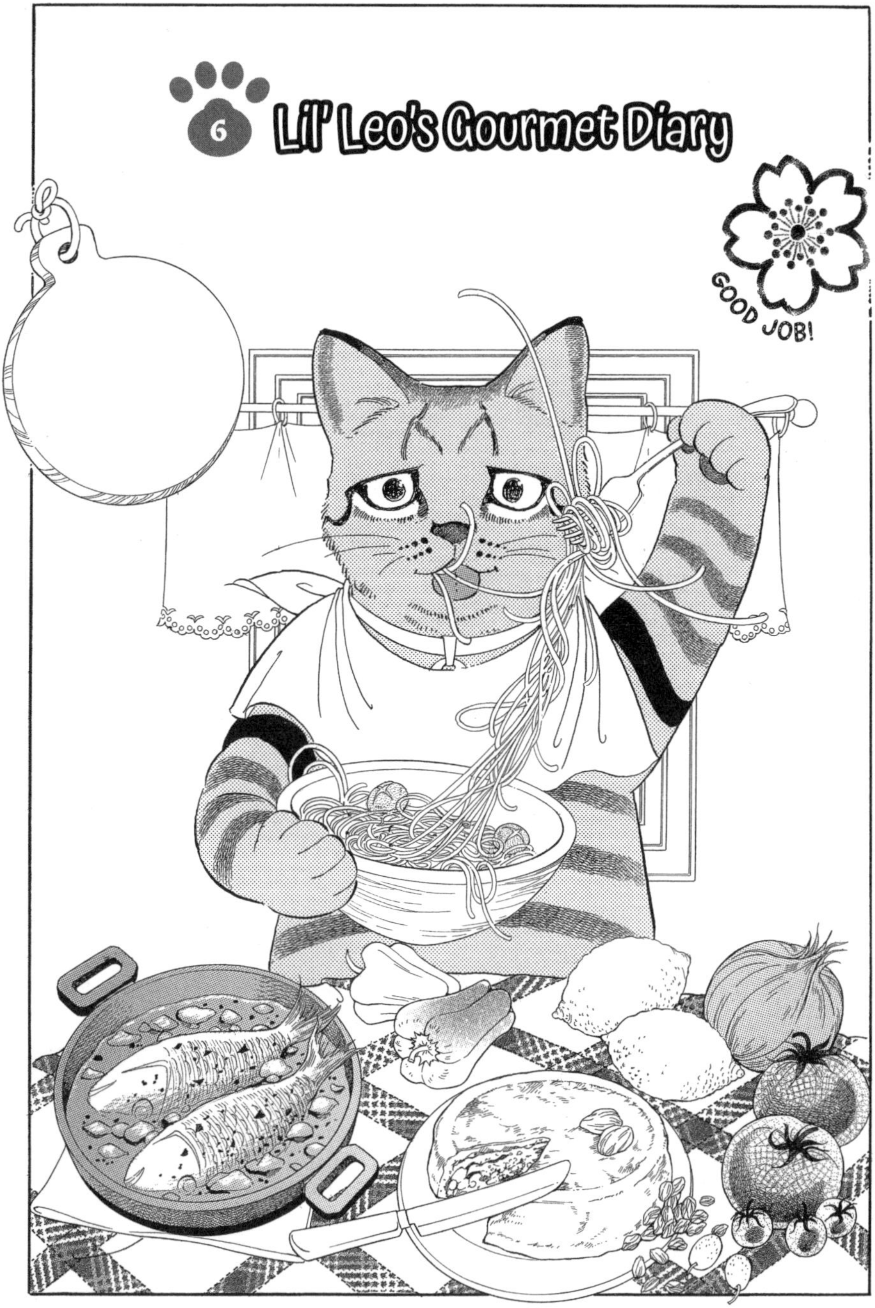
GOOD JOB!

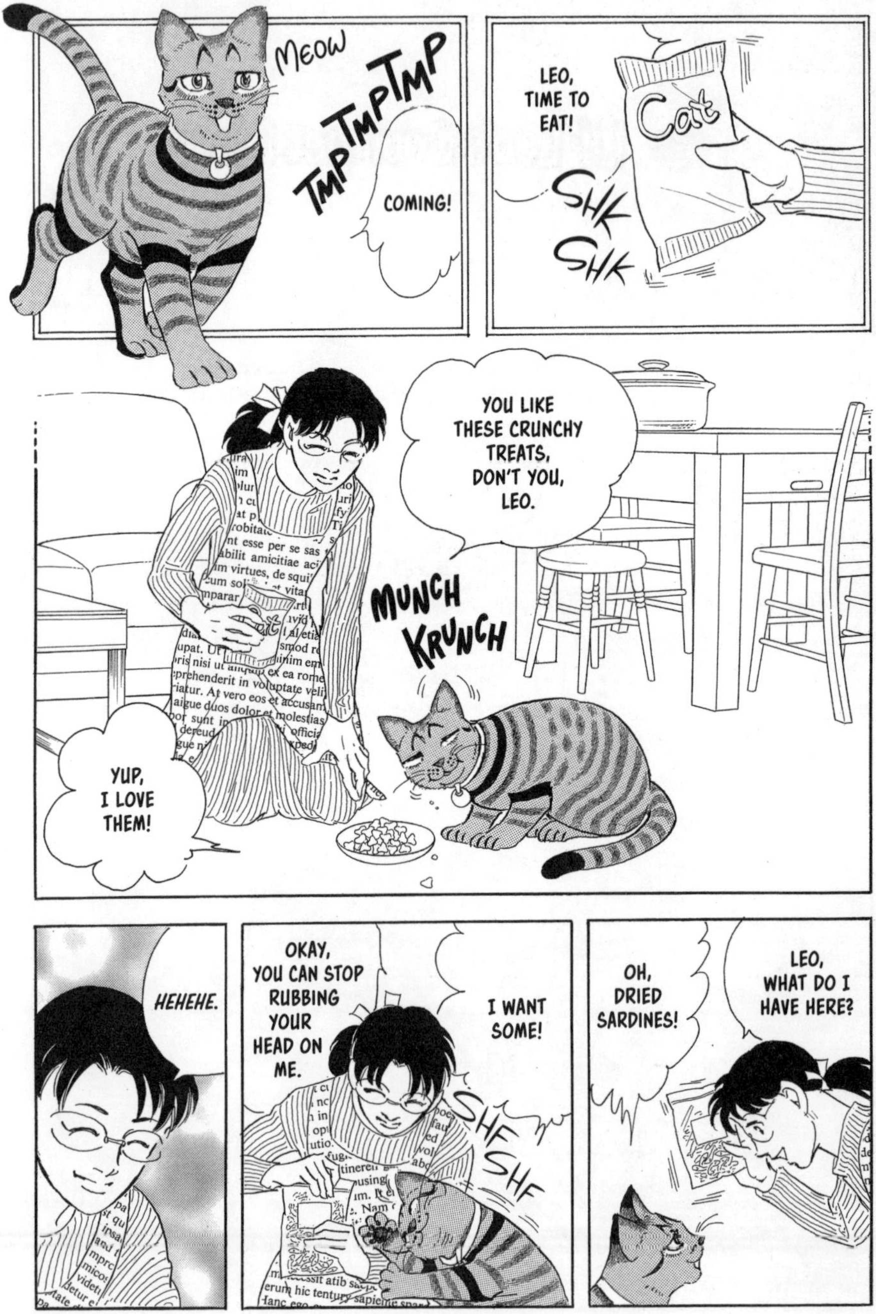
LEO, TIME TO EAT!
SHK SHK
TMPTMPTMP
COMING!
MEOW
YOU LIKE THESE CRUNCHY TREATS, DON'T YOU, LEO.
MUNCH KRUNCH
YUP, I LOVE THEM!
LEO, WHAT DO I HAVE HERE?
OH, DRIED SARDINES!
I WANT SOME!
OKAY, YOU CAN STOP RUBBING YOUR HEAD ON ME.
SHF SHF
HEHEHE.

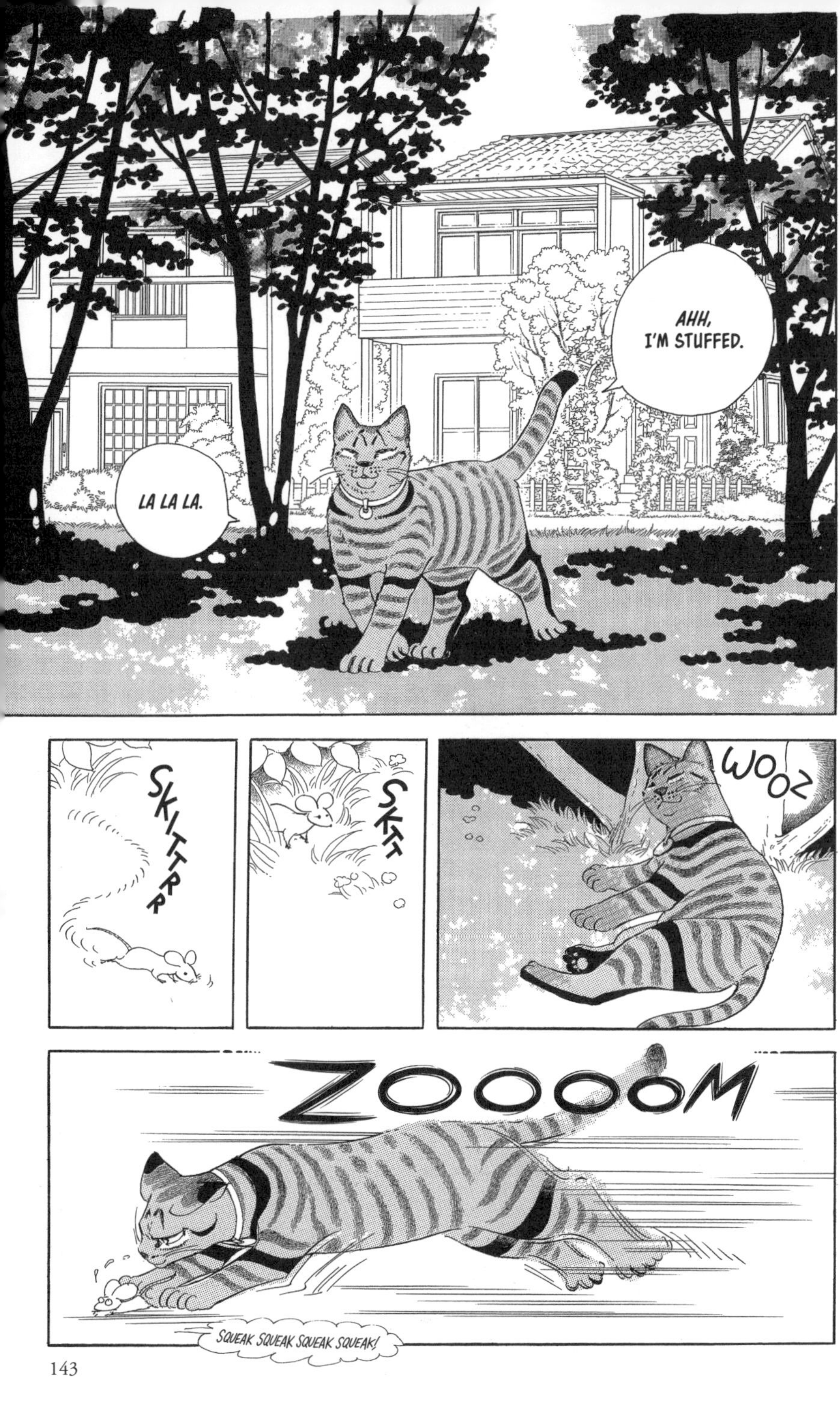
AHH, I'M STUFFED.
LA LA LA.
WOOZ
SKTTT
SKITTRR
ZOOOOM
SQUEAK SQUEAK SQUEAK SQUEAK!

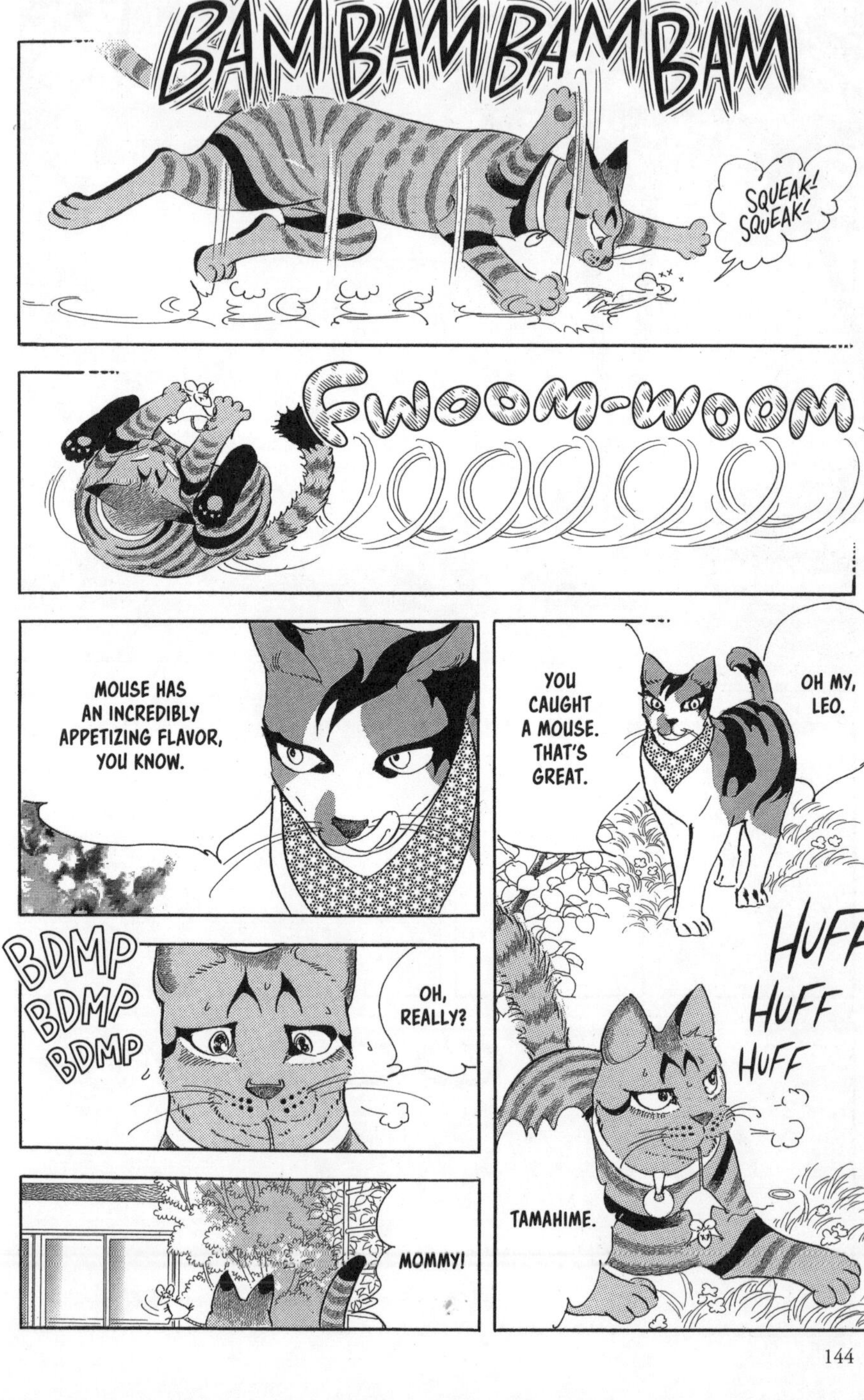
BAM BAM BAM BAM
SQUEAK! SQUEAK!
FWOOM-WOOM
OH MY, LEO.
YOU CAUGHT A MOUSE. THAT'S GREAT.
HUFF HUFF HUFF
TAMAHIME.
MOUSE HAS AN INCREDIBLY APPETIZING FLAVOR, YOU KNOW.
BDMP BDMP BDMP
OH, REALLY?
MOMMY!

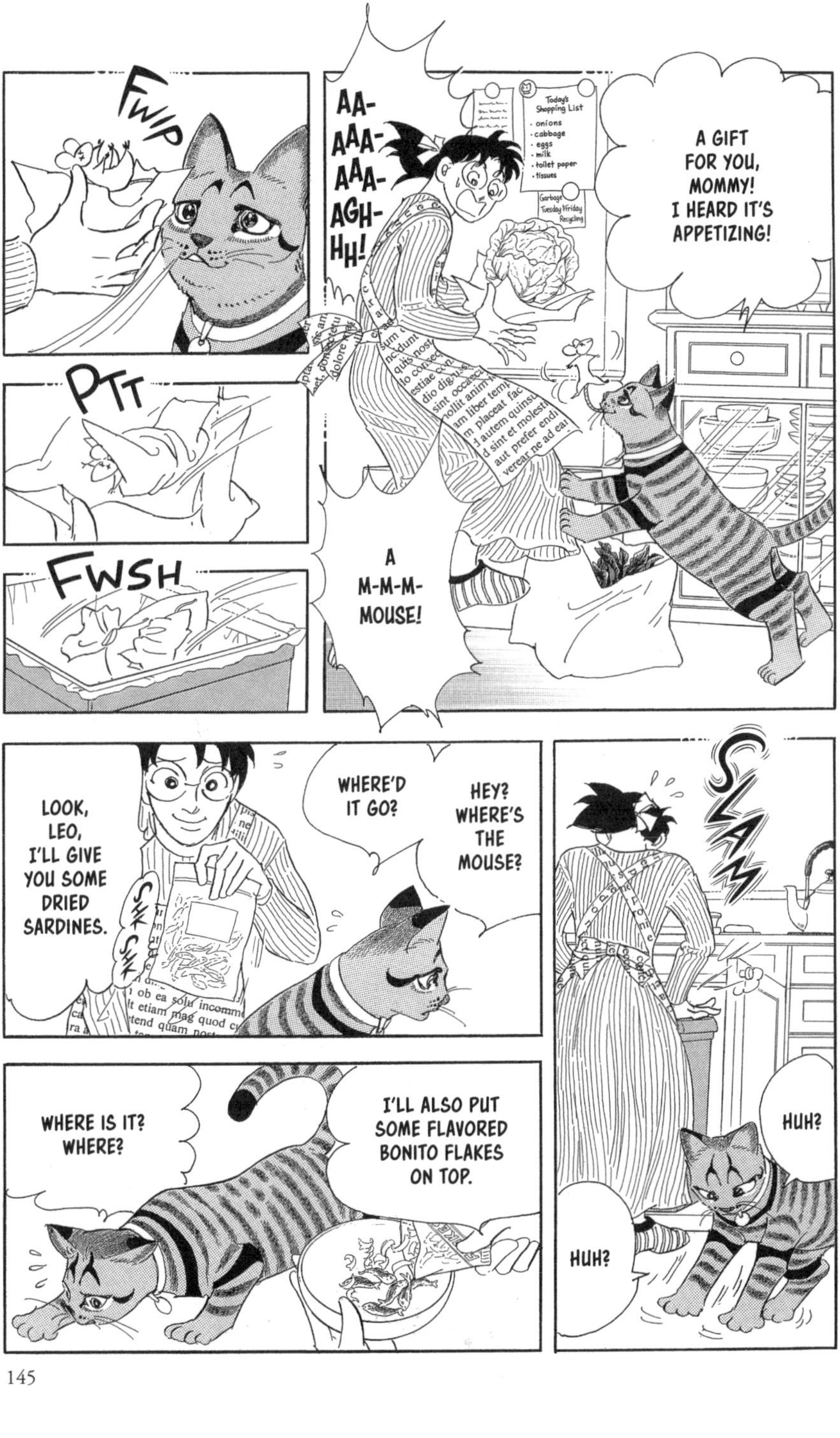
A GIFT FOR YOU, MOMMY! I HEARD IT'S APPETIZING!
Today's Shopping List
· onions
· cabbage
· eggs
· milk
· toilet paper
· tissues
Garbage Tuesday Friday Recycling
AA-AAA-AAA-AGH-HH!
A M-M-M-MOUSE!
FWIP
PTT
FWSH
SLAM
HUH?
HUH?
HEY? WHERE'S THE MOUSE?
WHERE'D IT GO?
SHK SHK
LOOK, LEO, I'LL GIVE YOU SOME DRIED SARDINES.
I'LL ALSO PUT SOME FLAVORED BONITO FLAKES ON TOP.
WHERE IS IT? WHERE?

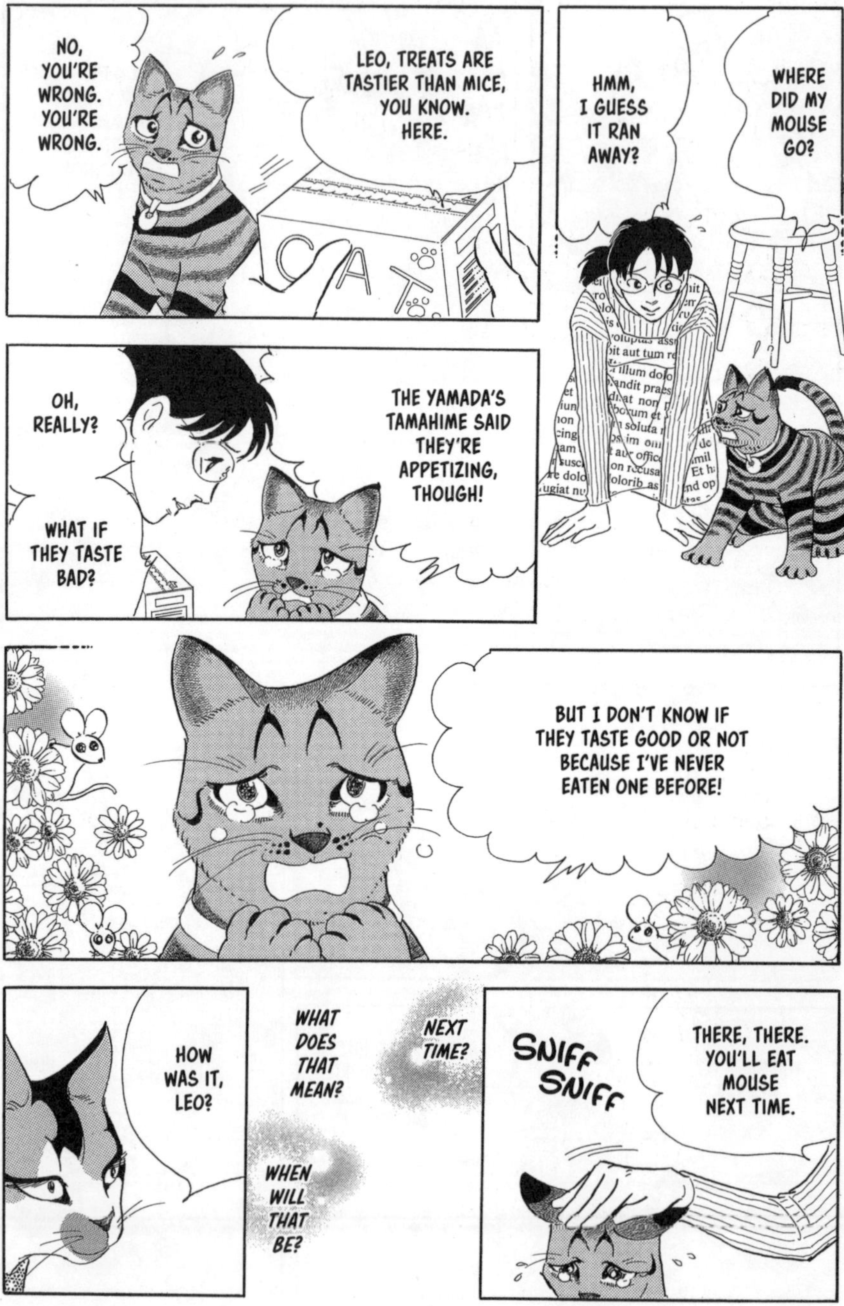
WHERE DID MY MOUSE GO?
HMM, I GUESS IT RAN AWAY?
LEO, TREATS ARE TASTIER THAN MICE, YOU KNOW. HERE.
CAT
NO, YOU'RE WRONG. YOU'RE WRONG.
THE YAMADA'S TAMAHIME SAID THEY'RE APPETIZING, THOUGH!
OH, REALLY?
WHAT IF THEY TASTE BAD?
BUT I DON'T KNOW IF THEY TASTE GOOD OR NOT BECAUSE I'VE NEVER EATEN ONE BEFORE!
THERE, THERE. YOU'LL EAT MOUSE NEXT TIME.
SNIFF SNIFF
NEXT TIME?
WHAT DOES THAT MEAN?
WHEN WILL THAT BE?
HOW WAS IT, LEO?

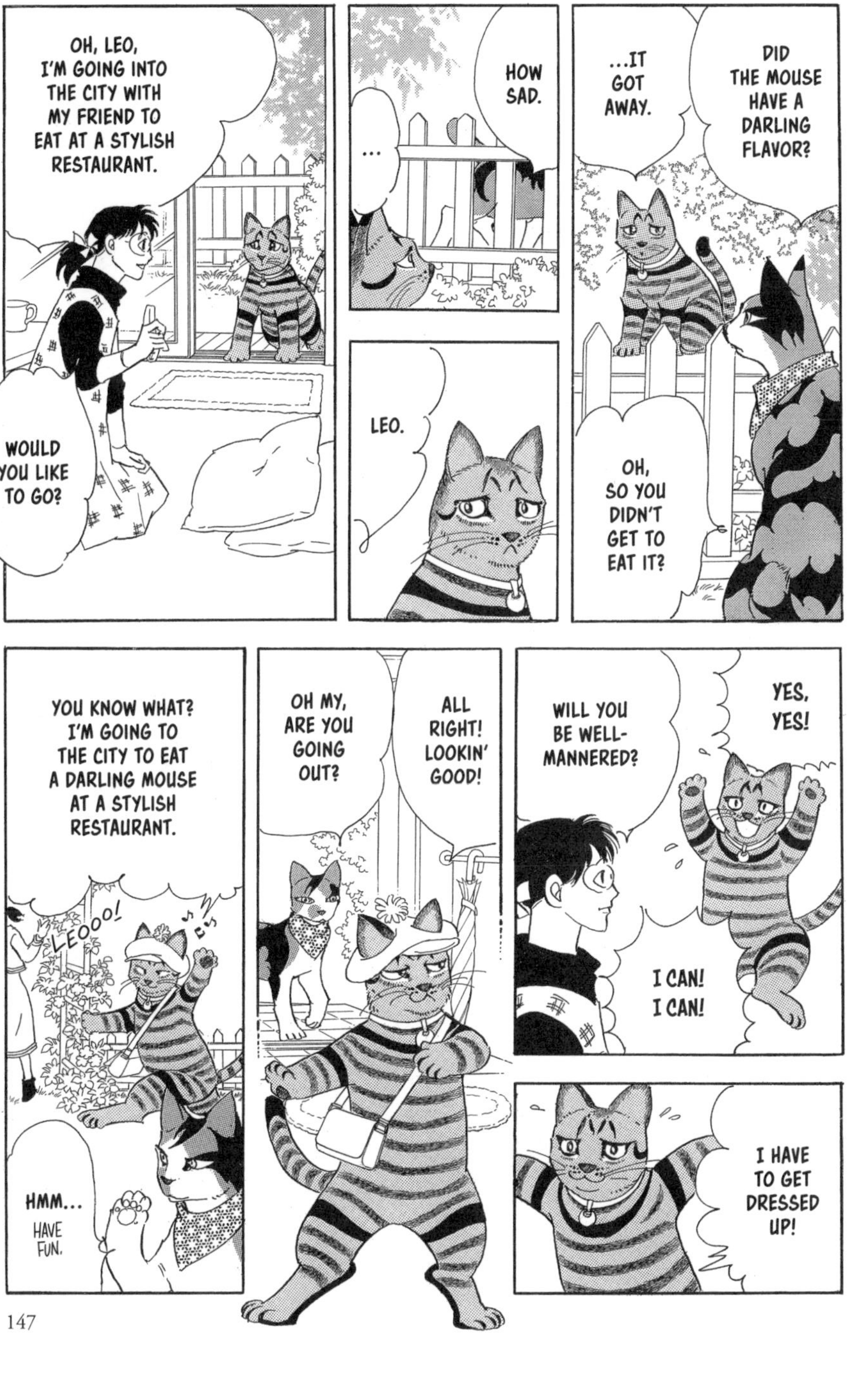

DID THE MOUSE HAVE A DARLING FLAVOR?
...IT GOT AWAY.
OH, SO YOU DIDN'T GET TO EAT IT?
HOW SAD.
...
LEO.
OH, LEO, I'M GOING INTO THE CITY WITH MY FRIEND TO EAT AT A STYLISH RESTAURANT.
WOULD YOU LIKE TO GO?
YES, YES!
WILL YOU BE WELL-MANNERED?
I CAN! I CAN!
I HAVE TO GET DRESSED UP!
ALL RIGHT! LOOKIN' GOOD!
OH MY, ARE YOU GOING OUT?
YOU KNOW WHAT? I'M GOING TO THE CITY TO EAT A DARLING MOUSE AT A STYLISH RESTAURANT.
LEOOO!
HMM... HAVE FUN.

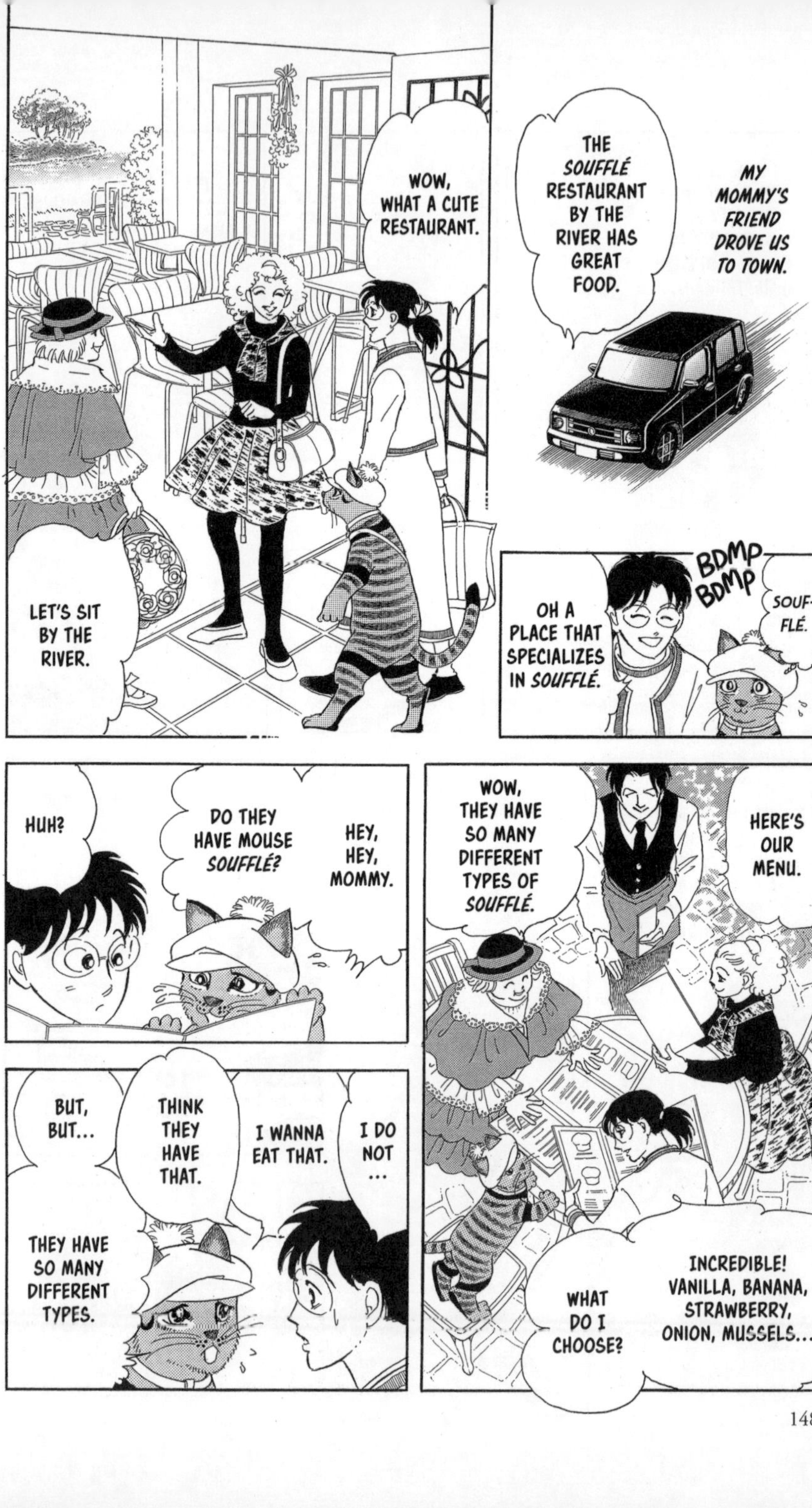
MY MOMMY'S FRIEND DROVE US TO TOWN.
THE *SOUFFLÉ* RESTAURANT BY THE RIVER HAS GREAT FOOD.
BDMP BDMP
SOUF-FLÉ.
OH A PLACE THAT SPECIALIZES IN *SOUFFLÉ*.
WOW, WHAT A CUTE RESTAURANT.
LET'S SIT BY THE RIVER.
HERE'S OUR MENU.
WOW, THEY HAVE SO MANY DIFFERENT TYPES OF *SOUFFLÉ*.
INCREDIBLE! VANILLA, BANANA, STRAWBERRY, ONION, MUSSELS...
WHAT DO I CHOOSE?
HEY, HEY, MOMMY.
DO THEY HAVE MOUSE *SOUFFLÉ*?
HUH?
I DO NOT ...
I WANNA EAT THAT.
THINK THEY HAVE THAT.
BUT, BUT...
THEY HAVE SO MANY DIFFERENT TYPES.

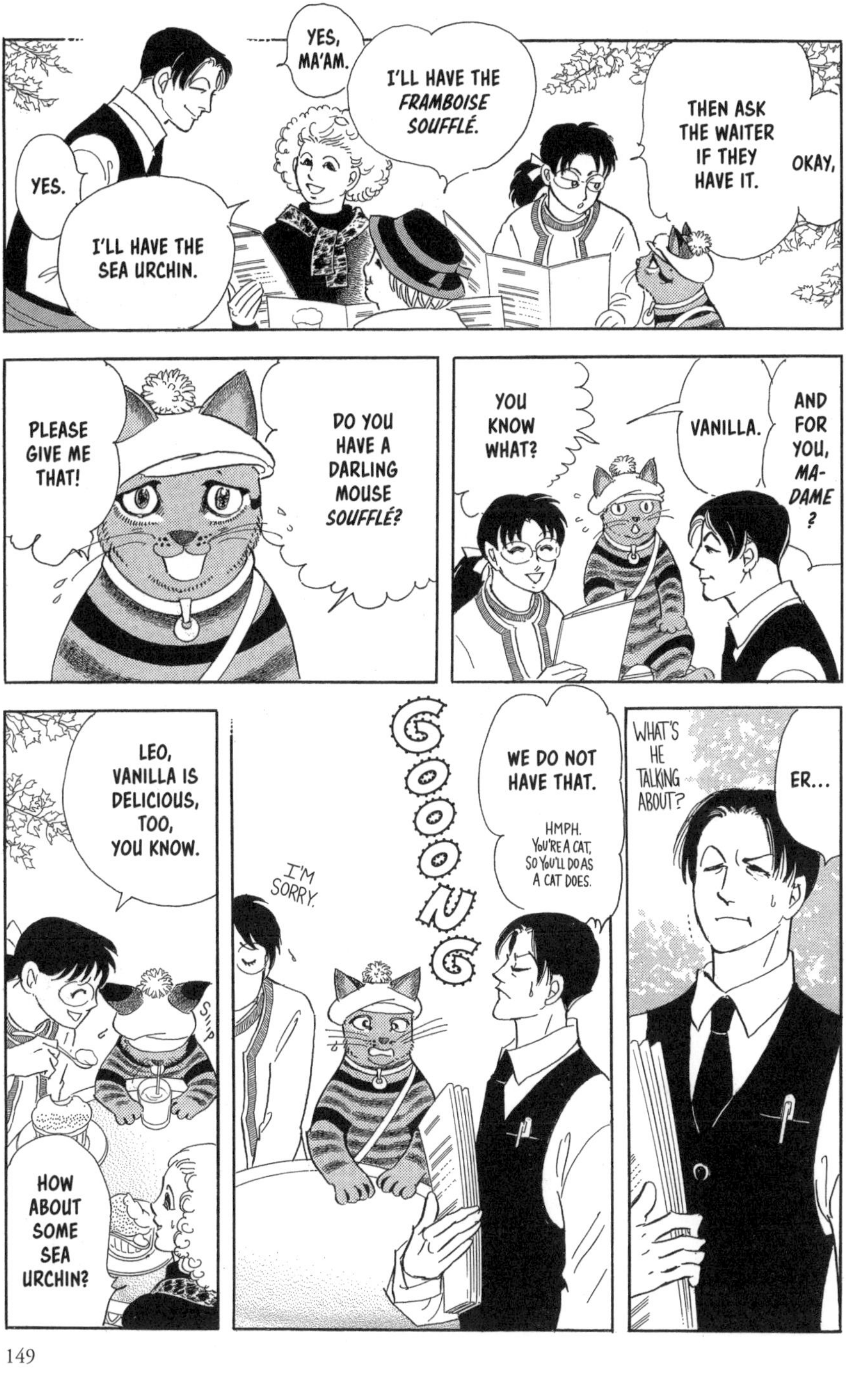
OKAY,
THEN ASK THE WAITER IF THEY HAVE IT.
I'LL HAVE THE *FRAMBOISE SOUFFLÉ.*
YES, MA'AM.
YES.
I'LL HAVE THE SEA URCHIN.
AND FOR YOU, *MADAME*?
VANILLA.
YOU KNOW WHAT?
DO YOU HAVE A DARLING MOUSE *SOUFFLÉ?*
PLEASE GIVE ME THAT!
ER...
WHAT'S HE TALKING ABOUT?
WE DO NOT HAVE THAT.
HMPH. YOU'RE A CAT, SO YOU'LL DO AS A CAT DOES.
GOOOONG
I'M SORRY.
LEO, VANILLA IS DELICIOUS, TOO, YOU KNOW.
HOW ABOUT SOME SEA URCHIN?

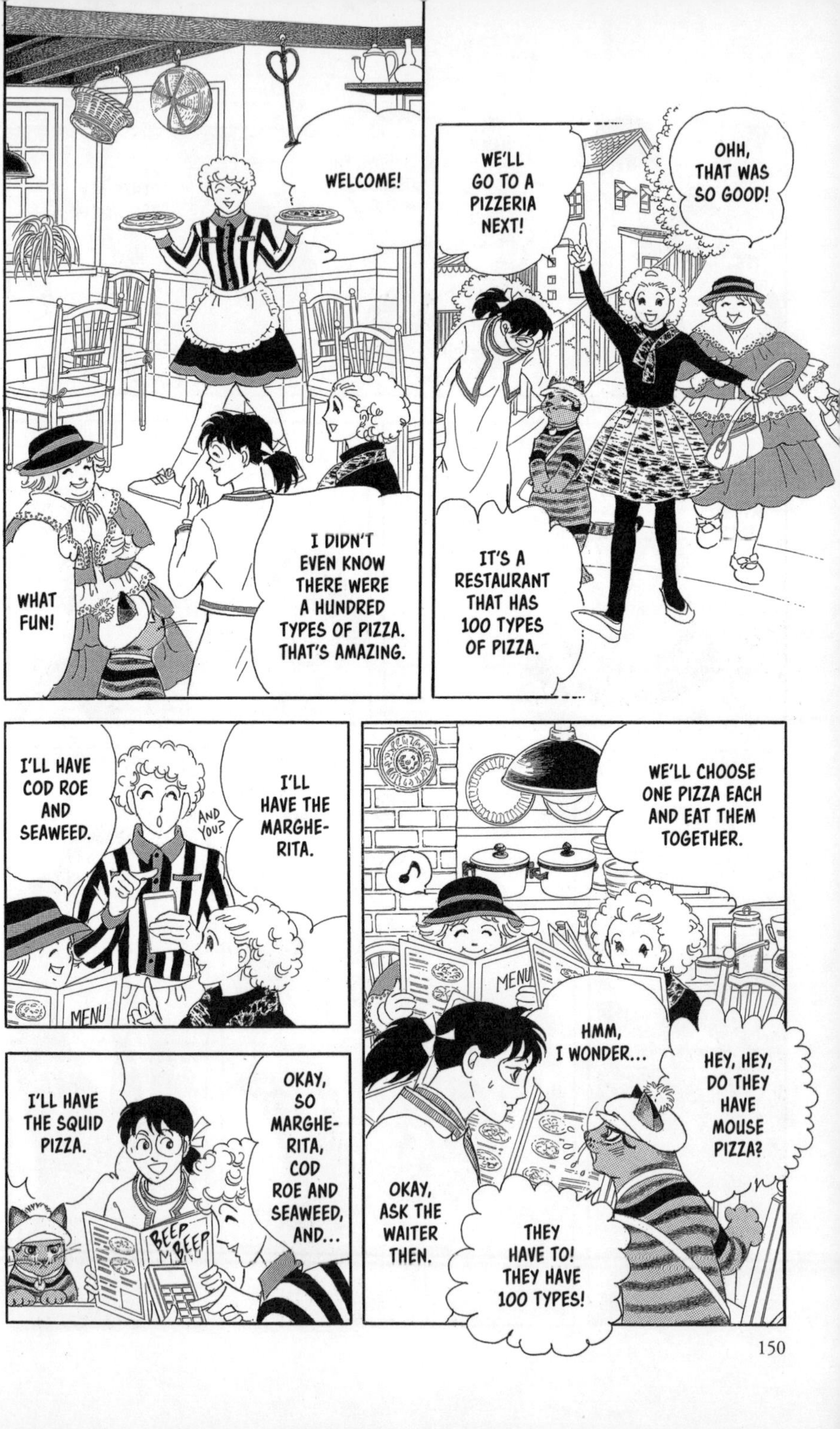
OHH, THAT WAS SO GOOD!
WE'LL GO TO A PIZZERIA NEXT!
IT'S A RESTAURANT THAT HAS 100 TYPES OF PIZZA.
WELCOME!
I DIDN'T EVEN KNOW THERE WERE A HUNDRED TYPES OF PIZZA. THAT'S AMAZING.
WHAT FUN!
WE'LL CHOOSE ONE PIZZA EACH AND EAT THEM TOGETHER.
HEY, HEY, DO THEY HAVE MOUSE PIZZA?
HMM, I WONDER...
THEY HAVE TO! THEY HAVE 100 TYPES!
OKAY, ASK THE WAITER THEN.
MENU
MENU
I'LL HAVE THE MARGHE-RITA.
AND YOU?
I'LL HAVE COD ROE AND SEAWEED.
MENU
OKAY, SO MARGHE-RITA, COD ROE AND SEAWEED, AND...
BEEP BEEP
I'LL HAVE THE SQUID PIZZA.

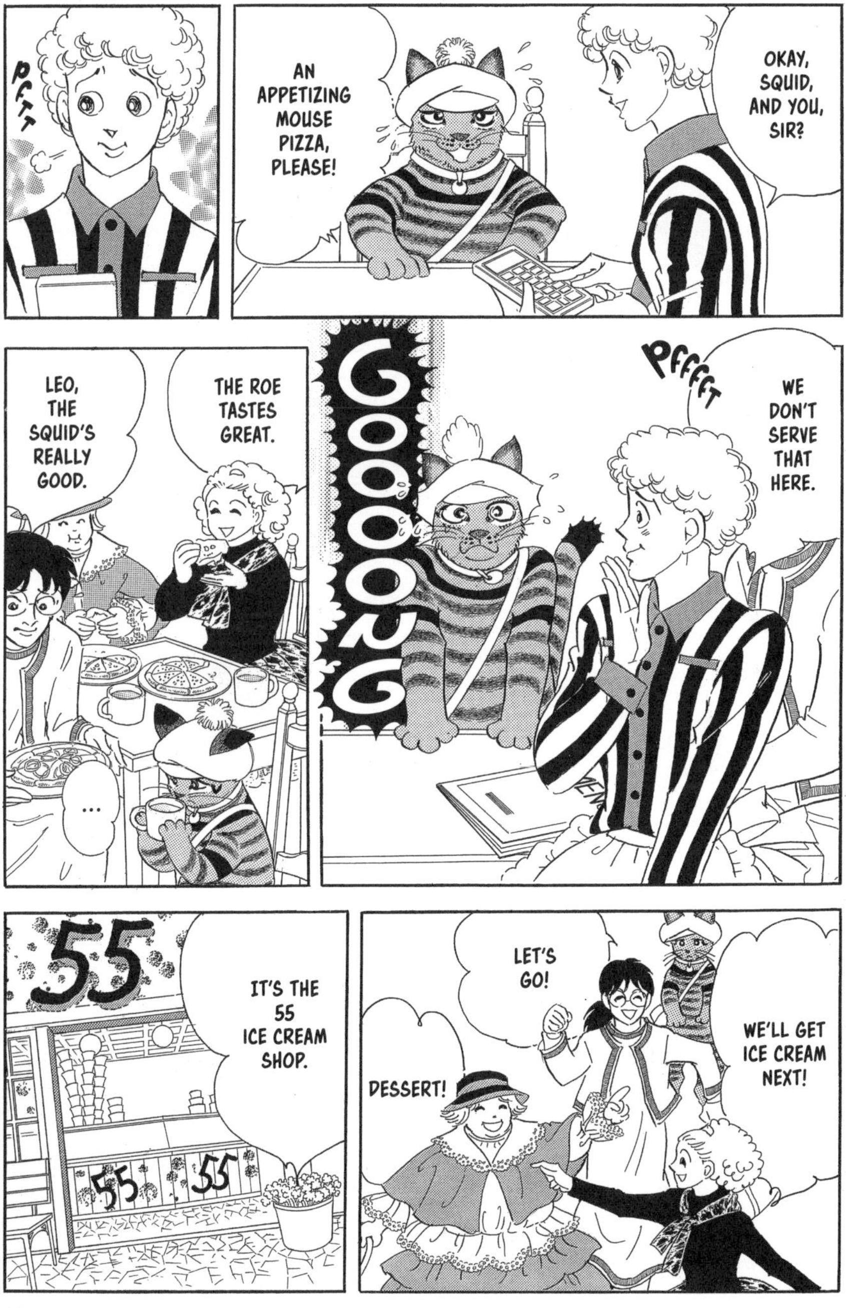
OKAY, SQUID, AND YOU, SIR?
AN APPETIZING MOUSE PIZZA, PLEASE!
PFTT
PFFFFT
WE DON'T SERVE THAT HERE.
GOOOOONG
THE ROE TASTES GREAT.
LEO, THE SQUID'S REALLY GOOD.
...
WE'LL GET ICE CREAM NEXT!
LET'S GO!
DESSERT!
55
IT'S THE 55 ICE CREAM SHOP.
55
55

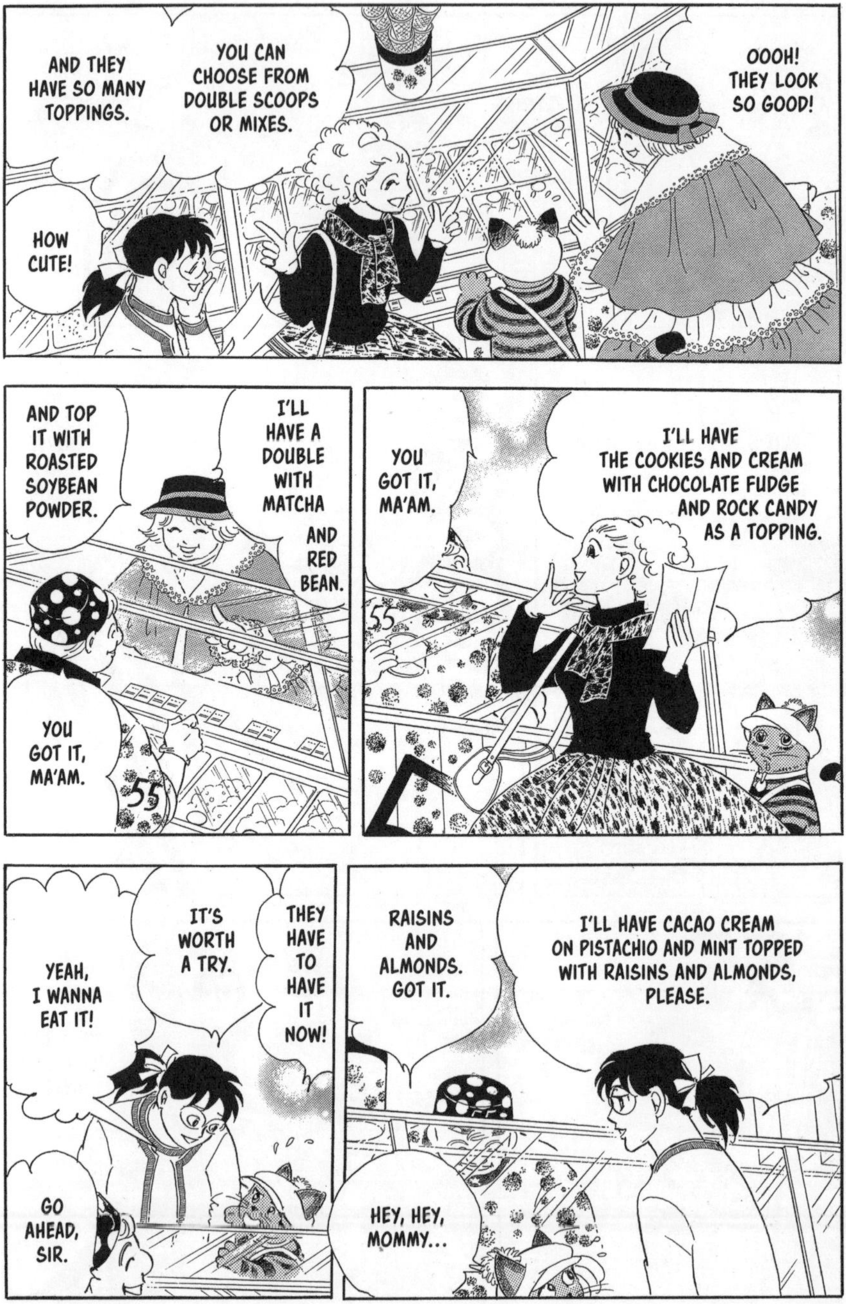
OOOH! THEY LOOK SO GOOD!
YOU CAN CHOOSE FROM DOUBLE SCOOPS OR MIXES.
AND THEY HAVE SO MANY TOPPINGS.
HOW CUTE!
I'LL HAVE THE COOKIES AND CREAM WITH CHOCOLATE FUDGE AND ROCK CANDY AS A TOPPING.
YOU GOT IT, MA'AM.
I'LL HAVE A DOUBLE WITH MATCHA
AND RED BEAN.
AND TOP IT WITH ROASTED SOYBEAN POWDER.
YOU GOT IT, MA'AM.
I'LL HAVE CACAO CREAM ON PISTACHIO AND MINT TOPPED WITH RAISINS AND ALMONDS, PLEASE.
RAISINS AND ALMONDS. GOT IT.
HEY, HEY, MOMMY...
THEY HAVE TO HAVE IT NOW!
IT'S WORTH A TRY.
YEAH, I WANNA EAT IT!
GO AHEAD, SIR.

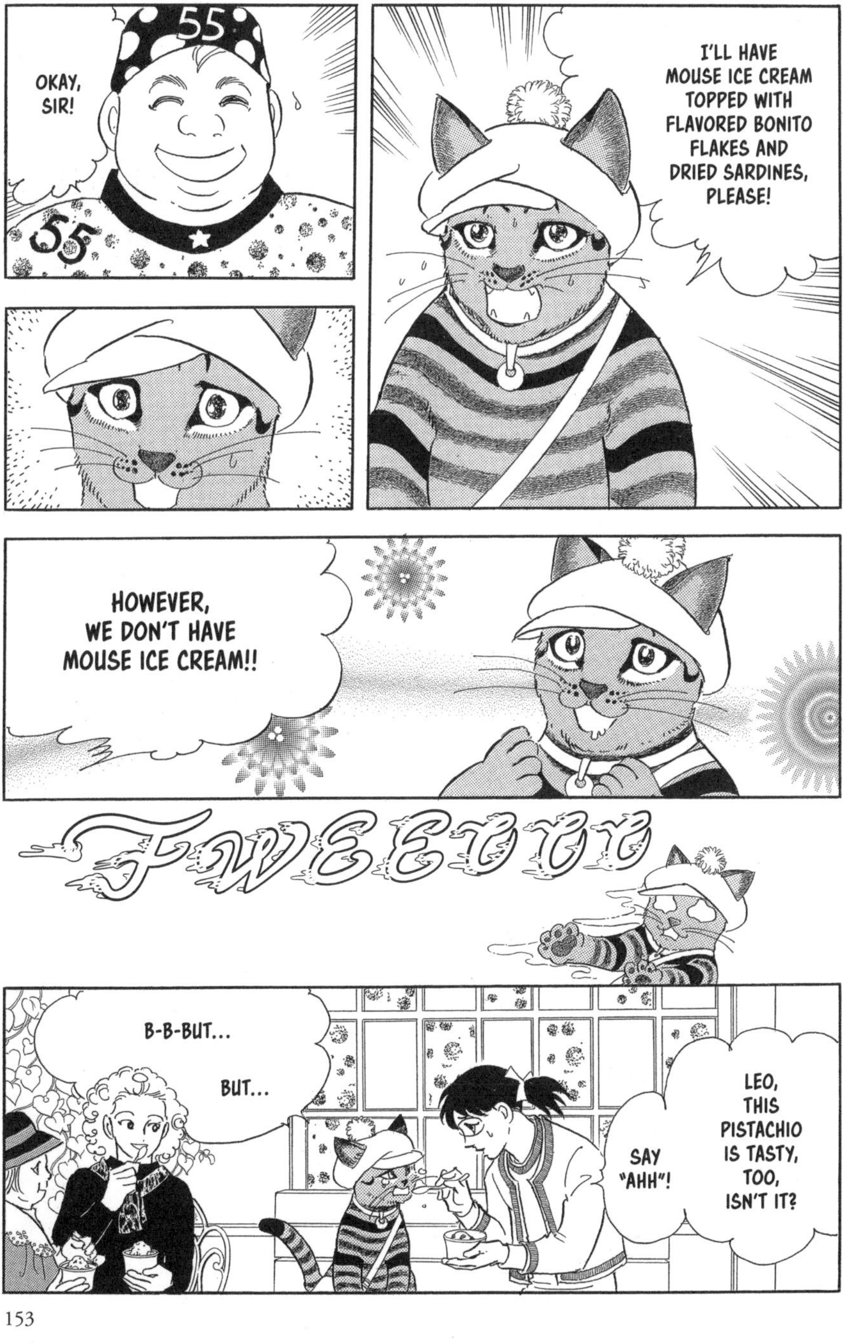
I'LL HAVE MOUSE ICE CREAM TOPPED WITH FLAVORED BONITO FLAKES AND DRIED SARDINES, PLEASE!
OKAY, SIR!
HOWEVER, WE DON'T HAVE MOUSE ICE CREAM!!
FWEEUUU
LEO, THIS PISTACHIO IS TASTY, TOO, ISN'T IT?
SAY "AHH"!
B-B-BUT...
BUT...

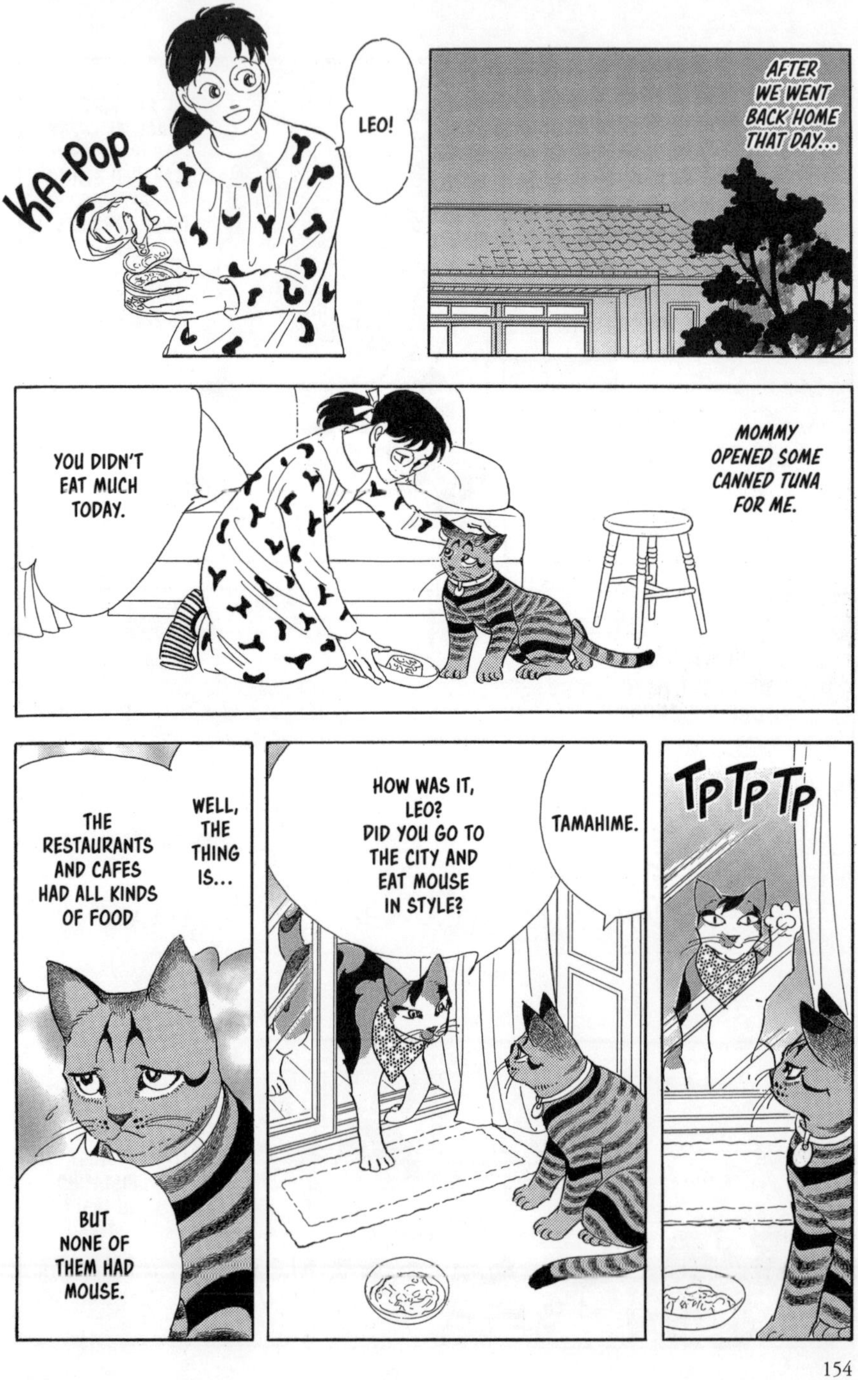
AFTER WE WENT BACK HOME THAT DAY...
KA-POP
LEO!
MOMMY OPENED SOME CANNED TUNA FOR ME.
YOU DIDN'T EAT MUCH TODAY.
TP TP TP
TAMAHIME.
HOW WAS IT, LEO? DID YOU GO TO THE CITY AND EAT MOUSE IN STYLE?
WELL, THE THING IS...
THE RESTAURANTS AND CAFES HAD ALL KINDS OF FOOD
BUT NONE OF THEM HAD MOUSE.

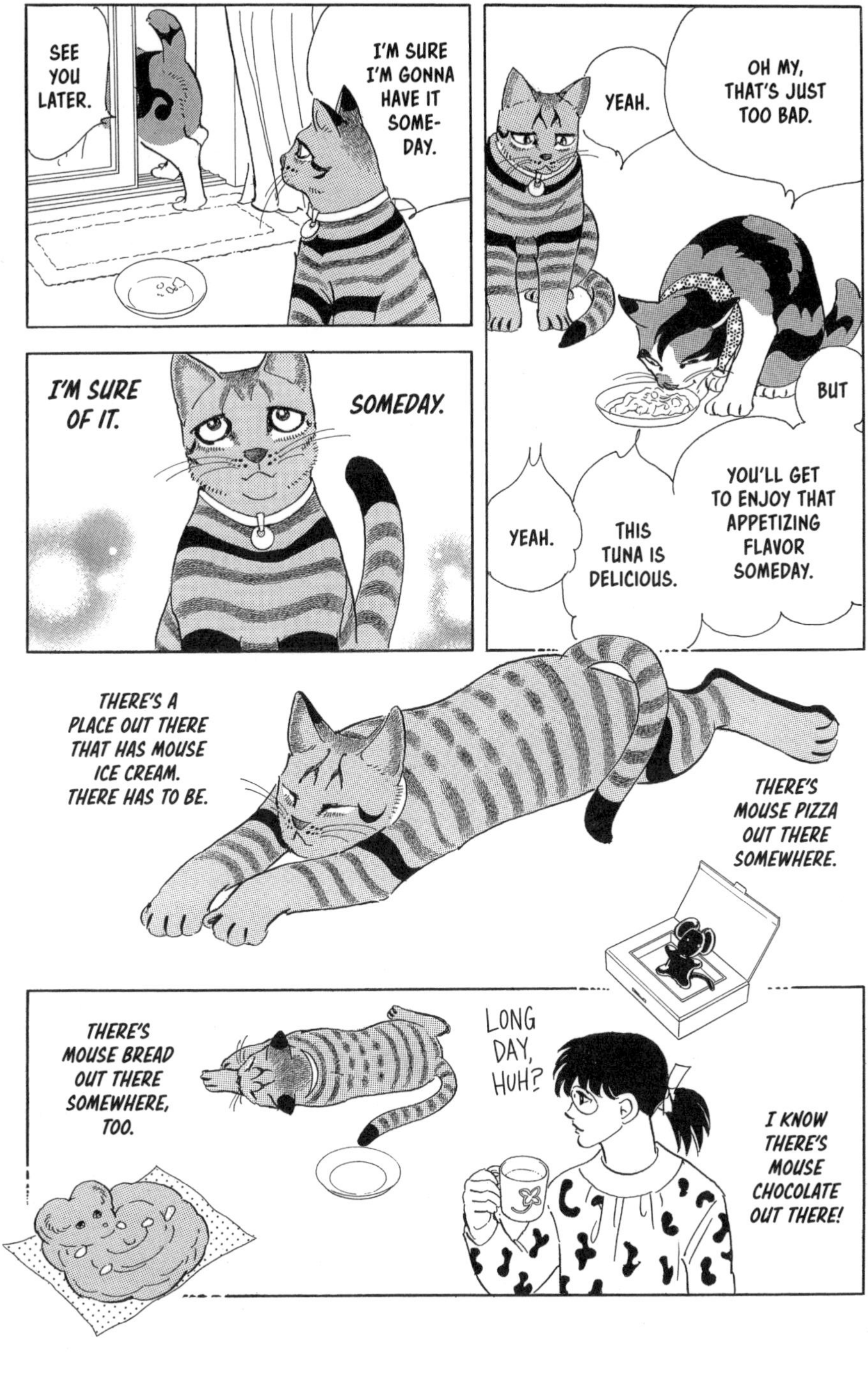
OH MY, THAT'S JUST TOO BAD.
YEAH.
BUT
YOU'LL GET TO ENJOY THAT APPETIZING FLAVOR SOMEDAY.
THIS TUNA IS DELICIOUS.
YEAH.
I'M SURE I'M GONNA HAVE IT SOME-DAY.
SEE YOU LATER.
SOMEDAY.
I'M SURE OF IT.
THERE'S MOUSE PIZZA OUT THERE SOMEWHERE.
THERE'S A PLACE OUT THERE THAT HAS MOUSE ICE CREAM. THERE HAS TO BE.
I KNOW THERE'S MOUSE CHOCOLATE OUT THERE!
LONG DAY, HUH?
THERE'S MOUSE BREAD OUT THERE SOMEWHERE, TOO.

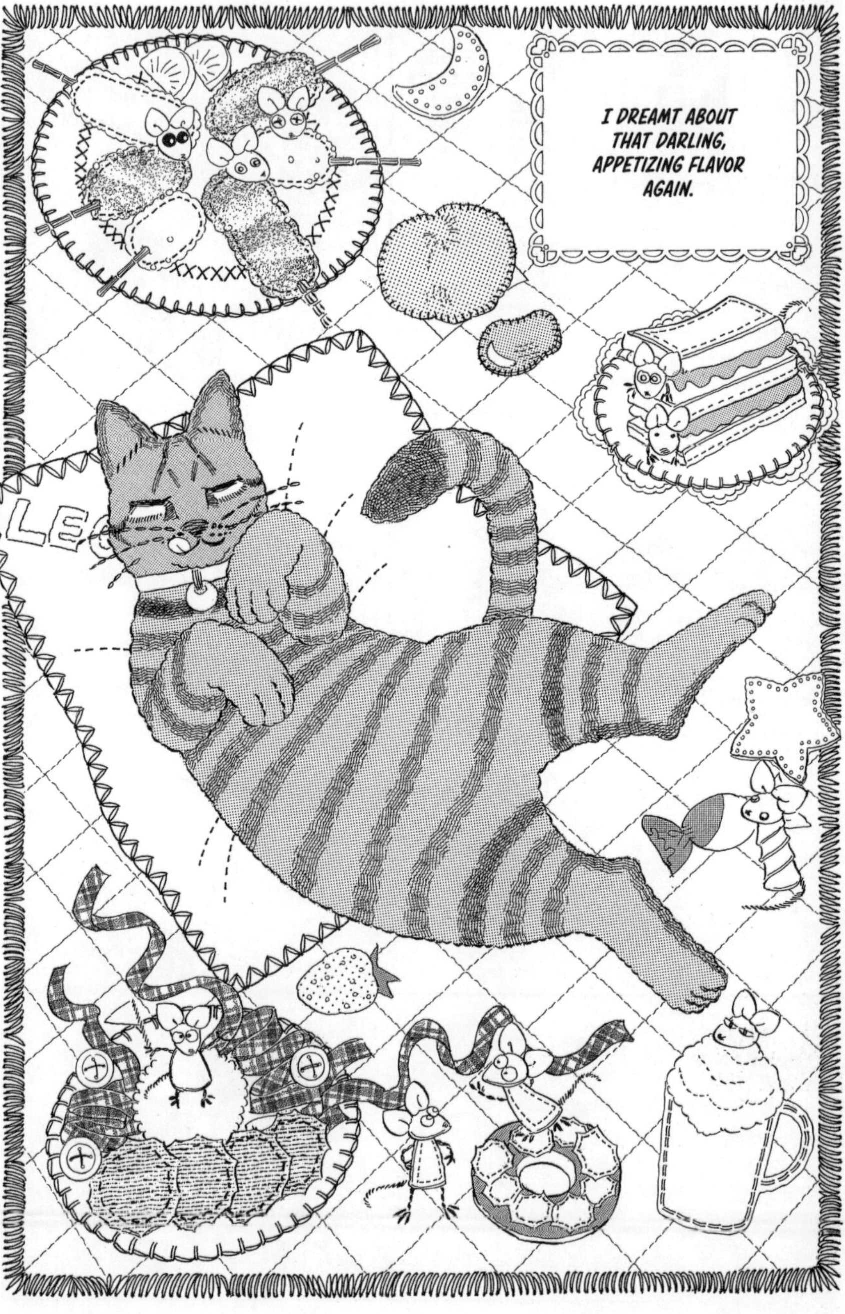
I DREAMT ABOUT THAT DARLING, APPETIZING FLAVOR AGAIN.
LE

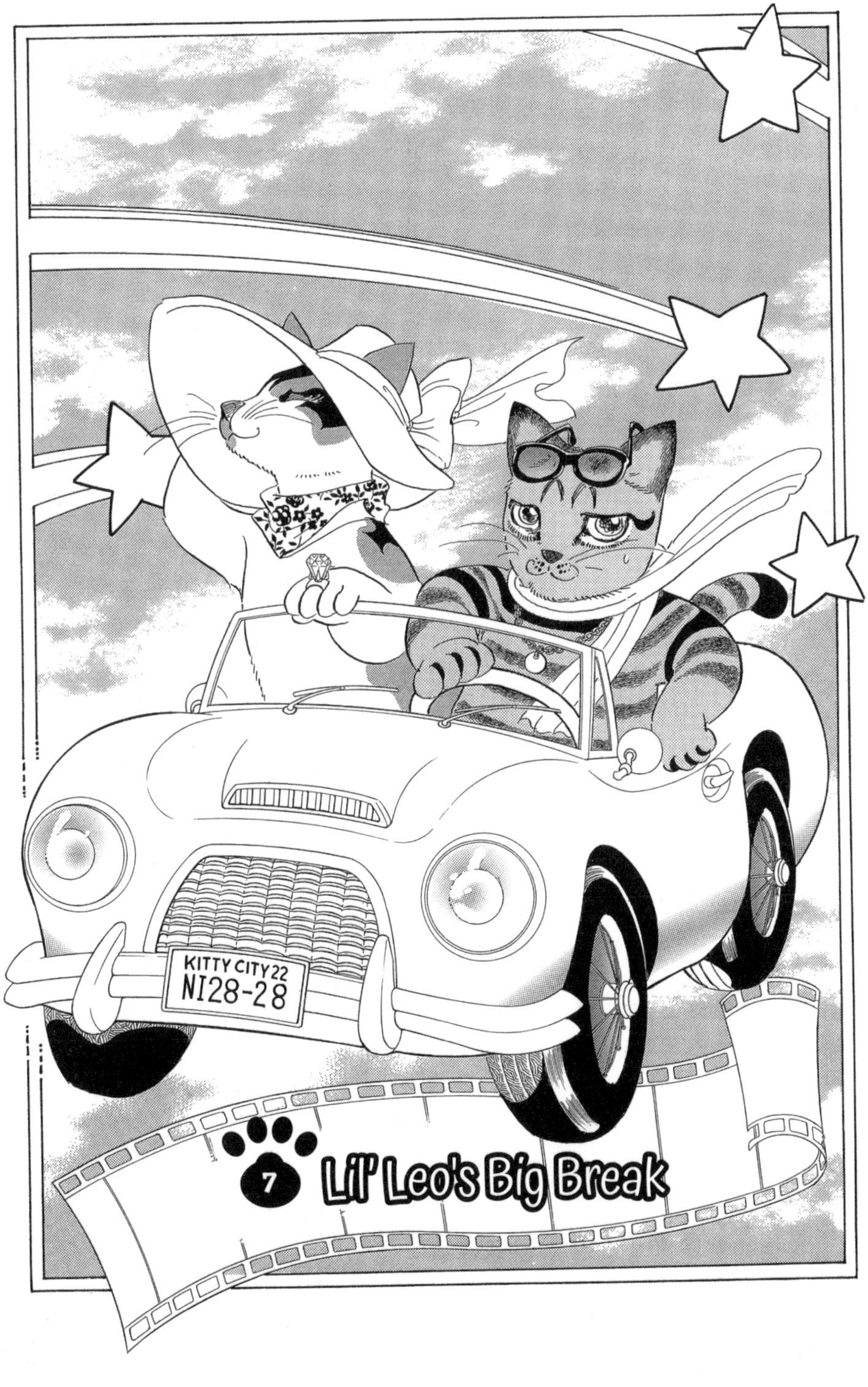
KITTY CITY 22
NI28-28
7
Lil' Leo's Big Break

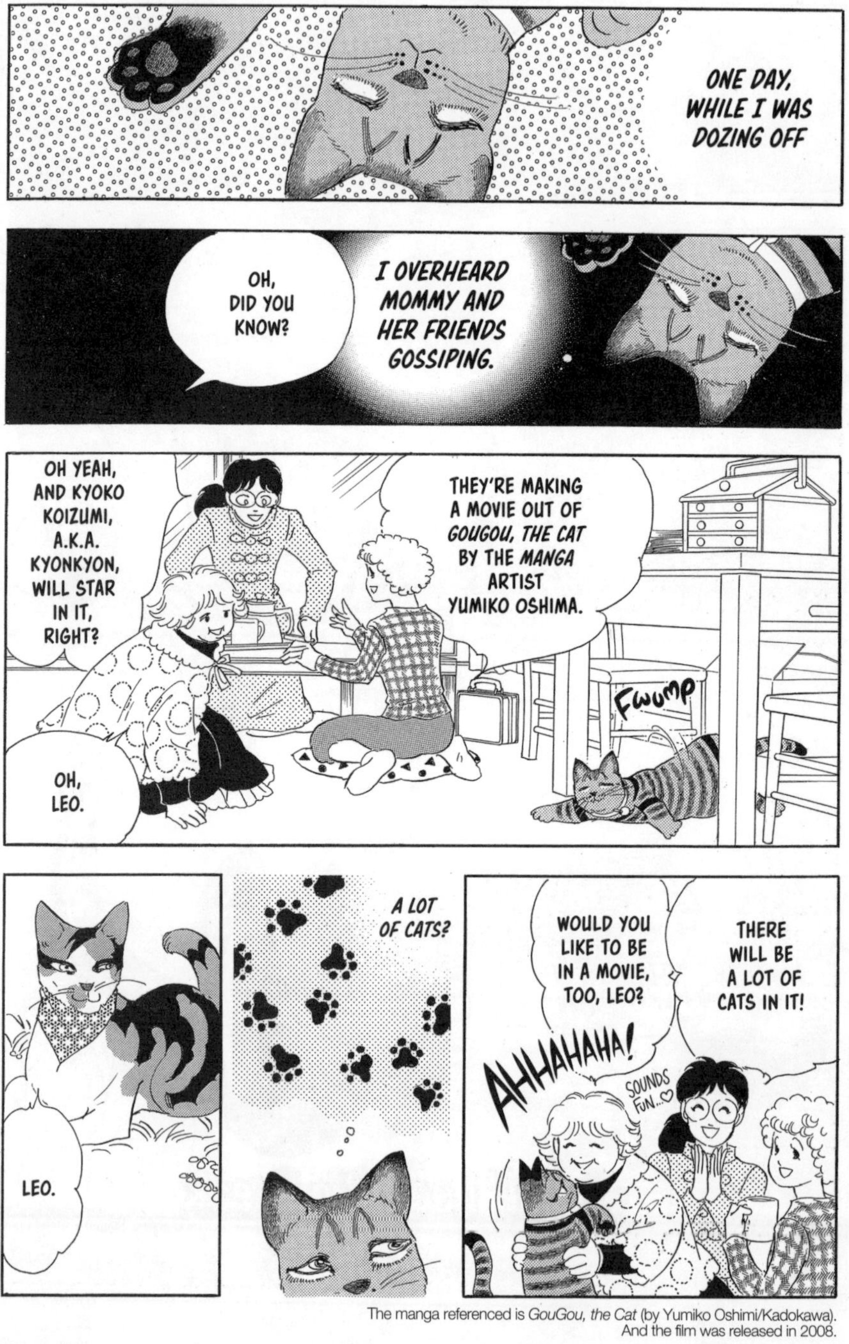
ONE DAY, WHILE I WAS DOZING OFF
I OVERHEARD MOMMY AND HER FRIENDS GOSSIPING.
OH, DID YOU KNOW?
THEY'RE MAKING A MOVIE OUT OF *GOUGOU, THE CAT* BY THE *MANGA* ARTIST YUMIKO OSHIMA.
OH YEAH, AND KYOKO KOIZUMI, A.K.A. KYONKYON, WILL STAR IN IT, RIGHT?
FWUMP
OH, LEO.
THERE WILL BE A LOT OF CATS IN IT!
WOULD YOU LIKE TO BE IN A MOVIE, TOO, LEO?
AHHAHAHA!
SOUNDS FUN...♡
A LOT OF CATS?
LEO.

The manga referenced is *GouGou, the Cat* (by Yumiko Oshimi/Kadokawa). And the film was released in 2008.

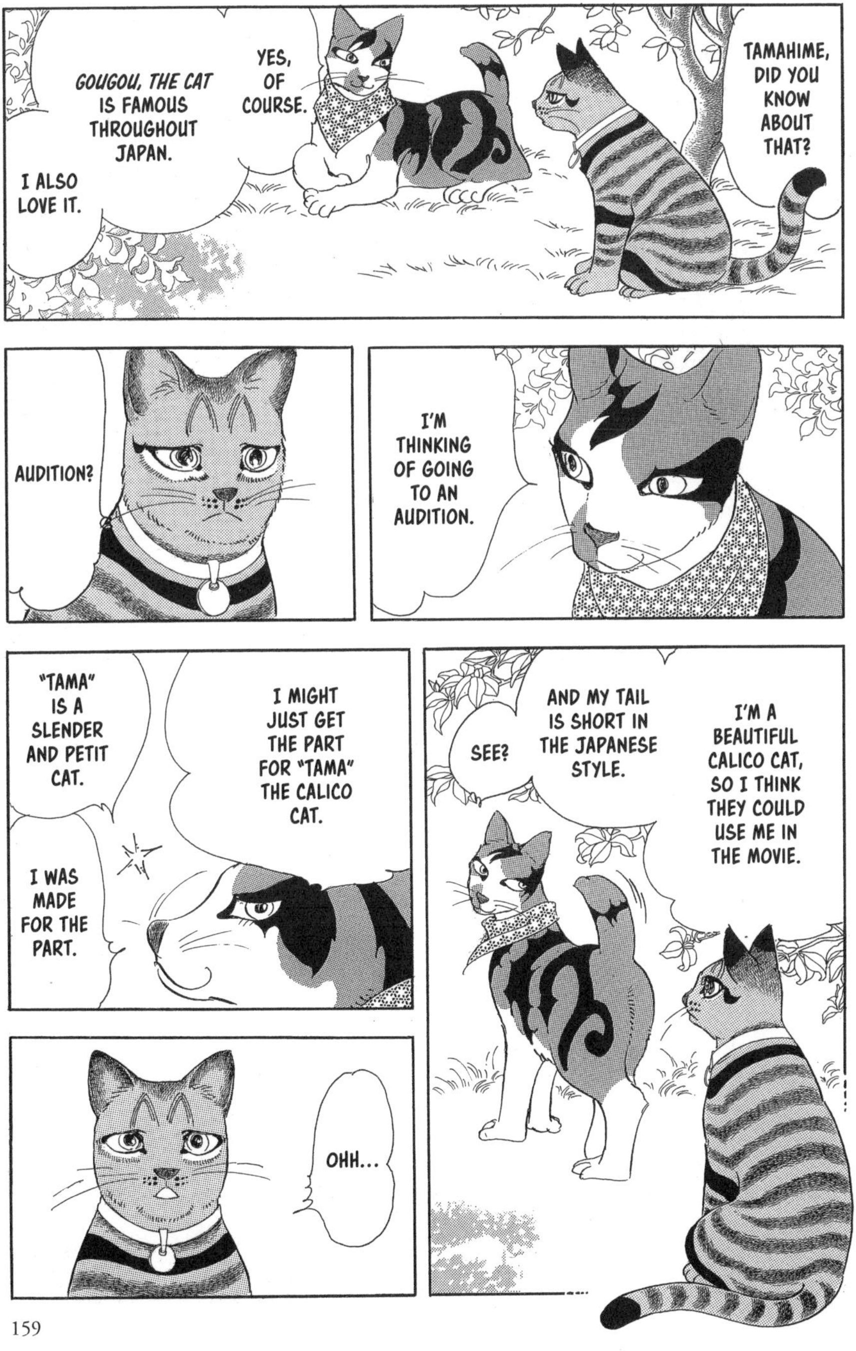
TAMAHIME, DID YOU KNOW ABOUT THAT?
YES, OF COURSE.
GOUGOU, THE CAT IS FAMOUS THROUGHOUT JAPAN.
I ALSO LOVE IT.
I'M THINKING OF GOING TO AN AUDITION.
AUDITION?
I'M A BEAUTIFUL CALICO CAT, SO I THINK THEY COULD USE ME IN THE MOVIE.
AND MY TAIL IS SHORT IN THE JAPANESE STYLE.
SEE?
I MIGHT JUST GET THE PART FOR "TAMA" THE CALICO CAT.
"TAMA" IS A SLENDER AND PETIT CAT.
I WAS MADE FOR THE PART.
OHH...

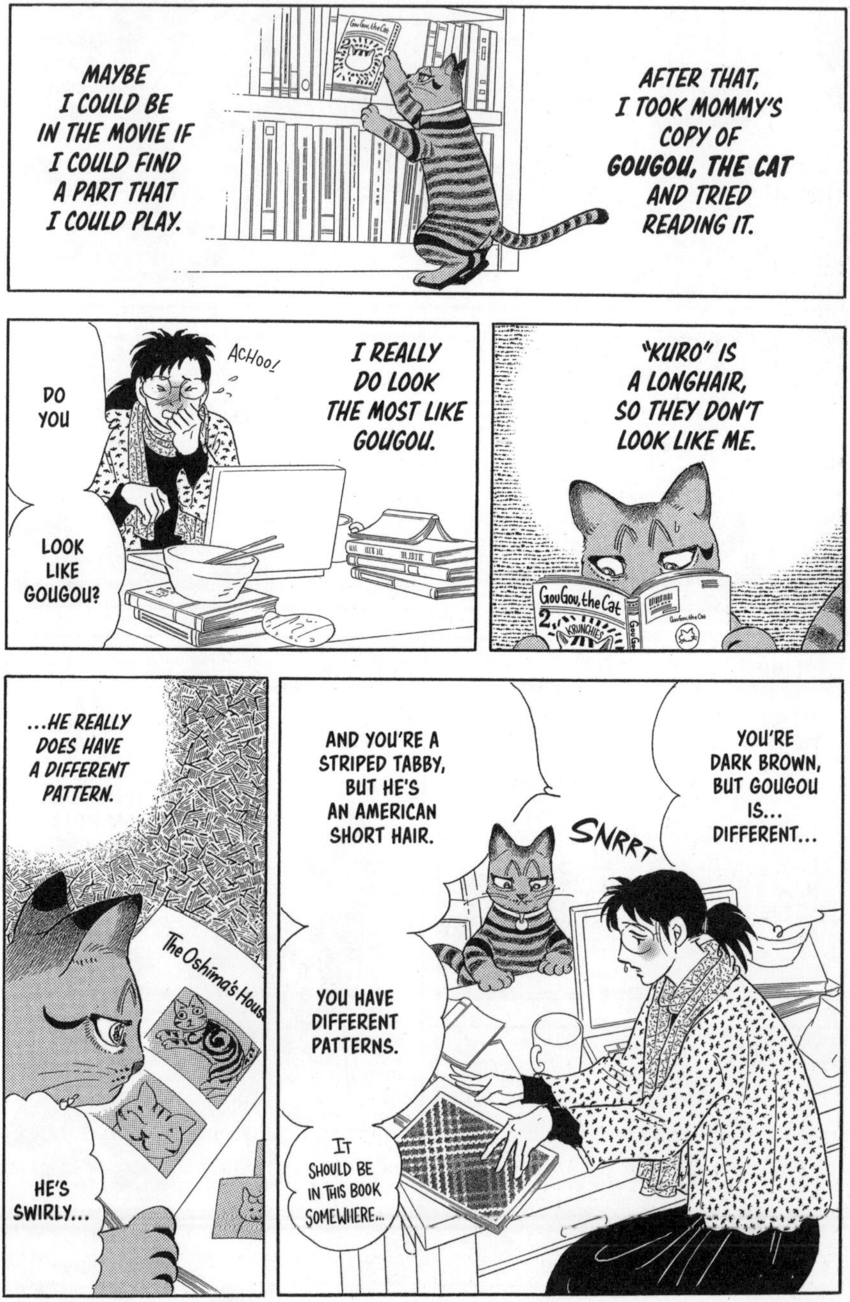
AFTER THAT, I TOOK MOMMY'S COPY OF GOUGOU, THE CAT AND TRIED READING IT.
MAYBE I COULD BE IN THE MOVIE IF I COULD FIND A PART THAT I COULD PLAY.
"KURO" IS A LONGHAIR, SO THEY DON'T LOOK LIKE ME.
GouGou, the Cat 2
KRUNCHIES
I REALLY DO LOOK THE MOST LIKE GOUGOU.
ACHOO!
DO YOU
LOOK LIKE GOUGOU?
YOU'RE DARK BROWN, BUT GOUGOU IS... DIFFERENT...
SNRRT
AND YOU'RE A STRIPED TABBY, BUT HE'S AN AMERICAN SHORT HAIR.
YOU HAVE DIFFERENT PATTERNS.
IT SHOULD BE IN THIS BOOK SOMEWHERE...
...HE REALLY DOES HAVE A DIFFERENT PATTERN.
The Oshima's House
HE'S SWIRLY...

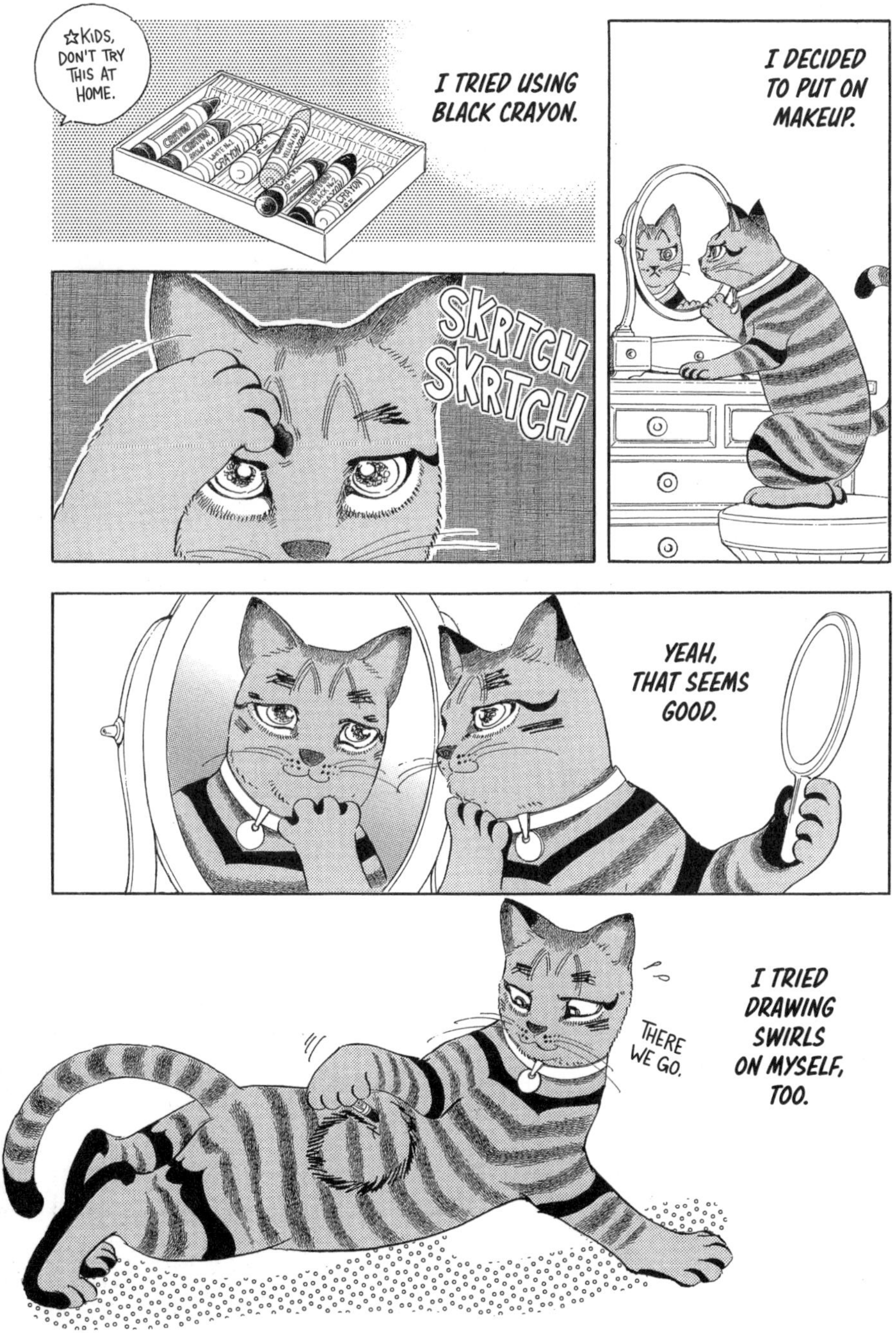
I DECIDED TO PUT ON MAKEUP.
I TRIED USING BLACK CRAYON.
☆KIDS, DON'T TRY THIS AT HOME.
SKRTCH SKRTCH
YEAH, THAT SEEMS GOOD.
I TRIED DRAWING SWIRLS ON MYSELF, TOO.
THERE WE GO.

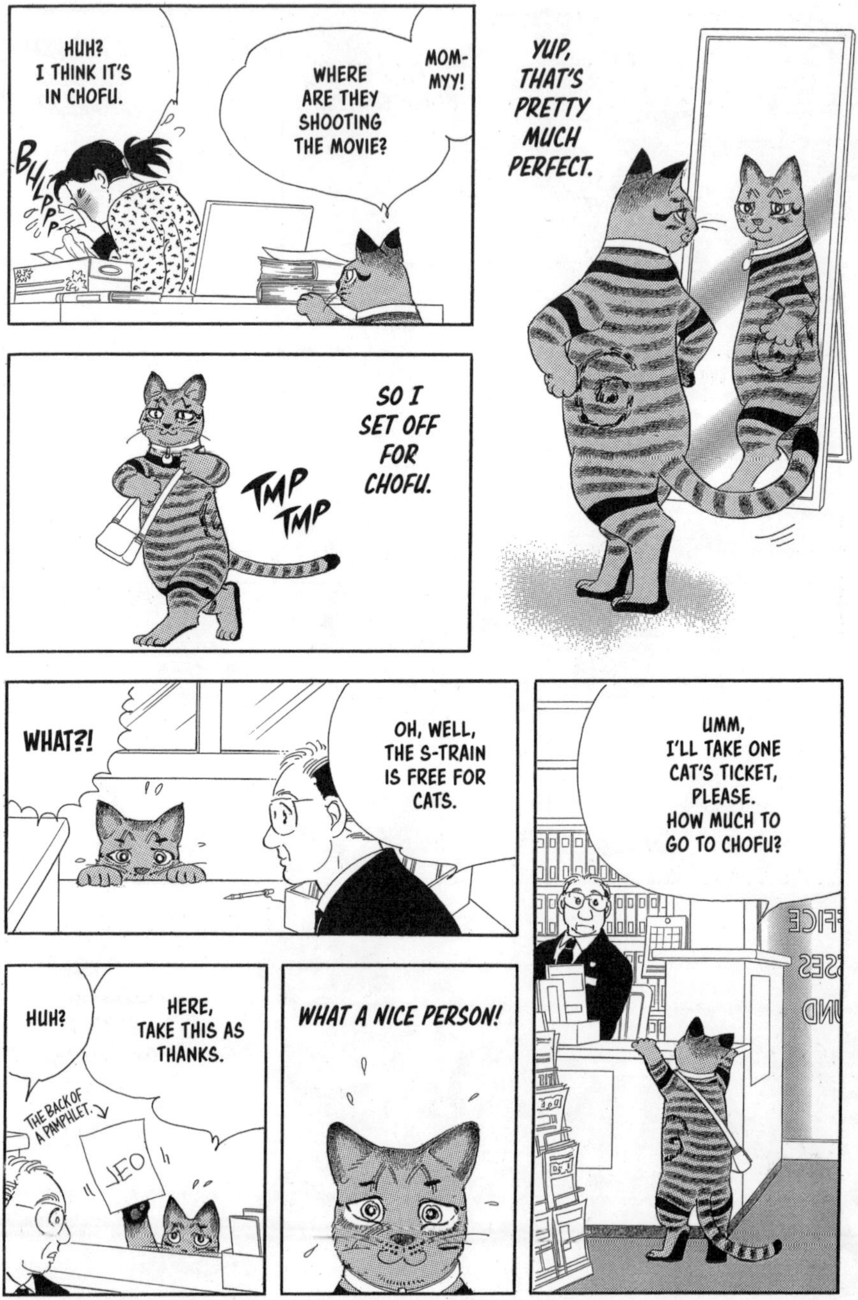
YUP, THAT'S PRETTY MUCH PERFECT.
MOM-MYY!
WHERE ARE THEY SHOOTING THE MOVIE?
HUH? I THINK IT'S IN CHOFU.
BHLPPP
SO I SET OFF FOR CHOFU.
TMP TMP
UMM, I'LL TAKE ONE CAT'S TICKET, PLEASE. HOW MUCH TO GO TO CHOFU?
OH, WELL, THE S-TRAIN IS FREE FOR CATS.
WHAT?!
WHAT A NICE PERSON!
HERE, TAKE THIS AS THANKS.
HUH?
THE BACK OF A PAMPHLET.
LEO

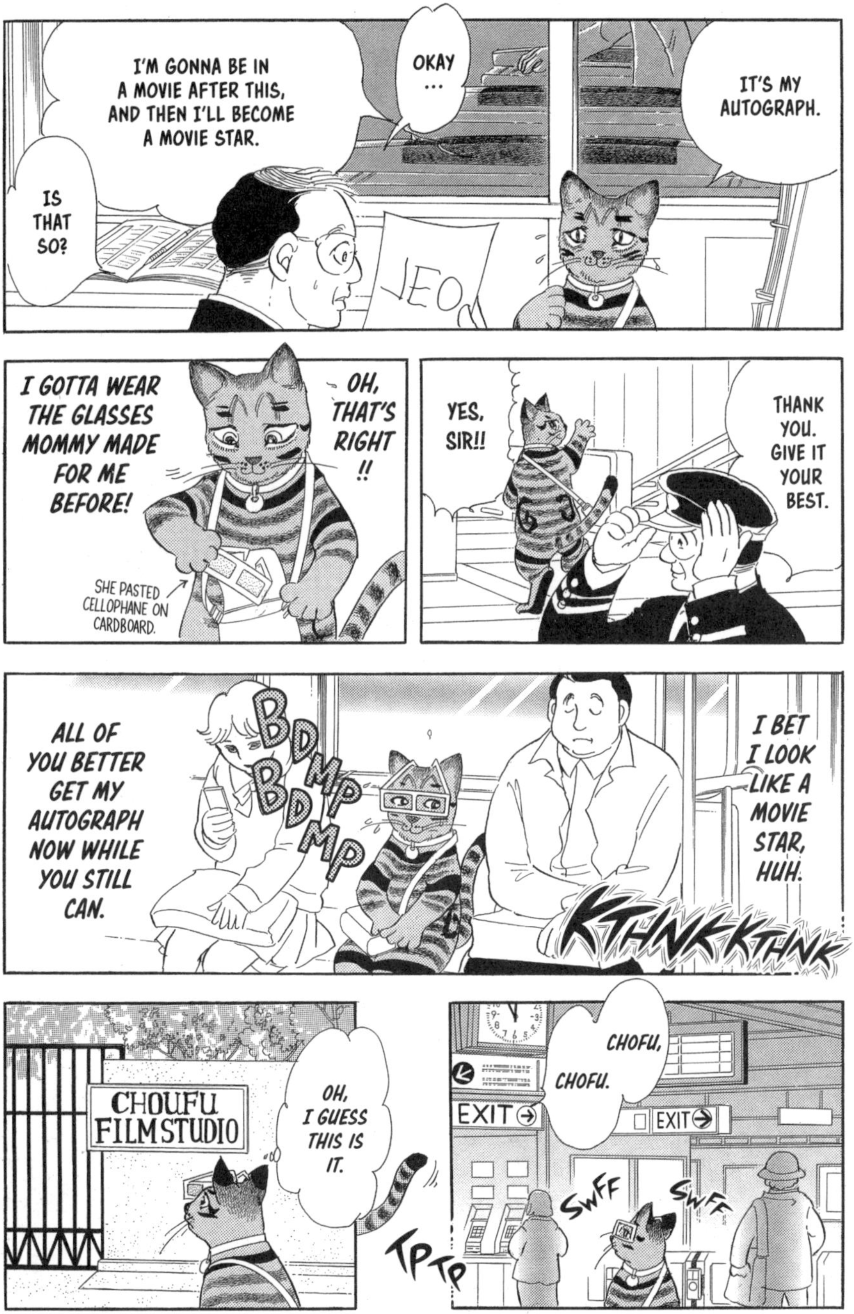
IT'S MY AUTOGRAPH.
OKAY ...
I'M GONNA BE IN A MOVIE AFTER THIS, AND THEN I'LL BECOME A MOVIE STAR.
IS THAT SO?
JEO
THANK YOU. GIVE IT YOUR BEST.
YES, SIR!!
OH, THAT'S RIGHT !!
I GOTTA WEAR THE GLASSES MOMMY MADE FOR ME BEFORE!
SHE PASTED CELLOPHANE ON CARDBOARD.
I BET I LOOK LIKE A MOVIE STAR, HUH.
KTHNK KTHNK
BDMP BDMP
ALL OF YOU BETTER GET MY AUTOGRAPH NOW WHILE YOU STILL CAN.
CHOFU, CHOFU.
EXIT
EXIT
SWFF
SWFF
TPTP
OH, I GUESS THIS IS IT.
CHOUFU FILM STUDIO

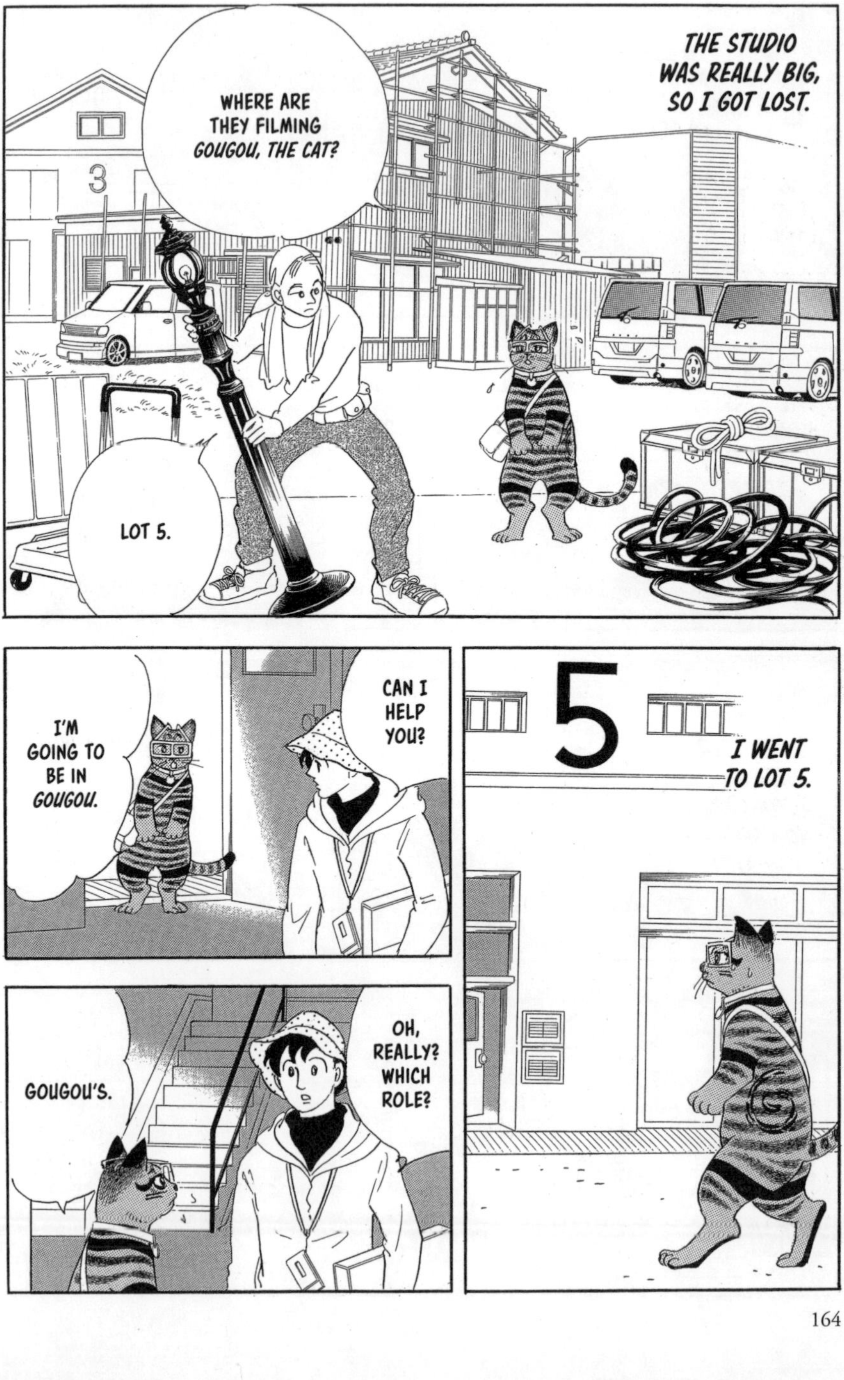
THE STUDIO WAS REALLY BIG, SO I GOT LOST.
WHERE ARE THEY FILMING GOUGOU, THE CAT?
3
LOT 5.
5
I WENT TO LOT 5.
CAN I HELP YOU?
I'M GOING TO BE IN GOUGOU.
OH, REALLY? WHICH ROLE?
GOUGOU'S.

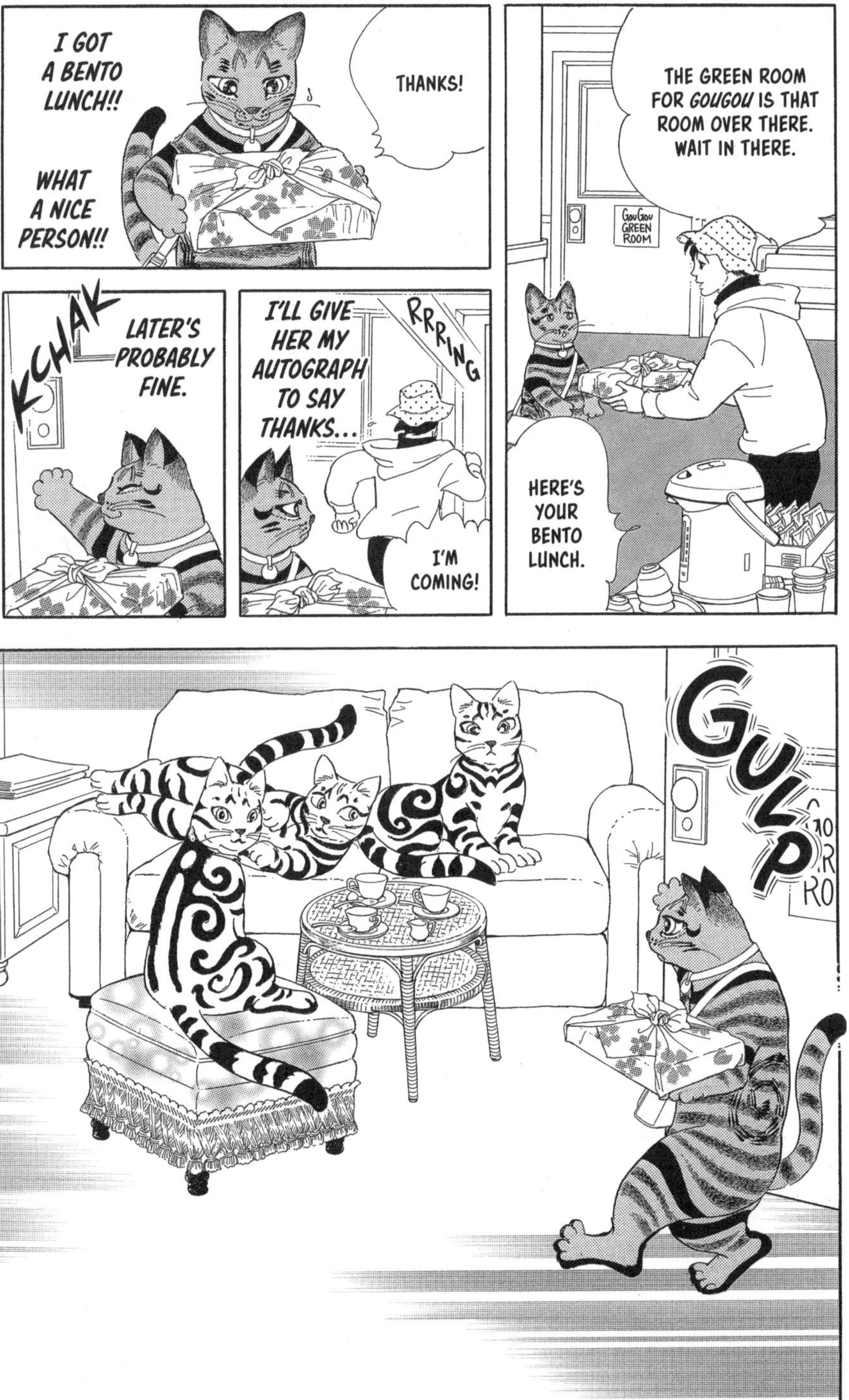
THE GREEN ROOM FOR GOUGOU IS THAT ROOM OVER THERE. WAIT IN THERE.
GouGou GREEN ROOM
HERE'S YOUR BENTO LUNCH.
THANKS!
I GOT A BENTO LUNCH!!
WHAT A NICE PERSON!!
RRRING
I'LL GIVE HER MY AUTOGRAPH TO SAY THANKS...
I'M COMING!
LATER'S PROBABLY FINE.
KCHAK
GULP

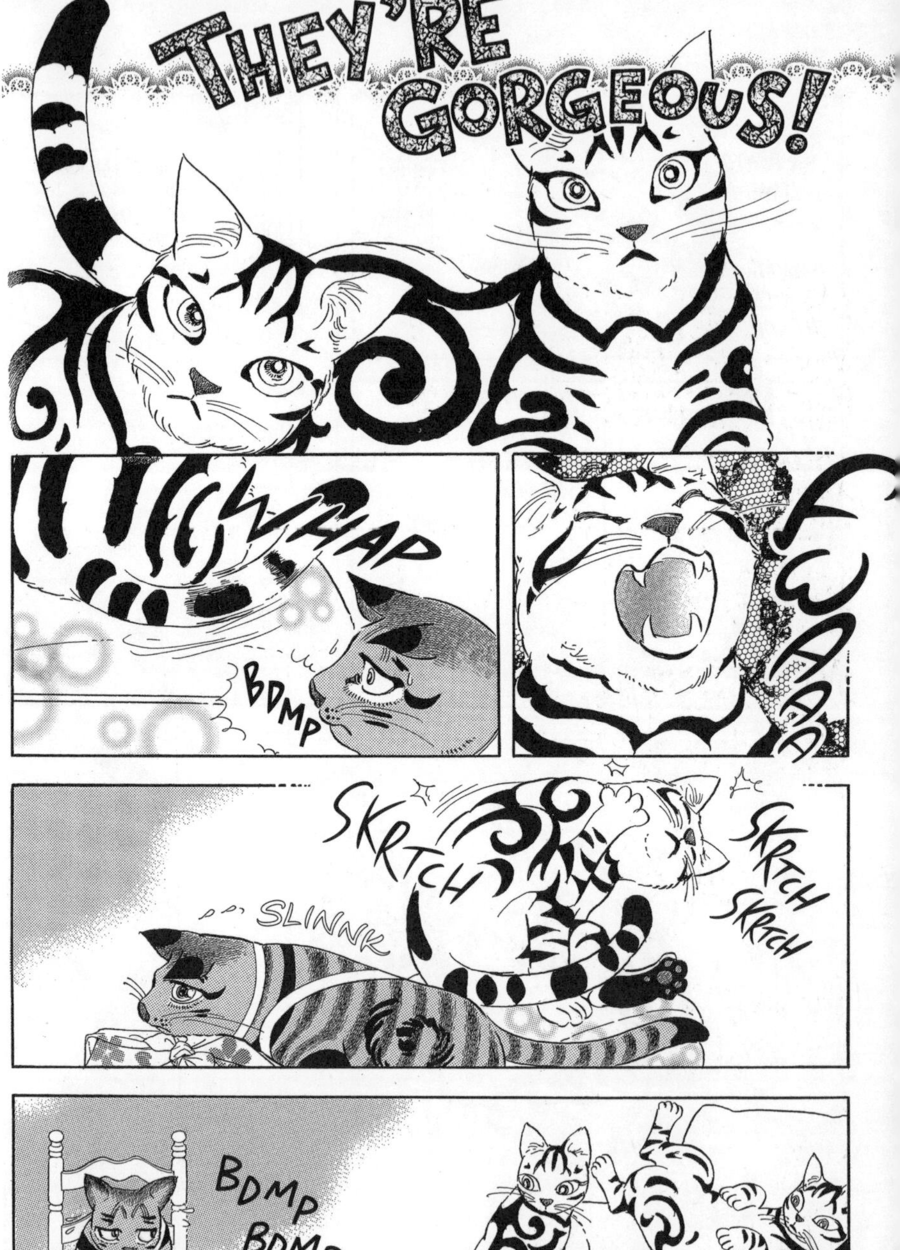
THEY'RE GORGEOUS!
SWAAAA
WHAP
BDMP
SKRTCH SKRTCH
SKRTCH
SKRTCH
SLINNK
BDMP BDMP BDMP

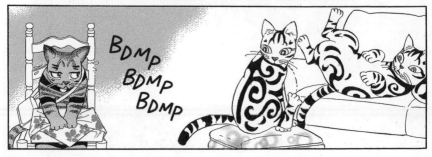

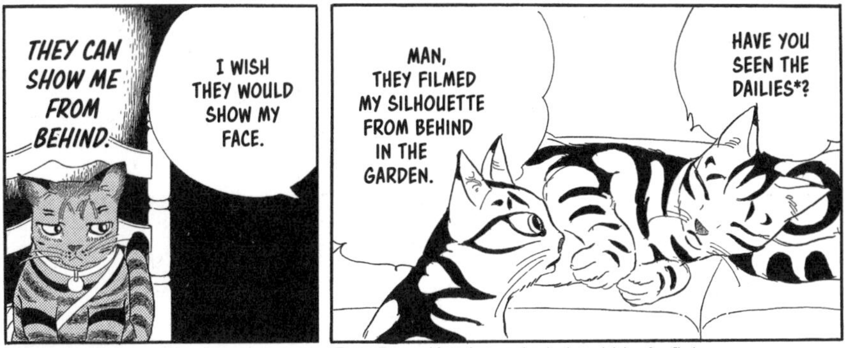
HAVE YOU SEEN THE DAILIES*?
MAN, THEY FILMED MY SILHOUETTE FROM BEHIND IN THE GARDEN.
I WISH THEY WOULD SHOW MY FACE.
THEY CAN SHOW ME FROM BEHIND.

*The video used for reference that is viewed right after filming.

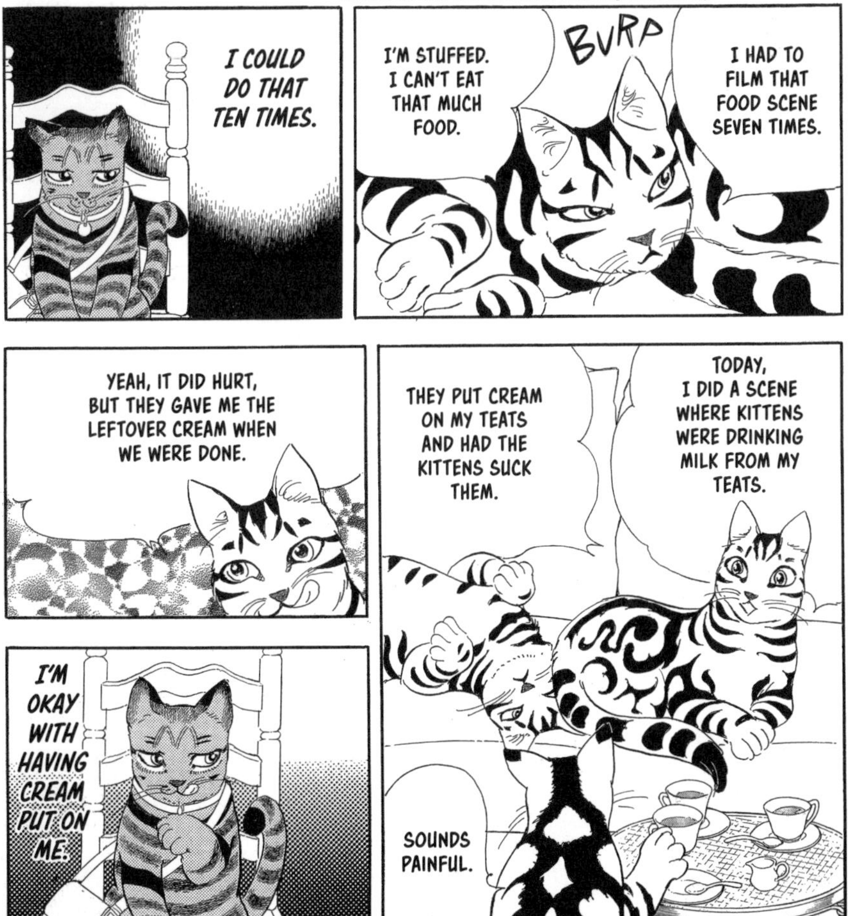
I HAD TO FILM THAT FOOD SCENE SEVEN TIMES.
BURP
I'M STUFFED. I CAN'T EAT THAT MUCH FOOD.
I COULD DO THAT TEN TIMES.
TODAY, I DID A SCENE WHERE KITTENS WERE DRINKING MILK FROM MY TEATS.
THEY PUT CREAM ON MY TEATS AND HAD THE KITTENS SUCK THEM.
SOUNDS PAINFUL.
YEAH, IT DID HURT, BUT THEY GAVE ME THE LEFTOVER CREAM WHEN WE WERE DONE.
I'M OKAY WITH HAVING CREAM PUT ON ME.

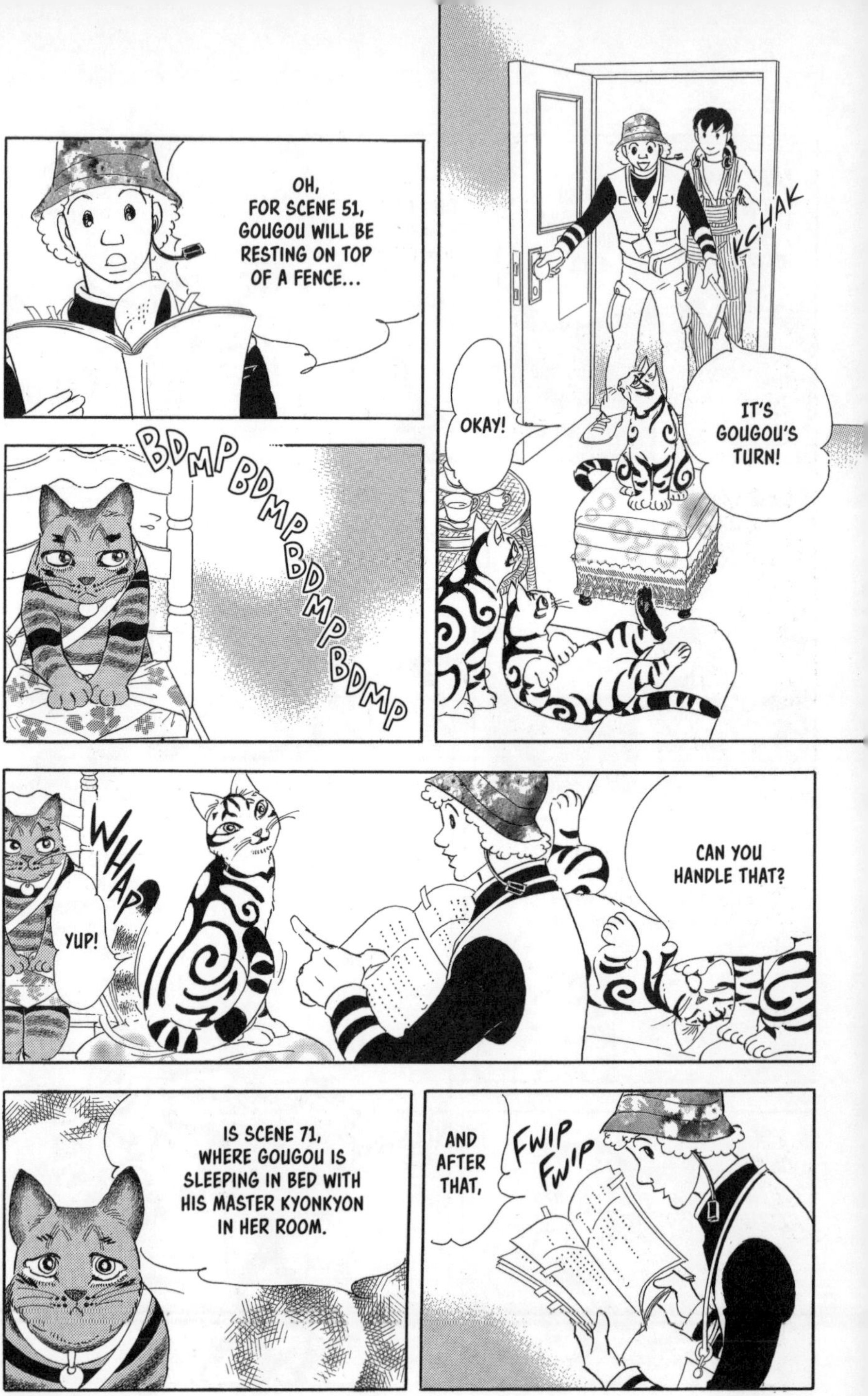
KCHAK
IT'S GOUGOU'S TURN!
OKAY!
OH, FOR SCENE 51, GOUGOU WILL BE RESTING ON TOP OF A FENCE...
BDMP BDMP BDMP BDMP
CAN YOU HANDLE THAT?
WHAP
YUP!
FWIP FWIP
AND AFTER THAT,
IS SCENE 71, WHERE GOUGOU IS SLEEPING IN BED WITH HIS MASTER KYONKYON IN HER ROOM.

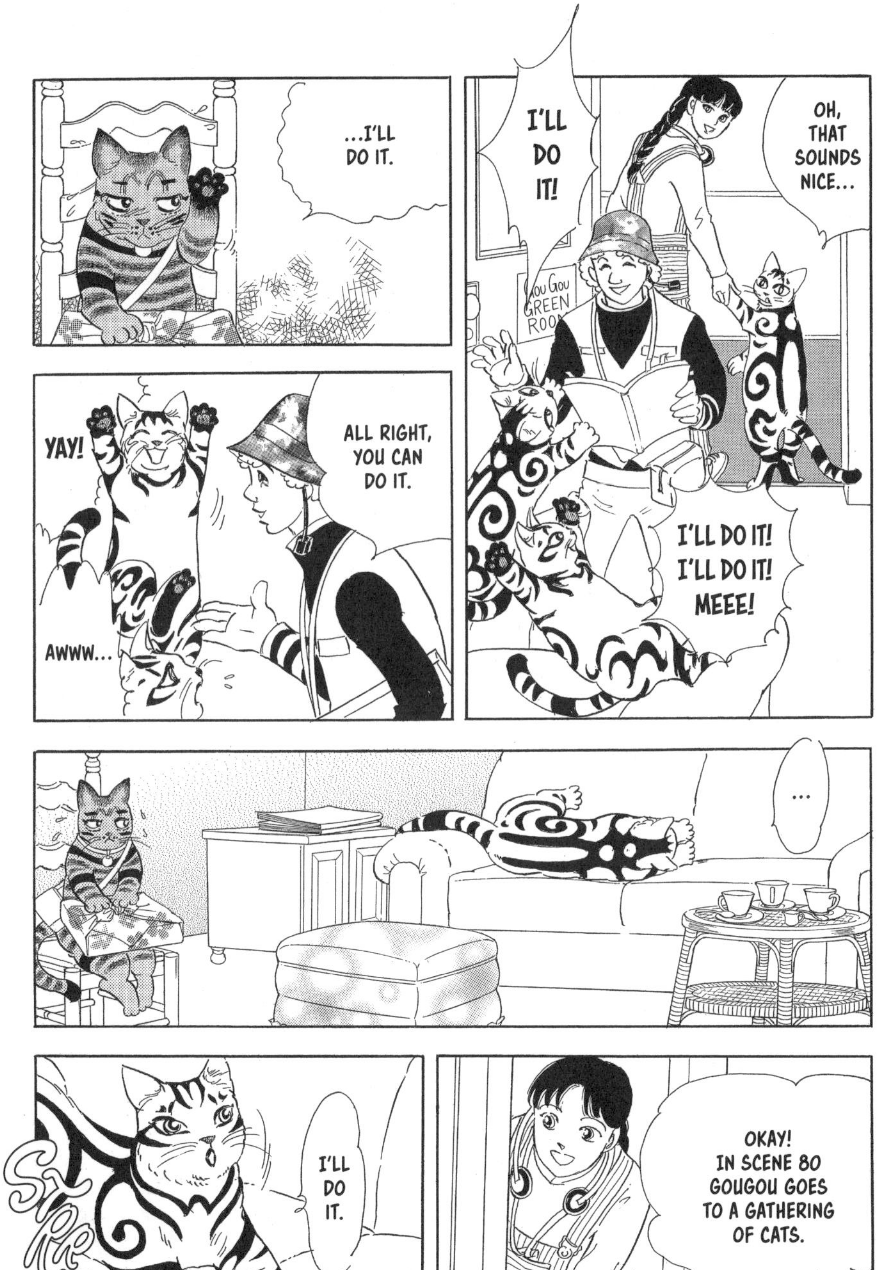
OH, THAT SOUNDS NICE...
I'LL DO IT!
I'LL DO IT! I'LL DO IT! MEEE!
...I'LL DO IT.
ALL RIGHT, YOU CAN DO IT.
YAY!
AWWW...
...
OKAY! IN SCENE 80 GOUGOU GOES TO A GATHERING OF CATS.
KREEK
I'LL DO IT.
STRETCH

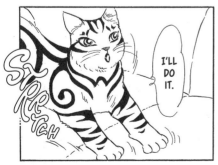

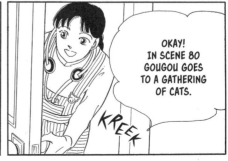

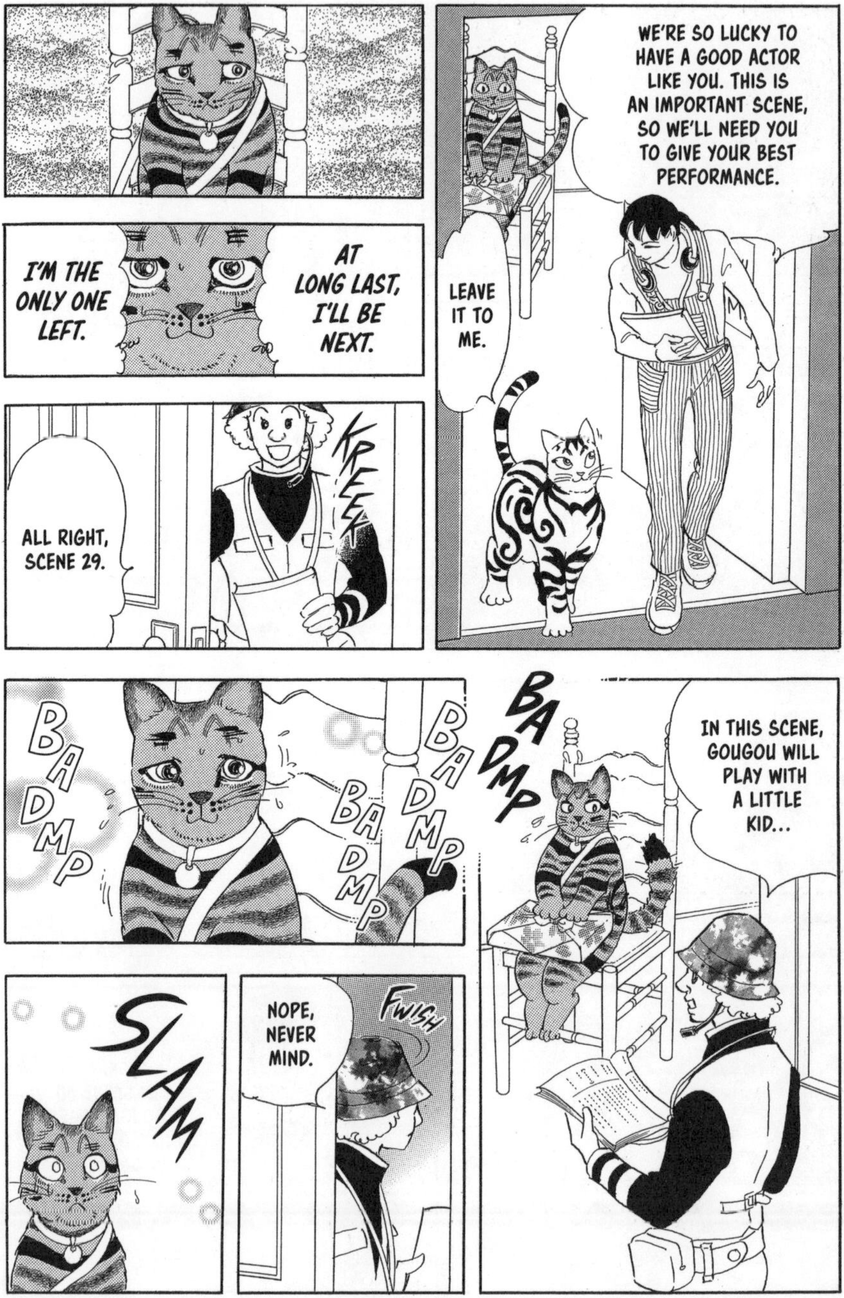
WE'RE SO LUCKY TO HAVE A GOOD ACTOR LIKE YOU. THIS IS AN IMPORTANT SCENE, SO WE'LL NEED YOU TO GIVE YOUR BEST PERFORMANCE.
LEAVE IT TO ME.
AT LONG LAST, I'LL BE NEXT.
I'M THE ONLY ONE LEFT.
KREEEK
ALL RIGHT, SCENE 29.
BADMP
IN THIS SCENE, GOUGOU WILL PLAY WITH A LITTLE KID...
BADMP
BADMP
BADMP
BADMP
FWISH
NOPE, NEVER MIND.
SLAM

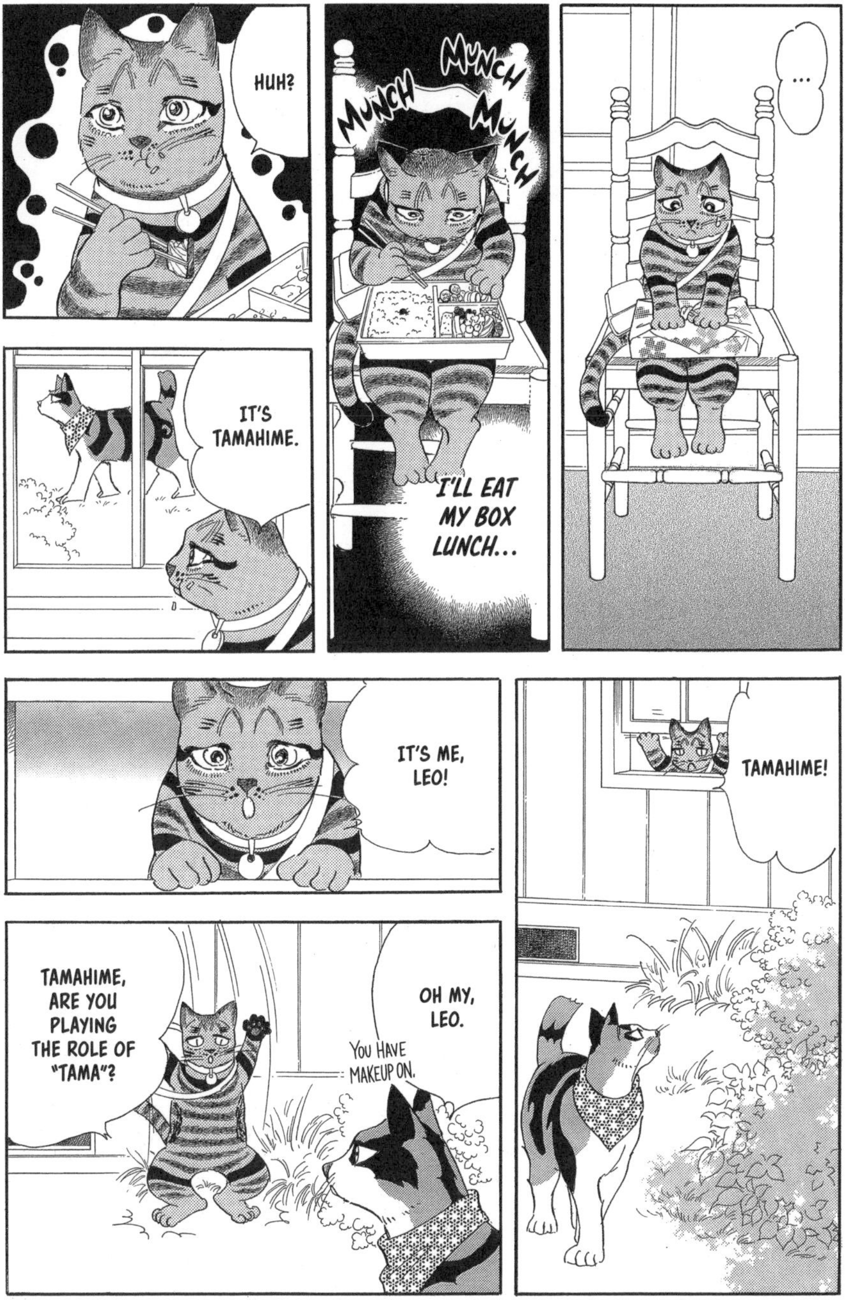
...
MUNCH MUNCH MUNCH
I'LL EAT MY BOX LUNCH...
HUH?
IT'S TAMAHIME.
TAMAHIME!
IT'S ME, LEO!
OH MY, LEO.
YOU HAVE MAKEUP ON.
TAMAHIME, ARE YOU PLAYING THE ROLE OF "TAMA"?

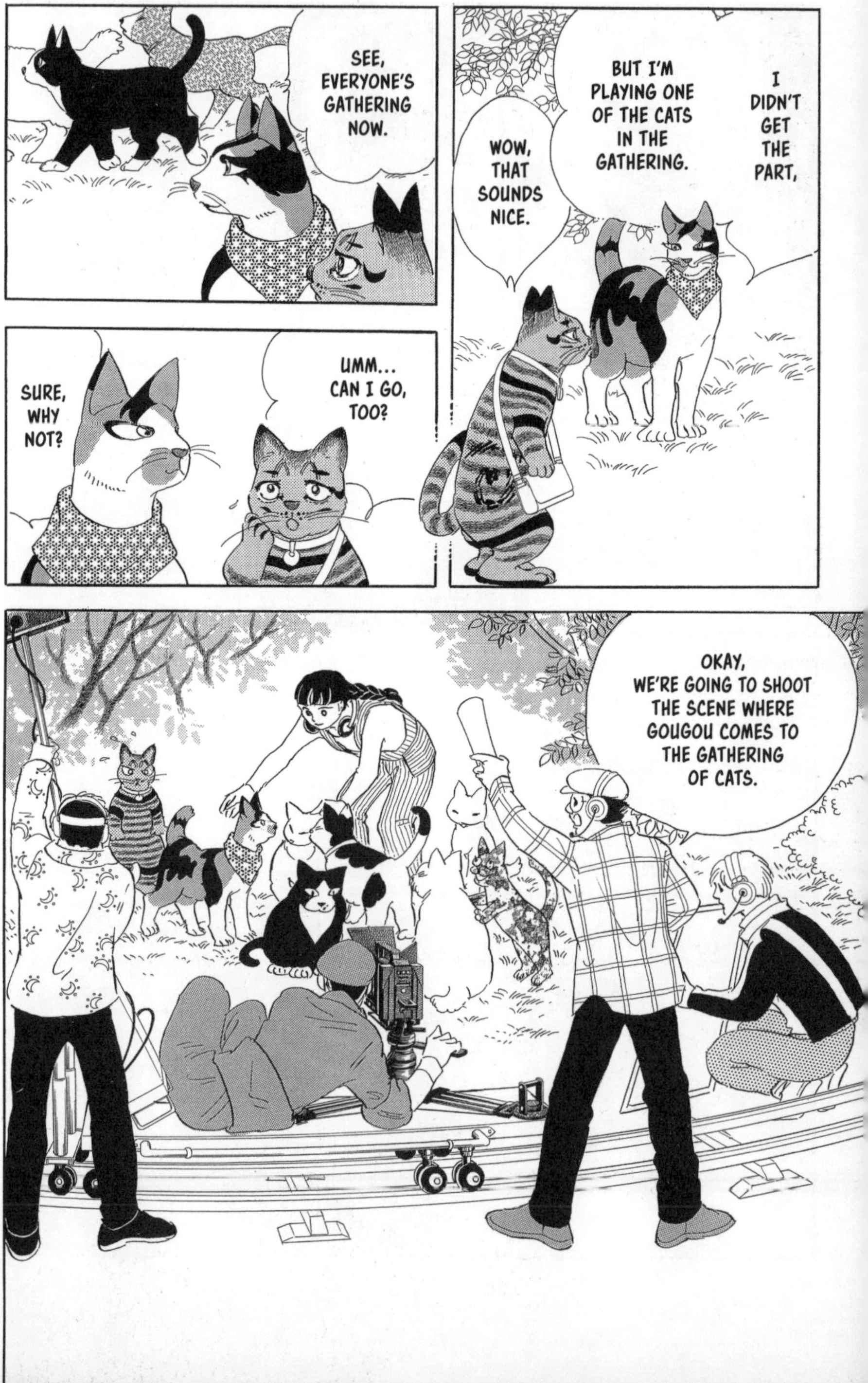
I DIDN'T GET THE PART,
BUT I'M PLAYING ONE OF THE CATS IN THE GATHERING.
WOW, THAT SOUNDS NICE.
SEE, EVERYONE'S GATHERING NOW.
UMM... CAN I GO, TOO?
SURE, WHY NOT?
OKAY, WE'RE GOING TO SHOOT THE SCENE WHERE GOUGOU COMES TO THE GATHERING OF CATS.

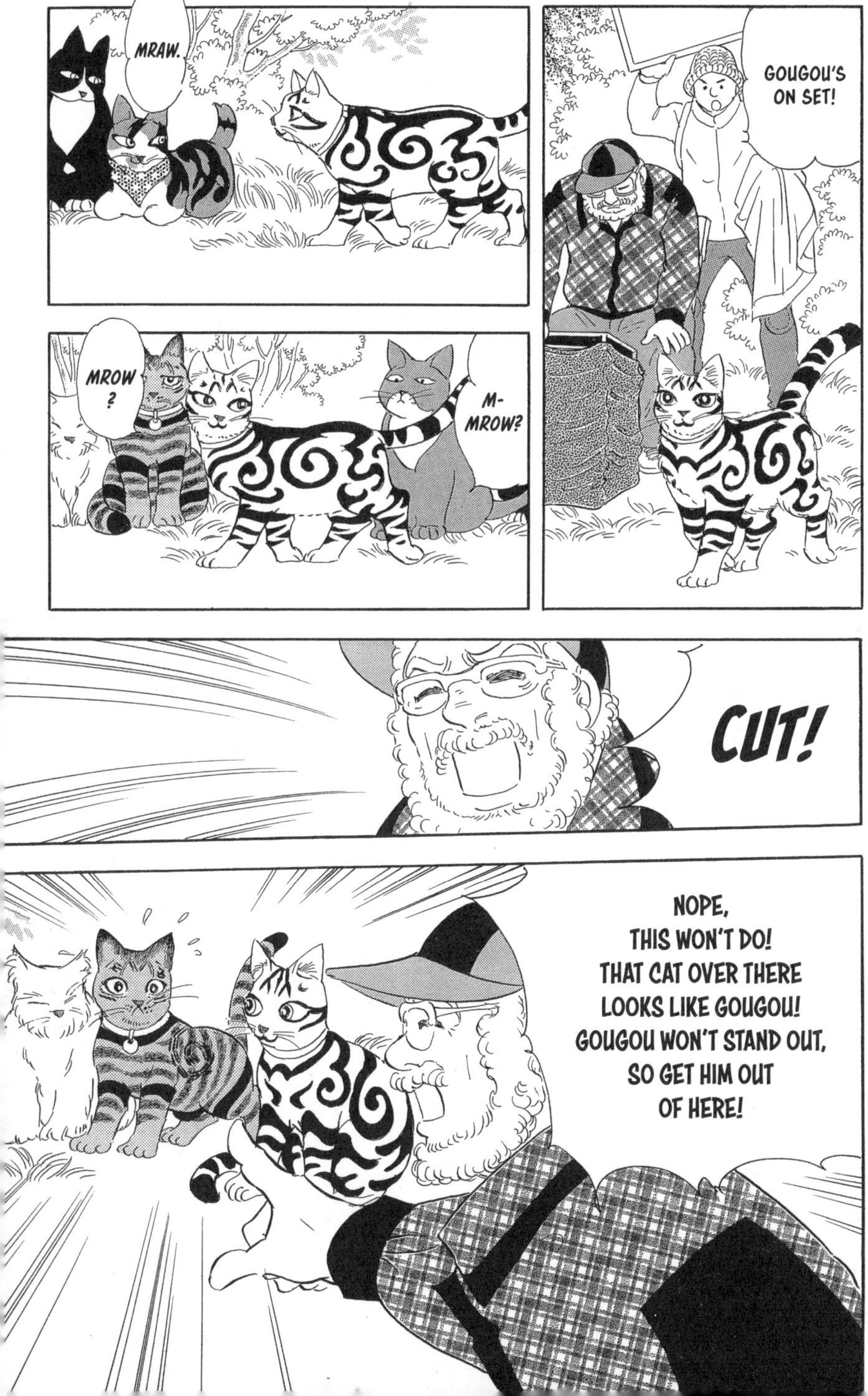
GOUGOU'S ON SET!
MRAW.
M-MROW?
MROW ?
CUT!
NOPE, THIS WON'T DO! THAT CAT OVER THERE LOOKS LIKE GOUGOU! GOUGOU WON'T STAND OUT, SO GET HIM OUT OF HERE!

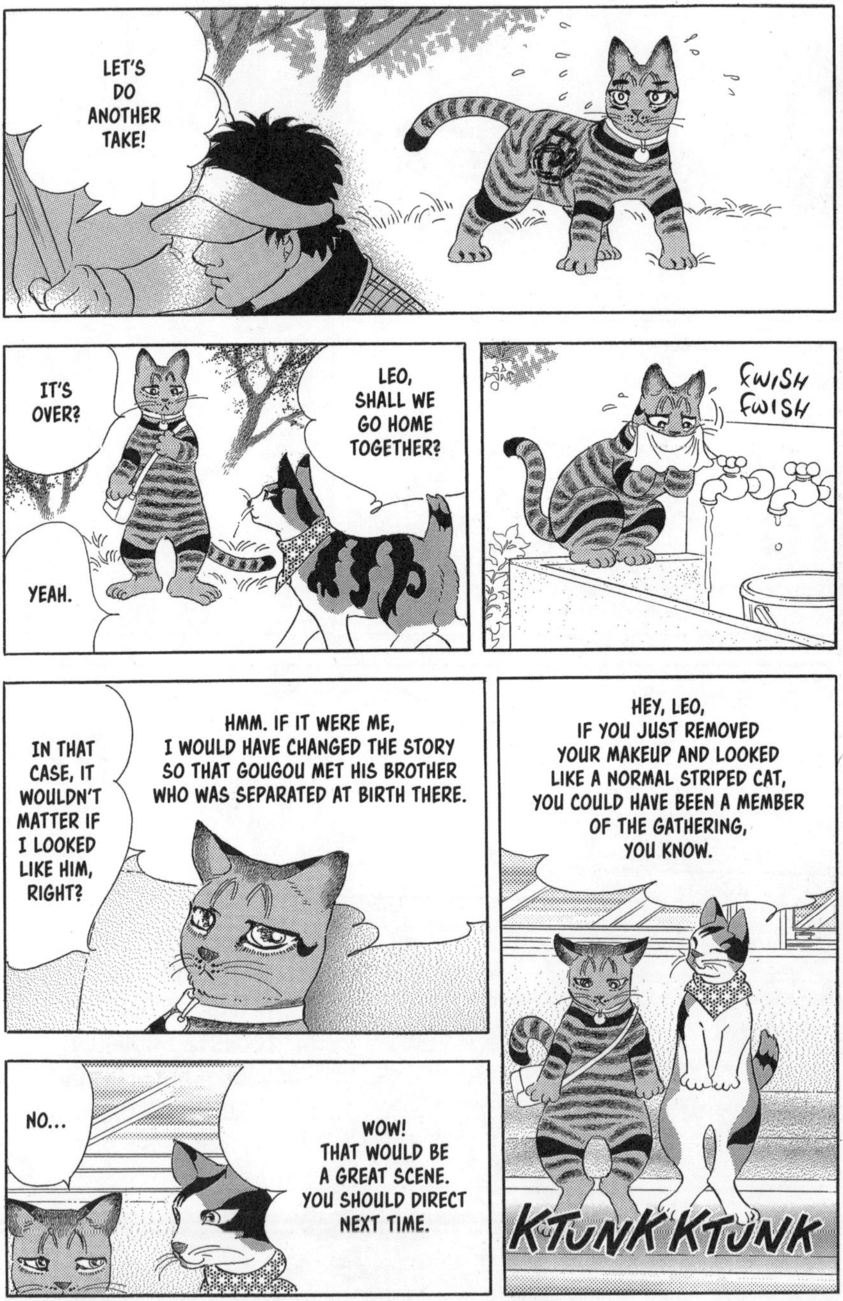
LET'S DO ANOTHER TAKE!
FWISH FWISH
LEO, SHALL WE GO HOME TOGETHER?
IT'S OVER?
YEAH.
HEY, LEO, IF YOU JUST REMOVED YOUR MAKEUP AND LOOKED LIKE A NORMAL STRIPED CAT, YOU COULD HAVE BEEN A MEMBER OF THE GATHERING, YOU KNOW.
KTUNK KTUNK
HMM. IF IT WERE ME, I WOULD HAVE CHANGED THE STORY SO THAT GOUGOU MET HIS BROTHER WHO WAS SEPARATED AT BIRTH THERE.
IN THAT CASE, IT WOULDN'T MATTER IF I LOOKED LIKE HIM, RIGHT?
WOW! THAT WOULD BE A GREAT SCENE. YOU SHOULD DIRECT NEXT TIME.
NO...

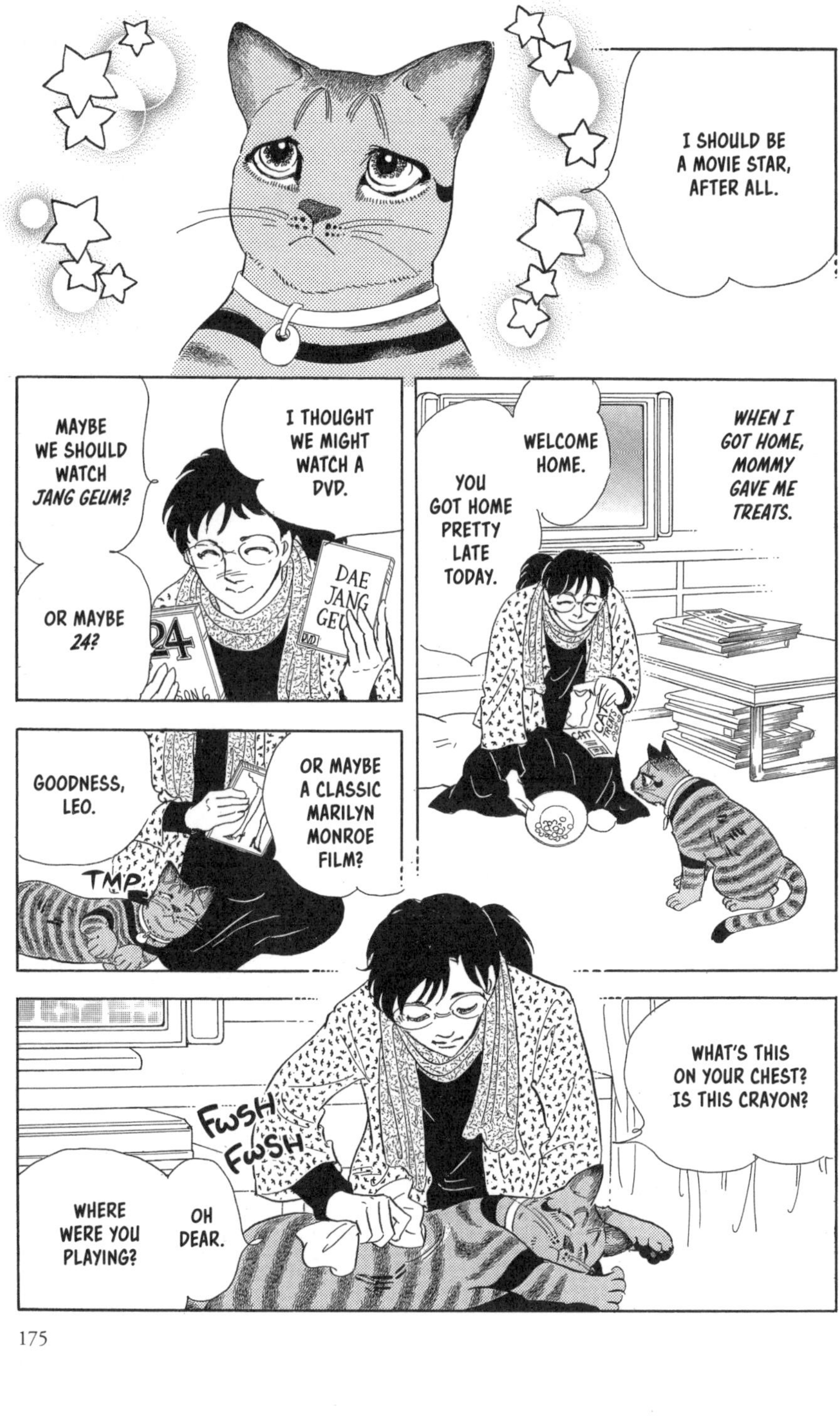
I SHOULD BE A MOVIE STAR, AFTER ALL.
WHEN I GOT HOME, MOMMY GAVE ME TREATS.
WELCOME HOME.
YOU GOT HOME PRETTY LATE TODAY.
I THOUGHT WE MIGHT WATCH A DVD.
MAYBE WE SHOULD WATCH *JANG GEUM?*
OR MAYBE *24?*
OR MAYBE A CLASSIC MARILYN MONROE FILM?
GOODNESS, LEO.
TMP
WHAT'S THIS ON YOUR CHEST? IS THIS CRAYON?
FWSH FWSH
OH DEAR.
WHERE WERE YOU PLAYING?

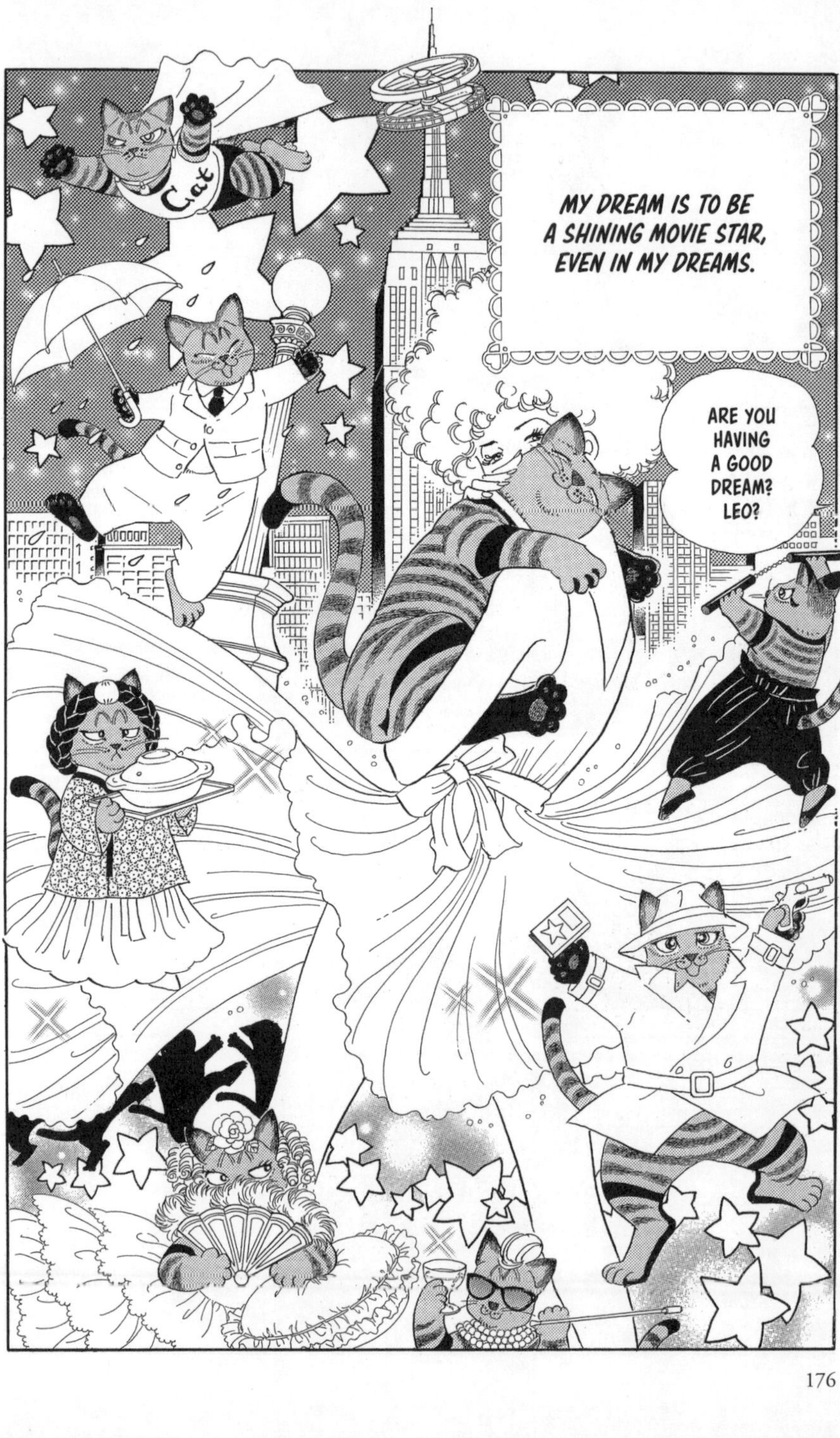
MY DREAM IS TO BE A SHINING MOVIE STAR, EVEN IN MY DREAMS.
ARE YOU HAVING A GOOD DREAM? LEO?

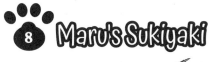

8 Maru's Sukiyaki

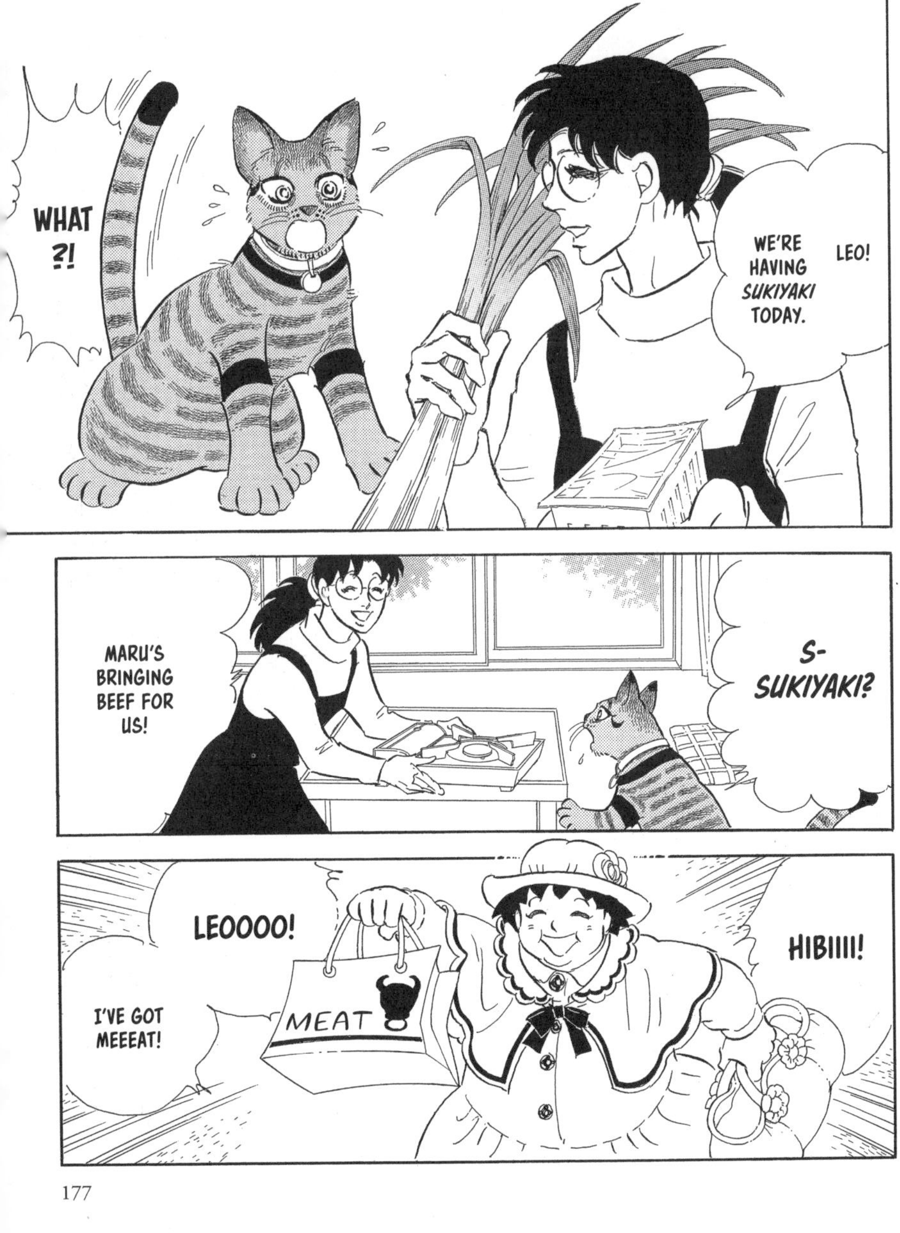
LEO!
WE'RE HAVING SUKIYAKI TODAY.
WHAT ?!
S- SUKIYAKI?
MARU'S BRINGING BEEF FOR US!
HIBIIII!
LEOOOO!
I'VE GOT MEEEAT!
MEAT

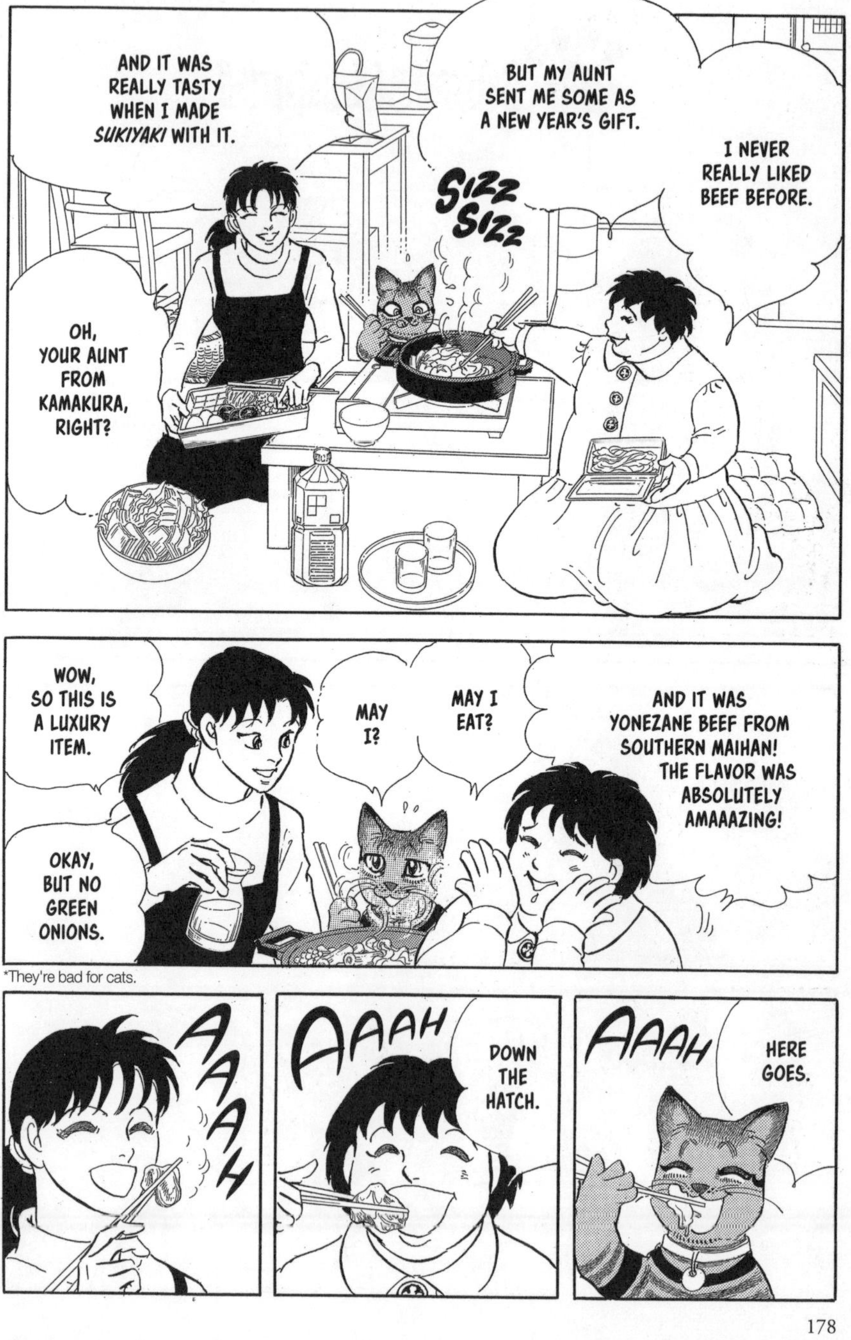
I NEVER REALLY LIKED BEEF BEFORE.
BUT MY AUNT SENT ME SOME AS A NEW YEAR'S GIFT.
SIZZ SIZZ
AND IT WAS REALLY TASTY WHEN I MADE *SUKIYAKI* WITH IT.
OH, YOUR AUNT FROM KAMAKURA, RIGHT?
AND IT WAS YONEZANE BEEF FROM SOUTHERN MAIHAN! THE FLAVOR WAS ABSOLUTELY AMAAAZING!
MAY I EAT?
MAY I?
WOW, SO THIS IS A LUXURY ITEM.
OKAY, BUT NO GREEN ONIONS.
AAAH
HERE GOES.
AAAH
DOWN THE HATCH.
AAAAH

*They're bad for cats.

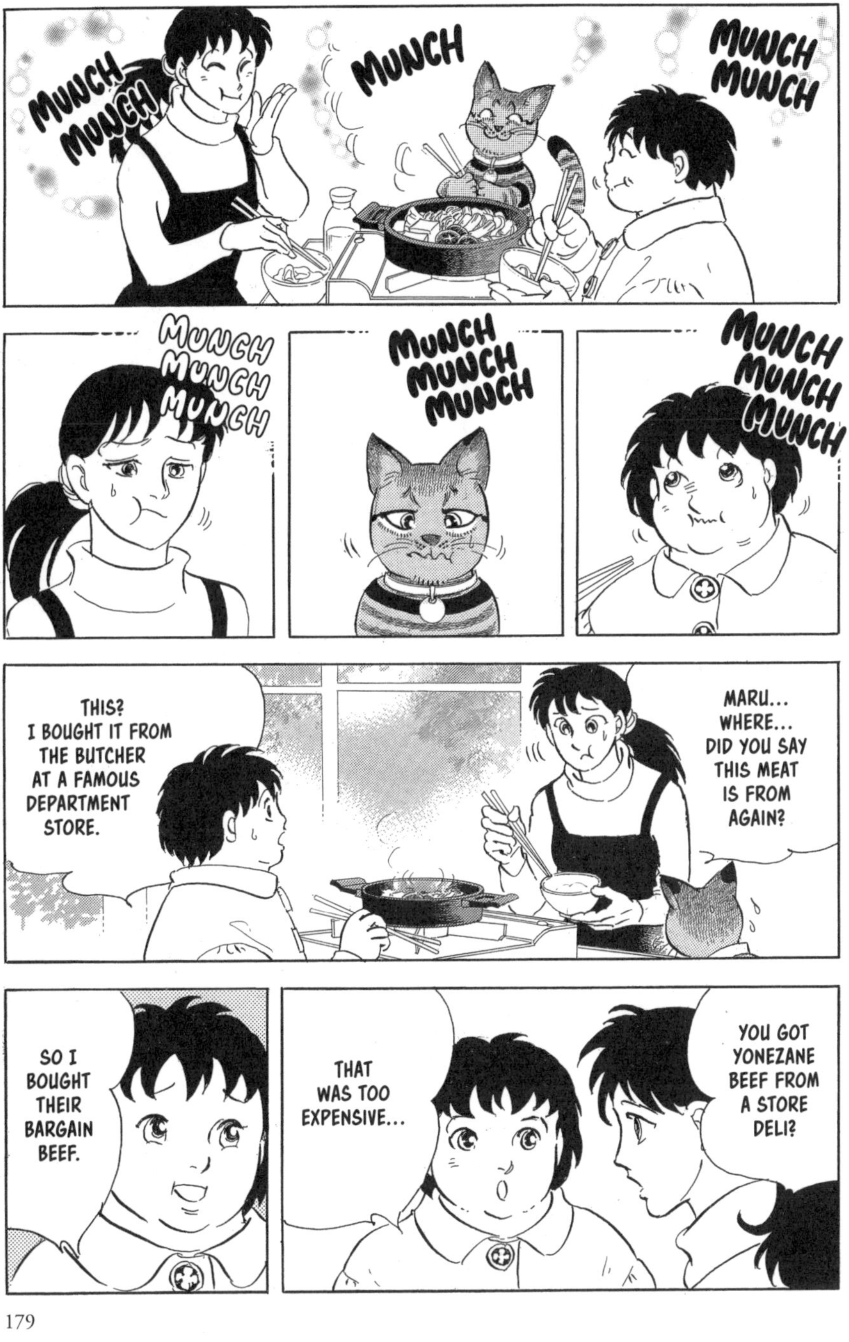
MUNCH MUNCH
MUNCH
MUNCH MUNCH
MUNCH MUNCH MUNCH
MUNCH MUNCH MUNCH
MUNCH MUNCH MUNCH
MARU... WHERE... DID YOU SAY THIS MEAT IS FROM AGAIN?
THIS? I BOUGHT IT FROM THE BUTCHER AT A FAMOUS DEPARTMENT STORE.
YOU GOT YONEZANE BEEF FROM A STORE DELI?
THAT WAS TOO EXPENSIVE...
SO I BOUGHT THEIR BARGAIN BEEF.

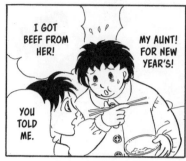

THIS IS PRETTY GOOD FOR BARGAIN BEEF...
BUT THERE'S SOMETHING OFF ABOUT IT.
MOMMY, I CAN'T STOP CHEWING THIS MEAT.
BUT, BUT...
MY AUNT! FOR NEW YEAR'S!
I GOT BEEF FROM HER!
YOU TOLD ME.
AND WHEN I MADE *SUKIYAKI* WITH IT...
IT WAS TASTY!
YOU TOLD ME.
I NEVER LIKED BEEF BEFORE!
THAT NEW YEAR'S *SUKIYAKI* WAS ABSOLUTELY AMAZING!
RTTL RTTL RTTL RTTL
AND SO IT BEGINS ...

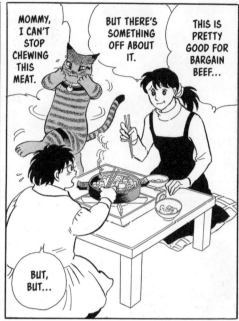

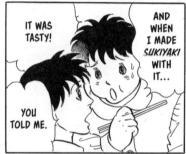

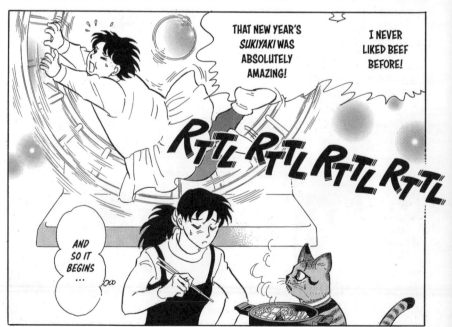

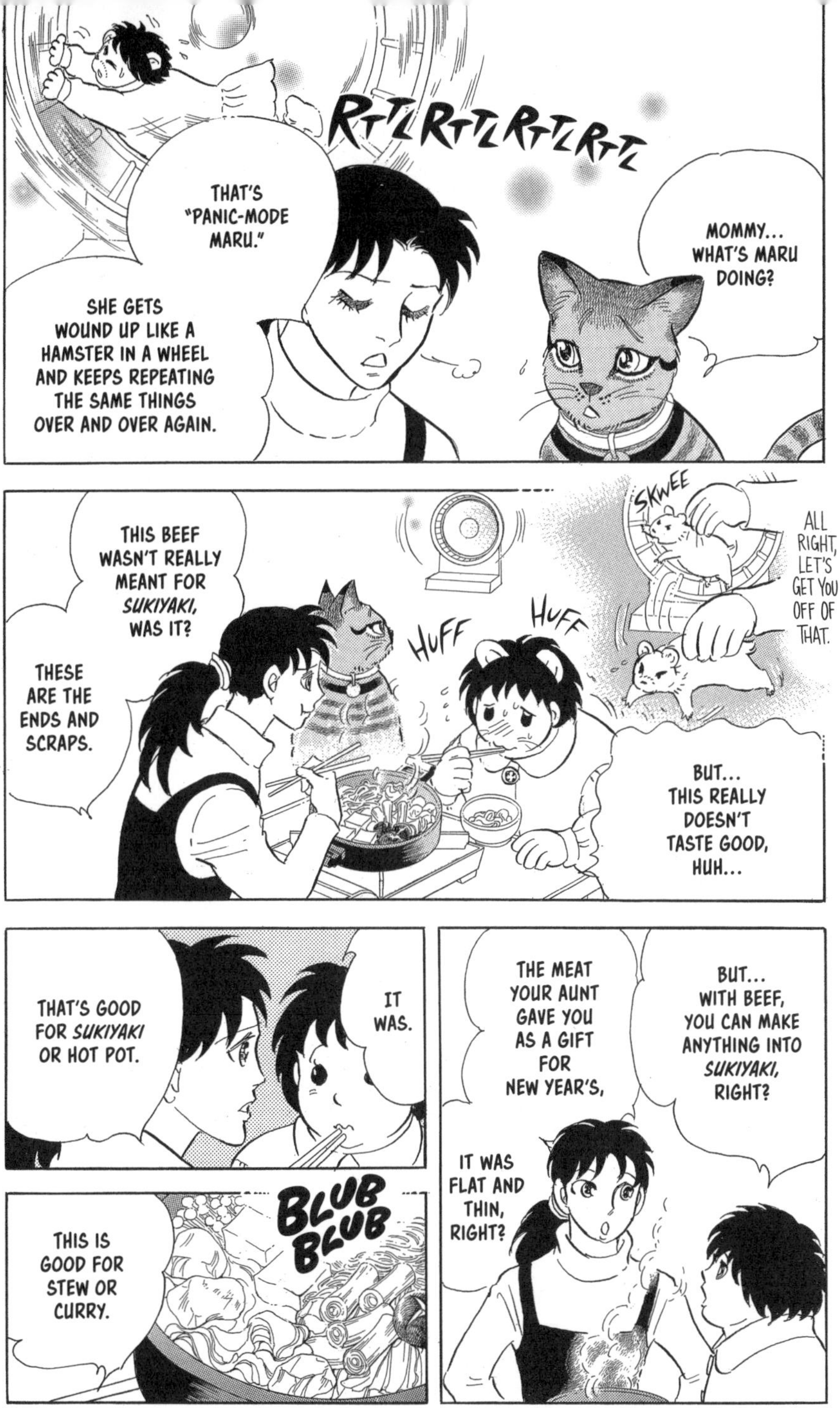
RTTLRTTLRTTLRTTL
MOMMY... WHAT'S MARU DOING?
THAT'S "PANIC-MODE MARU."
SHE GETS WOUND UP LIKE A HAMSTER IN A WHEEL AND KEEPS REPEATING THE SAME THINGS OVER AND OVER AGAIN.
ALL RIGHT, LET'S GET YOU OFF OF THAT.
SKWEE
HUFF HUFF
BUT... THIS REALLY DOESN'T TASTE GOOD, HUH...
THIS BEEF WASN'T REALLY MEANT FOR *SUKIYAKI,* WAS IT?
THESE ARE THE ENDS AND SCRAPS.
BUT... WITH BEEF, YOU CAN MAKE ANYTHING INTO *SUKIYAKI,* RIGHT?
THE MEAT YOUR AUNT GAVE YOU AS A GIFT FOR NEW YEAR'S,
IT WAS FLAT AND THIN, RIGHT?
IT WAS.
THAT'S GOOD FOR *SUKIYAKI* OR HOT POT.
BLUB BLUB
THIS IS GOOD FOR STEW OR CURRY.

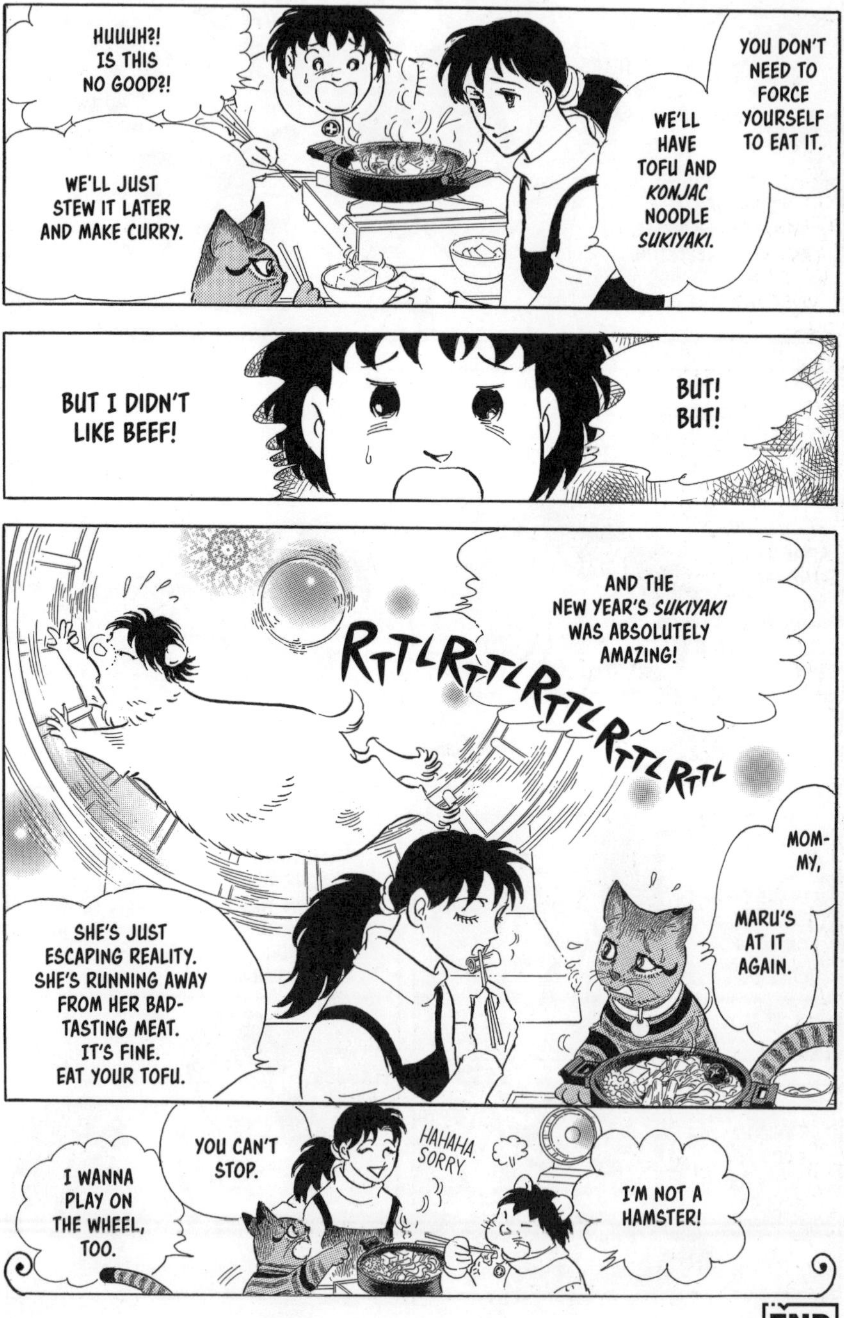
YOU DON'T NEED TO FORCE YOURSELF TO EAT IT.
WE'LL HAVE TOFU AND *KONJAC* NOODLE *SUKIYAKI*.
HUUUH?! IS THIS NO GOOD?!
WE'LL JUST STEW IT LATER AND MAKE CURRY.
BUT! BUT!
BUT I DIDN'T LIKE BEEF!
AND THE NEW YEAR'S *SUKIYAKI* WAS ABSOLUTELY AMAZING!
RTTLRTTLRTTLRTTLRTTLRTTL
MOM-MY, MARU'S AT IT AGAIN.
SHE'S JUST ESCAPING REALITY. SHE'S RUNNING AWAY FROM HER BAD-TASTING MEAT. IT'S FINE. EAT YOUR TOFU.
I'M NOT A HAMSTER!
HAHAHA. SORRY.
YOU CAN'T STOP.
I WANNA PLAY ON THE WHEEL, TOO.

END

IT'S LEO'S PHOTO DIARY!

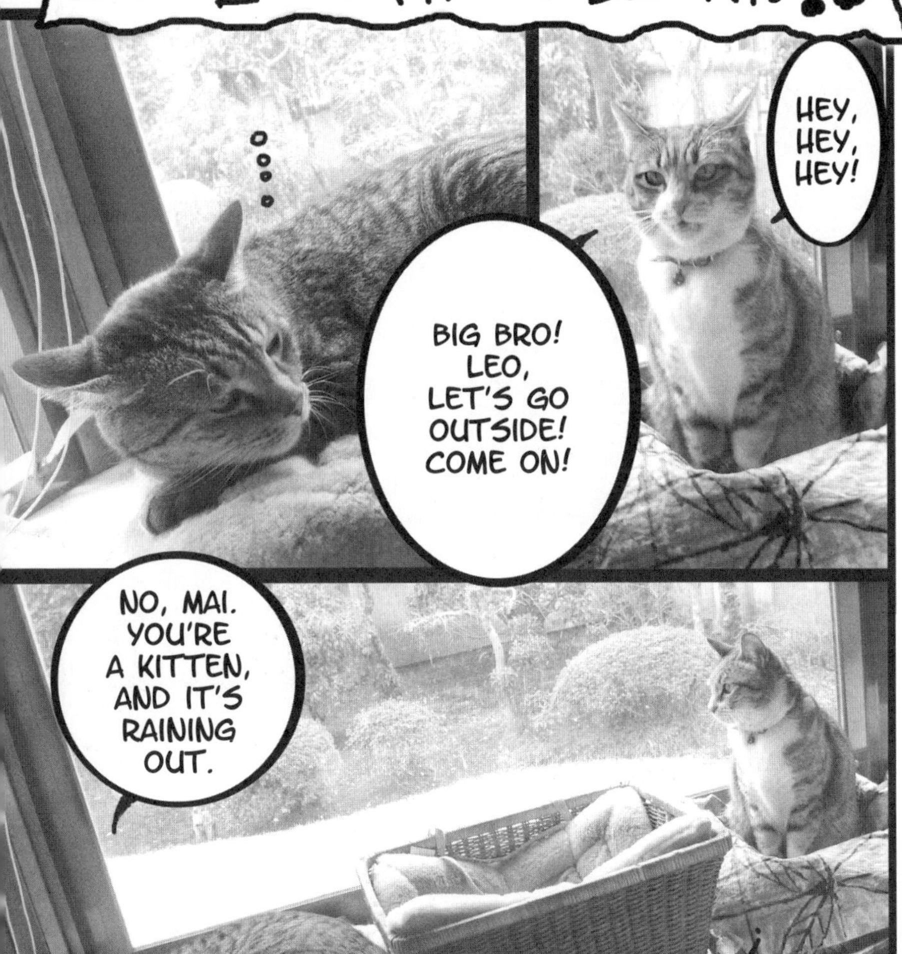

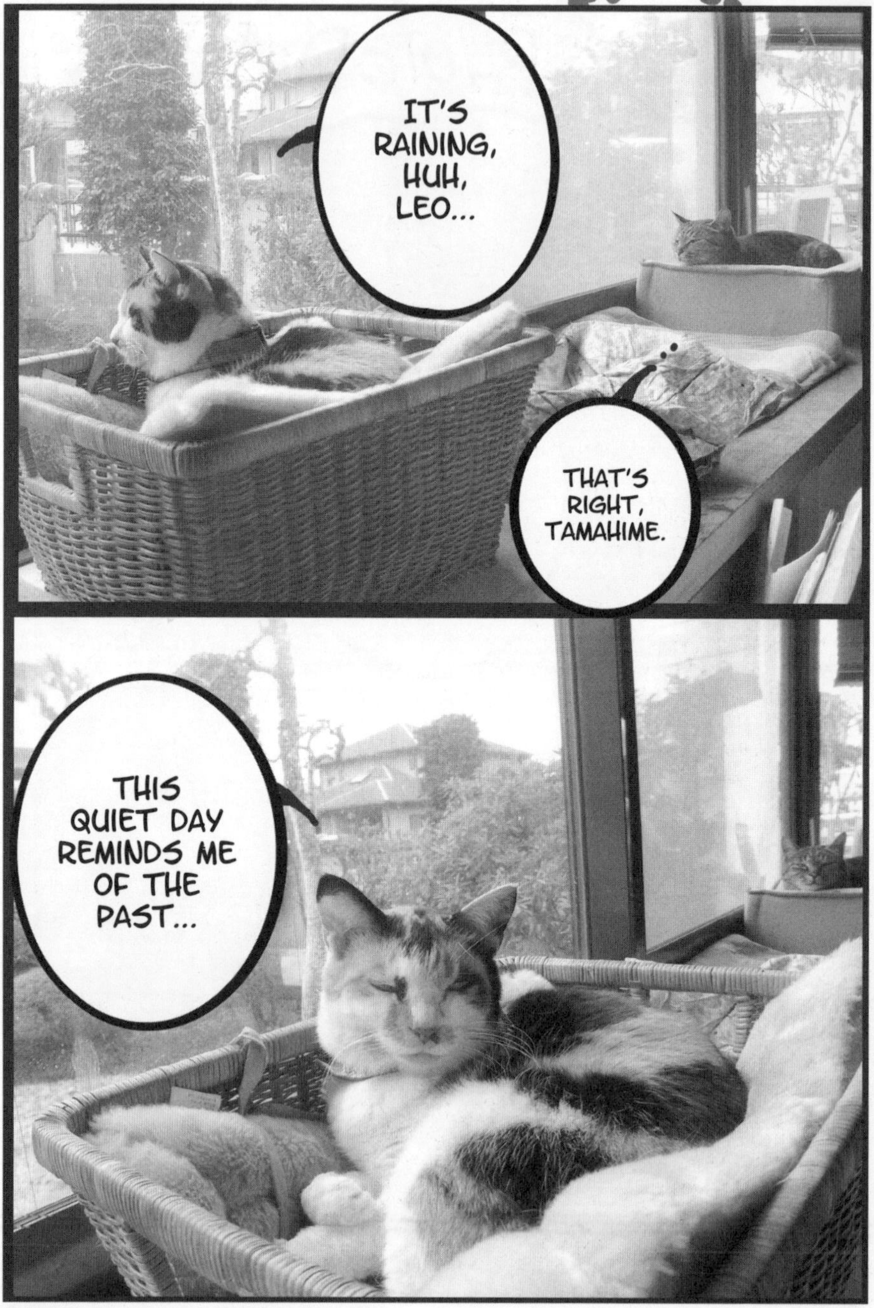
IT'S RAINING, HUH, LEO...
THAT'S RIGHT, TAMAHIME.
THIS QUIET DAY REMINDS ME OF THE PAST...

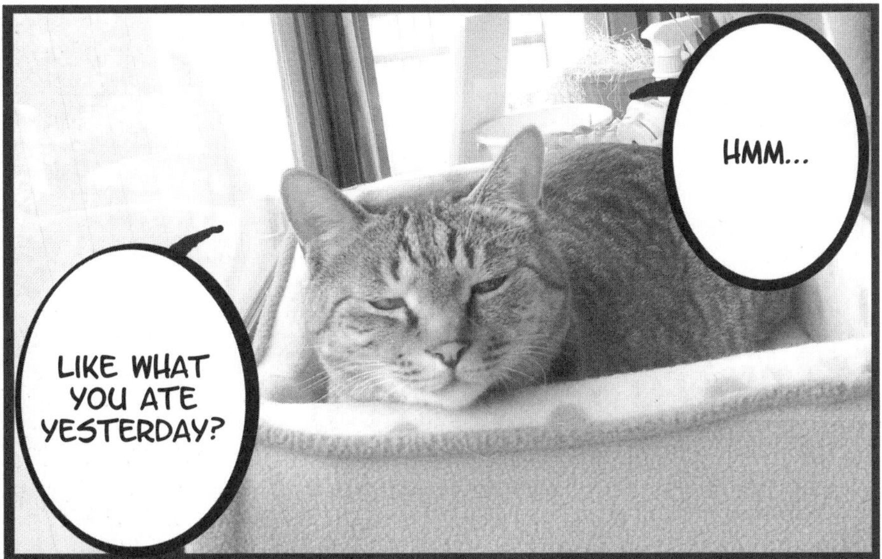
HMM...
LIKE WHAT YOU ATE YESTERDAY?

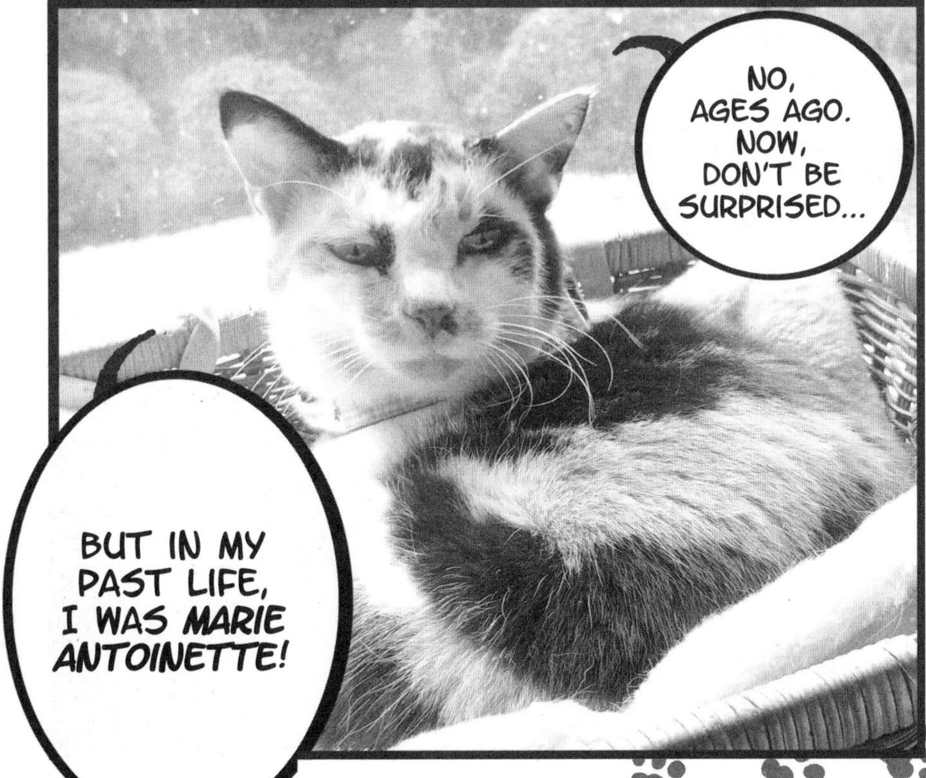
NO, AGES AGO. NOW, DON'T BE SURPRISED...
BUT IN MY PAST LIFE, I WAS *MARIE ANTOINETTE*!

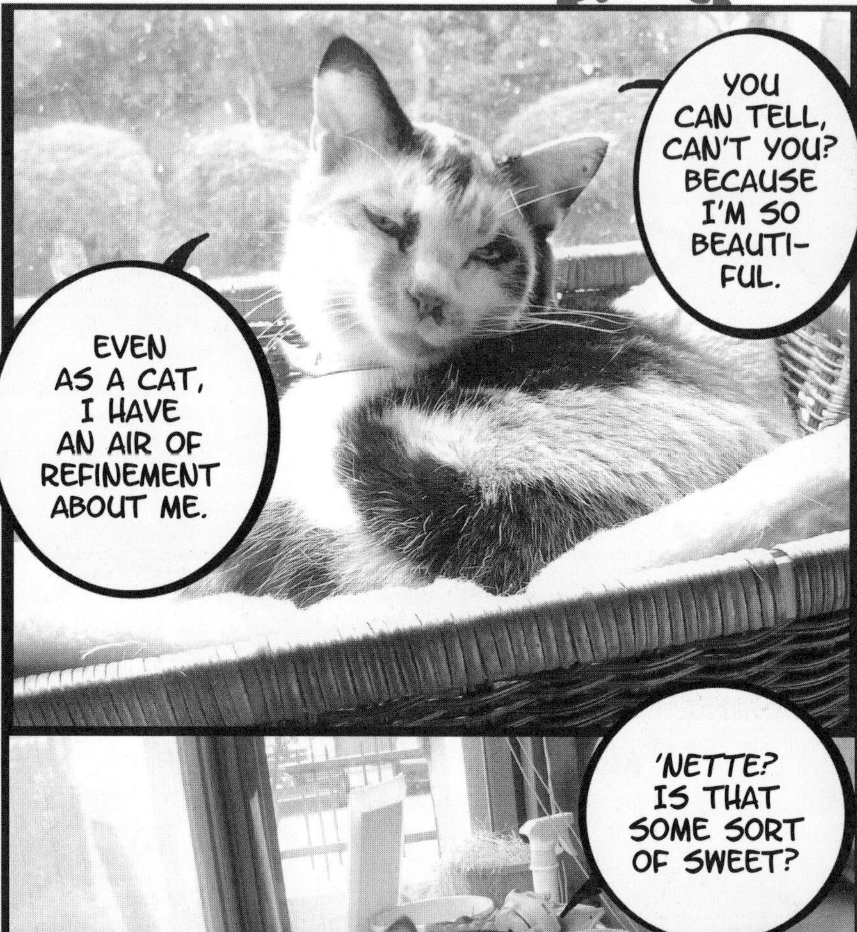
YOU CAN TELL, CAN'T YOU? BECAUSE I'M SO BEAUTI-FUL.
EVEN AS A CAT, I HAVE AN AIR OF REFINEMENT ABOUT ME.
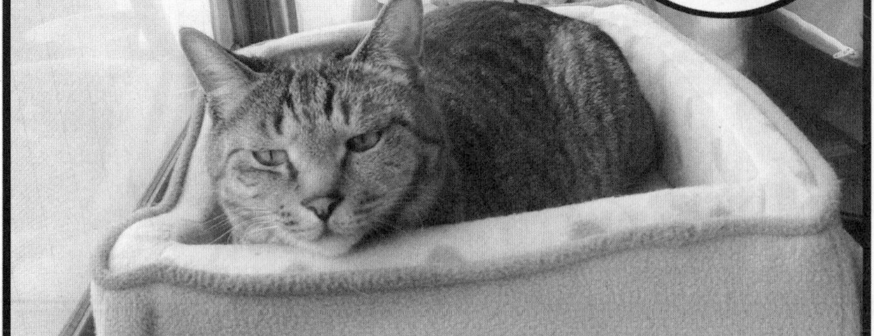
'NETTE? IS THAT SOME SORT OF SWEET?

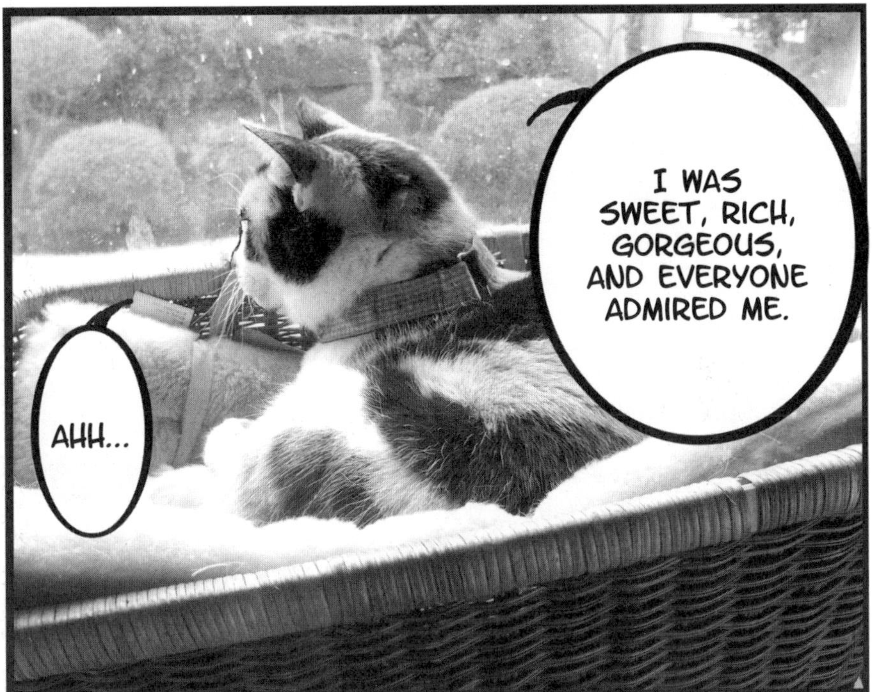
I WAS SWEET, RICH, GORGEOUS, AND EVERYONE ADMIRED ME.
AHH...

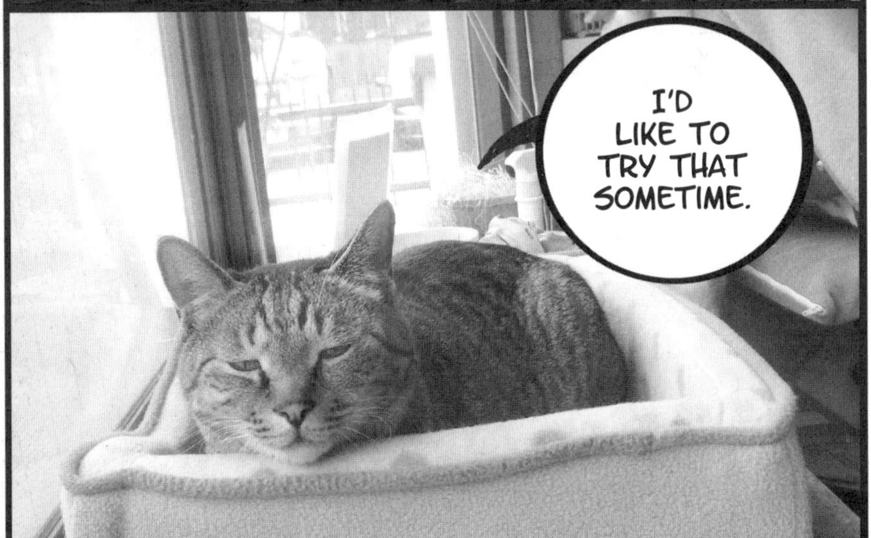
I'D LIKE TO TRY THAT SOMETIME.

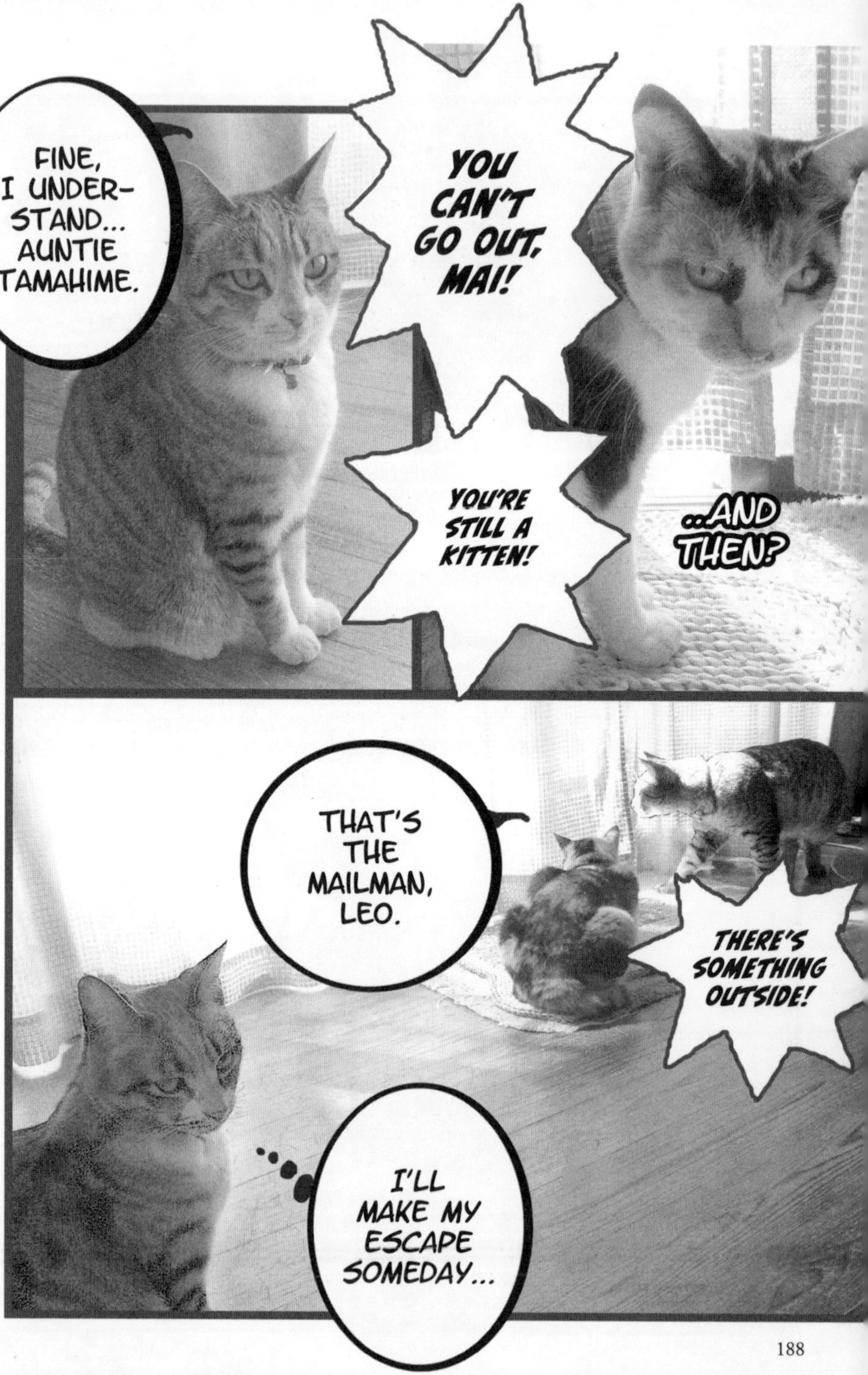
YOU CAN'T GO OUT, MAI!
YOU'RE STILL A KITTEN!
...AND THEN?
FINE, I UNDERSTAND... AUNTIE TAMAHIME.
THERE'S SOMETHING OUTSIDE!
THAT'S THE MAILMAN, LEO.
I'LL MAKE MY ESCAPE SOMEDAY...

🐾 A Few Words from Lil' Leo

I'm the model for *Lil' Leo*. I'm a striped, dark brown, male cat with straight lines above my eyes, and a weird face. But when I'm surprised, my eyes go wide like a normal cat.

(As interpreted by Moto Hagio)

Profile of Moto Hagio 🐾

- From Omuta City, Fukuoka Prefecture.
- Born May 12 and a Taurus.
- Type O blood.

Her debut title was *Ruru and Mimi* (1969). She was awarded the 21st Shogakukan Manga Award for *The Poe Clan* (Fantagraphics) and *They Were Eleven!* (DENPA), as well as the 27th Nihon SF Taisho Award for *Otherworld Barbara* (Fantagraphics).

Lil' Leo

Translator: Ajani Oloye
Proofreading: Patrick Sutton
Production: Nicole Dochych

LEO-KUN
by Moto HAGIO
© 2009 Moto HAGIO
All rights reserved.
Original Japanese edition published by SHOGAKUKAN.
English translation rights in the United States of America, Canada,
the United Kingdom, Ireland, Australia and New Zealand arranged with
SHOGAKUKAN through Tuttle-Mori Agency, Inc.

Published in English by DENPA, LLC., Portland, Oregon 2021
Lil' Leo originally serialized in *flowers* Feb., Mar., Jul., Aug., Dec. 2008
and Mar., Apr., Jun. 2009 by SHOGAKUKAN.

This is a work of fiction.

ISBN-13: 978-1-63442-978-8
Library of Congress Control Number: 2021932766
Printed in China

First Edition

Denpa, LLC.
625 NW 17th Ave
Portland, OR 97209
www.denpa.pub

WARNING!

← Read right-to-left!

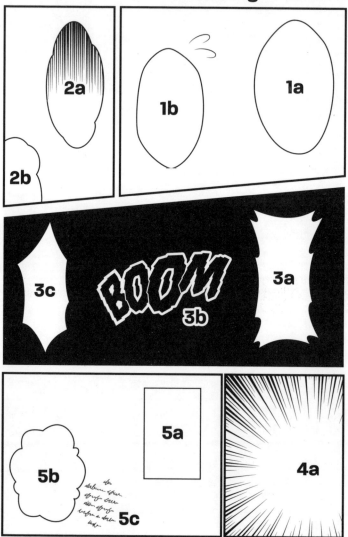

Lil' Leo is presented in its original Japanese reading orientation.
Japanese comics, or *manga*, read right-to-left and top-to-bottom.
We've given an example to follow above. Turn the book over to
start from page 1!

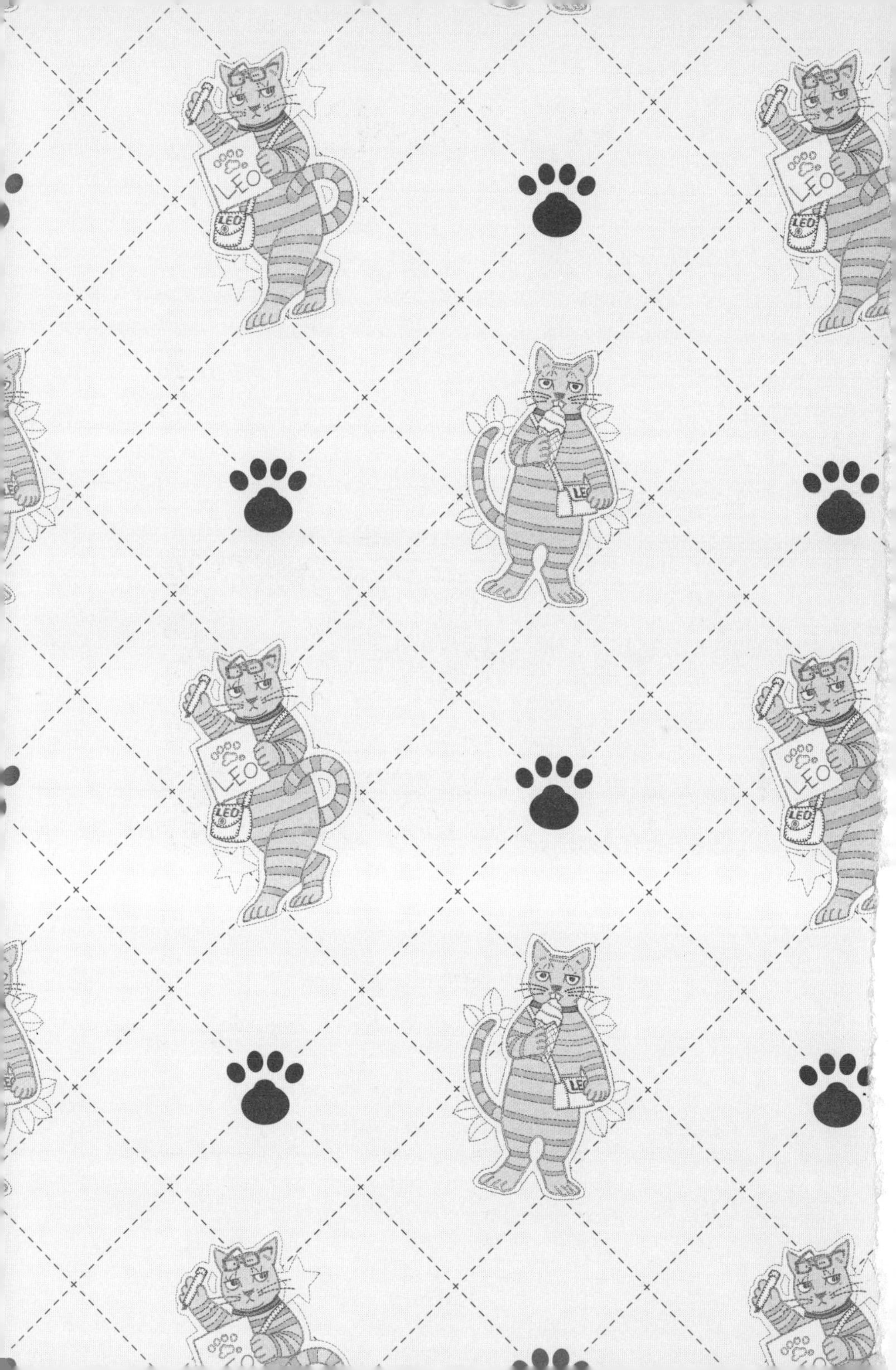
LEO

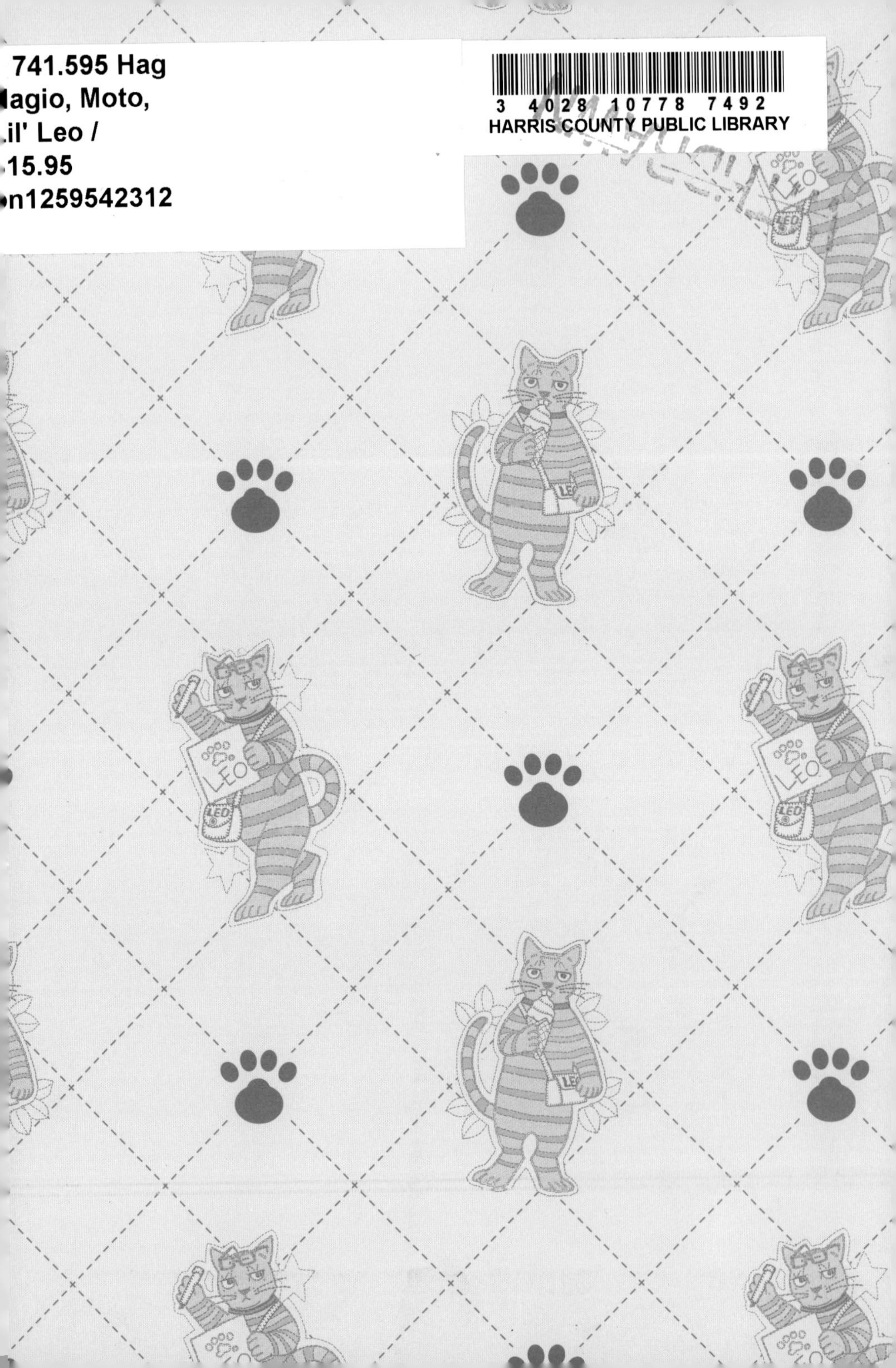